A PHILOSOPHY OF CINE

A Philosophy of Cinematic Art is a systematic study of cinema as an art form, showing how the medium conditions fundamental features of cinematic artworks. It discusses the status of cinema as an art form, whether there is a language of film, realism in cinema, cinematic authorship, intentionalist and constructivist theories of interpretation, cinematic narration, the role of emotions in responses to films, the possibility of identification with characters, and the nature of the cinematic medium. Groundbreaking in its coverage of a wide range of contemporary cinematic media, it analyses not only traditional photographic films, but also digital cinema, and a variety of interactive cinematic works, including videogames. Written in a clear and accessible style, the book examines the work of leading film theorists and philosophers of film, and develops a powerful framework with which to think about cinema as an art.

BERYS GAUT is Professor of Philosophy at the University of St Andrews. He is the author of *Art, Emotion and Ethics* (2007) and co-editor of *The Creation of Art* (2003) and *The Routledge Companion to Aesthetics* (2nd edn, 2005).

A PHILOSOPHY OF CINEMATIC ART

BERYS GAUT

CAMBRIDGE
UNIVERSITY PRESS

CAMBRIDGE UNIVERSITY PRESS

Cambridge, New York, Melbourne, Madrid, Cape Town, Singapore, São Paulo, Delhi

Cambridge University Press
The Edinburgh Building, Cambridge CB2 8RU, UK

Published in the United States of America by Cambridge University Press, New York

www.cambridge.org
Information on this title: www.cambridge.org/9780521529648

First published 2010

Printed in the United Kingdom at the University Press, Cambridge

A catalogue record for this publication is available from the British Library

ISBN 978-0-521-82244-2 Hardback
ISBN 978-0-521-52964-8 Paperback

For Morag

Contents

Illustrations

Preface

In 1987 I was working towards my PhD at Princeton and was surprised to discover that the Department of Philosophy was offering a course on the philosophy of film. I had no idea that such a subject existed. I was interested in the philosophy of art and had a passing interest in film, so I decided to sit in on the lectures. The course was a revelation: one could actually do philosophy about film and moreover do it in a way that was both intellectually rigorous and also acutely sensitive to the aesthetic qualities of individual films. The visiting professor who taught that course was George Wilson, who has been a friend and something of a mentor ever since. My greatest intellectual debts in the philosophy of film are to him. Had he not taught that course, this book would probably never have been written.

Having been inspired by George's course, I attended several film courses run by P. Adams Sitney and Tony Pipolo at Princeton. I sat well back in a large lecture theatre, and I suspect that they never knew I was there. But their lectures showed me, along with George's wonderful interpretations of films, how powerful and interesting films could be and that films were capable of far greater depth than I had previously imagined. My debts to these two scholars are considerable.

On moving to St Andrews in 1990, I was delighted to discover that my new colleagues encouraged me to start a philosophy of film course, and they have been unfailingly supportive of my endeavours since then. I also owe a great deal to several generations of St Andrews undergraduates and postgraduates, who have attended the various philosophy of film courses I have taught. Most of the material in this book has been, in various versions, road tested on them. They no doubt suffered through early drafts of this material, but several of them, as well as some of my erstwhile colleagues who taught the course when I was on leave, have gone on to teach philosophy of film courses since then, so I suppose that I must have been doing something right. Roy Cook, Brandon Cooke, Matthew Kieran, Kathleen Stock, Hamish Thompson and Kate Thomson-Jones were among my victims.

I would also like to thank the many philosophers and film theorists who have over the years given me comments on papers or talks, material from which has been incorporated into this book. These include Noël Carroll, Diarmuid Costello, Greg Currie, Julian Dodd, Jonathan Friday, Peter Goldie, John Hyman, Andrew Kania, Jerry Levinson, Paisley Livingston, Dom Lopes, Patrick Maynard, Bence Nanay, Alex Neill, Michael Newall, Carl Plantinga, Greg Smith, Murray Smith and Kendall Walton. I am particularly grateful to Richard Allen and David Davies, who read a draft of the entire manuscript and provided many helpful comments on it. I am also grateful for the comments on the book by members of my M.Litt. seminar on the philosophy of film in 2008. I also owe a special debt of gratitude to Noël Carroll, whose work on the philosophy of film played a critical role in convincing me early on that the subject is one that can support serious philosophical endeavours, and whose writings and friendship have been of great importance to me in helping me to develop my own philosophy of cinema.

I would like to thank the University of St Andrews for funding two periods of research leave and the Leverhulme Trust for granting me a Research Fellowship to work on the book. I am also very grateful to Hilary Gaskin and Gillian Dadd at Cambridge University Press, whose encouragement for me to write this book has been much appreciated. And I am indebted to the staff at the Kobal Collection for being unfailingly helpful and efficient in providing the illustrations for this book.

This book draws in part on several of my previously published papers, though this material has been extensively revised and augmented. I have used material from the following by kind permission of Oxford University Press: 'Film' in Jerrold Levinson (ed.), *The Oxford Handbook of Aesthetics* (2003); 'Film Authorship and Collaboration' in Richard Allen and Murray Smith (eds.), *Film Theory and Philosophy* (1997); and 'Making Sense of Films: Neoformalism and its Limits', *Forum for Modern Language Studies*, 31 (1995), pp. 8–23. I am grateful to Blackwell Publishers for permission to use material from: 'The Philosophy of the Movies: Cinematic Narration' in Peter Kivy (ed.), *The Blackwell Guide to Aesthetics* (Blackwell, 2004); 'Interpreting the Arts: The Patchwork Theory', *Journal of Aesthetics and Art Criticism*, 51 (1993), pp. 597–609; and 'Cinematic Art', *Journal of Aesthetics and Art Criticism*, 60 (2002), pp. 299–312. I would like to thank Routledge for permission to use material from 'Digital Cinema' in Paisley Livingston and Carl Plantinga (eds.), *The Routledge Companion to Philosophy and Film* (Routledge, 2009). I have also used material from 'Identification and Emotion in Narrative Film' in Carl Plantinga and Greg M. Smith (eds.),

Passionate Views: Film, Cognition and Emotion, pp. 200–16; © 1999 The Johns Hopkins University Press, reprinted with permission of The Johns Hopkins University Press. I am grateful to the Association for Media Education in Scotland for permission to use material from 'Film and Language', *Media Education Journal*, 38 (2005), pp. 19–20. I have used parts of 'Imagination, Interpretation, and Film', *Philosophical Studies*, 89 (1998), pp. 331–41, with kind permission of Springer Science and Business Media. Finally, I am grateful to *Presses Universitaires de France* for allowing me to use material from 'Opaque Pictures', *Revue Internationale de Philosophie*, 62 (2008), pp. 381–96.

Finally, as always, my thanks go to my parents, and to Morag, Suzanne and Robert. The dedication of the book speaks for itself.

Introduction

This book addresses some central issues in the philosophy of cinema: the role of expression, realism, authorship, theories of interpretation, the nature of narration, character identification and audiences' emotional responses. In developing theories of these phenomena, two broad themes emerge. The first is a concern with cinema as an art. The second is an argument that the cinematic medium plays a role in explaining and evaluating central features of cinematic works. In both respects, the book reveals a strong debt to classical film theory, which was concerned with the question of what makes film an art, and argued that the nature of the film medium plays a central role in understanding and evaluating films. Contemporary film theory lost interest in the question of whether film is an art and in some of its modes was little concerned with the nature of the film medium, assimilating it instead to semiotic phenomena. And some contemporary philosophers of film, notably Noël Carroll, have argued at length both that there is no role for medium-specific explanations in film and also that, partly as a result of this, we should abandon the attempt to construct grand film theory, and instead adopt piecemeal theorising.[1] If the argument of this book is successful, the classical film theorists were much closer to the truth in holding that medium-specific explanations and evaluations, as well as a good degree of systematising theory about cinema, are possible.

The scope of the discussion of cinema in this book is broad. Cinema is the medium of the moving image. In the etymologically rooted sense of the word, 'cinema' is related to the notion of kinematics, the study of things that move. 'Movies' and 'motion pictures' are terms that capture the phenomenon: we are discussing pictures that move. Moving images come in many kinds, a fact of which it has been easy to lose sight until recently, given the dominance of traditional photochemical, celluloid-based film for most of the period in which moving images have been subject to theorising. Indeed,

[1] Noël Carroll, *Theorizing the Moving Image*, especially Part I.

sometimes the word 'film' is used simply to mean photochemical, celluloid-based moving images, a usage I will not respect. When I need to single out photochemical films, i.e., films composed of images made by exposing certain photosensitive chemical salts to light, I will refer to 'traditional' films or cinema. As we shall see, cinema never was confined to photochemical images. The variety of the kinds of cinema has become obvious within the last fifteen years with the rise of digital cinema, both in its non-interactive and interactive forms; the latter encompasses a range of cases from videogames to digital interactive dramas to virtual reality displays.

Since the role of the medium plays a central part in the book's argument, the question arises of what to say about digital cinema, in particular, in relation to the traditional cinematic medium. Digital cinema is in salient ways different from traditional cinema, particularly in its interactive possibilities, so it is important to consider in what ways its differences condition artistic features of cinematic works. So in most chapters a separate section considers how the argument advanced in that chapter applies to digital cinema. The upshot is a systematic investigation of some central features of digital cinema, both interactive and non-interactive, in addition to those of traditional film. Both digital and interactive cinema have earned a great deal of attention from new media theorists and game studies scholars, but these scholars have shown little interest in how classical film theory might be of assistance in understanding them. Philosophers have scarcely even begun to address the issue of digital cinema. This book, I hope, will help remedy this situation and show how questions, concepts and tools partly derived from classical film theory can fruitfully be applied to the wide variety of cinema that is now available to us.

The rest of this Introduction sketches in some necessary background to the argument advanced in this book. The first section adumbrates the development of film theory and the philosophy of film. The second provides an overview of the development of the cinematic medium, including traditional, digital and interactive cinema. Given the importance of the cinematic medium to the argument of this book, it is vital to understand the technical aspects of the medium.

I.I FILM THEORY AND PHILOSOPHY

Today the philosophy of film is a wide and growing discipline, and exhibits a striking feature that, though not unique amongst the philosophies of the arts, is at least unusual: many philosophers and film theorists are interacting with and learning from each other's work. Much, though certainly not all, of the work of philosophers has been critical of aspects of film theory, but the interaction has been fruitful for both disciplines. This interplay is witnessed by several anthologies in which both film theorists and philosophers of film are included.[2] And probably the most widely used introductory film anthology includes writings by the philosophers Noël Carroll, Stanley Cavell, Gilles Deleuze, Cynthia Freeland and Jerrold Levinson.[3]

Philosophy of film is almost as old as the medium of photographic film (which was invented around 1890): Hugo Munsterberg, a philosopher and psychologist, wrote a pioneering work on film in 1916.[4] However, film only began to attract wide philosophical attention in the 1970s, which saw seminal books and articles appear by Stanley Cavell, Francis Sparshott, Alexander Sesonske, and Arthur Danto.[5] Since then, writings in the philosophy of film have burgeoned; more recent important philosophical monographs on film include those of Noël Carroll, Gregory Currie and George Wilson.[6] Besides books and articles on the philosophy of film in general, there have also been many studies of individual films by philosophers.

Since film theory has played a central role in setting the agenda for the philosophy of film, it is worth briefly rehearsing film theory's development.[7] Classical film theory began shortly after the invention of film. Its concerns were broadly threefold. First, a new medium had been born: but was it art? Its roots in scientific experiments and its mechanical means of recording seemed to rule out any role for individual expression or for created form, which argued against its artistic status. Classical film theorists such as Rudolf Arnheim (who is a major influence on the present book) were keen to defend film against such charges and show that it was indeed an

---

[2] David Bordwell and Noël Carroll (eds.), *Post-Theory*; Richard Allen and Murray Smith (eds.), *Film Theory and Philosophy*; Carl Plantinga and Greg M. Smith (eds.), *Passionate Views*; and Paisley Livingston and Carl Plantinga (eds.), *The Routledge Companion to Philosophy and Film*.

[3] Leo Braudy and Marshall Cohen (eds.), *Film Theory and Criticism*.

[4] Hugo Munsterberg, *The Photoplay*.

[5] Stanley Cavell, *The World Viewed* (the first edition was published in 1971); Francis Sparshott, 'Basic Film Aesthetics' (first published in 1971); Alexander Sesonske, 'Cinema Space'; and Arthur Danto, 'Moving Pictures'.

[6] Noël Carroll, *Philosophical Problems of Classical Film Theory*; Noël Carroll, *Theorizing the Moving Image*; Gregory Currie, *Image and Mind*; and George Wilson, *Narration in Light*.

[7] Influenced by film theory, but distinct from it, is the field of game studies, including the study of videogames. The most prominent theoretical division in this field concerns the possibility of interactive narration, an issue that divides narratologists from ludologists, and which I discuss in detail in Section 5.7. Other issues addressed by game studies have direct analogues within traditional film studies, such as the status of videogames as an art, the role of authorship and the nature of audiences' emotional engagement with works. These aspects will also be addressed in the present book, but only insofar as they rest on the interactive element of videogames, rather than on their status as games.

art form.[8] Second, because of its photographic basis film seemed to be in some sense a pre-eminently realist medium and therefore to have new artistic resources distinct from earlier art forms: André Bazin and Siegfried Kracauer investigated the nature of film realism.[9] Third, if film is an art, then it seemed to many that there must be an identifiable artist responsible for each film; hence proponents of the auteur theory, such as Andrew Sarris and Victor Perkins, argued for the existence of a single author of a film, normally identified as the director.[10] As we shall see, all of these issues have been of interest to philosophers. Indeed, in its central concerns, in its clarity of expression and in its precision of argument, classical theory bears some affinity to contemporary philosophy of film.

The second kind of theory, so-called contemporary film theory, came to prominence in the mid-1960s. Its central claim was that film is a kind of language. That idea had been mooted by some classical theorists, such as Sergei Eisenstein.[11] But it received its most sustained defence at the hands of Christian Metz.[12] To this claim was later added the thesis that psychoanalysis, in particular that form represented by the works of Jacques Lacan, is central both to the understanding of the film medium and to understanding viewers' responses to films.[13] Contemporary film theorists also argued for the pervasiveness of ideology in film in virtue of certain features of the medium or of certain major kinds of films, such as realist ones.[14] Several philosophers have been intensely critical of the three claims just outlined.[15] However, though this kind of film theory is still a very influential force in cinema studies, of late the field has grown more pluralistic and somewhat less interested in building grand theory, and has become more attentive to the varieties of ways that individual films and national cinematic traditions represent their subjects.

Within the last twenty years or so, there has grown up a third kind of film theory: cognitive film theory. Its most influential exponent is David Bordwell, who has used findings from cognitive psychology to support a neoformalist aesthetics.[16] Some cognitive theorists, such as Torben Grodal, have also drawn on findings in neural science and others, such as Murray

---

[8] Rudolf Arnheim, *Film as Art*; the book was first published in German in 1933, the enlarged edition in 1957.
[9] André Bazin, *What is Cinema?*; and Siegfried Kracauer, *Theory of Film* (first published in 1960).
[10] Andrew Sarris, 'Notes on the Auteur Theory in 1962'; and V. F. Perkins, *Film as Film*, chapter 8.
[11] Sergei Eisenstein, 'Beyond the Shot [The Cinematic Principle and the Ideogram]'.
[12] Christian Metz, *Film Language*.   [13] Christian Metz, *The Imaginary Signifier*.
[14] James Spellerberg, 'Technology and Ideology in the Cinema'.
[15] For instance, Currie, *Image and Mind*, Preface; and Carroll, *Mystifying Movies*.
[16] David Bordwell, *Narration in the Fiction Film* and *Making Meaning*.

Smith, on work in analytic philosophy to throw light on viewers' emotional responses to films and on how these responses are guided by film genres and narrative patterns.[17] Cognitive film theory is still a minority position within film studies, though its influence is growing and it has benefited the philosophy of film through its receptivity to a dialogue with analytic philosophy. Its interest in how viewers interpret films and emotionally respond to them has also helped shape some of the issues in the philosophy of film.

The contribution of philosophy to our understanding of film so far has not lain chiefly in identifying new issues or puzzles about film, which have been largely set by film theory.[18] Rather, philosophers have chiefly contributed by bringing greater conceptual sophistication to the debate. Notions of realism, language and interpretation are of central concern to philosophy in general, and it is unsurprising if philosophers have succeeded in identifying a great deal of confusion in how they have been handled in film theory. Philosophers have also addressed a wide range of issues that have been identified by film theory. In addition to those discussed in this book, these have included the tenability of the concept of non-fiction cinema and the phenomenology of cinematic space and time.[19]

Perhaps the most salient feature of the philosophy of film at present is that, while most analytic philosophers have rejected the psychoanalytic and 'film as a language' paradigms that are embodied within contemporary film theory, we are still at best in the early stages of laying out a comprehensive alternative theory. Indeed, as noted earlier, some philosophers, most prominently Noël Carroll, have argued against the very possibility of a comprehensive and correct theory of film, defending instead the development of piecemeal accounts of different aspects of film.[20] However, Wilson's *Narration in Light* goes some way to developing a theory of cinematic point of view and narration, and Currie's *Image and Mind* advances a comprehensive theory of cinematic representation. Currie's theory also draws

[17] Torben Grodal, *Moving Pictures*; and Murray Smith, *Engaging Characters*.
[18] An exception is the discussion of whether films can philosophise, a topic largely pioneered by philosophers; see, for instance, Thomas Wartenberg, *Thinking on Screen*.
[19] On non-fiction cinema, see Noël Carroll, 'From Real to Reel: Entangled in Nonfiction Film'; and on the phenomenology of time and space, see Alexander Sesonske, 'Cinema Space' and 'Aesthetics of Film, or A Funny Thing Happened on the Way to the Movies'. Other works by philosophers that adopt a broadly phenomenological approach include Noël Carroll, *Comedy Incarnate*; and Allan Casebier, *Film and Phenomenology*. Film music has also been discussed in some respects which I will not discuss here: see Jerrold Levinson, 'Film Music and Narrative Agency'; and Peter Kivy, 'Music in the Movies: A Philosophical Enquiry'.
[20] Carroll, *Theorizing the Moving Image*.

heavily on cognitive psychology, which has been influential on cognitive film theory. The approach taken in the present book is more systematic than piecemeal and is one which, though influenced by cognitive psychology, is based on an investigation of the role of the medium in conditioning features that cinema shares with other art forms, such as narration, expression and representation. Such a theory both reveals what film has in common with other art forms, and also show what distinguishes it from them, and why.

1.2 MOVING IMAGE TECHNOLOGIES

Cinema comes in many kinds. The oldest kind is object-generated moving images. Within the Hindu religious tradition, shadow plays have existed in Java since at least the tenth century AD, involving flat puppets, manipulated by thin rods, with their shadows projected onto a screen by a light source. Some of these shadow plays have been extremely elaborate, involving staging, for instance, entire scenes taken from the great Hindu epic, the Mahabharata. Object-generated cinema is closely akin to theatre, since it requires the physical presence of the object that is generating the images (the paper cut-out) and of the performers, who manipulate the puppets and speak their parts. It is thus ill suited to mass reproduction: each performance is unique and requires the presence of the performers. Moreover, the motion projected onto the screen is real, and not the apparent motion of rapidly changing still images, since the puppets are really moving.[21]

A more recent kind of cinema is handmade cinema. In 1833 the Zoetrope was invented, a rotating disk inscribed with individual drawings, which were viewed through slots in the circumference of the disk that appeared to make the drawings move. In 1877 Émile Reynaud invented a related device, the Praxinoscope, composed of a revolving drum with drawn images on the inside, viewed through a set of mirrors, so that the drawings seemed to move. From about 1882 Reynaud combined this device with a projector, eventually projecting moving images onto a screen using a long roll of hand-drawn images. From 1892 onwards in Paris he regularly screened these movies. Reynaud's problem was in reproducing them: since they were individually hand painted, they were expensive to replicate, and the paper

---

[21] Plato's parable of the cave in the *Republic* would also count as a kind of object-generated cinema, albeit one where the audience is suffering from an extreme delusion about the reality of the images projected. Ian Jarvie in *Philosophy of the Film*, p. 46, calls Plato's parable an 'Astounding … anticipation of the cinema'.

rolls on which they were painted were fragile. With the first public screening of a photographic film in December 1895 by the Lumière brothers, the commercial pressures increased on Reynaud and he started using cameras to make films. By 1900 he had exited the business, undermined by competition, and he destroyed his equipment in disillusion.[22]

Reynaud's career, though short, is significant for thinking about the philosophy of cinema. His films strikingly reveal the fact that movies are not necessarily photographic. Indeed, one can construct an alternative hypothetical history of film from Reynaud's brief career. It was bad luck that photographic cinema was invented so close in time to his handmade cinema. The problem of reproducing handmade films was in fact solvable: printing techniques, such as lithography, could have been used to make multiple copies of his films, so that we would have talked of 'film prints' in the sense that we talk of handmade prints, rather than in the sense that we talk of photographic prints. In this alternative history of film, photography would have played no role in cinema, and we would have thought of film as closely akin to handmade visual media. Indeed, digital cinema can be thought of as Reynaud's revenge on photographic film, since digital cinema need not be photographic at all (images can be and sometimes are entirely hand drawn using image editing software). It thus reactivates a possibility that earlier technological history seemed permanently to have obliterated. Reynaud's cinema also shows that certain kinds of cinema need not possess even the possibility of live action – the photographic recording of real people and events – but rather might be essentially animated. In Reynaud's cinema, lacking photography, live action could play no part: all of his films were and had to be animated films. So animation might have played a central part in the history of movies, unlike the relatively peripheral role it actually played, given the dominance of live action films, which were made possible by photographic recording means. (And note too that until the rise of digital cinema, animated films were standardly photographically based, since they were photographs of drawings.)

The remaining kinds of cinema are all mechanically generated. The most familiar is cinema based on traditional photographs, photochemical images. In the latter half of the 1880s and the first half of the 1890s several people had developed this medium – Louis Le Prince, W. K. L. Dickson (working for Thomas Edison) and the Lumière brothers. Its possibility rested on the confluence of several inventions: short enough exposure times to allow multiple exposures per second to be taken (silent films generally were

---

[22] Kristin Thompson and David Bordwell, *Film History*, p. 16; and Perkins, *Film as Film*, pp. 41–2.

recorded at 14 to 16 frames per second), the invention of a flexible, transparent film base (developed by George Eastman in 1889) and the adaptation of the Maltese cross drive mechanism (as previously used in machine guns and sewing machines) to move forward the film roll and hold it still for a fraction of a second. Most significant for our purposes is the fact that the photographs used were photochemical: they were made by exposing to light silver salts (silver halides), which darken in the presence of light. The salts were then fixed (to stop them further darkening when taken out of the camera) and developed (to enlarge the darkened salts and remove the ones that had not darkened). The resulting negative was then re-photographed to make a positive print. Thus the resulting original print is a second generation photograph – a photograph of a photograph.

Unlike object-generated cinema, but like Reynaud's, this kind of cinema does not require the presence of the depicted people and objects; and the motion shown, being generated by a sequence of still images, is only apparent, not real.[23] The appearance of movement, as with photographic film, was achieved through the psychological mechanisms of critical flicker fusion and apparent motion. The former occurs when lights are rapidly switched on and off, and at about fifty flashes per second the spectator seems to see a continuous beam of light; the latter occurs due to our tendency to see a set of stationary lights as moving when they are illuminated one after another in sequence (as in the display lights sometimes used outside theatres, where we interpret the sequence of flashing lights as moving).

The use of a photochemical process for generating images had important implications for film as an art and for film theory. This imaging process is ineliminably marked by its chemical origins: different film stocks, involving different kinds of chemicals, have different looks that matter aesthetically. For instance, fast film stocks, composed of fewer and larger silver granules, are suitable for shooting in low light and for recording fast-moving objects; since there are fewer granules, these kinds of film stock give a film a 'grainy' look. Given their sensitivity to low light, fast stocks were often used in newsreels, and Italian Neorealist filmmakers in the 1940s used fast stock to give their fiction films a documentary feel. In contrast, slow film stock is composed of many more, smaller film granules, and so can register far more detail in a scene with less grain; it was generally used in classical Hollywood cinema to show off the opulence and beauty of its sets and stars. So different film styles, through the constraints of photochemical processes, had a slightly different granular look. And the development of colour film, with

---

[23] See Section 2.3.1 for an argument that the motion of cinematic images is not real.

its use of colour dyes in association with silver halides, also produced distinctive aesthetic features: for instance, 1950s Technicolor films, using a dye-transfer process, could produce a deeply saturated yellow that other colour film stocks, such as Eastmancolor, were unable to emulate.

The photochemical process also had important implications for the way that film theory, with its focus until very recently on traditional photographic films, thought about cinematic representation and manipulation. Given the photochemical process, there are very limited possibilities for altering an image once taken: one can hand retouch these images, and use mattes (masks) to screen out part of the image, so that different images can be composited together. But when these kinds of changes are made, the process of photographing the photograph generally has to be repeated, and each new photograph leads to loss of detail and information (generational loss), so that manipulation of the image is generally at the expense of optical sharpness. Thus image manipulation has its limits. In contrast, it is easy to manipulate this sort of film by literally cutting one image from another and then gluing or taping it to another one: so sequence manipulation is simple. Hence film theorists tended to accord both realism to the content of the individual image, since it was relatively resistant to manipulation (a feature noted by realist film theory) and to celebrate the manipulative capacities of the medium in respect of editing (a feature stressed by the Soviet montage school of theorists, such as Kuleshov, Pudovkin and Eisenstein).

The other kind of mechanically generated cinema is electronic cinema, or video. Electronic cinema stores images not by photochemical, but by electronic means. Its roots go back to a patent filed in 1884 by Paul Nipkow, who developed the first prototype of a television, and the first successful television camera was invented by John Logie Baird in 1925. Video systems work by electronic scanning, at first of a set of phosphors on a camera pick-up tube, where the light value of each phosphor is read by an electronic beam. Then in 1969 the charge-coupled device (CCD) was invented at Bell Labs, a device that consists of a set of photosensitive diodes that convert light to an electric pulse, and the resulting array of values is stored in a capacitor. Video can employ analogue or digital images. An analogue image is one that is completely specifiable only by continuously varying values. (Object-generated, handmade and photochemical images are also analogue.) In analogue video, continuously varying signals are produced and recorded on some storage device, such as VHS tape. Its besetting problem is that the only way to edit it with any ease is to employ linear editing: rather than editing involving cutting up the tape, so that the original tape can be employed, it involves recording the tape again, thus making the generational loss problem worse. Analogue video's great advance was that it allowed live broadcasting, since electronic processing is far more rapid than the slow processing of photochemical film. And its social impact through television was, of course, immense. But I will say little about it here, since its salient new features relative to traditional film are its capacities for live broadcast, for enhanced image manipulation and for a degree of interactivity. Digital cinema also possesses the first of these features, while taking the latter two to wholly new heights. So for the purposes of exploring differences between cinematic media, digital cinema is a more striking and useful contrast with traditional film than is analogue electronic cinema.

My main point of comparison with traditional photographic cinema, then, will be digital cinema. Digital cinema, like analogue electronic cinema, employs a CCD when it is recording real objects, but it *digitises* the output of the CCD, converting it into a stream of integers. Before addressing these technical features of digital cinema, let us look briefly at its history so that we can better understand its significance and range.

In discussing digital cinema, we need to distinguish between full and partial digital cinema. The cinematic process from planning to screening can be divided into five phases: pre-production, production, post-production, distribution and exhibition. Partial digital cinema is digital at one or more of these phases, but not at all of them; full digital cinema is digital at all of these phases.

Digital sound arrived in the 1980s. In respect of the visual dimension, digital cinema began in the post-production arena, where films were digitally processed and manipulated, usually as a way of creating special effects or animation. One of the earliest partially digital films was *TRON* (1982), which employed digital sequences to simulate a kind of computer game. *Jurassic Park* (1993) and *Forrest Gump* (1994) brought digital special effects to popular awareness, and George Lucas' Industrial Light and Magic studio created the effects in these and many other pictures. Digital colour grading or timing (the manipulation of film colour by digital means) was widely employed from the late 1990s in preference to chemical grading and digital editing gradually became standard through the popularity of the Avid editing machine. *Toy Story* (1995) was the first digital animated feature film, created by Pixar Studios (originally Lucasfilm Computer Development Division). In the production process, some of the first widely distributed films to be shot with digital cameras were the two earliest *Dogma 95* films, *The Idiots* (1998) and *The Celebration* (1998), and many independent filmmakers adopted digital shooting thereafter. In distribution and exhibition, 1999 saw four widely publicised digital

Figure 1. The four-way split screen in *Time Code* (2000).

screenings of Lucas' *Star Wars: Episode I – The Phantom Menace* (though the film was shot on conventional film and later digitised) and also the Sundance Film Festival's acquisition of a digital projector. (Before this point digitally produced films were transferred by laser recording back onto celluloid for commercial screenings.[24]) And in pre-production, animatics (animated storyboards) were increasingly employed in the 1990s. By the late 1990s there were experimental fully digital films, and the first commercial fully digital films appeared in the new century: Mike Figgis' *Time Code* (2000) was one of the earliest (see Figure 1). It used a four-way split screen and foregrounded its digital nature by being one continuous take, something that is not in practice possible for a feature-length film in traditional cinema. George Lucas' *Star Wars: Episode II – Attack of the*

[24] It is now fairly common to use the Digital Intermediate process: a film shot on celluloid is digitised by a laser scanner, manipulated digitally (for instance, in respect of its colours, adding special effects, and so on) and then transferred back to celluloid by a laser recorder. Hence the film is recorded in an analogue medium, converted to digital (analogue-to-digital conversion) and manipulated, then converted back to an analogue medium (digital-to-analogue conversion) for purposes of screening in conventional cinemas.

Clones (2002), shot on digital video, later brought fully digital cinema to popular attention.

So fully digital cinema, involving all parts of the filmmaking and distribution process, is a very recent phenomenon. But it is likely to become the dominant form of cinema within the next two decades, given its exclusive adoption by influential filmmakers, such as George Lucas and Robert Rodriguez, and because it is cheaper to produce and distribute than is conventional film. It is also likely to accelerate the dispersion of filmmaking practice away from Hollywood, and to lead to an increasing democratisation of the filmmaking and film distribution process, particularly over the internet.

This brief history of digital cinema has been concerned with the kind of cinema screened in movie theatres. But cinema is the medium of the moving image and the digital moving image includes interactive images. Interactive digital cinema comes in a wide variety of forms. The most familiar are videogames, including Massively Multiplayer Online Role-Playing Games, such as *World of Warcraft*. The notion of a game is not sharply delimited; but in a narrow sense of the term, games are rule-governed practices that specify certain outcomes as winning or losing ones (for instance, chess); in a wider sense they are activities of make-believe that need not specify any outcomes as winning or losing ones (for instance, children playing with dolls).[25] There are many kinds of interactive cinema that are not videogames on the narrow construal of 'game'. There are virtual worlds that support role-playing activities, such as *Second Life*, but which have no winning and losing outcomes; there are interactive fictions that support a completely 'free play' or 'sandbox' mode, such as the various incarnations of *The Sims* (2000 onwards); there are flight simulators and walkthroughs of designs created within CAD (Computer Assisted Design) software; there are gallery artworks that incorporate interactive moving images, such as Camille Utterback and Romy Archituv's *TEXT RAIN* (2000), which allows viewers to catch and move text that falls like gentle rain down a projected display; and there are experimental interactive dramas that allow the user partly to determine the outcome while shaping the overall course of the drama in light of her choices, such as Michael Mateas and Andrew Stern's *Façade* (2005). There are even live action interactive films, such as *I'm Your Man* (1992), which allow the viewer to choose among several possible story developments,

---

[25] The distinction between the narrower and broader sense of 'game' is often discussed in game studies in terms of *ludus* and *paidea*: see James Newman, *Videogames*, pp. 18–22.

endings and viewpoints.[26] Surprising as it may seem, videogames and other interactive works fall within the domain of digital cinema. So I will discuss videogames here insofar as they demonstrate the aesthetics of interactivity, one of the most important features made possible by digital cinema.[27]

Videogames predate the rise of non-interactive digital cinema by some decades: the first videogame was *Spacewar*, which ran on a mainframe at MIT in 1962 (though there is an argument for 1958 being the point of origin of videogames). The 1970s saw the rise of arcade games and the first home consoles, which were chiefly deployed to run the ubiquitous *Pong*, a simple game involving batting a dot representing a ball back and forth across the screen. In the 1980s and the early 1990s the introduction of home computers and of more powerful consoles allowed for the playing of games that looked a little like traditional animated 2D films, albeit cruder and at a far lower resolution. But the most significant moment in this story was reached in 1995–6 when the processing power of consoles, such as the Sony PlayStation and the Nintendo 64, and the storage capacities of their optical media reached the point where they could display coloured and textured 3D graphics, which gave the player's character greater freedom to move around in the fictional world and permitted games to display with some richness themes and devices drawn from traditional film genres, particularly action adventure and horror genres. Videogames started to look like a kind of cinema, with interesting, rich and explorable fictional worlds. The next generation of consoles in 2000–1, chiefly the PlayStation 2 and the original Xbox, further enhanced graphic quality and ran games that granted players almost unconfined freedom to roam fictional worlds, notably in the 'sandbox' modes of *Grand Theft Auto III* (2001) and its successors. Thus, though videogames predate digital, non-interactive cinema by some decades (since the simplicity of the early graphics required comparatively little processing power) the late 1990s saw the rise of videogames that had a graphical and thematic richness that made them comparable to animated digital cinema but with additional interactive possibilities. Given the ever-advancing processing power and storage capacities of computers and consoles (which are

[26] *Façade* can be downloaded from www.interactivestory.net; for a discussion of *I'm Your Man*, see Marie-Laure Ryan, *Narrative as Virtual Reality*, pp. 271–80; and for *TEXT RAIN*, see Jay David Bolter and Diane Gromala, *Windows and Mirrors*, chapter 1.

[27] In discussing videogames I will not address the many philosophical issues they raise that derive from their status as games: their definition, the relation of their game aspect to their status as art, the relation of games to fiction, the concept of gameplay, and so on. Only the aspects related to their interactivity will be directly addressed here. For a philosophical discussion of videogames that examines their game aspect in detail, see Grant Tavinor, *The Art of Videogames*.

simply computers specialised for playing videogames), we are now at the point where the quality and detail of the graphics, rendered in real-time, that can be displayed by the PlayStation 3 (introduced in 2006–7) look more impressive than the pre-rendered graphics of *Toy Story*. And some videogames, including *Ico* (2001) and *Bioshock* (2007), display an artistry and thematic richness that make them interesting and powerful works of art in their own right. So videogames should not be ignored as a kind of cinema.

I have been talking about digital cinema in its interactive and non-interactive forms: but what precisely is digital cinema? In contrast to an analogue image, a digital image is one that is specified by a set of discrete values, typically integers (whole numbers). These integers are stored as a bitmap. A bitmap is composed of a grid of picture elements (pixels), and each point of the grid has an integer assigned to it. These integers are stored as binary digits ('bits', which is a contraction of 'binary digits'), i.e., as integers to base 2. At each point of the pixel grid, one out of millions of integers, representing colours, is stored: a common digital standard is 24-bit colour: i.e., any one of 2^{24} (over 16.7 million) colours can be represented at any point in the pixel grid. The bitmap corresponds to, and is used to generate, an image displayed on a digital display device (such as a monitor or digital projector), each value at the pixel grid corresponding to the appropriate colour on the display. A bitmap image is sometimes referred to as a 'raster image', 'raster' being an older term for a digital screen. Given the essential role of the bitmap in digital cinema, we can thus define digital cinema as the medium of moving images generated by bitmaps.

Note the formulation 'generated by'. A visual image by definition is visible, i.e., can be seen, and that requires it to have visual properties. But a bitmap is a mathematical, abstract entity – an ordered set of integers – and numbers (as distinct from numerals) cannot be seen. So a bitmap is not an image: rather, it is a *mathematical representation*, i.e., a mathematical model, *of* an image. The digital image itself is an image generated by a bitmap that specifies it.

Digital images (bitmap images) are one type of computer graphic.[28] Other important types employed in making digital movies are vector graphics and 3D graphics. A vector graphic is an image that is specified

---

[28] Sometimes 'digital image' is used interchangeably with 'computer graphic', but, strictly speaking, the former is a kind of computer graphic specified using an array of integers (hence the term 'digital'), whereas computer graphics can be specified by other mathematical means, such as functions. So I will not use the terms interchangeably here.

by mathematical functions, rather than by assigning integers to pixel elements (examples of vector graphics are the images produced in Flash and in Adobe Illustrator). This allows the vector image, unlike the bitmap image, to be scalable: whereas the bitmap image will pixellate (look blocky, so one can see individual pixels) when enlarged, the vector image will smoothly rescale: when enlarged or reduced, the image is recalculated using the functions and the appropriate size adjustments are made. A vector image, like a bitmap image, is specified by a mathematical representation, but in this case the representation employs mathematical functions, rather than an array of integers. Vector graphics are often employed in making digital movies, but their use does not impugn the definition of digital cinema in terms of moving images generated by bitmaps, since, to be displayed by a digital device, vector graphics must first be *rasterised*, i.e., converted into bitmap (raster) images. The proximate cause of the image in digital cinema is always a bitmap image, whatever its distal causes.[29]

The other kind of computer graphics that plays a prominent role in making digital movies is 3D graphics, such as those produced by Maya, a 3D graphics editor that is widely used in making both films and videogames. A 3D image in this sense is so called, not because it is composed of two overlapping images that give the perceptual illusion of depth (these are used in 3D cinema); nor because the image seems to have depth rather than looking flat (the appearance of depth is common in bitmap and vector images). Rather, it counts as 3D because it is specified by a mathematical representation (model) that represents objects by all three spatial dimensions, along their x, y and z axes. It is often displayed as a wireframe image, which shows the lines where the planes of the object intersect. As with vector graphics, the representation employs mathematical formulae, so the images produced are scalable (though bitmap information is sometimes also used to represent textures). The model of an object standardly specifies its spatial properties, colours, textures, lighting conditions, and so on. Specification of a point of view (a virtual camera) on that object allows the computer to create an image using the model, a process called *rendering*. Again, to be shown on a digital display device, this image must be rasterised, i.e., converted to a bitmap image.

---

[29] One can directly display vector graphics on analogue display devices, such as graph plotters or laser light beams, without rasterising the images; but in such cases the result is not fully digital cinema, since the display is not digital.

Digital images can be made in three ways, any or all of which can be employed in creating a single image and which can be combined seamlessly. The first method employs a mechanical capture device automatically to assign integers to pixel positions. This works by digitising a continuously varying value, the light waves emanating from objects. A CCD records the light levels as voltages, stores them, and then the values are digitised. Sampling happens thousands of time a second (the standard rate for DVDs is 96kHz, i.e., 96,000 times per second), and the amplitude of the wave at each sample point is recorded as an integer. The integer is stored at each pixel, which encodes information about the light emanating from the part of the object that the pixel represents. The most common form of capture device is the digital camera, but scanners can also be employed, as can motion capture techniques, which record a performer's body and/or facial motions by capturing the values of light bounced off reflective markers placed on her. Striking examples of the use of full body and facial motion capture are *The Polar Express* (2004) and *Beowulf* (2007).

The second method is by creating images by hand using a software editing tool. This can be done by directly constructing the digital image as a kind of digital 'painting', by assigning pixels by hand (for instance, one can change the colours of individual pixels by hand using Adobe Photoshop or Corel Painter). This technique is sometimes employed, for instance, to paint in backgrounds behind characters. Or it can be done indirectly by manually constructing the vector graphic or 3D model that is used to generate the bitmap – one can, for instance, hand-construct a wireframe model of an object, as was done by Gray Horsfield in making the digital model of the Barad-dûr tower in *The Lord of the Rings: The Return of the King* (2003).

The third method is computer synthesis, by which the computer runs a series of algorithms to generate a digital image from a 3D model, or some other digital image or vector graphic. The most common example is rendering, which, as noted, involves a computer producing a two-dimensional image from the mathematical model of a three-dimensional space with its contained objects. Other examples of computer synthesis are *procedural animation*, where a set of rules is iterated by the computer to generate animated processes, such as fire, wind or wave movements; and also animation employing artificial intelligence (AI) techniques to impart, for instance, different individual movements to characters in crowd scenes or to make combat opponents in videogames act with more apparent intelligence and skill.

Several important implications for the philosophy of cinema follow from this account of the digital image and how to generate it. First, digital images can be directly subject to computational manipulation: digital images, as well as the vector and 3D graphics that can be used to produce them, are, as we noted, generated by mathematical representations that specify them. Analogue images, in contrast, can be subject to computational manipulation only indirectly, after they have been digitised.

Second, it follows from their computability that digital images can be easily and infinitely manipulated without degradation. For any numerical array, there is an algorithm that can transform it into any other numerical array, and information stored as numbers suffers no degradation in being reproduced. Likewise, one can replace mathematical functions that specify images with other functions by computational means without information degradation. In contrast, analogue images, such as traditional photographs, are, as we noted, relatively difficult and cumbersome to manipulate, and their reproduction, involving an analogue copy of an analogue original, leads to generational loss. The fact that digital images can be easily manipulated means that the traditional dichotomy noted by film theory between the relative difficulty of manipulating an image and the ease of editing breaks down: both image- and sequence-manipulation are easy in digital cinema.

Third, whereas there is a fixed and finite amount of information in a digital image (given by its bitmap), this is not true for the analogue image, since there is an infinite amount of information in a continuously varying value.

Fourth, some of the aesthetic features of traditional film, linked in part to its chemical basis, fall away. There is no film stock in digital cinema: so there is no film grain, nor are there colour differences resulting from the chemical composition of stock. Digital cinema thus has a kind of purity from its physical origins, a point sometimes put in terms of the 'weightlessness' of the digital image. Indeed, the processing of digital films sometimes involves adding back the appearance of grain so as to give the image the look of traditional film.

Fifth, as earlier noted, the digital image is not necessarily photographic: only one kind of capture technique is photographic, and the hand construction and computer synthesising methods are not photographic at all. This is not to deny that there are digital photographs (see Chapter 1), but it is to show that the exclusive hegemony of the photograph in cinema has been undermined. Whereas in traditional animation there is always a drawing or painting that is photographed (in the case of 2D animation) or a set of objects that are photographed (in stop-motion animation), this need not be true of digital animation, if it employs digital painting or computer synthesising. Thus animation is intrinsic to the medium in such cases: there need be no drawings that are photographed and the animation may be produced as a set of digital images, rather than being a recording of independently existing images.

Finally, given the possibility of direct computer processing in real-time, digital cinema can be interactive, whereas traditional photochemical film cannot be. Interactivity requires a set of algorithms (precise rules) that specify outputs, given inputs. The inputs in the case of interactive cinema include visual and auditory images, which can be crafted by the variety of means that we have discussed for digital cinema in general. For interactivity to take place, the user must also provide some input by manipulating a device, such as a computer keyboard or a console controller. Both the input state and the user-provided information are processed by the algorithm to generate an output state, another image, which in turn will serve as the input for the next iteration of the operation. Computer programs in general are nothing more than implementations of algorithms: so computers support interactivity. The same algorithm can run in different programs, so that, for instance, the same videogame, specified by its algorithms, can run on different computer operating systems and on different consoles. But a specific *implementation* of a videogame runs in a specific program – most commonly written in the C++ programming language, using either DirectX or OpenGL Application Programming Interfaces (APIs), if 3D graphics are required. Thus, whereas non-interactive digital cinema is in part the *product* of a computer program, implementations of videogames *are* in part computer programs. That means that making a videogame (and any other type of interactive cinema) is in part a matter of designing a set of algorithms that are implemented in a program, as well as crafting the images. The aesthetic aspects of interactivity will be addressed at several points in this book.[30]

[30] For some of the technical aspects of digital cinema and imagery, see Brian McKernan, *Digital Cinema*; and James Monaco, *How to Read a Film*, chapter 7. For a comparison of digital and analogue images, see W. J. T. Mitchell, *The Reconfigured Eye*, chapter 1. For practical guides to digital animation that also provide good accounts of the concepts and methods, see Isaac Kerlow, *The Art of 3D Computer Animation and Effects*; and Dariush Derakhshani, *Introducing Maya 2008*. For interactivity and computers, see Dominic McIver Lopes, *A Philosophy of Computer Art*; and for a practical and theoretical introduction to 2D games programming, see Michael Morrison, *Beginning Game Programming*. For a useful overview of the technical aspects of both digital and traditional film, see David Bordwell and Kristin Thompson, *Film Art*, chapter 1.

I end with two remarks about the relations of this discussion of moving image technologies to the positions defended in this book. First, I have spoken of cinema as a medium, but also of different kinds of cinema, such as digital cinema, as media. One might suppose that this usage is inconsistent: either cinema is a medium or particular kinds of cinema are media. The general type cannot be a medium, as well as the more specific types categorised under it. But this objection is mistaken. I will discuss the notion of a medium in Chapter 7, but at this point we can simply note that ordinary usage allows us to speak of one medium containing several others. For instance, one can talk of prints as a medium, as distinct, say, from the media of paintings or literature. Yet the medium of print itself contains etchings, woodcuts, engravings, lithographs, each of which can also be properly termed a medium. And the medium of print is itself contained in the broader medium of visual imagery, alongside other media, such as painting and cinema. So media can contain other media, a phenomenon that I term *nesting*. Hence there is nothing suspect about talking about the medium of cinema, as well as, say, the medium of digital cinema or photo-chemical cinema.

Second, this idea of nesting lays out some of the methodology for the study of cinema. For in asking whether a particular feature is specific to film, we need to be clear about what is the contrast involved. Certain features are specific to moving images in general, in contrast to other media, such as literature and still images. So we might ask, for instance, what are the differences, if any, between the way that novels and movies in general narrate. Other features are specific to digital images in contrast to, say, traditional photographic images or handmade pictures. For instance, from the fact that a photograph is a causally generated image, as we will see in Chapter 1, it follows that its object existed at (or before) the time the photograph was made. But it does not follow of purely handmade moving images that their objects ever existed. (If the drawings were photographi-cally recorded and the photographs projected, as is the case with many animated films, it follows only that the *drawings* existed at the time they were recorded.) Nor does the existence of a purely digitally generated image entail that its object existed – such images need not be based on a recording of some object, but can be handmade or generated by a computer program. The philosophy of film has concentrated almost exclusively on traditional photographic images. But as should now be clear, photographic film is only one of a broader range of moving image media. So we need to disentangle systematically which aspects of photographic films depend on their photo-graphic nature, and which on their being moving images. Such a project allows us better to understand traditional photographic film itself, as well as digital cinema. In subsequent chapters, then, I will generally devote a section to digital cinema, in order to bring out some of the differences from traditional film, as well as showing those of its features that are similar to it, due to the two media being species of the general medium of the moving image.

CHAPTER I

The challenges to cinema as an art

Filmmakers during the first two decades of the new medium's existence thought of themselves sometimes as scientists, sometimes as explorers, sometimes as entertainers, but hardly ever as artists, as pioneers of a new artistic medium. D. W. Griffith in his earliest Biograph films from 1908 did not dare put his name on the credits, lest his ambitions in the legitimate theatre be undermined by his low-life escapades with celluloid. Only gradually did he come to think of his films as works of art; and if *Birth of a Nation* (1915) and *Intolerance* (1916) look now like deeply problematic achievements, they did at least represent the self-conscious striving to make films that are art. Though filmmakers took some time to think of their activity as a kind of art, theorists took longer. Hugo Munsterberg's pioneering *The Photoplay: A Psychological Study* (1916) represents the first sustained attempt to defend film as an art.[1] But even in 1933 Rudolf Arnheim in his *Film* (revised as *Film as Art* in 1957) could think that the leading issue in film theory was whether film is an art.[2] Indeed, Arnheim famously defended silent film as an art, but looked with some apprehension at the newly invented sound film, which he thought of as a threat to the artistic status of cinema. A great deal of classical film theory, as we noted in the Introduction, was concerned with arguing that cinema, despite its mechanical, photographic basis, is an art form.[3]

That is a matter of history, but what has this to do with us today? I argue in this chapter that the historical challenge to cinema as an art form still has a surprising degree of force; I investigate the nature of that challenge, show that it has two distinct though related versions, and reply to them both. Investigation of the twin challenges will establish that cinema can satisfy an important criterion for being an art: that it be able to communicate thoughts about its subject matter, or put another way, that it has a

---

[1] Hugo Munsterberg, *The Photoplay*.   [2] Rudolf Arnheim, *Film as Art*.
[3] See also Noël Carroll, *Philosophical Problems of Classical Film Theory*, p. 4.

representational capacity, in a sense to be explained shortly. The chapter will also establish something about the features of the film medium that are partly responsible for film being an art form. By meeting the two challenges, the chapter will thus provide part of the answer to what makes film an art form; completing the argument will involve showing what makes film distinctive as an art form, and this will be undertaken in Chapter 7, in light of the investigation into the cinematic medium in the rest of the book. The discussion in the first three sections of the present chapter is focused on traditional photographic film; in the last section I turn to examine digital images and cinema, to see how the arguments discussed bear on these.

I.I THE CAUSAL CHALLENGE

It might be supposed that an examination of whether cinema is an art form is nowadays completely otiose. For whereas in Arnheim's day cinema's artistic achievement might be disputable, surely nowadays it is not. Simple consideration of the great films which are undoubtedly works of art shows that cinema is an art: *Rules of the Game* (1939), *Citizen Kane* (1941), *Rashomon* (1950) and *Tokyo Story* (1953) constitute the best possible argument that cinema is an art form. Just as G. E. Moore answered idealism by brandishing his hand in the air and noting that his hand indisputably existed, so one can brandish a list of the great films as proof that cinematic art undoubtedly exists. And for the same reason, classical film theory can be held to be of only historical interest, since its leading question has been definitively answered by the progress of the cinematic art. For once, art itself gives a decisive answer to a philosophical question.

But such a response, apparently so compelling, misses the subtlety of the challenge to the status of cinema as an art. For suppose that someone wanted to show that compact discs are an art form. He could point to the undeniably great works that are there on compact disc: works by Beethoven, Mozart, Bach and Coltrane are not seriously disputable as great artistic achievements, so the CD is an art form. Yet such an argument would clearly be fallacious: the CD is not an art form. Of course, someone might object that this misses a crucial disanalogy: works by Beethoven *et al.* are only contingently on CD, and are also instantiated in other media, such as the printed score and the live performance. True enough: but if as may increasingly become the case, musical pieces were written specifically for CD-only distribution, would that go to show that CDs would thereby become an art form? Rather, the moral of the comparison is that the mere fact that a medium (whether acoustic or visual) *records* artistic works does not thereby make it into an art form. Likewise, consider photographs of paintings that illustrate art textbooks. These photographs are undoubtedly of artworks, but that does not thereby make the photographs themselves artworks. Indeed, someone might be alarmed to hear that the photographer intended to make an artwork: is he presenting us with a faithful copy of the original painting, one might wonder? Now call it the *transfer fallacy* when genuine features of content are *ipso facto* ascribed to the vehicle carrying that content. Then we have an instance of the transfer fallacy when the artistic status of cinematic content is *ipso facto* ascribed to the photographic vehicle carrying that content. So merely noting the existence of films that are undoubtedly works of art does not in itself show that films are an art form.

Interestingly, at least one modern writer, Roger Scruton, has pressed a related point, and has questioned the status of cinema as an art. Scruton's views on photography have been the subject of a great deal of critical discussion.[4] But their evident bearing on cinema, stressed by Scruton himself, has earned less attention, and it has also often been missed that Scruton's objections are closely related to the sort of worries that early film theorists such as Arnheim were trying to silence. But Scruton somewhat shies away from the full implications of his view as far as films are concerned. He holds that 'A film is a photograph of a dramatic representation; it is not, because it cannot be, a photographic representation. It follows that if there is such a thing as a cinematic masterpiece it will be so because – like *Wild Strawberries* and *La règle du jeu* – it is in the first place a dramatic masterpiece'.[5] He holds that cinema is not an independent art form: 'independent, that is, of the theatre, from which it borrows so many conventions'.[6] So his position appears to be that cinema is a dependent art form – presumably, that it is an art form if it fulfils certain conditions, such as recording something with artistic content. But as the examples of CDs and catalogue photographs show, the fact that something is a recording of a work of art does not thereby make it into a work of art. So the radical challenge is this: given that the photographic basis of cinema is simply a recording device, however can cinema be an art form?

---

[4] Roger Scruton, 'Photography and Representation', 'Fantasy, Imagination and the Screen' and 'The Photographic Surrogate'. For critical discussion of Scruton's views on photography, see David Davies, 'How Photographs "Signify": Cartier-Bresson's "Reply" to Scruton'; William L. King, 'Scruton and Reasons for Looking at Photographs'; Dominic McIver Lopes, 'The Aesthetics of Photographic Transparency' and Robert Wicks, 'Photography as a Representational Art'. Though Scruton's work is not explicitly discussed by them, for points pertinent to his claims, see also Barbara Savedoff, 'Transforming Images: Photographs of Representations' and Nigel Warburton, 'Photographic Communication'.
[5] Scruton, 'Photography and Representation', p. 102.   [6] *Ibid.*

It is worth examining Scruton's arguments in detail, since they throw much light on how one might flesh out the challenge to the status of cinema as an art. His claim about film rests on the photographic basis of the medium. He holds that photography is not a representational art, i.e., an art of representations. (He allows that one could take an aesthetic interest in photographs conceived merely as lines and shapes, i.e., photography conceived as an abstract art.[7]) This is, in the first instance, because photographs are not representations at all. He holds that for something to be a representation requires that it express or communicate thoughts.[8] For an image to express a thought about a subject it must stand in an intentional relation to that subject, since intentionality is the general mark of thought. In contrast, if an image stands in a merely causal relation to its subject, it cannot express thoughts about it. Paintings stand in an intentional relation to their subjects and thus are representations; photographs stand in a causal relation to their subjects and thus are not representations, but mere simulacra. However, Scruton is careful to qualify this claim by saying that he is referring to 'ideal' photography, by which he means a logical fiction, a type of photography unpolluted by the attempts of photographers to ape the methods of painting, by manipulating photographs through touching them up, using multiple exposures or montage, etc.[9]

Scruton understands the difference between causal and intentional relations in the following way, instanced by the two kinds of images. Since a causal relation obtains, from the existence of an (ideal) photograph of a subject it logically follows that its subject exists, that the subject appears roughly as it appears in the photograph, and that its appearance in the photograph is its appearance at a particular moment.[10] In contrast, (ideal) painting stands in an intentional relation to its subject: it does not logically follow from the existence of the painting that its subject exists, or that the painting represents its subject as it is, or that there is some particular of the type the painting represents.[11]

So because photography essentially involves a causal relation to its subject and painting an intentional relation to its subject, (ideal) photographs, unlike (ideal) paintings, do not express thoughts and therefore are not representations. There are two further points to note. First, though Scruton's argument employs the notion of intentionality in a general sense, he takes intentions in the narrow sense (a particular kind of intentional state) to be the crucial psychological states involved in differentiating

---

[7] *Ibid.*, p. 115.   [8] *Ibid.*, p. 105.
[9] *Ibid.*, pp. 103 and 117–18.   [10] *Ibid.*, p. 112.   [11] *Ibid.*, p. 103.

between the two kinds of images: 'the painting stands in this intentional relation to its subject because of a representational act, the artist's act, and in characterizing the relation between a painting and its subject we are also describing the artist's intention'.[12] Given Scruton's focus on artists' intentions, I will mainly concentrate on them too for purposes of examining his argument. Secondly, it is because the thoughts conveyed about a subject can be different from the properties of a subject that the properties of a representation can be radically different from those of its subject: a martyrdom is horrifying, and therefore so must a photograph of it be; but a painting of it could be serene.[13] And likewise 'if one finds a photograph beautiful, it is because one finds something beautiful in its subject. A painting may be beautiful, on the other hand, even when it represents an ugly thing'.[14] We can call this feature of a representation the possibility of *aesthetic transformation*.

The conclusion is that ideal photography cannot be a representational art form. Of course, actual photographs can aspire to be art, by attempting to be representations, but if this happens, as for instance in the use of photomontage, 'one must then so interfere with the relation between the photograph and its subject that it ceases to be a *photograph* of its subject'.[15] And in the case of cinema, any such artistic effect must also depart from the photographic basis of the medium.

Scruton's argument clearly articulates a version of the worry that photography, and therefore cinema, cannot be an art form because of its essentially causal nature. Indeed, Scruton's version of the argument touches on earlier accounts at more than one point. His notion of a perfect simulacrum is closely related to what Arnheim calls the 'complete' film – a film that is indistinguishable from reality, because it is so complete a copy of it. Likewise, Scruton's claim that (non-abstract) art requires representation in the sense indicated earlier is closely connected to Arnheim's view that art requires expression, since by the latter Arnheim appears to have in mind the communication of thoughts generally, not just of feelings. But whereas Scruton holds that ideal photography cannot overcome its representational incapacity, Arnheim holds that film has an expressive capacity.

If we refute Scruton's argument, we will have answered a powerful articulation of the traditional worry that film cannot be an art because of its causal basis. Begin by noting that even if Scruton is correct about photography's representational incapacity, his argument does not generalise to cinema, despite his claim to the contrary. For he holds that actual

[12] *Ibid.*   [13] *Ibid.*, p. 115.   [14] *Ibid.*, p. 114.   [15] *Ibid.*, p. 120.

photography can become representational only by moving away from ideal photography, by adopting non-photographic techniques. He mentions in this respect photomontage: one might put together photographs of people in such a way that they appear to be quarrelling, but the result is not a photograph of a quarrel; rather, 'it is, to all intents and purposes, a paint-ing'.[16] Suppose that one conceded that the picture is a representation of a quarrel only by virtue of its non-photographic properties. A parallel argu-ment would not show that a film putting together different shots of people so that they seemed to be quarrelling is not a film of a quarrel. For montage (editing) is one of the central features of cinema, taken to its greatest heights by the Soviet school, and it certainly cannot be regarded as a non-cinematic technique. Indeed, given that the normal length of a photographic film roll (about ten minutes of running time) is considerably less than the length of the average film, it is not just possible, but actually necessary, to use montage to produce a traditional, i.e., photochemical, film. So there is no plausibility in saying that a film of a quarrel produced by montage is somehow something else – 'to all intents and purposes a moving painting', perhaps? The use of montage may (perhaps) produce something that is not strictly speaking a photograph, but it certainly does not produce something that is not strictly speaking a film.[17]

Scruton also holds that not only can cinematic art at best depend only on the drama which it photographs, but that its chance of dramatic success is a remote one; for unlike theatre it has no clear criterion for establishing which aspects of what is screened are of aesthetic relevance.[18] Yet this argument also fails; for even if one believed that a film had no clear way of showing which features of the filmed scene were of aesthetic relevance, this could in fact form the basis of an argument that cinema is superior to drama. For lack of a criterion of relevance might contribute to the richness of the work of art, allowing an endless set of interpretations to develop, each locating different features of the film as of aesthetic significance. Such a situation would

---

[16] *Ibid.*, p. 118.

[17] Scruton discusses a famous case of Eisenstein's use of montage in *Battleship Potemkin*, a short sequence which is comprised of three shots of stone lions, the first asleep, the second with open eyes, the third rampant. He remarks that this is a powerful comment on the impotence of imperial splendour, but that this is achievable only because of the intentional juxtaposition of the images, which goes beyond a strictly causal relation (this isn't a photograph of a stone lion roaring) (*ibid.*, p. 125). The point is correct, but the concession that this is an instance of genuine cinematic commentary undermines his claim that 'whatever representational properties belong to it [a film] belong by virtue of the representation that is effected in the dramatic action, that is, by virtue of the words and activities of the actors in the film' (*ibid.*, p. 122).

[18] *Ibid.*, pp. 123–5.

certainly reduce the control of the artist, but that might in certain ways be to the good: a work can be aesthetically richer than its maker intended. But in any case, it is evident that films do have some techniques for determining what is of aesthetic relevance: for instance, characters and objects filmed in close-up, or those towards which the camera is moving, or those picked out in bright light, or in contrasting colours to their backgrounds, are those to which the viewer is supposed to attend.[19]

So even if Scruton were correct that photographs are not representational, this would not show that cinema is not an (independent) representational art, because the purportedly non-photographic element of montage is certainly not non-cinematic. However, this point in itself would restrict cinematic artistry to the editing, which is something that theorists such as Pudovkin came close to suggesting,[20] but which would severely curtail the scope of the claim of cinema to be an art. So we need to examine Scruton's claims about photography.

One might begin by suggesting that it is not true that for something to be a representation requires it to involve the expression of a thought. We say, for instance, that the level of mercury in a thermometer represents the temperature. And cognitive science talks of representations in the mind at the sub-personal level: modular theories of the mind talk of modules forming representations of colours, shapes and sizes, for instance. Yet arguably nothing at the sub-personal level has thoughts, for thoughts are properties of conscious beings, not of components of such beings (which is not to say that thoughts do not supervene on sub-personal facts). Hence it cannot be a necessary condition of something being a representation that it be the expression of a thought.

However, though this is true, there is also a legitimate sense of 'representation' that requires that thoughts be expressed. Moreover, a variant of Scruton's argument against photographic art would still go through if talk of representations were dropped entirely and the argument were reformulated thus: it is a necessary condition for a medium to constitute a (non-abstract) art form that it be the vehicle for the expression of thoughts about its subject-matter; and (ideal) photographs, being causally generated, are not capable of expressing thoughts. Hence there would be little advantage to be gained for our present purposes by attacking Scruton's construal of

[19] Scruton also holds that cinema tends to induce a kind of fantasy, which is a non-aesthetic phenomenon (*ibid.*, p. 125–6; and 'Fantasy, Imagination and the Screen'). For a critique of the claim that film as a medium somehow tends to encourage or be an expression of perversion, see my 'On Cinema and Perversion'.

[20] See Vsevolod Pudovkin, *Film Acting and Film Technique*.

representations, and in discussing his view I will, for the sake of the argument, understand a representation to require the expression of thoughts.

Taking this construal of representations as given, are photographs representations? Some of Scruton's observations about ideal photographs are clearly correct. He identifies what we can call a truth of *logical ontology*: if P is a photograph of O, then O existed at the time P was taken, and P is a photograph of the appearance of O at that particular time.[21] This is of course compatible with the existence of fakes – they seem to be photographs of O, but are not. (However, it does not follow that O is broadly as it appears to be in the photograph: one could in principle employ cunningly designed distorting lenses which transformed a photograph of what is in fact a dog into what appears to be a photograph of a cat.)

But the difference of logical ontology between photographs and paintings does not prove what Scruton thinks it does. What it does show is that whereas there can be no natural paintings (i.e., paintings formed without intentional agency), there could be natural photographs: for instance, there could be a shallow pool of naturally formed photographic salts in deep hollows, below a crystal roof which functioned as a lens, and which was briefly exposed to sunlight through a land slippage; such a natural formation might fix the image of some passing elephant on the floor of the pool. We would have no conceptual reason for denying that this is a photograph of the elephant, any more than we have reason for denying that a lump of clay trodden on by the elephant is a cast of the elephant's foot. In contrast, a storm that blew pigments together so that they looked like a painting of an elephant would not be one. Since a photograph can stand in a purely causal relation to its subject, it can be the product of purely causal forces; but, since a painting stands in an intentional relation to its subject, it must be the product of an intentional agent.

Besides these fantasy cases, the difference in logical ontology does have some consequences in practice. For instance, it shows that there is a certain sense in which all films are documentaries: any fiction film involving actors is necessarily a documentary about what certain actors did on certain soundstages at certain times in the past (though the documentary is rather peculiar in that what they doing is usually shown out of temporal order). For many purposes thinking of fiction films in this way is likely to be distracting or

---

[21] Strictly speaking, from the existence of a photograph, *P*, of *O*, it follows that *O* existed at *or before* the time *P* was taken, since it is possible to take photographs of stars that have ceased to exist by the time that their light reaches us. And the second claim should be construed so that, though the photograph captures the appearance of *O* on film *at that particular time*, the appearance of *O* on film need not be the same as how it would appear to the naked eye.

irrelevant, but for some purposes it can very be useful – for instance, in showing how the technique of certain actors developed over time. In contrast it is not true that any painting of an individual is necessarily a painting of a particular individual (a painting of Hercules need not have used any particular man as a model).

However, this contrast, while apposite, does not prove what Scruton hopes to prove by using it: namely, that with ideal photographs intentions are not expressed. For whilst no intentions figure in the naturally occurring photographs mentioned above, in practice no photographs are like this, being rather the products of intentional acts. Such real-life photographs may still be ideal in Scruton's sense, for they are not the products of manipulation via photomontage, or touching up of photographic plates, etc. Nevertheless they can display a manifold of intentions: someone intended to photograph something, the subject was perhaps posed or arranged in a certain way, a certain aperture f-stop, shutter exposure and type of photographic stock were chosen, etc. These activities are not extra-photographic manipulation, but they are on the contrary core activities in producing a photograph. One suspects that Scruton commits, or comes perilously close to committing, a modal scope fallacy in his claims about ideal photographs: it is true that intentions are not necessarily expressed in an ideal photograph; but it does not follow that intentions are necessarily not expressed in it. Only if 'ideal' meant not 'non-manipulated', but 'naturally occurring' would it be true that ideal photographs necessarily do not express intentions. But why ever should the logical possibility of naturally occurring photographs show that non-manipulated photographs do not involve the expression of intentions?[22]

Scruton has a further defence here: he holds that the kinds of intentions involved in posing a subject and choosing a point of view cannot make something a representation, since they might be present when someone chooses a subject before whom he places a mirror, setting up the mirror to show a certain point of view on the subject; yet a mirror is not a representation.[23] However, this only shows that such intentions may not be sufficient on their own to make something a representation; but it may be that such intentions are sufficient given the presence of other features as

[22] Note that a parallel point applies to intentionality in general, not just to intentions as a specific kind of intentional state. It is true that ideal (i.e., non-manipulated) photographs do not necessarily stand in intentional relations to their subjects, because of the point of logical ontology which Scruton notes – and hence natural photographs are possible. But this is compatible with photographs, in addition to the purely causal relation in which they stand to their subjects, also contingently standing in intentional relations to them – i.e., it is compatible with photographs conveying thoughts. And real-life non-manipulated photographs do stand in such intentional relations.

[23] Scruton, 'Photography and Representation', p. 119.

well – i.e., such intentions may not be individually sufficient, but may be jointly sufficient with some other conditions. For instance, the reason why a mirror is not a representation, even if such intentions are manifested, is plausibly because a mirror, unlike a photograph, cannot *fix* an image. If it could, then it is hard to see why a mirror could not be a representation.

It is worth developing the thought that photographs can be representations (i.e., representations expressing thoughts). Scruton's position is designed to show that (ideal) photographs, unlike paintings, cannot communicate thoughts about their subject. How might in fact they do so? Let us first examine how painting achieves this. Consider Ingres' magnificent *Madame Moitessier* (1851, National Gallery of Art, Washington DC). She stands before us resplendent in a black lace dress, gazing out calmly and dispassionately at the viewer, her left shoulder inclined towards us, the beringed hand cradling a gold fan, her right arm across her waist, her thumb linked through her long chain of pearls. She is standing apparently in her drawing room, with a low empanelled section below the dado, and a rich velvet embroidered wallpaper above; she is positioned carefully between her chair and fireplace. Clearly Ingres is communicating to us several ideas through this image: *Madame*'s posture is derived from the contrapposto stance of the Italian Renaissance, and her skin is the cool purity of marble. She is thus visually linked to Renaissance and Classical ideals of beauty: she is the acme of a traditional ideal of beauty. Wealth, displayed on her person and around her, is linked with taste and beauty in an indissoluble whole; so we are being told that wealth and beauty belong intimately together. Ideas of the rightness of social hierarchy, the proper role of painting in celebrating it, and the nobility of painting derived from its embeddedness in the classical tradition, are all being conveyed by this image. Now imagine *Madame* painted by Oskar Kokoschka: her poise is uncertain and unbalanced, she has lost quite a lot of weight, the careful tonal gradations of the flesh have yielded to a flame-like structure of strong colour contrasts furiously battling for prominence, the background is now indeterminate and grey. Not the power of privilege, but its perhaps imminent demise; not the greatness of the classical tradition, but the importance of immediate raw observation; not the serenity of beauty, but the nervous flickerings of desire are now being conveyed to us. Or consider the same figure painted by Lucian Freud. Let us allow *Madame* to preserve her modesty and retain her clothes: still, the flesh that we can see seems almost like meat, its surface translucent, revealing the veined reds and slab-like blues below; the figure is now twisted and uncomfortable, stripped of her finery, poised in a bare and anonymous room; she is no longer the sublime and confident returner of the viewer's gaze, but its uneasy and uncertain recipient. This is the world of humankind as the displayed object of the artist's unwavering attention, a world in which social class counts for nothing, where the sense of mortality weighs on subject and artist alike.

As even these straightforward observations make clear, painting can convey intricate thoughts about the personality of its subjects, about social class, about ideals of beauty, about the role of painting and the artist's place in tradition. Painting is, in Scruton's sense of the term, undoubtedly a representational art. But it should also be clear that photography can perform the same tasks. Imagine Ingres' subject portrayed by photographers. As photographed by Sir Cecil Beaton, Moitessier might be surrounded by a splendid set, richly bedecked with drapery and with intricate, luxuriously carved detail; she is attired in the latest Parisian finery, a coquettish gleam in her eye, illuminated by an elegant three-point lighting set-up, her image printed in subtly modulated tones on glossy paper. Here beauty is seen not as something intimately related to classical ideals, but as something always of the moment; the beautiful object is not unattainable, but is closely linked to just having fun; and the task of the photographer is not searchingly to dig up truth, but to celebrate, to exult in, the sheer surface beauty of the world. *Madame*, we can be sure, would approve. Suppose, in contrast, that she instead found herself invited down to the Isle of Wight, and were caught before Julia Margaret Cameron's camera. Now only her head is shown; she is lost in sepulchral gloom, lit from a single point source up and to her right; her image is slightly blurred, and she seems to be lost in faraway and despondent reflections, perhaps brought on by reading just a little too much Tennyson. *Madame* aspires to mental depth. Here we have the thought conveyed of the human face as the picture of the human soul, a soul concerned with large and vague reflections, focused on grave and eternal matters. We have the idea imparted of photography not as the recorder of glittering surfaces, but as a stripping away of those appearances to reveal the spiritual life shimmering beneath them. Or imagine our subject now spirited away to be captured by Diane Arbus' camera – *Madame* would not like this at all. She is posed full on against a neutral background, standing awkwardly and slightly off balance, her skin surprisingly blotchy (a defect previously masked by Ingres' pearly translucence of tone and by Cameron's forgiving shadows). She seems very uncomfortable in front of the camera, somehow out of harmony with her world, blankly uncomprehending of how miserable her situation really is. Photography is here deployed as the revealer of the sheer ungainliness, the brute ugliness of the human condition, a painful reminder of how shallow and impotent our illusions really are.

One could go on, but *Madame* has done sterling work and she deserves a rest. Photography, it should be clear, can convey a similarly rich set of thoughts as painting – thoughts concerning the personality of its subjects, the nature of life, the role of photography, the place of tradition, and so forth. The means available to the photographer for conveying these thoughts are various: through the choice, posing, and dressing of subjects, the adoption of means of lighting and printing, the selection of lenses, the building-up of an artistic *persona* across a multiplicity of photographs, in the light of which we interpret the photographer's individual images, and so on. Further, that photographs are representations is witnessed by the fact that they too have the capacity for aesthetic transformation. Scruton correctly notes that paintings are capable of aesthetic transformation – a painting of a horrifying martyrdom can be serene, and a painting that represents something ugly can be beautiful. But the same holds true of photographs: a photograph of a crucifixion might be serene, where the scene is shown from a great distance, set against a pure blue, tranquil sky; and a photograph of ugly coal slag-heaps might be seductively beautiful if shot through colour filters or when the setting sun colours the scene. So on the test of aesthetic transformation, we should conclude that if paintings are representations, photographs are as well.

Photographs are, then, representations in Scruton's sense of being expressions of thought, and nothing it seems prevents us from concluding that photography (and cinema) is a representational art. But Scruton has another argument available that would allow him to block this last claim, even if he were forced to concede that photographs are representations. For he holds that a representational art requires one to have an aesthetic interest in representation, and an aesthetic interest is an interest in something for its own sake; thus for something to be a representational art requires one to be interested in the representation for its own sake.[24] But with a photograph, unless we have a merely abstract aesthetic interest in its formal properties, we are interested in it merely insofar as it tells us about its subject and not insofar as it is a representation, i.e., we are not interested in how it presents its subject; and the latter claim he supports by denying the possibility in photographs of what we earlier termed *aesthetic transformation*.[25]

However, as we saw, aesthetic transformation can and does occur in photographs. And whilst it may be true that the untrained eye's interest in photographs is usually centred on what they show about their subject, it is an important aim of training in photographic (and cinematic) appreciation

[24] *Ibid.*, pp. 108–10.   [25] *Ibid.*, pp. 114–16.

to shift attention to the question of *how* the photographer presents her subject, to focus on the ways in which she manages to achieve effects and to convey thoughts about it. And, as our imagined scenario of Madame Moitessier's posthumous photographic career illustrates, there is every reason to think that photographs can reward this kind of attention.[26] Scruton also claims that the photographer does not have that degree of control over the detail of the image which the painter possesses, and which is required for construing the image as transparent to human intentions and so as being the fitting object of interest in representation for its own sake.[27] But, as the Moitessier examples also illustrate, photographers can have enough control over detail for the images to count as the expression of sometimes quite rich and intricate thoughts, and so the resulting photographs can amply reward aesthetic attention to their mode of representation.

We should conclude, then, that photography is a representational art. Our main question is the broader one of whether photography (and traditional cinema) is an art *tout court*; and a positive answer to this follows of course from the fact that photography (and traditional cinema) is a representational art. Concerning this broader question, there are two observations worth adding. Firstly, as Scruton concedes, even if photography were not a representational art, it might still be an art, because of its formal properties – so we might be interested in it as an abstract art. And this is correct: one can display an interest in the intrinsic aesthetic features of an artwork; in the case of a painting or a photograph, one can be interested in the formal balance and unity of the composition, its tonal harmonies, and so on. These acts of attention all have features of the artwork as their objects, yet none is in itself a way of attending to how the work represents its subject.[28] Thus even if one thought that photographs were not representations, in the sense of having the capacity to communicate thoughts, it would not follow that they could not be artworks, since they might have other artistic properties. This further strengthens the case for photography (and cinema) being an art.

Secondly, if, as I have argued elsewhere, the correct account of art is specified by a cluster concept, then the communication of thoughts (which

---

[26] King, 'Scruton and Reasons for Looking at Photographs' also discusses some real-life examples of interest in photographs in respect of the manner in which they represent their subjects.

[27] Scruton, 'Photography and Representation', p. 117.

[28] Further, attention to how a subject is presented by an artwork need not always be attention to a communicated thought which the photographer *intended* to convey. A photograph may present its subject in ways that the photographer did not intend – a high angle may make the subject look insignificant, for instance, even though the photographer was trying to exalt it. So certain features of modes of presentation need not always be intended, and therefore Scruton's equation between thoughts communicated and the artist's intentions, breaks down.

is essential to something being a representation on Scruton's view) will plausibly be just one ground for holding an object to be an artwork, and should not be held to be a necessary condition for something to be an artwork.[29] For a cluster account holds that there are no necessary conditions for something to be art. However, some of the plausible criteria for an object's being an artwork – such as being expressive of emotion, being intellectually challenging (questioning received views and modes of thought), and having a capacity to convey complex meanings, for instance – of necessity require the artwork to communicate thoughts. So it must be the case that having a communicative capacity is criterial for something to be art. And others of the criteria – possessing aesthetic properties, being formally complex and coherent, and being the product of a high degree of skill, for instance – are such that they can qualify the communication of thoughts (for instance, communication can be elegant, complex and skilful). In these cases, having a communicative capacity widens the range of possible features of the art object which can instantiate these criteria, and may thus indirectly contribute to something being an artwork. So on the cluster account of the concept of art, there are grounds for rejecting the claim that it is a *necessary* condition for something to be an artwork in general that it communicate thoughts; but such an account also supports the claim that this is an important *criterion* for something to be an artwork. Applying this weaker claim to the case of film, we get the following position: film is an art form *partly* by virtue of its representational capacities.

I.2 THE REPRODUCTION CHALLENGE

Scruton articulates in sophisticated fashion a version of the traditional challenge to cinematic art deriving from its status as a medium of causally generated images. However, there is a further challenge to cinema as an art that is almost invariably run together with this causal challenge, and both challenges are to be found in the traditional concern about cinema as an art. Arnheim put the concern this way: 'Film cannot be art, for it does nothing but reproduce reality mechanically'.[30] The first challenge contained herein is that film is mechanical: i.e., it is generated by a causal process, and therefore has no room for the expression of artistic intentions. Scruton's objection is mainly an elaboration of this version of the worry. But the other

---

[29] See my '"Art" as a Cluster Concept' and 'The Cluster Account of Art Defended' for a defence of a criterial account of the concept of art.

[30] Arnheim, *Film as Art*, p. 8.

aspect of the challenge is that film *reproduces* reality. Reproduction of some item occurs when someone produces another one of it. This challenge is that film does no more than produce an exact copy of reality, and therefore purportedly has no role for the expression of artistic intentions. Consider the case of waxworks: Arnheim in discussing the spectre of the complete film – a film which is perceptually indistinguishable from the reality it films – says that 'the film is on its way to the victory of wax museum ideals over creative art'[31]; and Scruton in arguing that film tends to encourage and satisfy fantasy, argues that film is a simulacrum which is the object of fantasy, just as a waxwork is, since it is a copy of reality.[32] The reproduction challenge is based on the thought that if an object is an exact copy of reality, there is no room for artistic manipulation of it, and therefore no room for the expression of artistic intentions or the communication of thoughts. Intentions are expressed only if there is a deviation between the copy and its model, which allows a suitably informed spectator to infer their presence from comparison of the two.

The causal challenge, we can now see, is distinct from the reproduction challenge: causal copies need not be exact likenesses (photographic images can be severely distorted by using anamorphic lenses, for instance); and whilst a high-quality waxwork of a person is certainly a good reproduction of his appearance, it need not be causally generated (by, for instance, taking a mould of him), but rather can be intentionally, meticulously crafted, and so can stand in an intentional relation to him. So the traditional challenge to cinematic art has two distinct strands: the causal challenge and the reproduction challenge. How is the latter to be answered?

Though Arnheim, like Scruton, tends to run together the two versions of the objection, his main focus is on answering the reproduction objection. And his chief move in answering it is unobjectionable. He notes that 'even at the most elementary level there are significant divergences between the image that the camera makes of reality and that which the human eye sees'.[33] We could put the point this way: an exact (visual) reproduction of x is one that is visually indiscriminable from x (where 'x' is a variable ranging over objects and events). So if a film were an exact reproduction of x it would be the case that the film of x would be visually indiscriminable from x. But this is obviously not the case: we have no difficulty at all in distinguishing

[31] *Ibid.*, p. 154.
[32] Scruton, 'Fantasy, Imagination and the Screen', p. 129. Scruton in fact tends to run together the two distinct aspects of the objection that are disentangled above.
[33] Arnheim, *Film as Art*, p. 127.

between films and what they are films of. And the same is of course true of photographs: a photograph of an apple is rectangular, flat, and perhaps in black and white; an apple is none of these things.

So the reproduction challenge is easily answered; but then a further more difficult question naturally presents itself: given that a film fails in certain respects to be an exact copy of reality, in which particular respects is failure required in order for the film to be a work of art? Or in the light of our answer to the first challenge, we can put the question this way: given that film is an art partly by virtue of its capacity to be a representation, in what particular respects is failure of reproduction required in order for a film to be a representation? After all, not just any failure of a film exactly to reproduce reality will qualify it as a work of art. A badly maintained photocopier may produce smeary copies of the papers put into it; such copies are not exact reproductions of their input, yet neither are they works of art.

Arnheim answered the question in part in this way: film can be an art because of the divergences between film and reality, where these divergences are used for artistic ends.[34] In contrast, the complete film – a film perceptually indistinguishable from its subject – cannot be a work of art, precisely because it does not diverge at all from reality.

There is something important and correct about this claim, but in Arnheim's hands it goes astray. For he famously concludes from it that the sound film is inherently aesthetically inferior to the silent film. If the complete film is the antithesis of the film as art, then the closer a film comes to completeness, he believed, the greater must be its artistic failure, other things equal. Hence the sound film is inherently aesthetically inferior to the silent film. Yet that, in the light of subsequent cinematic developments, is a hard claim to swallow. So how can we disentangle what is correct about Arnheim's claim from what leads him astray?

Arnheim gives several examples of the divergence between silent film and reality and of the artistic exploitation of these divergences. These divergences he generally thinks of as limitations that film has compared to reality: for instance, silent films lacks sound, reality does not; black and white films lack colour, reality does not; film lacks a space–time continuum (they can move from one represented point of time or space to another point instantaneously), reality does not; film has a delimited frame, reality (and our visual field) does not; film is limited to one point of view at a time, reality is not, etc. The film artist uses these limitations for artistic purposes. The lack of

[34] The other part of his claim is that the divergences must be in ways distinctive to the cinematic medium; I defend the distinctiveness claim in Section 7.5.

sound is used by Josef von Sternberg in *The Docks of New York* (1928) to create a striking effect: a revolver shot is illustrated by the sudden rise of a flock of birds.[35] The lack of colour can aid compositional unity in the creation of the shot, and to create an effective symbolism of light versus darkness, again as illustrated by Sternberg's film.[36] The lack of the space–time continuum allows the artist to use montage, by which a film can flip from one represented point of space or time immediately to another one, and so to create a representation radically different from the reality filmed.[37] The existence of the film frame allows the artist to show us a part of a scene, and then only later to show the whole of it – as when Chaplin has a medium-shot from the waist up of himself turned out in top hat and tails, and then the next shot shows that he has no trousers on, and is standing there in his underpants.[38] The fact that a shot is always taken from one point of view can similarly be exploited for artistic effect, as when in another film Chaplin, who has been deserted by his wife, shows us a shot of himself taken from the back, his shoulders heaving up and down, apparently sobbing; he then turns around to reveal that he is vigorously manipulating a cocktail shaker.[39]

These examples leave no doubt that artistic effects are possible by manipulation of features of the cinematic medium. But not all the features concerned are happily described as limitations of film as compared to reality. Certainly, early projected films could not employ colour or sound, and were therefore limited, i.e., had a representational incapacity in these respects. But absence of the space–time continuum is not correctly described as a limitation. Rather, by using it films can do something that one cannot do in reality: they can flip from one represented point of time or space to another point instantaneously. This is an extra capacity, not a limitation. So the divergence between film and reality is sometimes a matter of limitation, sometimes of an extra capacity.[40]

Secondly, mere divergence together with artistic use cannot be sufficient to make a film an artwork. Cinema diverges from our usual everyday situation in that we are in a darkened room with a beam of light coming in from behind us. But that is something completely fixed by the technology of cinema if good viewing conditions are to be achieved – it is not the

---

[35] *Ibid.*, p. 107.   [36] *Ibid.*, pp. 66–7.   [37] *Ibid.*, pp. 87–102.   [38] *Ibid.*, p. 78.   [39] *Ibid.*, p. 51.
[40] In fact, Arnheim himself also writes at several points of capacities, rather than limitations (e.g., at *ibid.*, p. 111), so he was aware of the point made above. But my point is that his argument for the aesthetic inferiority of sound and colour film requires him to think in terms of limitations, not in terms of capacities. Once we appeal to capacities, we can correctly identify those divergences of cinema required for it to be an art.

case, for instance, that sometimes the beam moves around, coming in from the side rather than the back, or that the lighting level is constantly fluctuating. The fact that this is a fixed divergence means that it cannot be exploited for artistic expression, for we cannot think of the filmmakers as trying to communicate something to us through it. For instance, we cannot appropriately think of the beam of light coming over our heads as a metaphor for spiritual transcendence, even if the film being screened is about such transcendence. Consider another divergence between film and reality fixed by technology: the film image is always bounded in some way by a screen, and lacks genuine depth, being only two-dimensional (and this is true of course even of 'three-dimensional' films, which consist of overlapping two-dimensional images). So the mere facts that the projected image has spatial limits and lacks genuine depth cannot be used to convey, for example, a sense of restriction and oppression in a film. In contrast, the shape of the image, which is variable, can be used for expressive purposes. For instance, in *Rebel Without A Cause* (1955) the exceptionally wide screen is employed to convey a sense that the characters, particularly Jim, the young man played by James Dean, are oppressed by their society and surroundings.[41] This is a genuine case of cinematic commentary and it depends on the fact that the image can have different dimensions (i.e., the aspect ratio of the image is variable). It is because the divergence is variable that image dimensions can be used for expressive purposes; but the mere fact that the image is bounded by a screen cannot be, for that is a given.

These claims might seem false. After all, could one not draw attention to the fact that there is a beam of light projected over the audience's head, by showing such a beam in the film and giving it an expressive role? Or could one not draw attention to the image's boundaries by having characters prominently set half in and half out of the image or constantly crossing and recrossing the boundary?[42] The answer is that one could do these things; but this does not undermine the claim that fixed divergences cannot be used for expressive purposes: for in these cases, it is features of the image's content (the image of a beam of light, or of characters straddling the boundary) that are doing the expressive work, and of course the content of the image is variable. So the claim about fixed divergences stands.

Thus, not only can divergence from reality be a matter of extra capacities rather than limitations, it must also be *variable* divergence if artistic employment is to be possible. And further examples illustrate that for this variable

---

[41] George Wilson, *Narration in Light*, p. 170.   [42] The objection is due to Patrick Maynard.

divergence to be fully understood it must be specified in terms of variation relative to some culturally and/or historically specified norm.

Consider first the case of lenses. Shooting a scene through a normal lens produces a film image that diverges, i.e., is perceptibly discriminable, from the actual scene, but nevertheless strongly resembles it in certain respects.[43] What allows the divergence to be used for expressive purposes is that there is a variety of lenses, which can instead be employed to shoot the scene. Wide-angle (short-focal length) lenses produce a characteristic 'fish bowl' effect, bowing out lines located in a plane before the camera into a convex effect and expanding space on an axis running away from the camera. They are often employed to make characters loom towards the viewer, perhaps slightly threateningly, or to open up space in a confined room. Long lenses in contrast bend lines in a plane before us into concave shapes, and collapse the spatial dimension running along an axis away from the camera. The effect is to flatten space and to dynamise movement against a background. Variation of lenses can achieve striking effects: in *Twelve Angry Men* (1957) as the tension increases in the jury room over the jury's decision, the increasingly confrontational scenes are shot with progressively longer lenses. The strategy conveys the sense that the characters have less and less space in which to move and are pressed up one against the other. Here again we see the importance of not simply deviation, but of variable deviation (being able to shoot through different lenses) for the possibility of artistic communication. But note as well that what matters is that the variation is relative to a norm – the normal lens – which allows us to identify the different expressive effects.

A second example concerns camera movement. One striking difference between looking at a film and looking at a bit of reality is that the shot in the film has an intrinsic perspective, whereas reality does not. In both cases there is the viewer's point of view on the object, but only the shot has an intrinsic perspective. (Thus when I move around a cinema, my point of view on the film shifts, but the intrinsic perspective of the image does not.) The intrinsic perspective of the shot can be mobile or not: the shot can be from one fixed position, or the camera may move. Early films such as those of the Lumière brothers employed a fixed camera. Early cameras were too delicate and cumbersome to move easily. Thus the fact that the camera stayed put was simply a given in these films and had no expressive meaning. However, now that camera movement has become a commonplace, holding the camera stationary for very long periods of time is correctly construed

---

[43] See Section 2.3.6 for a discussion of what these respects are in which resemblance holds.

as making an expressive point. For instance, in Chantal Akerman's *Jeanne Dielman, 23 quai du Commerce, 1980 Bruxelles* (1975) the camera is stationary in each interior shot in the film, and this comments on the trapped existence of the eponymous character: the camera cannot move, Jeanne Dielman cannot escape. For Akerman, employing a stationary camera was a matter of choice, whereas for the Lumière brothers it was not.[44] Because *variable* deviation was possible for Akerman, she could use lack of camera movement for expressive effect. And we interpret the lack of movement here against a norm of the general degree of camera movement in feature-length films. It is again variation relative to a norm that allows expression to occur here, and one must understand the historical context in order to grasp when such variation is to be interpreted expressively.

A third example concerns the use of low-angle shots. One standard use of these shots is as 'power shots', to convey the power or threat of an individual, who is shot from below. Think of the looming, threatening shots of Charles Foster Kane's face towards the end of his life taken from a position almost on the floor. These shots are variations relative to a norm: we do not in real life usually observe individuals while lying on our backs on the floor (except perhaps when we are very drunk). Western cinema takes roughly the height of an adult as the height from which the camera usually films. And in the shots of Kane just mentioned, variation from this real-life observation point is used to convey a certain expressive point. In Japanese films, particularly those of the classical period, similarly low-angle shots of individuals abound. But they do not convey a threat: they are known as *tatami* shots, and are taken as if the viewer were sitting on a *tatami*, a floor mat, observing someone – which was a normal observation point for Japanese society of that time. Hence the norm, variation relative to which is at issue here, must be at least partly culturally specified – the normal viewing point of Japanese society of a certain period differs from the normal viewing point of Western societies.

So Arnheim's view that film can be an art form by virtue of diverging from mechanical reproduction of reality is not strictly speaking correct, given that he tends to construe divergence in terms of fixed limitations on the reproductive capacities of the medium. What matters is not exploitation of limitations, but rather exploitation of the medium's presentational capacities – and specifically the medium's capacities to record reality in

---

[44] This point should not be construed to hold that an agent expresses something only if the agent chooses to express that thing. One can express one's anger, for instance, unintentionally – one can let slip how annoyed one really is. The point is simply that the agent must have control over the means of expression (e.g., facial expression and tone of voice), not that all expression is intentionally chosen.

different ways, where these different ways can vary relative to a norm of how reality is recorded. It is by virtue not of the limitations of the medium, but by virtue of the medium's capacities to record reality in different ways that film can possess expressive properties, can communicate thoughts.

It is partly because it is capacities that matter and not limitations that Arnheim's views about sound and colour films are badly grounded. Employing sound and colour reduces the divergence between film and reality (for they become less perceptually discriminable from each other), but using sound and colour also grounds new capacities to record reality in different ways. Consider Hitchcock's expressive use of colour: in *Vertigo* (1958) before Scottie meets Madeleine/Judy, the film is predominantly filmed in shades of brown. But afterwards it blossoms into green, expressing his newfound happiness. Likewise, sound creates a new set of ways in which the world can be recorded: a voice can be recorded in a hollow, booming fashion, or in a dry precise sound mix, and so on. Think of the way Kane's voice sounds in the resounding emptiness of Xanadu, for instance. The fact that a section of a film is in black and white can in a black and white film have no expressive power; likewise the fact that there is silence on the sound track can in a silent film have no expressive power. In contrast, in a colour film, a black and white sequence can have expressive force – recall the opening and closing sequences of *The Wizard of Oz* (1939); and in a sound film, silence can have considerable expressive impact. It is not because film is limited in what it can record of reality that it is expressive, but rather because it has recording capacities that can be varied: the same piece of reality can be recorded in different ways.

This also explains why in fact a complete film in Arnheim's sense could, despite what he maintains, also have expressive properties. For if filmmakers chose to make a complete film, then this would be one way of filming a story out of other technically possible ways to do so. And thus their choice of means would be capable of conveying a message – of saying something about the scenes depicted. Only if there were no option but to make the film complete would we be unable to interpret the film as expressing anything. Indeed, to return to one of Arnheim's analogies, it is not even true that waxworks can have no expressive power. For provided that their makers had the option of producing something other than a speaking likeness, the production of such a likeness may express perhaps an objective or ironical or humorous point of view on the subject.[45] This

---

[45] In a related point, Carroll notes that mechanical recordings can have expressive properties, such as matter-of-factness; see his *Philosophical Problems of Classical Film Theory*, p. 78.

is part of the explanation for why artists such as Duane Hanson can make an artistic point by placing extraordinarily lifelike reproductions of real human beings in art galleries. So the condition of variable divergence can be satisfied even if the reproduction is an exact one, provided that it was possible to make the copy look other than exactly the same as the original.

1.3 FILM AND COMMUNICATION

We are now in a position to answer the challenge to the status of traditional film as an art form. That challenge when analysed has two aspects: how can film be an art form, given that it stands in a causal relation to its subject matter? And how can film be an art form, given that it is a mere reproduction of reality? The first part of the challenge was met by showing that there is no reason to deny that, despite their causal generation, films can express thoughts. Films (and photographs) can be representations, in Scruton's sense. The mere logical possibility of naturally occurring photographs does not show that photographs, and therefore films, as they actually exist are not representations. The second part of the challenge was met by noting that films are not exact copies of reality, and hence thoughts can be expressed by the mode of filming reality. Pursuing this second issue, we discovered that it is not because of film's recording limitations that it can be an art. Rather, film can convey thoughts because it has the capacity to record reality in different ways. It is because of the *plasticity* of its recording capacities that film can be representational – that is, scenes can be filmed in different ways: by selecting different optical points of view, different lenses, different camera movements, different film stocks, different techniques of editing, different aspect ratios, and so on. These variations in ways of recording can communicate something about the scenes recorded. Thus photography and film are representations (i.e., they can communicate thoughts), and can do so because objects and events can be recorded in different ways.

This point links to a very general observation about the conditions required for communication. Any communicative act must involve some means of communication – language, gestures, smoke signals, or whatever. For information to be transferred, it must be possible to produce variations in the signals within that means of communication. There must be available very many words, types of gestures or smoke shapes. And it must be possible for an agent to control which of these various signals are produced, for otherwise one cannot infer the expression of thoughts (intentional states in general) by the agent from the variation within the signals produced.[46]

Films clearly satisfy these conditions, since a variety of signals in the medium can be produced. One can communicate thoughts. But crucially for our purposes, the variations in the signals are producible not just by filming different objects or events, but by filming any given object or event in several different ways. And it is because of this variation in the *mode* of filming, rather than in the *content* that is filmed, that we can properly hold the artistry to reside in the mastery of the medium and not just in the mastery exhibited in what is being filmed. Film is an art, not simply the recording of an art: communication occurs via the mode of presentation of content, not simply via the presentation of different contents. And because communication requires control over the means of communication, we must be able to attribute control of the mode of presentation to a film-maker, if she is to be seen as communicating by means of it: that is why we can correctly interpret Akerman's stationary camera as expressive, whilst the same is not true of the Lumières' stationary camera. And this too is why fixed limitations in our practices, such as the beam of light projected over our heads at the cinema, cannot be employed for communicative purposes.

Film, then, is an art form partly by virtue of its representational capacity: its capacity to communicate thoughts about its subject matter. This in turn is made possible by the plasticity of the cinematic recording medium, the fact that it can record its subject matter in a variety of ways. Film, in short, is an art form partly by virtue of its representational capacity, grounded on its plasticity as a recording medium.

1.4 DIGITAL CINEMA AS ART

So far, we have been discussing traditional cinema (i.e., cinema using photochemical images). How far do the arguments considered apply to

---

[46] Note that this claim does not entail the truth of intentionalism about artistic meaning. Firstly, thoughts are intentional states, but it does not follow from this that the agent necessarily intends to express the thought that his utterance in fact expresses – one can communicate either more or less than one intended. So though very often agents intend to express the thoughts that they do express, this is not necessarily so. Secondly, artistic meaning is a broad notion, which encompasses many artistic properties beyond those that are happily assimilated to communicative content. My point here is that the agent must have control over the means of communication in order to express thoughts by means of them, not that all aspects of communicative content are intended. In fact, I will argue against intentionalism in Chapter 4. Also note that if communication occurs, it does not follow that only one person is doing the communicating: there are joint communications. So there is no requirement that all films have a single author – in Chapter 3 I will argue that mainstream films are always collectively authored.

Figure 2. Frodo (Elijah Wood), Gollum and Sam (Sean Astin) in *The Lord of the Rings: The Return of the King* (2003).

digital cinema? We will consider first whether Scruton's arguments apply to digital cinema and if so, whether there is an effective reply to them, and then whether the neo-Arnheimian defence we have employed for traditional film also works for digital cinema.

To examine the application of Scruton's arguments to digital cinema, we need to return to the technical discussion begun in the Introduction. As noted there, one can generate digital images by three main methods: mechanical capture (using cameras, scanners or motion capture), hand construction (using a graphics editing tool) and computer synthesis. All three basic techniques can be combined seamlessly. For instance, the character of Gollum in *The Lord of the Rings* trilogy (2001–3) was generated by motion-capturing the body movements of Andy Serkis, editing them, and then using them to control a largely hand-constructed 3D computer model of Gollum (it was also partly produced by scanning in sculptures of Gollum); the model's movements and expressions were then further adjusted manually using digital tools; a computer algorithm rendered the 3D model into a series of 2D views; and these were then further manually adjusted by digital 'painting' techniques (see Figure 2).[47] These techniques were pushed further in *King Kong* (2005), where motion capture was used

---

[47] See Peter Jackson, *The Lord of the Rings*, Special Extended DVD Edition (2004), especially 'The Taming of Sméagol', Appendix III; and 'Visual Effects' on MASSIVE, Appendix VI.

on Serkis' face as well as his body.[48] The resulting images come across largely as seamless, in the sense that the viewer can see no trace of the separate techniques that were used in their making. So the digital image can be produced by three kinds of techniques (capture, hand making and computer-synthesis) in any proportion, and with a seamlessness to the image that does not betray its origins. Given this mixture of techniques, we can refer to the digital image as a *mélange* (or blended) image – that is, it can be produced by any of three distinct techniques and each technique may vary in the proportion it has in the making of a particular image.

Now consider each of these techniques in terms of Scruton's theory. Clearly the painting (handmade) technique employed to generate a digital image would count as generating an intentional relation to its object on his view, and so would not impugn the status of this kind of digital image as representational in his sense of the term.

Digital photographs, since the essential causal relation is present as with traditional photographs, would not be representations according to Scruton. But the same basic reply employed in the case of the traditional photograph would also work here: the essential presence of a causal relation between a photograph and its subject is consistent with the contingent presence of many intentional relations, capable of expressing thoughts. Moreover, the possibilities of different ways of recording a subject are even greater in the case of the digital than in the case of the traditional photograph, since software packages allow for a greater plasticity of recording means than is possible with the traditional photograph. For instance, lighting levels across different parts of the image can be set with greater exactitude in the case of the digital photograph than is easily achievable by the chemical means of the traditional photograph. Control of details is also greater, so that, for instance, models' skin blemishes can be removed, as can actors' support wires in special effects scenes. And the possibilities of aesthetic transformation are also more striking for the same reasons. One can also show just as much of an interest in the digital photograph for its own sake as one can in the traditional photograph for its own sake.

Finally, consider the computer synthesis aspect: does it cast any doubt on the representational status of the digital image? Computer synthesis simply consists in the computer implementing a series of algorithms, and an algorithm is a precise rule; whether the resulting image has an essentially causal or intentional relation to its subject will depend on whether the

---

[48] See Peter Jackson, *King Kong*, DVD Disc 2 (2006): *Post-Production Diaries*, especially 'Bringing Kong to Life: I and II'.

original input (image or mathematical model) stood in a causal or intentional relation to its subject. If an image is a digital painting, then it does not follow from the existence of the image that the subject existed; implementing, say, a brightening algorithm on the image does not alter that fact. Likewise, if a 3D model (3D graphic) is built by hand using computational tools, then its relation to its subject is intentional and remains so despite the running of an algorithm on it. On the other hand, if the originating image is a digital photograph, then it follows that its subject existed; implementing a brightening algorithm results in a brighter image of the subject, but it is still an image of that subject, so that the necessary existence of the subject, given the existence of the photograph, is not gainsaid. And likewise if a 3D model is built not by hand, but by mechanically scanning an object, that object existed, and if a rendering algorithm generates a 2D image of the object from that model, it still follows that the object existed. Hence whether or not computer synthesis generates an intentional or causally grounded image of the subject depends on the nature of the originating image or model. So one or other of the replies to Scruton just canvassed would apply to the synthesised image too. And the point that one cannot infer from any supposed representational incapacity of a photograph to this incapacity in cinema applies even more strongly to digital cinema, given the greater possibilities for representational transformations in the case of digital cinema. So Scruton's arguments fail for digital images and digital cinema.

Scruton might reply by holding that his arguments do not fail, but rather are inapplicable, because the digital image is not photographic in any of its manifestations: it is entirely handmade, or is computer synthesised on the basis of a handmade image. This is because the possibility of computer manipulation means that one is never dealing with an ideal photograph in the case of the digital image. Digital images are all like paintings and have an intentional relation to their subject because one can manipulate them within graphics editing applications, changing their colours, shapes and so on. This reply would be similar to his claim that techniques such as photomontage transform photographs into non-photographs.

However, it is not true that manipulating a photographic image necessarily makes it into a non-photograph. Printing a photograph on high contrast paper to make its subject look more striking does not transform the photograph into a non-photographic image. Only some kinds of manipulations make a photograph into a different kind of image: for instance, overpainting the image transforms the overpainted parts of the photograph into a painting, and all causal linkage between the subject of the image and the image is lost. Certainly, digital imaging software makes available painting techniques that break the essential causal link between a photograph and its subject. But the mere possibility of using such techniques does not show that, if they are not employed, the resulting image is like a painting, any more than the possibility of overpainting a traditional photograph shows that traditional photographs are like paintings. Moreover, many digital editing methods are akin to traditional darkroom techniques; such techniques include cropping, adjusting exposure times to change the overall lightness of an image, dodging (reducing light to part of an image) or burning in (increasing light to part of the image), the use of texture screens (to impart a particular texture to the photograph), the choice of paper for printing to adjust contrast and other features, combination printing (combining two negatives to make one print), and so on. If such darkroom techniques do not make traditional photographs into paintings, the same is true of the equivalent digital techniques.

There is a more radical move that Scruton might make to support the inapplicability defence: rather than claiming that the digital image is akin to a painting, he might hold that his arguments are inapplicable because the digital image is neither a photograph nor a digital painting, but something radically different from either. Here he could borrow from the work of W. J. T. Mitchell, an important pioneer of the study of digital imagery. According to Mitchell, the digital image is a radically distinct type of image from ones existing prior to it. He holds that talk of digital photographs is only metaphorical: 'Although a digital image may look just like a photograph when it is published in a newspaper, it actually differs as profoundly from a traditional photograph as does a photograph from a painting'.[49] In support of this claim, he appeals, first, to various features of the digital image that we noted in the Introduction, such as the existence of a fixed amount of information and the ease and speed of manipulation with which this fixed information can be manipulated. This contrasts with the indefinite amount of information in a traditional, analogue photograph and the comparative difficulty of manipulating it. Second, he notes that Scruton is correct about the importance of the distinction between causal photographic relations and intentional non-photographic ones in the case of traditional photographs. But in the case of digital photographs 'The distinction between the causal process of the camera and the intentional process of the artist can no longer be drawn so confidently and categorically. Potentially a digital "photograph"

[49] Mitchell, *The Reconfigured Eye*, p. 4.

stands at any point along the spectrum from the algorithmic to the intentional'.[50] This is because of the three generative techniques noted earlier and their seamless combination that can produce the digital image. The result is what he calls 'electrobricollage'.[51] So Mitchell in effect notes the existence of what I am calling a mélange image and holds that, since digital images are mélange images, they are never photographs.

The view that there are no digital photographs is not quite as wildly counterintuitive as one might suppose. Mitchell briefly mentions an analogy: automobiles were initially thought of as horseless carriages but we now think of them as a different mode of transport.[52] To expand on his point, suppose that someone in 1900 sees a car for the first time, and wonders whether it is like a horse-drawn carriage but with a motor in place of the horse, or like a train, but one that does not run on tracks, and concludes that it is a kind of blend of both transportation devices. The correct conclusion is that it is neither the one nor the other, but a radically new kind of thing. In the same way, Mitchell holds that the digital image should not be thought of as a photograph nor as a blending of a photograph with a painting, but as a new kind of thing that is neither the one nor the other.

However, Mitchell's claim that there are no digital photographs should be resisted. First, the difference between the fixed information of the digital photograph and the indefinite amount of information of the traditional photograph does not show that the former is not really a photograph: it merely shows that photographs come in different kinds, digital and analogue. Second, the fact that, as we saw, digital images can be produced by three, possibly seamlessly blended techniques, does not show that when digital images are produced by purely capture techniques, perhaps with some computer manipulation of the results, that what results is not a photograph. A digital photograph is one form that the mélange image can take. The crucial difference between a digital camera and a traditional camera is the replacement of a photochemical film with an electronic sensor (a CCD); the lenses, optical systems, shutter mechanisms, and so on, can be identical. Given the similarity of generative methods, it is implausible to claim that one is a photograph and the other is not. The important difference lies in the means of recording the light and the digitising of the subsequent information; but the root feature of photography, that it is the mechanical recording of the appearance of things by fixing a record of the light emanating from them, applies in both cases. So we should allow that digital photographs exist, while holding that the digital image can take

[50] *Ibid.*, p. 31.   [51] *Ibid.*, p. 7.   [52] *Ibid.*, p. 4.

other forms too. This is not to deny what is radically new about the digital image: it is rather to note that the digital image, in some of its modes, is similar enough to a traditional form of image to count as a photograph.

So Scruton's arguments against traditional photography and cinema being representational arts also fail for digital photography and cinema; nor should he hold that his arguments do not fail, but rather do not apply because digital photography is really a kind of painting or at least not a kind of photography.

The neo-Arnheimian defence of cinematic art advanced earlier also applies to digital cinema: indeed, the greater range of ways of recording reality made possible through digital manipulation and control of details strengthens the claims of digital cinema to be an art form. Interestingly, though, Arnheim himself would view digital cinema with some dismay. For in several ways it lies closer than does even sound and colour traditional film to his nightmare of the complete film, which he holds is incapable of being art. For instance, digital cinema's interactive possibilities mean that its content, like many features of the real world, can be altered by the viewer's intervention; and its lack of film grain and its ability to be digitally colour graded to remove any inconstancies in the recording of colours from one scene to another make viewing it more like viewing the real world. Worse still, the advent of virtual reality systems means that, when they are perfected, Arnheim's artistic Armageddon of the complete film will have been realised.[53] The more encompassing versions of such virtual reality systems involve a head-mounted display that feeds data to the wearer's eyes and ears, and data gloves that feed touch data to her hands; such systems are also interactive, allowing multiple agents to participate in the generation of the shared representation. These systems may eventually achieve complete sensory immersion: that is, sensory input from a virtual reality display representing some world would be perceptually indiscriminable from the sensory input from that world itself. The complete film would have arrived.

We have already noted that the complete film would not be non-art if it were possible to film the reality recorded in different ways, so Arnheim's case against it as non-art would still fail. But it is worth pursuing the perfected virtual reality (PVR) scenario just sketched, since it discloses another way for cinema to be expressive and an art form. Suppose that someone created a *Munch world* in PVR. This world is not generated by

---

[53] For useful discussions of virtual reality, see Oliver Grau, *Virtual Art*, especially the Introduction; and Michael Heim, 'Virtual Reality'.

photographic or any other capture means, but by hand-constructed 3D digital 'paintings' and computer synthesis procedures running on them, and looks like the content of some of Edvard Munch's paintings. Gaunt men and women bend over the death beds of emaciated young girls, their staring eyes full of despair; and people cower on bridges, hands clapped to their ears, screaming in terror, as puffs of blue and red smoke billow around them. The PVR representation of the Munch world would be a complete film in Arnheim's sense, but would also be powerfully expressive; yet it lacks the limitations on recording required by Arnheim's account for expression to occur. Moreover, it does not achieve its expressive power by a particular way of recording reality, for none of the images is generated by capture techniques on real objects and indeed these objects do not exist. Cinematic expression is secured in this case not through the expressive recording of reality, but through the direct creation of expressive content. And that shows that there is another way for cinematic expression to occur, besides recording reality in different ways: cinema can be expressive by directly creating expressive content. This possibility depends in turn on the fact that the digital image in its 'painting' mode can stand in a purely intentional relation to the world, and so does not require the existence of some objects to be recorded. And this possibility (setting aside the PVR aspect) is not just a thought experiment, but is something that has actually been realised in respect of their visual dimension in many works of digital animation. For, unlike traditional animation, where there is a set of prior drawings or paintings, which have certain expressive properties and that are photo-graphed to make the film, there need be no independently existing drawings or paintings in the case of the digital animated film.

So cinematic art now deploys a possibility that painting already possesses, since it does not require some independently existing object in order to create expressive content. In contrast, traditional film always records some-thing in front of the camera; and, though there are of course fiction films, these films are, as earlier noted, also documentaries of what certain actors and other artists were doing in front of the camera (or are recordings of drawings and paintings in the case of animated films). But digital cinema possesses the possibility, in its non-photographic modes, of creating expres-sive content that does not require any recording of reality at all. So it possesses new possibilities for cinematic artistry.

CHAPTER 2

Language and realism

We saw in the previous chapter that it is in part the plasticity of the representational medium that gives film its expressive potential. This raises the question of how to characterise the representational capacities of film. There are two kinds of answers that have been given to this question. The first holds that film is a kind of language. This answer has been very influential in film studies, and will be criticised for traditional cinema in the first section below and for digital cinema in the second section. The second answer holds that film is a pictorial medium and that pictures are not language-like. This will be the answer returned in this chapter. It follows that we should pose the question of the nature of cinematic realism at least partly in pictorial terms. I consider seven kinds of realism in cinema, concentrating in particular on the view that pictorial images can be transparent.

2.1 FILM AS A LANGUAGE

Much in common thought about film supports the idea that film is a kind of language. We speak of the language of film, of film as text, of the development of new languages of film and of reading a film. The idea of film as a language has also received much (though not universal) support in film theory. The Soviet filmmakers and theorists Lev Kuleshov and Vsevelod Pudovkin held that the shot played the role of a word, and the edited sequence of shots the role of a sentence. Sergei Eisenstein thought of film as a kind of pictorial language, comparing it to hieroglyphics and pictograms. André Bazin talked of the development of the language of film, and Christian Metz, in perhaps the most influential of all accounts, developed a systematic theory of film as language.[1] The idea of film as a language

---

[1] Vsevolod Pudovkin, *Film Acting and Film Technique*; Sergei Eisenstein, 'Beyond the Shot [The Cinematographic Principle and the Ideogram]'; André Bazin, 'The Evolution of the Language of Cinema'; and Christian Metz, *Film Language*.

has also had a major impact on film education: a popular film textbook is entitled *How to Read a Film.*[2]

The notion of film as a language may be a useful metaphor for some purposes, but does it express a literal truth? Is film really a kind of language?[3] A language consists of a vocabulary and a grammar. Words have a fixed meaning; they have a purely conventional relation to the things they denote; the vocabulary of a language is finite; and there are minimal lexical units. Grammar, which joins together words, is also, at least in its surface structure, conventional; and there is a finite number of grammatical rules. By combining vocabulary using grammatical rules, a potentially infinite number of meaningful sentences can be produced by recursion, and the meaning of these sentences depends systematically on that of their component parts. We thus understand new sentences by virtue of their being composed of familiar words in grammatical relations.

This rough sketch of what a language consists in will suffice to answer our question about film. At first glance, film seems to fit the linguistic model: it is a medium of communication and so has meaning; shots are joined together by editing to create sequences, the meaning of which depends on the shots and their relations; and some sequences can involve mistakes, apparently like grammatical mistakes. For instance, it is sometimes held that it is mistaken to cross the axis of action when shooting a scene.[4]

But on closer inspection the disanalogy to language becomes striking. Consider first the individual shot. There is a finite number of words in a language, but there is no upper limit on the number of distinct photographs that can be taken. Moreover, traditional film has a causal relation to what it denotes: something is a photograph of some object only if that object caused a light pattern to be imprinted on the photographic emulsion. A causal relation is not a conventional, arbitrary, relation, but is fixed by empirical facts. So whatever other conventional aspects there are to a photograph, the

---

[2] James Monaco, *How to Read a Film.*

[3] This question is not the same as whether film semiotics is correct. Semiotics is the study of signs, and not all signs are linguistic. In Charles Peirce's classic distinction, signs can be symbols (standing in a conventional relation to things; an example is language), icons (based on resemblance; an example is, arguably, pictures), or indexes (standing in a causal relation; an example is photographs). See Justus Buchler (ed.), *Philosophical Writings of Peirce*, chapter 7. Some film semioticians oppose the linguistic model and argue that cinema is composed of signs that are indexes or icons. See, for instance, Peter Wollen, *Signs and Meaning in the Cinema.*

[4] If two people are talking, for instance, the axis of action is a straight line running from one to the other, and the camera is supposed to stay on one side of that line. See David Bordwell and Kristin Thompson, *Film Art*, p. 263.

core photographic relation is not conventional. Nor is there anything corresponding to a minimal lexical unit in the photograph. The word 'Socrates' contains the letters 'rat', but 'rat' does not denote anything in this context, so 'Socrates' is a minimal lexical unit. However, a photograph of Socrates could be subdivided repeatedly, with each part of the photograph denoting a part of Socrates. Nor is there anything in a photograph corresponding to the distinction between, say, nouns and adjectives: a photograph of a green apple has no separate parts that pick out its greenness and its being an apple: both are inextricably presented together. And what would the photographic "words" be that corresponded to 'is' and 'not'?

Photographs are pictures, and though plenty of conventions are involved in the making and reception of pictures, the core relation of depiction is also not conventional.[5] Suppose I show a few pictures to someone who has never seen pictures before. The pictures are of a man, a cow and a pig, and each time I point to the appropriate thing. Thus attuned to the pictorial style, she will, when presented with a picture of a horse, be able to recognise it as depicting a horse, if she has seen horses before. But suppose that I am trying instead to teach her French: I give her the words 'homme', 'vache' and 'cochon' and each time point to the appropriate thing. I then give her the word 'cheval': will she know that it denotes a horse? Evidently she will not. Pictures have what Flint Schier calls 'natural generativity': if we are given no more than a small sample of pictures, so as to get used to the pictorial style, we can go on to understand any number of other pictures in that style. And Schier argues plausibly that this is because we use our ability to recognise objects to recognise pictures of them. We cannot do that with words, since they are purely conventional and therefore arbitrary in the way they denote, so we must learn the appropriate meanings one by one. And this claim about pictorial understanding is not just a thought experiment: it is consistent with what psychologists have discovered. In one striking experiment, conducted by Julian Hochberg and Virginia Brooks, a nineteen-month-old child (their own son), who had not previously been allowed to see any pictures, was presented with a set of drawings and photographs of objects familiar to him, and he was able to recognise all of them. Clearly the core depictive relation cannot be conventional.[6]

---

[5] The conventionality of pictures is defended by Nelson Goodman, *Languages of Art*, chapter 1; a recent defence of some of Goodman's views, though with substantial recasting, is John Kulvicki, *On Images*.

[6] Flint Schier, *Deeper into Pictures*, especially chapter 3; Dominic Lopes, *Understanding Pictures*, chapter 7; and Gregory Currie, *Image and Mind*, pp. 80–9. The Hochberg and Brooks experiment is discussed in Stephen Prince, 'The Discourse of Pictures: Iconicity and Film Studies'; and in Noël Carroll, 'The Power of Movies', p. 80.

So the shot is not a word nor analogous to one, nor is it comprised of words. Because it lacks a vocabulary, the shot also lacks a syntax, since a syntax is a set of rules for combining words together. As we noted, there is, for instance, nothing corresponding to a subject–predicate distinction within a shot. And shots cannot generate an infinite number of meanings by virtue of recursive exploitation of their syntax and vocabulary, since they lack both.

What, though, of montage, the editing of shots together? The idea of montage as the centre of film language has been extremely influential within film theory, and Christian Metz is the most important proponent of the idea. Metz holds that the shot has only minimal language-like features: he concedes film's lack of lexical units and that the pictorial relation is analogical (based on resemblance). He also writes that 'The word, which is the unit of language, is missing; the sentence, which is the unit of speech is supreme. The cinema can speak only in neologisms. Every image is a hapax'.[7] Moreover, the image is a sentence only because of its function, not because of its internal structure. Instead, he thinks that the claims of film to be a language are primarily supported at the editing level. His best example is the 'alternate syntagma', parallel editing, which involves an A-B-A-B shot sequence. Parallel editing is a device that means that two or more events are proceeding at the same time, and therefore can be thought of as like the word 'simultaneously'.

The basic problem with the idea of montage as the core of film language is clear: we cannot think of the relations between shots (the montage relations) as constituting a grammar, since grammar is a relation between words, and shots as we argued above do not correspond to words. Metz agrees that shots are not analogous to words and that the word is missing in cinema, but he still wants to talk of sentences in cinema. Yet it is incoherent to talk of sentences in the absence of words, since sentences are by definition composed of words. Moreover, if each cinematic sentence is, as Metz claims, a hapax (i.e., has a unique occurrence), then without an internal structure, we would never be able to understand it. We can understand new sentences only because we recognise them as constructed of familiar words in recognisable grammatical relations. And parallel editing is not best thought of as being like the word 'simultaneously'. For this word, like all others, has a core, context-independent meaning, fixed by those letters in that sequence. In contrast, what an A-B-A-B shot sequence means has to be grasped from its context. It might indeed mean that the events are

---

[7] Metz, *Film Language*, p. 69.

happening simultaneously; but instead it could represent an alternating flashback (or flash forward); or it could represent an atemporal comparison of two scenes; or the scenes could be set in entirely different epochs, as in the four distinct historical eras of D. W. Griffith's *Intolerance* (1916); and so on. To discover which of these is the case, we have to understand the content of the images joined together. The sequence does not have a fixed meaning, unlike a word. So, while Metz's discussion of editing relations has merit as a classificatory scheme, it does not show that film is a kind of language.

It might be objected that this last point merely shows that the A-B-A-B sequence is ambiguous, but this does not show that the sequence is not word-like, any more than the ambiguity of 'bank' shows that it is not a word. However, 'bank' has two fixed meanings, and we consult the context to determine which of these is relevant in the situation. But in the case of the sequence, there is not a set of determinately fixed meanings; rather, we can imagine an indefinite number of other meanings for the sequence, depending on the contents of the images. Moreover, even if this were a case of ambiguity, this is Metz's most promising example, and other sequences could have even more purported ambiguities. But we could not in practice have a language in which every word had, say, five meanings, since then even a simple sentence of ten words would have 10 to the power of 5 possible meanings (100,000 meanings). No such language would be humanly usable.

Consider too the status of the rule not to cross the axis of action, which is sometimes held up as an example of a grammatical rule in cinema. It is a rule, but is it a convention? A convention exists, roughly, if there is a problem situation to which there are at least two equally good solutions but where one of these solutions has to be agreed on (a co-ordination problem); if there is a publicly acknowledged rule by which one of these solutions is generally followed; and if each participant follows the rule on condition that other participants follow it.[8] For instance, it is a convention to drive on the left in Britain: there is no more reason to drive on the left than the right side of the road, but there is reason for everyone to agree to drive on the same side; there is a publicly acknowledged rule stating that one should drive on the left; and drivers follow the rule on condition that other drivers do so. Likewise, at least in their surface structure the rules of grammar are conventional: in English the subject standardly comes before the predicate in sentence order, but other languages could standardly reverse this order. The demands of clear communication give reason for us to agree

---

[8] This is a rough characterisation of the account offered in David Lewis, *Convention*.

on some subject–predicate order; we have an agreed rule that generally places the subject before the predicate; and we use this rule on condition that other speakers do so.

Is the rule not to cross the axis of action conventional in this sense? Are there at least two equally good solutions: to ban crossing the axis of action, or to allow it with impunity? Not so, since the rule is partly based on optically determined facts. If the camera crosses the line of action from one shot to the next, then a movement running from the left of the screen to the right in one shot will appear as a movement running from the right of the screen to the left in the next shot. This will be confusing to spectators, absent any further information, since it suggests that there are two distinct movements taking place. So, given the communicative aim to get the spectator to understand the action, the two solutions are not equally good. Hence the rule is not purely a convention: it is partly determined by physical facts of the situation. Of course, this is not to say that there are no conventional aspects to classical continuity editing (the kind of editing typically employed in Hollywood films). But it does show that its choice is not purely arbitrary, given filmmakers' aims.

Even the role of film conventions, where they do exist (and parallel editing is an example), does not prove that film is a language. For there are conventions used in communication that are not linguistic. Bowing, handshaking and pointing at things are all communicative conventions, but none is language-like, none has a vocabulary and syntax. One can make mistakes with these conventions (for instance, pointing at the wrong thing), without these mistakes being in any sense grammatical ones. So we should agree that film can communicate and therefore has meaning. But the way it conveys meaning is not like the way language does.

2.2 DIGITAL CINEMA AND LANGUAGE

There are, then, good reasons to deny that traditional film is, or is closely analogous to, a language.[9] What, though, of digital cinema? Here the claim that cinema is a kind of language appears more promising.

First, as we have seen, not all of the images in digital cinema are happily described as photographic: rather than being captured by cameras, the images can be handmade, using computational tools such as paint

---

[9] For other discussions of the film as language thesis, see Currie, *Image and Mind*, chapter 4; Gilbert Harman, 'Semiotics and the Cinema: Metz and Wollen'; Wilson, *Narration in Light*, pp. 200–4; and William Rothman, 'Against "The System of the Suture"'.

programs, and further transformed by various algorithmic procedures. In the case of handmade images there need be no object of which the image is a recording. If so, the image cannot stand in a causal relation to that object. Hence the objection concerning causal relations not being conventional is rendered void.

Second, traditional photographs are analogue – the light intensity emanating from objects is recorded by the photographic salts in the emulsion as a continuous value. This allows the subdivision of a photograph to go on indefinitely, with each part of the photograph denoting a part of the subject. But the digital image (a bitmap image) is different. The grid of pixels (picture elements) has a discrete number of units, and each unit measures the light intensity (or the intensity of the red, green and blue primary colours) as a discrete integer. As can easily be seen on a computer screen, if one keeps enlarging a digital image, one is left with nothing but a grid of pixels, and these pixels are not recognisable as parts of an object. Thus, one might suppose that, unlike traditional photographs, digital photographs do have discrete units, and at the lowest level of subdivision, the pixel, these do not denote. In just the same way, 'Socrates' denotes, but neither the individual letters comprising the word, nor their various combinations, such as 'rat', denote anything.

Third, digital images do involve a language – the images are specified by computer code. Pixels need to have their horizontal and vertical position specified in the grid that is displayed on the screen, and their colour is also specified by a code. For instance, in standard 24-bit colour depth bitmaps, there are 256 possible values for each of the red, green and blue values associated with each pixel (making possible a total of over 16.7 million distinct colours per pixel). Which colour is associated with each numerical value for each primary colour is arbitrary: black is standardly designated in eight bit (binary digit) code by '00000000' and white by '11111111', but the reverse coding could have been chosen. And which of the three primary colours should be assigned to the first byte (the first eight bits), which to the second byte, and which to the third byte, is likewise arbitrary. Yet, though arbitrarily assigned, these numbers have meaning and their order matters: thus this seems to be a genuine language.

Finally, interactive digital works, as we noted in the Introduction, are constituted by a program that transforms initial images using user-provided input into output images. But programs, such as the C++ language commonly used for interactive works, are genuine languages, with a syntax and a vocabulary. So because of its programming basis, interactive cinema is language-like.

Suppose that these points were correct. They would prove that digital cinema is more like a language than is traditional film: they would still not prove, however, that it is, or is strongly analogous to, a language. For the point about pictures (including digital pictures) not being conventional, but possessing natural generativity, still stands; and the points about editing not being language-like also remain. So digital cinema would be nudged closer towards language than would traditional cinema, but that is all.

However, the only point that reduces the disanalogy between language and cinema is that digital images need not be causally connected to their objects: in digital animation there need be no drawings, paintings or maquettes that were photographed to produce the digital image, for the image may be hand constructed in a graphics editing program. (Recall, in contrast, that traditional animation involves photographs of drawings or paintings, so one can infer from the existence of the cinematic images that the drawings or paintings existed.) However, the lack of a causal relation does not secure the main claim that the digital image is therefore conventional; for, as just noted, visual images are naturally generative and therefore do not stand in a conventional relation to their subjects.

Consider next the divisibility question. In 'Socrates', 'rat' does not denote. But the pixel in a digital photograph does denote a part of its subject, even if the subject is not recognisable from that pixel alone. Moreover, it does this by denoting the light intensity falling on that point of the subject, and this light intensity is recognisable from viewing that pixel on its own. So the relation of the pixel to the digital image is not like the relation of 'rat' to 'Socrates'. The supporter of digital film language might reply by modifying her view and hold that therefore the *pixel* is the minimal denotative unit. It is the equivalent of 'Socrates' and like that word, it denotes something; and just as the parts of 'Socrates' do not denote, so the parts of the pixel do not denote. But that claim is also false. The parts of a pixel denote the parts of the area of the object that the pixel denotes. It is simply that the parts of the pixel denote the parts of the area of the object by taking the average light intensity over them, rather than by recording individual light intensities at each point – that is, the pixel has a uniform colour and tone that averages the colour and tone of the parts of the area of the object that it denotes, but nevertheless each part of the pixel denotes a part of the object. So the denotation relation still holds at the sub-pixel level. The parts of a pixel do denote, unlike the parts of a word.

Also, the digital photograph is not, in the respects relevant to the language debate, different from a traditional photograph. For the latter is comprised of sometimes billions of individual grains, which are the deposits of the photographic salts that are part of the photographic emulsion, after they have been developed and fixed, and the positive image printed from them. In this respect there is also an array of picture-elements in the traditional photograph, albeit one with vastly more elements than is usual in digital photographs, and which are not arrayed in a grid. Keep on enlarging such a photograph, and in the end one will see individual grains, from which the object is not recognisable, even though the grains denote parts of the object. This is the lesson of Michelangelo Antonioni's *Blow-Up* (1966): as Thomas, the photographer played by David Hemmings, keeps enlarging the image that he thinks shows a murder, the grains of film become more prominent and it becomes impossible in the end to tell what they denote. Of course, the digital photograph records the intensity of light at various picture points digitally, by sampling the continuous values of light falling on the charge-coupled device, whereas chemically based photographs store the light information as continuous, analogue values. But in both cases subdividing the image yields parts of the image that denote parts of the relevant object. And in this respect, they are both unlike the word, where the parts of the word do not denote parts of the object. So there is no relevant dissimilarity here that aids the supporter of digital cinema as a language.

The third point raised concerns the existence of codes for colours and spatial position in the pixel grid. One might deny that these are really a language: if computers understand the code, we must be able to attribute intentional states, such as beliefs, to them; yet there are reasons to deny that current computers can possess intentional states. But this objection, even if correct, should not undermine the claim, for there is no doubt that people have intentional states, and people can understand the code.[10] However, the coding issue does not help the supporter of film as a language. For if film were a kind of language (or closely analogous to one), it would follow that to understand a film one must understand film language, in the same way that to understand a novel one must understand the language of the novel. But that is not true of the computer code: no one needs to understand the image coding language to understand a digital film: indeed, the average moviegoer

---

[10] A delightful story illustrates the point: when the Mariner IV spacecraft transmitted images back from Mars, it did so by sending arrays of numbers, which were printed out on paper. Scientists at the Jet Propulsion Laboratory then coloured over them with crayons, using the specified colour-coding scheme. The scientists understood the code, even if the computers did not. See Mitchell, *The Reconfigured Eye*, p. 78.

likely has no understanding of the code at all. So it's not a *cinematic* code. The coding is at a more basic level, and determines the physical structure of the image (its colours and their spatial arrangement), not the *meaning* of the image. Computers have to "understand" the code to constitute the image, but filmgoers do not have to understand the code in order to grasp the meaning of the film. This becomes even clearer if we consider digital sound, which is generated by a digital code that represents sounds by integers. The existence of this code does not show that the sounds produced are linguistic: an explosion recorded in digital sound does not become language-like because it is recorded by a system that employs digital code. So digital cinema, just like traditional cinema, should not be considered as being, or as being analogous to, a language.

Finally, interactive digital cinema is not language-like. The images, information about which is stored in the program that implements the digital work, are not language-like for reasons we have discussed: understanding them requires one to draw on one's natural recognitional abilities. The program that implements the cinematic work is indeed a language, but it is not a *cinematic* language for the same reason that pixel grid codes are not cinematic languages. For one need not understand, say, C++ in order to understand what is going on in *Façade* (2005) nor in order to decide how to respond to events in that work: indeed, only a tiny fraction of videogame audiences understand the programming languages in which they are written. So the situation is not like that of, say, a reader of a novel who cannot understand its meaning unless she understands the language in which it is written. The programming language thus is not used for communicative purposes, unlike the language of the novel. Rather, the programming language of a videogame merely serves to constitute the images at the physical level of colours and sounds and to implement players' decisions about how to proceed in the game.

2.3 REALISM: TRADITIONAL AND DIGITAL CINEMA

Cinema is the medium of moving pictures. We argued in Section 2.1 that pictures are not akin to language, since they possess natural generativity and a plausible explanation for this fact is that we use the same abilities to recognise a picture of an object as we do to recognise the object depicted. So we should not look to the study of language to cast light on the notion of cinematic realism. Rather, the appropriate notion of realism to apply to cinema concerns the kinds of realism that can apply to pictures. As Walton remarks, 'Realism is a monster with many heads desperately in need of disentangling'.[11] We can identify at least seven distinct notions of realism that can fruitfully be applied to cinema. In the current section I will discuss six; I defer until Section 2.4 discussion of transparency, the seventh and most debated of these notions. In both sections I will examine how the relevant notions of realism apply to both traditional and digital cinema.

2.3.1 Content realism

We say of some fictional works, including fiction films, that they are realistic in respect of their content, and of others that their content is not realistic; in the latter category entire genres are held to be not realistic, such as fantasy fictions. But what does it mean to call a fiction realistic in respect of its content? One might suppose that fiction films by definition concern non-actual events and so cannot be realistic. But it is not a necessary condition of realistic content in fiction that the work deals with actual events or objects, for there are realistic fictions that treat of merely imagined events and objects. Nor does the representation of actual people or events in fiction suffice for realistic content, since they may be treated in unrealistic fashion, as in farce. Rather, the notion of content realism in fiction is that the *kinds* of people or objects, and the *kinds* of events represented are those that tend to occur in the real world. *King Kong* (2005) is unrealistic in its content, since there are no gorillas the size of houses in the real world: that kind of thing does not exist. And it is also unrealistic because the kinds of events depicted could not plausibly occur: no one could survive the sort of shaking and hurling to which Ann Darrow is subjected when she is first carried through the jungle of Skull Island grasped in Kong's hand. *Groundhog Day* (1993) is unrealistic in its content, not in respect of the kind of beings depicted, for they are fairly ordinary people, but in respect of the kind of events depicted, since eternal recurrence does not happen in the real world. *All about Eve* (1950), in contrast, is realistic in its content in both respects: the kinds of people it shows exist, and the kinds of events it depicts (revealing ambition, jealousy and rivalry) occur not infrequently. Realism of fictional content is a matter of degree: the more common the objects depicted and the more mundane the events shown, the more reason we have to say that the fiction is realistic.

Content realism concerns *what* is represented, not *how* it is represented: it concerns the fictional content of the work, not its mode of presentation. Content and mode of presentation can vary independently of each other.

---

[11] Kendall Walton, *Mimesis as Make-Believe*, p. 328.

Peter Jackson calls his aim in some of his films 'realistic fantasy'.[12] That may sound oxymoronic, but it is not. Films such as *King Kong* are fantasies, and so are unrealistic in many aspects of their fictive content; but they are realistic in how that content is depicted. For instance, Kong is given a photorealistic depiction (Section 2.3.3), as opposed to using traditional animation techniques that would not produce an image that looked exactly like a photograph of a huge gorilla. Conversely, one could film a fictional story that is extremely realistic in its content in a very unrealistic fashion: for instance, one could film it using anamorphic lenses, weirdly unmotivated lighting, extremely fragmented editing techniques, etc., so that looking at the resulting film would be very different from looking at the objects that it represents; hence the film would be in a very perceptually unrealistic style (Section 2.3.6).

2.3.2 *Illusionism*

The notion of the content realism of fiction has wide application: it applies to any medium that can support fictions, including novels, plays, dances and cinema. The other notions of realism that we will discuss are less wide-ranging, being more focally concerned with visual media. When many contemporary film theorists, and indeed ordinary viewers of film, talk of realism they often speak in terms of illusion. The second sense of realism, *illusionism*, holds that films standardly create an illusion in the minds of their spectators, a popular view with contemporary film theorists. To examine this claim, we need to distinguish between cognitive and perceptual illusions.[13]

Cognitive illusions involve a false belief. Not all false beliefs engendered by cinema should count, however, as germane to realism. If viewers of a film have false beliefs about what is fictional in the film, perhaps because the film's plot is hard to follow, those false beliefs are not relevant to the issue of cinematic realism. Rather, the content of the belief must involve the notion of the real. For instance, contemporary film theorists often hold that the spectator standardly has a false belief that represented events which are in fact fictional are real; this is generally coupled with the claim that the spectator also believes that she is in the presence of these events. It is extremely doubtful, however, whether spectators are under an illusion

---

[12] Brian Sibley, *Peter Jackson*, p. 360.
[13] For related discussions, see Currie, *Image and Mind*, pp. 28–9; and Richard Allen, *Projecting Illusion*, pp. 97–100.

with this content. The claim that viewers believe that the fictional events are present to them hardly squares with their standard reactions: were they really under the illusion that they were in the presence of an axe-wielding maniac depicted in a horror film, they would flee the cinema. There is, it is true, a (possibly apocryphal) story that the first viewers in 1895 of the Lumière brothers' film of a train drawing into a station ran away from the screen, lest they be killed by the oncoming train. If the story is true, they were suffering from an illusion of presence (though not of what was fictional being real, since it was a real train); but it is highly unlikely that many cinematic viewers have suffered from this illusion, and a brief experience of film watching would rapidly dispel it.[14] The version of illusionism which holds that spectators believe that the events are real but do not believe that they are in their presence also fails to square with viewers' reactions: if they believed that they were watching, say, a video feed of some scene of monstrous mayhem taking place elsewhere, they would be on the phones asking for help to be sent to the victims, not contentedly munching their popcorn. Nor do spectators standardly display a tendency to revise their overall beliefs about what is real in the light of cinematic fictions: they do not, for instance, come to believe that the world contains the monsters or aliens depicted in a film.

However, it is too easy to move from this thought to the claim that cognitive illusions are never involved in watching cinema. For example, many viewers of films may assume, when they see stunts in a film, that the actor himself did that stunt. In some cases they are correct; but in many others they are not. This is relevant to realism, since the thought-content is that the actor *really* did the stunt, rather than using a double (it is not a thought about what is fictional in the film). Or a spectator may believe that a film is *really* shot in, say, New York, where the story is set and which the onscreen images appear to depict, even though it is in fact shot in Toronto (a frequent substitute for New York in the 1990s, given the lower costs of filming in Canada). Hence determining whether spectators are subject to illusions crucially depends on the content that is being judged to be real.

The viewer of digital cinema may well be under illusions in respects that the viewer of traditional film standardly is not. For instance, the viewer may assume that she is seeing an image of an actor moving in a real location, but the set has in fact been created purely digitally. Or she may assume that she is seeing an image of actors moving, whereas she is seeing purely digitally

---

[14] Currie, *Image and Mind*, pp. 22–4.

created characters: in *The Lord of the Rings* and *King Kong*, for instance, 'digital doubles' are used at several points, where placing actors in the scene would have been too dangerous. Even close inspection fails to reveal whether a digital double is used at some points, especially in long shots. Digital creation and manipulation of characters and sets, then, give a much greater scope for illusionism in digital cinema than exists in traditional film. But again, this does not support the cognitive illusion of presence.

The second kind of illusion is a perceptual one. This need involve no false beliefs: I may know in the Müller-Lyer illusion that the two lines are of the same length, yet my experience represents them as being of different lengths. Dominic Lopes has argued that cinema involves perceptual illusions: for instance, in watching *Star Trek* I have an experience as of Spock on the bridge of the *Enterprise*, even though these entities are fictional.[15] However, this experience is not happily described as a type of illusion. For, as Currie has pointed out, in the case of the cinematic experience, unlike in the case of the Müller-Lyer illusion, 'we do not sit there struggling to maintain our beliefs in the face of a contradictory experience'.[16] For instance, we don't struggle to maintain our belief that we are only seeing an image of Spock against the contradictory experience that we are really seeing him. The content of our visual experience is an image, and on the basis of that we perceptually imagine Spock.[17]

However, this is not to say that perceptual illusions play no part in our experience of cinema. I claimed in Section I.2 that the apparent movement of still images in all kinds of cinema other than object-generated ones (shadow plays) is illusory. This is invariably a perceptual illusion, and for some viewers it may also be a cognitive one (they believe that the images really move). Currie has, however, argued against this claim: he holds that the movement of cinematic images is a real, though response-dependent, property.[18] He points out that the standard reason for thinking that cinematic motion is an illusion fails, since even though there are only static images on the celluloid roll, the claim is that it is what is on the screen that moves, not what is hidden in the camera. He also notes that holding that cinematic movement is a product of our perceptual system is compatible with its being a response-dependent property, not an illusory one.[19]

---

[15] Dominic Lopes, 'Imagination, Illusion and Experience in Film'.
[16] Gregory Currie, 'Reply to My Critics', p. 362.
[17] I will have more to say about the role of imagination in cinematic experience in Chapter 5.
[18] Currie, *Image and Mind*, pp. 34–47.　　[19] *Ibid.*, pp. 38–9.

Despite its considerable ingenuity, Currie's view that cinematic motion is not illusory should be rejected. Genuine movement is continuous: i.e., things do not jump from one spatial point to another without successively occupying all of the intervening points between the start and end points. Yet sequences of cinematic images, i.e., light-patterns on the screen, are not continuous in this sense. So they do not move: they are a succession of still images. Contrast the case with shadow plays: if I make the shape of a rabbit with my hands in a projector's light, then when the shadow moves, the shadow will occupy all of the intervening points between the start of the sequence and the end. A film of the shadow play might be perceptually indiscriminable from the shadow play, and so would present itself as if the image sequence were continuous: but it would not be continuous, and hence there would be a mere illusion of movement.

Currie would likely protest that this argument assumes that the light-pattern on the screen is identical with the cinematic image, whereas he holds that the latter merely supervenes on the former; and this allows him to hold that the cinematic image possesses properties, such as real movement, which its subvening basis does not.[20] I doubt whether Currie's non-identity claim is correct; but in any case we need not settle the issue here, given another point that he makes. He discusses a scenario where in a totally darkened cinema, a stationary point of light is projected onto the screen, and spectators have the illusion that the point is moving. This is an illusion, says Currie, since it is a necessary condition for genuine movement of an image that 'at each place on the screen occupied by the image as it moves, there should be illumination at that place (and at the relevant time) on the screen'.[21] But by the same criterion, cinematic images do not genuinely move. For when a cinematic image appears to move continuously, since the associated sequence of light-patterns is static and discontinuous, there will be many points on the screen where the image appears to be, but where there is no illumination at those times. Moreover, cinema images are projected in rapid bursts of light, and between exposures there is no light coming from the projector, so that audiences spend about half the time when they are watching films in darkness. During these times there appears to be a cinematic image, even though there is no light pattern anywhere on the screen. Not only is there an illusion of movement in cinema, there is also an associated illusion of continuous illumination of the screen.[22]

---

[20] *Ibid.*, p. 40.　　[21] *Ibid.*, p. 46.

[22] Andrew Kania has raised some related objections, as well as additional ones, to Currie's view; see Kania, 'The Illusion of Realism in Film'.

Figure 3. Ann (Naomi Watts) and Kong: photorealism in *King Kong* (2005).

2.3.3 Photorealism

A third sense of 'realism' is *photorealism*. This is a concept much used by practitioners of digital animation. Photoreal animation is animation where the animation image of something is visually indiscriminable from how a photograph of that thing would look, if the thing existed with the properties that the animation image ascribes to it. Much digital animation is now driven by the photoreal ideal, and it has been successfully realised several times, not least in *King Kong* (2005) (see Figure 3). The animation image of Kong here is visually indiscriminable from how a photograph of Kong would look, if he existed with the properties that the animation image ascribes to him. In contrast, a traditionally drawn cartoon of Kong could easily be visually discriminated from a photograph of what he would look like, if he existed, as can the stop-motion animation image in the original *King Kong* (1933).

What is striking about the notion of photorealism is that it does not employ a comparison of the image to how a real object would look to provide a standard of realism (the standard adopted by perceptual illusionism), but rather compares the image to a *photograph* of an object. This notion of realism is, then, a derivative one. The use of the photograph as the standard is illustrated by the introduction by digital animators of such things as film grain, motion blur (introduced by John Lasseter in 1984) and lens flare into digital images. These are not things that accompany our normal seeing of an object, but are artefacts of photography. Often the standard of photorealism is set by the traditional photograph, rather than the digital one. For instance, film grain is a feature of traditional film, because of the silver salt deposits used, but does not occur in digital photographs (these may look blocky when enlarged, but that is a different phenomenon). Other features employed in digital animation are common to traditional and digital photography: motion blur occurs because the exposure time of a shot is sufficiently lengthy that the object has discernibly moved during it; and lens flare happens when some light from a light source bounces away from the lens, instead of going through it. In the case of digital animation, there is no film grain, no motion blur (the represented objects are constructs, rather than independently existing), and no lens flare, since the lens is a 'virtual' one, being merely a point of view onto the constructed digital world. So adding all of these features takes the experience of watching a film further away from the experience of watching the represented object and closer to that of watching a traditional or digital photographic film of that object.

Photoreal animation is an artistic achievement, affecting how one responds to the image in artistically relevant ways (for instance, the greater realism of the animation helps promote empathy with Kong and engagement with his plight). However, photoreal animation is all but impossible in traditional animation: imagine the superhuman difficulty of drawing frames of Kong so that they look like photographs of him. Photoreal animation is aesthetically important, and is a central means for achieving the realism of fantasy and special effects digital movies. So there is at least one aesthetically relevant effect that is distinctive of the medium of digital cinema. (There are others too, deriving, for instance, from the potential interactivity of the digital image.) This is a point to which we will return in Chapter 7.

2.3.4 Ontological realism

A fourth sense of 'realism' in play in cinema is what we might call *ontological realism*. Recall the discussion of Scruton in Section 1.1: from the existence of a photograph, it follows that its subject existed. Photographs have a causal relation to their subjects, handmade pictures have an intentional relation to them. From the obtaining of a causal relation, it follows that the subject of the photograph existed at the time the photograph was made: one cannot photograph something that does not exist, such as Kong. From the obtaining of an intentional relation, in contrast, it does not follow that the subject existed at the time that the picture was made: I can make a painting of Kong or a digital non-photographic image of him.

So photographs, whether traditional or digital, can only be of what is actual (though they can, of course, be photographs of people, such as actors, who are make-believedly someone else; and the audience can also make-believe that photographs are images of fictional things). Non-photographic digital images or aspects of digital images that are not photographic, in contrast, can be of what is not actual. So traditional film is ontologically realistic, but digital film is not in all cases. The traditional film image is, in Charles Sanders Peirce's terms, an index (it has a causal relation to its referent), whereas some digital images are merely icons (resembling their subjects but lacking a causal relation to them).[23]

It does not follow from the ontological realism of photographs that they cannot be misleading or that there are no photographic fakes. From the existence of a photograph of a strangely shaped piece of driftwood floating on a lake it follows that the driftwood existed. The photograph may be presented as a photograph of Nessie, the famed Loch Ness monster, and may be widely taken to be such. But Nessie, sadly for the Scottish tourist industry, does not exist. So ontological realism does not entail that viewers cannot mistake photographic content nor that photographs provide indefeasible evidence for the existence of what their apparent content shows.

2.3.5 Epistemic realism

This point brings us to a fifth notion of realism, what I will call *epistemic realism*. An image is epistemically real just in case it provides strong (though defeasible) evidence that the object or event that it apparently depicts really was like that or really happened.[24] Traditionally, photographs have been accorded great evidential authority: we accept a photograph as providing much stronger evidence for something's having occurred than we would a handmade drawing or painting, however meticulous, of that thing. And a traditional film can be viewed as constituting good evidence that certain actors were on certain locations in the past.

What is the source of the epistemic authority of photography as opposed to handmade pictures? Some have argued that this is to be explained in

---

[23] Stephen Prince, 'True Lies: Perceptual Realism, Digital Images, and Film Theory'.

[24] It may seem odd to count this epistemic feature as a kind of realism, since the latter is normally understood as a metaphysical category, not an epistemic one. Nevertheless, the notion of evidential authority is part of the lay notion of realism applying to photography and I will so treat it here.

part by the different background beliefs we have about photographs and handmade pictures.[25] But there are at least two substantive differences on which the epistemic difference is grounded. First, handmade pictures and photographs fall into different epistemic types. A handmade picture records what the artist *believes* he sees, and not necessarily what is in front of him: if he hallucinates a white rabbit, then that is what he will draw or paint. But a photograph of the same scene will show only what is actually there, the vacant lawn. So, while what the artist sees and therefore draws is counterfactually dependent on his beliefs about the scene, what the camera shows is independent of the photographer's and others' beliefs about what is there.[26] This means that the evidential authority of hand-made pictures derives from testimony, while the authority of photography derives from non-belief mediated contact with the world. Testimony is an essential source of knowledge of the world. Nevertheless, it suffers from epistemic handicaps that do not afflict causal contact unmediated by beliefs.

The second source of greater photographic epistemic authority lies in the relative difficulty of manipulating traditional photographs. A painting of a nonexistent object or person can as easily be made as can one of an actual object or person, at least if the artist is endowed with a modicum of visual imagination. And there is no necessary difference between the look of the one and the other. But in the case of a photograph, there must be some real object that is being photographed (this follows from ontological realism) and this object must be made, in the case of fakes, to look like something else, for instance, Nessie, or JFK caught in a compromising entanglement. Fakery can be accomplished either by manipulation of what is in front of the camera, such as the use of cosmetics and prosthetics for people, special lighting, etc; or it can be achieved by special intervention in the photographic process. Techniques for photographic intervention include combination printing, using multiple negatives to combine shots together (which was used, for instance, by Henry Peach Robinson to make *Fading Away* [1858]); multiple exposures of a single negative; hand painting of part of the negative; use of mattes (masks) to combine parts of shots together; and so on. These processes are technically difficult and also leave traces of their use, for instance, in the generational loss

---

[25] Jonathan Cohen and Aaron Meskin, 'On the Epistemic Value of Photographs'.
[26] This distinction is due to Kendall Walton, who uses it to argue for photographic transparency. I will argue against transparency in the next section; in the current subsection I explore the real implications of the distinction.

that afflicts photographic reproduction, in mismatches between perspectives taken from different shots, in the visibility of matte lines, and so forth.

All this applies to traditional photographs. What of digital photographs, though? As we saw in Section 1.4, the digital image is a mélange image, which can be made by hand, by mechanical capture or by computer synthesis, in any proportion and which can be combined seamlessly. It follows that digital photographs lack the evidential authority of traditional photographs. For the handmade elements and computer synthesis introduce elements into the digital photograph that are capable of undetectable manipulation. If one is dealing with a photograph, as opposed to the wider category of the digital image, there is a conceptual constraint, albeit one with a fuzzy boundary, on how much synthesis and hand intervention can occur before one ceases to be able to talk of the image being a photograph. The problem, though, is that it may be impossible to tell from inspection of the digital image whether this boundary has been crossed. One cannot necessarily tell by close inspection which aspects of the digital image were made by which technique: there is no generational loss through repeated reproduction of the digital image for processing purposes, and the photoreal ideal is achievable. So we may think that we are looking at a digital photograph of something, though it is in fact a mere animation frame, which provides no evidence of anything having actually occurred in front of the camera. And since many digital special effects are partial animations built around live action, special effects in live action movies similarly mean that one cannot with any confidence tell what really happened by careful inspection of a film still. Worse, only the closest inspection of film stills or photographs may show whether one is looking at a digital or a traditional photograph, so the evidential weakness of digital photographs endangers one's epistemic relations with traditional photographs. As Barbara Savedoff has noted, the rise of the digital photograph threatens the general 'destruction of photographic credibility'.[27]

So digital photographs lack the evidential weight of traditional photographs. But one should not exaggerate this fact. One can still in many cases detect digital fakery: this may be because of the content – despite that convincing image, you know my sedentary nature makes it unlikely that I really did climb Everest and plant the Scottish saltire on the top. Or it may be because of the pictorial properties of the image – the point

[27] Barbara Savedoff, 'Escaping Reality: Digital Imagery and the Resources of Photography', p. 212.

of view from which the image of me and the flag appears is different from that from which the mountain appears, the shadows fall differently, and so on. Digital manipulation is a highly skilled art, which may require the co-operation of literally thousands of talented artists on an animated or special effects film. Nevertheless, it is far easier to manipulate digital than traditional film, which is why digital cinema or the Digital Intermediate process is the method of choice for animated and special effects films.

This fifth sense of realism yields an irony. Digital cinema has greater powers to achieve realistic-looking images than does traditional film, but when viewers come to know of these powers, they have every reason to be suspicious about whether what they seem to have evidence for happening really did happen. In this sense, digital cinema's pursuit of realism is a self-defeating project: the informed viewer increasingly has reason for a suspension of judgement about the evidential authority of the digital image.

2.3.6 Perceptual realism

A sixth kind of realism mooted for cinema is what has been called *perceptual realism* (it is also been termed *pictorial realism*, but since all of the notions of realism that I are examining can also apply to pictures, I will not employ that term here). This notion of realism can be applied to cinema as a medium, or may be applied to distinguish certain cinematic styles as realist from those that are not. The root idea of perceptual realism is that realist pictures look more like their objects (what they depict) than do nonrealist pictures. But this apparently simple and plausible idea needs careful specification if it is to be defended.

One general difficulty infects the notion of looking like, for it seems vacuous: as Nelson Goodman famously objects, everything resembles everything else in some respect or other, since with a little ingenuity one can always find properties which two things, however different, have in common. A more specific difficulty is that what has counted as a realistic style has varied widely across history. This is true for pictures in general, where styles as various as European Neoclassicism and Japanese woodcuts have been counted as realist. And it is also true of cinema, where Soviet 1920s films, classical Hollywood films from the 1920s to 1950s, Italian Neorealist films of the 1940s and 1950s, French Poetic Realist films of the 1930s and 1940s, and 1960s *cinéma vérité* films have all been classified as realist, despite their huge variations in style. In the face of such variations, some have suggested that realism is no more than a convention: Goodman holds that 'realism is a matter of habit'.[28]

The first step in addressing such worries is to return to the general issue of depiction and to the notion of natural generativity. As we saw, the fact that one can, from at most a small sample of pictures in a particular style, go on to interpret other pictures in that style, is best explained by holding that one employs one's capacities to recognise objects in order to recognise pictures of those objects. But, one might wonder, what in turn explains the fact that one can employ one's recognitional powers in this way: why, for instance, can one use one's ability to recognise dogs to recognise pictures of dogs? By far the most plausible answer is that dog-pictures and dogs have something in common, i.e., they resemble each other, in such a way that one's ability to recognise dogs can be triggered by dog-pictures. Otherwise, the fact that dog-pictures can do this just looks like magic. So dog-pictures and dogs both have whatever properties trigger the dog-recognising disposition in us. Note that this account does not require that we are able to specify these properties independently of the disposition, short of engaging in detailed psychological investigations. But it does require that there must be some resemblances – call these *recognitionally relevant resemblances* – between pictures and their objects. So the answer to Goodman's triviality objection is that pictures and their objects resemble each other in recognitionally relevant ways.

Not all pictures are realistic; but one can apply the notion of recognitionally relevant resemblance, which concerns depiction in general, to the specific class of realist pictures. A picture P of an object O is more realistic than a picture P^* of O just in case P resembles O in more recognitionally relevant ways than P^* resembles O. This gives an account of the realism of individual pictures; the realism of pictorial types and styles can be handled with the same basic mechanism, since types and styles can be thought of as classes of actual and possible pictures. It follows from this account that realism is a matter of degree, since a picture may share more or less of these recognitionally relevant properties with its object. When we say that a film is realistic or unrealistic *simpliciter*, we have chosen some threshold of degree of resemblance at which to make the judgement, and this can vary in different contexts, including the comparison class. It also follows that realism is a comparative notion (we compare one picture, or pictorial

---

[28] Goodman, *Languages of Art*, p. 38. Dominic Lopes, 'Pictorial Realism' and Catherine Abell, 'Pictorial Realism' also draw attention to the variety of styles that have counted as realist, though they do not endorse Goodman's conventionalism about realism.

style, with another in respect of realism) and that there can be legitimate disputes about whether a picture is realist or not, for one may be comparing different recognitionally relevant properties in weighing up whether one picture is more realist than another. All of these consequences are to be welcomed and allow us to explain why realism has been ascribed to such varying pictorial styles.[29]

This sketch of perceptual realism, albeit brief, suffices for our purposes. Is cinema a realist medium on this account? Realism is a matter of degree, and is a comparative notion. Still photography was hailed on its invention as a great advance in realism over handmade pictures. And that is correct: for still photographs can effortlessly produce extraordinary detail, whereas producing equivalent detail with handmade pictures is extremely time consuming and therefore very unusual. If the visual detail of a picture is accurate, the number of recognitionally relevant features that it shares with its object increases. So it is true that photographs, as a class, are more realistic than handmade pictures as a class. Moreover, cinema on its invention was seen as an advance on the realism of still photographs. And that is also true: temporal relations between different events are captured in the cinematic shot that are not recorded in the still shot; so cinema resembles reality in more recognitionally relevant ways than does still photography, for it records temporal relations of real events that still photographs do not.[30]

This conclusion applies to cinema as practised in standard ways. Cinema is standardly shot using conventional lenses, ground according to the rules of classical perspective, and it standardly uses editing techniques that preserve basic temporal order, normally with overt markers for deviations from that order, such as flashbacks. But one can imagine a cinematic practice that used only anamorphic lenses that made each image look like a Cubist picture and employed nothing but jump-cuts and random temporal orderings of shots. The standard kind of cinema is realist, but the latter Cubist cinema would not be or would be far less realistic, because its recognitionally relevant resemblances to the real world would be far fewer

---

[29] For similar accounts of perceptual realism, to which I am indebted, see Crispin Sartwell, 'What Pictorial Realism Is'; and Currie, *Image and Mind*, pp. 80–90. However, Sartwell's account lacks the comparative element of the account described above. A comparative account of realism is defended by Noël Carroll, *Philosophical Problems of Classical Film Theory*, pp. 142–3.

[30] Perfected virtual reality (PVR) would be even more realistic than conventional cinema, because the PVR images would be perceptually indiscernible from real objects, so they would resemble those objects in all recognitionally relevant ways. And interactive cinema is in one respect more realistic than non-interactive cinema, since what we perceive is, as in the real world, partly up to us and depends on our actions.

Figure 4. Deep focus in *Rules of the Game* (1939).

than in the case of standard cinema. So cinema is more perceptually realistic than is still photography and handmade pictures, but its degree of realism depends on the nature of the individual image (as is also true of still photography) and also on the editing relations between those images. So questions of the nature of cinematic realism cannot be entirely divorced from the question of the realism of the individual cinematic styles that are practised within the medium.

The most influential account of the realism of cinematic styles is due to André Bazin. Bazin holds to be realistic what we may dub the 'deep-focus' style of Jean Renoir's films, most famously in *Rules of the Game* (1939) (see Figure 4). In contrast, Bazin holds that films in the montage style of Sergei Eisenstein, such as *October* (1928), or the Expressionist style, such as that of *The Cabinet of Dr Caligari* (1920), are not realistic.[31] The deep-focus style is characterised by a number of features, most obviously depth of focus. Depth of focus occurs when all objects in front of the camera, no matter

---

[31] André Bazin, *What is Cinema?* and especially 'The Evolution of the Language of Cinema'. For an extended, useful discussion of Bazin's views on cinematic styles, see Noël Carroll, *Philosophical Problems of Classical Film Theory*, chapter 2. See also Currie, *Image and Mind*, pp. 106–8.

how distant from it, are in focus, as opposed to shallow focus, when only those objects at a certain distance (either close or further away) from the camera are in focus. The style is also characterised by the preponderance of medium long shots over close-ups and by the long take (keeping the camera running for a long period of time). Bazin holds that this style preserves the unity of space and time, does not impose an interpretation on the spectator, allows the spectator to scan the image on her own and allows the action to occur independently of the spectator. These features are the reasons that he offers for holding that the style is realist. In contrast, the montage style destroys the unity of space and time, he holds: it is characterised by a greater use of close-ups, so that the spatial relations of objects are often not shown; it uses much shorter takes, so that the temporal relations of events have to be inferred rather than simply observed; it imposes an interpretation on the spectator by juxtaposition of images; the spectator is not so free to scan the image; and the action depicted seems to be partly dependent on the spectator.

Evidently the different aspects of each style are logically independent from each other: for instance, one could use deep-focus images in a film with short takes and therefore many edits. Nevertheless, these groupings of individual features do represent a reasonably accurate account of two distinctive and important styles, so let us preserve Bazin's groupings.

Using our account of perceptual realism, overall Bazin's view of the comparative realism of the two styles can be defended. Looking at a deep-focus film is more like looking at the events represented than is looking at a montage film of those same events, because of the greater recognitionally relevant resemblances between the deep-focus film and the events shown. If I am observing those events in reality, I can directly observe the temporal relations between them; if I am watching a long take of those two events, I similarly can directly observe the temporal relations between the events depicted. But if I am watching a film sequence composed of a series of short, edited shots of the same events, I have to infer, rather than directly observe, the temporal relations between the depicted events. So observing the series of short shots is less like observing the real temporal events than is observing the long take. Likewise, in the case of a deep-focus shot I can directly observe the spatial relations between the figures in the foreground and the background (provided I understand perspective), just as I can in reality. But in the case of a shallow focus shot, I may be unable to see what is going on in the background, and a distinct set of shots may be required to show these events in focus. So, again, I have to infer the spatial relations between the foreground and the background events; and, again, this is less like observing reality directly. So Bazin's basic point, that the preservation of the unity of space and time in the deep-focus style shows that this style is realist, is correct – or, to put it more carefully in terms of our comparative notion, the deep-focus style is more realistic than the montage style.

However, whilst Bazin's basic claim about the two styles is correct, some of his more detailed points require a more careful statement, or even misfire. The audience is indeed free to scan the image in a deep-focus film – but it is also free to scan the image in a montage film. Bazin's claim should be stated in terms of being free to scan the *scene* (what was in front of the camera): it is this that a medium long shot and deep-focus image of a scene permits, whereas a montage of close-ups of the scene can prevent this. It may also be objected that we do not see in deep focus. Hold up your hand in front of your face, focus on the background and your hand goes out of focus: there is limited depth of field in human vision. So would not a shallow-focus image more accurately reflect our visual relations to reality? But Bazin can be defended here: for a shallow-focus shot of a scene results in the background being intrinsically out of focus – nothing you can do will bring it into focus. But looking at an object always allows you to focus sharply on any part of it. So there is a greater recognitionally relevant resemblance between looking at a deep-focus shot and looking at its object than there is between looking at a shallow-focus shot and looking at its object.

Bazin also holds that the deep-focus style, unlike the montage style, preserves ambiguity, and so no interpretation is imposed on the spectator, unlike in the montage style. He gives the example of the Kuleshov experiment as an instance of montage removing ambiguity and imposing an interpretation.[32] The Kuleshov experiment consisted of three shots of an actor's face; these shots were intercut with a shot of hot soup, a girl playing with a teddy bear and of a woman lying dead in a coffin. Audiences reportedly reacted with amazement that the actor was able so subtly to convey shifts in emotion between hunger (this was a time of food shortages), happiness and restrained sorrow. In fact, the three shots of the actor were the same shot repeated three times and he had a neutral expression on his face. The Soviet montage school presented the experiment as proof of the constructive possibilities of montage: Bazin regards it as a proof that, unlike the deep-focus style which would have preserved the neutrality of expression, the montage style forces an interpretation on the spectator. This is not only a bad thing, he believes, but also shows that the montage style is not a realist style.

---

[32] Bazin, 'The Evolution of the Language of Cinema', p. 36.

However, Bazin's point misfires. It is true of this particular experiment that it imposes an interpretation, unlike reality. But montage need not be employed in this way: sometimes it can foster ambiguity, as in the radical uncertainties imposed by the montage relations in Buñuel and Dalí's *Un Chien andalou* (1928), a film where it is unclear what the plot is, how many protagonists there are, what the timescale is, where it is happening, and much else. Conversely, long takes and deep focus may show who, say, committed a murder, whereas a montage edit of the same scene might be artfully constructed so as to occlude the identity of the murderer, hence keeping information from the audience (perhaps because this is crucial to achieving suspense). So montage can be used to avoid imposing an interpretation, while using a long take would impose that interpretation on the audience.

Though Bazin is wrong on the ambiguity point, his other points can be defended, albeit sometimes in modified form. So we should conclude that overall he is correct in holding that the montage style is less realistic than the deep-focus style.

How does the notion of perceptual realism apply to digital cinema? Digital cinema has the option of being shot in montage or deep-focus style, so one might suppose that digital and traditional cinemas are on a par here. However, in several respects digital cinema has a greater capacity for perceptual realism than does traditional film. It can construct takes of much greater length than can traditional film, which is limited to a film length of about 10–15 minutes, due to the bulkiness of the film roll in the camera. Indeed, digital films have been composed of one take that is the length of the entire film, that is, over one-and-a-half hours long: for instance, both *Time Code* (2000) and *Russian Ark* (2002) are composed of a single, extended shot. (In the former case this is combined with a four-way split screen, which counts against the film's realism.) Further, some digital films are 3D in a way that is far more perceptually effective than traditional 3D films; and perfected virtual reality (PVR), which would involve touch as well visual and acoustic perceptions, may be achievable within the near future by digital means. Clearly 3D films and virtual reality environments are more perceptually realistic than are standard 2D films: as we noted in Section 1.4, PVR yields sensory immersion, where one cannot perceptually distinguish between the virtual reality representation and what it is a representation of. Digital cinema has greater representational capacities than traditional film, and one of those capacities is to achieve greater perceptual realism.

2.4 TRANSPARENCY: TRADITIONAL AND DIGITAL CINEMA

We can now turn to the seventh and final form of realism. According to some philosophers, when we look at photographs we literally see the objects photographed. Look at a photograph of your dead grandmother and you literally see her. Photographs are in this sense transparent. The most prominent defender of this view is Kendall Walton, and his position has received a great deal of critical attention.[33] Far less discussed is a striking extension of the transparency claim to paintings and drawings by Dominic McIver Lopes. Lopes argues that when we look at a painting or drawing of an actual object, we literally see that object.[34] Lopes' position will strike many as severely counterintuitive, and even those who believe in photographic transparency tend to recoil from it. Walton, for instance, argues that transparency applies to photographs and at best only to some 'mechanically executed' drawings, such as tracings. Yet Lopes marshals some powerful and intriguing arguments in favour of his claim for general pictorial transparency. His position also has the merit of providing a unitary account of pictorial transparency, holding that both mechanically produced and handmade pictures are transparent. And, as we have seen, with digital imagery the contributions of mechanical reproduction and of handcrafted elements in a single image may be indistinguishable even to a tutored eye, so a unitary theory is to be welcomed. The alternative would be to hold that in the case of a complexly produced digital image, some aspects are transparent, others are not, and that standardly the viewer, lacking detailed knowledge about production history, does not know which aspects are transparent and which are not. There might of course be good arguments for why the unitary account is false, but considerations of simplicity favour the unitary account if there are no good arguments against it.

I will analyse Lopes' extension of transparency to pictures in general and argue that, even if one accepted some Walton-type arguments for photographic transparency, it would be a mistake to hold that handmade pictures,

---

[33] Kendall Walton, 'Transparent Pictures'. Critics of the view include Nigel Warburton, 'Seeing Through "Seeing through Photographs"'; Currie, *Image and Mind*, chapter 2; and Noël Carroll, 'Towards an Ontology of the Moving Image'. Walton's position has points of contact with Bazin's 'The Ontology of the Photographic Image'. However, the precise commitments of Bazin's position are unclear; for an argument that Bazin has been misinterpreted by Carroll, Currie and others, see Jonathan Friday, 'André Bazin's Ontology of Photographic and Film Imagery'.

[34] Lopes, *Understanding Pictures*, chapter 9.

and therefore the handmade components of digital cinema, are transparent too. But I will also argue that one should reject Walton's arguments for photographic transparency. Thus, though I reject Lopes' position, its merit of offering a unitary account of pictures in respect of transparency is preserved. The truth, however, is not that all pictures are transparent. They are all opaque. It follows that both traditional and digital cinema are opaque.

2.4.1 Walton on transparency

Lopes proceeds by challenging some of Walton's arguments, but also by employing modified versions of others to argue for general pictorial transparency. So I will first outline Walton's position.

Walton offers two kinds of general considerations in favour of photographic transparency. The first is a slippery slope argument: we see things with our naked eyes, but we also see them through spectacles, telescopes and mirrors. It is no strain to talk of seeing things on live television. Why resist then taking literally our talk of seeing someone through a photograph? The fact that a person is long dead is no obstacle to seeing her: we can see stars in the night sky, some of which have long ceased to exist. Why not, then, slide further down the slope: why not hold that we see through paintings and drawings too? This is where Walton's second argument applies. Seeing is a causal process, by which one has visual experiences that are counterfactually dependent on the visible properties of objects. These counterfactual relations must, however, be independent of others' beliefs (and other intentional states). Consider Helen, whose optic nerve is disconnected from her eyes, but who is given visual experiences by a neurosurgeon corresponding to what she would see were her eyes connected. This does not count as seeing, holds Walton, since Helen's visual experiences are dependent on the surgeon's beliefs, rather than being directly counterfactually dependent on features of the world. Now photographic content is also belief independent. Suppose that an explorer claims to see a dinosaur in a forest. He can produce a photograph to show that he was correct, if he was, since the dependence of the photograph on the scene is not mediated by his beliefs. But if the explorer produced a drawing of the dinosaur, then, even were he honest, this would merely show that he believed that a dinosaur was present, not that one actually was. If he had hallucinated a dinosaur, his sketch would show the hallucinated dinosaur; but a photograph would show merely the empty forest. So the counterfactual relations of paintings and drawings are mediated by the picture-maker's beliefs; hence we do not see through paintings and drawings to the world.[35]

Belief-independent counterfactual dependence does not suffice for seeing, however. A computer, which has no beliefs, could print out verbal descriptions of a dinosaur, yet looking at the descriptions would not count as seeing the dinosaur. So we need to add that seeing requires preservation of real similarity relations too. This notion is cashed out by Walton in terms of the errors of discrimination we can make. We can easily confuse a house and a barn in looking at them, and likewise we can easily confuse a photograph (and a picture) of a house with that of a barn. But we are more likely to confuse the word 'house' with 'hearse', than with 'barn'. Photographs preserve the real similarity relations of things, but descriptions scramble these similarity relations. Hence one does not see an object through its description, even if that description is mechanically generated; but one does see it through its photograph. Photographs satisfy the similarity-preservation condition for seeing something.

Walton denies that belief-independent counterfactual dependence and similarity preservation of visual experiences suffice for seeing something.[36] So these arguments cannot amount to a *proof* that, given the presence of these conditions, someone seeing a photograph literally sees its subject. Rather, Walton construes himself as issuing a 'challenge' to his opponents: given that we see through mirrors and telescopes, the challenge is to find a rationale for saying that we do not see through photographs. The role of the belief-independence and similarity-preservation conditions is to provide a principled rationale for drawing the point at which transparency ceases as between photographs and handmade pictures.[37] Later I will attempt to meet Walton's challenge, arguing that there is a principled distinction for holding that we see through mirrors and telescopes, but not through photographs or handmade pictures.

2.4.2 *Lopes and transparency*

Lopes thinks that the principled distinction should be drawn further down the slippery slope. He offers three considerations for maintaining that one can see through handmade pictures.

[35] Note that Walton's claim is that seeing must be independent of *others'* beliefs, and correspondingly that the viewer sees through a photograph because its content is not dependent on the *photographer's* beliefs. Walton does not hold that seeing requires independence of *the viewer's* beliefs, nor correspondingly that seeing through a photograph must be independent of the viewer's beliefs ('Transparent Pictures', pp. 264–5).

[36] Walton, 'On Pictures and Photographs: Objections Answered', p. 74 n. 36.   [37] *Ibid.*, p. 69.

First, he thinks it implausible that our discovery that what we thought was a photograph is in fact a painting could transform our experience of it and attitudes towards it. If a computer were programmed to wield a paintbrush to produce a picture of irises in the style of Van Gogh, Walton should hold that one can see through this picture (since its counterfactual dependence on the irises' properties is belief independent and so it would be like a photograph in this respect). Yet if a person followed the computer's precise paint-by-numbers instructions to produce a painting of the irises, Walton would have to hold that one no longer literally sees the irises through the picture. And that, says Lopes, is counterintuitive. Further, lots of photographs are touched up, though we sometimes do not realise this. If we suspect that this is so, our sense of seeing through such a photograph should weaken, he says, but it does not.[38]

Since I believe that both handmade and photographic pictures are opaque, I agree that there ought to be no transformation in one's experience of transparency between the different cases. However, my goal in this subsection is to examine whether believers in photographic transparency can resist the slide down the slippery slope to general pictorial transparency. And they would have no difficulty in doing so in respect of this argument.

First, Walton thinks that certain 'mechanically executed' drawings are transparent: place transparent paper on a window and trace the outlines of an object seen through it, or copy a photograph without realising what it represents, and one may produce transparent drawings.[39] Presumably Walton's test is whether or not the picture maker is employing a belief about the picture's subject. If that is so, he could agree that the picture made by a human following the computer's paint-by-numbers instructions may be transparent, while denying that all handmade pictures are transparent, since they standardly involve a belief about the painting's subject.

Second, and more importantly, Lopes seems to appeal to a general principle that our experience and attitudes should not be transformed when we discover that what we thought was a photograph is in fact a painting. But that general principle is false: it is common for our experience of pictures to be transformed when we understand that they are made in different ways. Suppose that I mistake a photorealist painting for a photograph: on finding out the truth my experience should be transformed in several ways. Questions about choice of style, for instance, now become pertinent, where they were not before. A photograph is always in a 'photographic' style, but a painting is not: so why, I might wonder, did the

---

[38] Lopes, *Understanding Pictures*, p. 182.   [39] Walton, 'Transparent Pictures', p. 267.

painter choose this particular style? And questions about the artist's motivation now become salient when we construe the work as a painting, which is produced by meticulous and hard labour, whereas these questions do not arise in the same way for a photograph, which can be made in a moment. So if this transformative experience occurs for some properties, why should it not occur in respect of transparency too?

Perhaps, though, Lopes is merely reporting his intuitions about transparency, without putting much weight on the general principle. But if this is so, those who do not share his intuitions have been given no reason to agree with him. Consider his example of discovering that a photograph has been touched up and his claim that this does not weaken our sense that we see through it. This will not challenge the intuitions of those who find the handmade/photographic distinction crucial for transparency. A touched-up photograph is an amalgam of a photograph and a handmade picture: gradually increase the area that is touched up, and one finally has a painting covering the photograph. So Walton's supporters can simply note that all the claimed intuition does is to contradict their own intuitions, rather than giving them a reason to reject them.

Lopes' second argument is more theoretically weighty. Walton holds that belief independence is a requirement if one is genuinely to see: Helen does not see, because her visual experiences are dependent on the neurosurgeon's beliefs, not directly on the visible features of the world. But Lopes endorses Currie's argument that belief independence is not a necessary condition for seeing. Malebranche believes that there are no genuine causal relations: all of our perceptions are mediated by God. So in the world as Malebranche construes it, all our visual experiences are dependent on God's beliefs, but nevertheless we still see in this world.[40] So even insofar as pictures are dependent on their makers' beliefs, notes Lopes, this is no reason to deny their transparency.[41]

Call the world as Malebranche construes it, the 'Malebranche-world'. Two replies to the argument are possible. First, even if inhabitants of the Malebranche-world say that they see, this does not show that they mean by 'see' what we do. Suppose we mean this word to pick out a kind of belief-independent counterfactual dependence of visual experiences on visible properties of the world. Discovering that there is no such dependence in the Malebranche-world, its inhabitants choose the best successor-concept to 'see' in their world, which is mediation by God's beliefs. That they mean this by 'see' does not show that we, not living in a Malebranche-world,

[40] Currie, *Image and Mind*, p. 62.   [41] Lopes, *Understanding Pictures*, pp. 182–3.

mean the same by it.[42] Nor, we can add, does it even show that the Malebranche inhabitants would judge differently about the Helen case than does Walton: the neurosurgeon is not God, and mediation by his beliefs does not count as seeing on the successor-concept.

A second, rather different, reply holds that the relevant belief-independent counterfactual dependence does in fact hold in the Malebranche-world, and this is why we are tempted to agree that we would see (in our sense) in this world. For the Malebranche thought experiment is supposed to generate a more robust set of intuitions than does the Helen case. But if this is so, it is because it is God who is doing the mediating, not a neurosurgeon. God is omniscient, morally perfect and omnipotent. It follows from his omniscience that if state of affairs p obtains, then he believes that p, and conversely that if he believes that p, then p. It follows from his moral perfection that he would not systematically deceive us, and it follows from his omnipotence that he can make effective his will not to deceive us. Since God possesses these three properties by necessity, we have a metaphysical guarantee that our visual experiences are also directly dependent on the state of affairs that p, as well as being mediated by God's belief that p. So both the relevant kind of belief independence, as well as belief dependence, obtain in the Malebranche-world. And thus, insofar as the inhabitants refer to the former in using 'see', they speak as we do, and we can agree with them that in this respect they see in their world. Only insofar as they refer to mediation by God's beliefs do they use the successor-concept to *see*.[43] So, again, the Malebranche-world does not undermine the claim that seeing, in our sense, requires belief-independent counterfactual dependence.

Lopes' final argument for descending the slippery slope to handmade pictures is the most interesting and important of the three arguments. It holds that even if, *pace* the previous argument, seeing requires belief-independent counterfactual dependence, handmade pictures can satisfy that requirement, and so be transparent. The counterfactual dependence between handmade pictures and their subjects is not necessarily mediated by the picture-maker's beliefs, but may instead be directly dependent on her experience. This belief independence holds in two respects. First, what

---

[42] Walton makes much the same point in 'On Pictures and Photographs', p. 75 n. 47.

[43] Does not the obtaining of direct counterfactual dependence on states of affairs undermine the initial stipulation that there is no genuine causality in a Malebranche-world? This is not so, if we analyse causation in terms other than counterfactuals. But if we do analyse causation in these terms, then the argument shows that there would be genuine causation in the Malebranche-world, and so the idea of such a world is incoherent. But if it is incoherent, then it cannot function as a counterexample to claims about seeing.

a handmade picture represents is its source, its subject, and its source is not determined by the artist's beliefs or intentions, any more than is the subject of a photograph. Second, the process of drawing is simply a recognition-based skill, and recognition is a perceptual, experiential process. Experience, Lopes believes, has non-conceptual content, that is, concepts play no necessary role in it. I can experience a vast number of different colours without having a concept of each one; I can draw Piccadilly Circus without knowing its name; and I can draw a square in perspective by marking on the paper a particular trapezoidal shape, of which I have no concept.[44] Since beliefs are constituted by concepts, it follows from the claim that experience has non-conceptual content that one can experience something without having a belief about that thing. So an artist's drawings may reflect simply her experience of the world, without being dependent on her beliefs: 'In drawing the eye and the hand work together, perhaps bypassing the mind, or rather that portion of the mind that deals in concepts and beliefs'.[45] Handmade pictures thus satisfy Walton's belief-independence requirement, and so are transparent.

This argument is interesting and subtle, and has the merit of resting on the widely held, though disputed, claim that experience has non-conceptual content. Nevertheless, it does not prove the transparency of handmade pictures.

First, suppose that it does show that handmade pictures can stand in belief-independent counterfactually dependent relations to their subjects. Does that condition (given the fulfilment of other conditions such as the preservation of similarity relations) prove that handmade pictures are transparent? Walton generally presents his requirement in terms of beliefs, though he adds that the independence must be from other intentional states too.[46] But why be so parsimonious? Why not include independence from others' visual experiences as well? Consider Helen again: suppose that the surgeon feeds her visual experiences based on his own experiences, rather than on his beliefs. Then the intuition that Helen is not genuinely seeing seems just as strong as in the case in which the surgeon's beliefs control Helen's visual input. Likewise, consider again the dinosaur scenario: if the explorer hallucinates a dinosaur, his belief that there is dinosaur in front of him will be manifest in his sketch, but not in a photograph of the scene. But what ultimately makes the difference between the sketch and the photograph is that the former, but not the latter, is dependent on the

[44] Lopes, *Understanding Pictures*, pp. 184–6.   [45] *Ibid.*, p. 186.
[46] Walton, 'Transparent Pictures', p. 264.

explorer's *visual experience*, his hallucination, for his experience also explains his beliefs. Thus modified, the Helen case shows that seeing requires independence not only of others' beliefs (and other intentional states), but also of others' visual experiences. And the dinosaur case shows that a photograph's content is independent of the picture maker's visual experience, but that a handmade picture's content is dependent on his experience. So we cannot see through a handmade picture on the modified, experiential requirement. Thus broadened out to include others' visual experiences, as well as intentional states, such as beliefs, Walton's argument against the transparency of handmade pictures goes through. And Lopes' objection cannot undermine it, for Lopes agrees that the relations in which a handmade picture stands to its subjects are mediated by the artist's visual experiences.[47]

This point suffices to undermine Lopes' third argument. However, I will also consider how it could be answered if we kept the relevant constraint formulated in terms of independence from others' beliefs and intentional states in general, rather than extending it to include others' visual experiences as well. Doing so not only reveals further objections to the third argument, but also allows us to consider the nature of the drawing and painting process.

Consider first the subject of a painting. Lopes, as we saw, holds that what a painting represents is its source, the object that plays a certain role in its production, where this role is independent of the artist's intentions and beliefs, as is also true of a photograph. Now consider a painter who is commissioned to produce a portrait of Rich. Being cash-rich but time-poor, Rich asks his identical twin, Poor, to sit for the portrait. The painter then paints Poor. Who is the subject of the painting? The person before the canvas, and whose appearance guided the artist's actions, was Poor; but the intended subject is Rich; and both Poor and Rich can be seen in the portrait. A plausible verdict is that both are the subject: Poor is the model of the painting, Rich is the person depicted, in the same way that an artist's model can be the model for a picture of Julius Caesar, and both are depicted in the picture. Poor stands in a relation to the painting not too dissimilar to that in which he would stand to a photograph, since he is present before the picture maker, and one might try to make out a case that the artist's beliefs are

---

[47] Intriguingly, in 'Transparent Pictures', p. 276 n. 22, Walton says that *in some cases* the relevant counterfactual dependence may rest 'not so much on the picture maker's *beliefs* as on his visual experience, or his thoughts, or possibly his intentions'. He does not explain why he restricts this claim to some cases: as just argued, the requirement of independence from others' visual experiences should be universal.

irrelevant in depicting Poor. But what of Rich? The relevant relation here is plausibly one of intention: it is only because the artist intends to depict Rich that the portrait is also of him. Suppose that the painter, being no friend of rich folk, decided to depict only Poor and ignore Rich's desires. Then the subsequent painting is straightforwardly one of Poor, funded by the deluded Rich. Lopes discusses the twin case, and holds that Rich is depicted by virtue of his standing in an information-transmitting causal chain to the picture.[48] But even if we accept this claim, it would still ground the conclusion that beliefs and intentions are necessarily involved in establishing pictorial content, since the relevant causal relations hold between the beliefs and intentions of the painter and Rich. Also, contrast the painting case with photography, where intentions may play no role. Suppose Rich asks a photographer to have Poor sit in his place; no matter what the participants' intentions, the resulting photograph is of Poor, and solely of him. So at least in some cases the artist's intentions play an ineliminable role in fixing the content of a handmade painting, but this is not true in equivalent cases in photography. Hence the depictive content of handmade pictures is not independent of all intentional states.

Lopes also argues that the nature of the drawing process is such that beliefs play no necessary role in it: 'Drawing is simply applied recognition'.[49] Since recognition is an experiential process, and experience has non-conceptual content, the drawing process can be independent of the artist's beliefs.[50]

Now I do not deny that experience in general has non-conceptual content.[51] But the pertinent issue concerns whether drawings can possess non-conceptual depictive content. It could be that experience in general has non-conceptual content, but that in making drawings the artist must apply some concepts. Lopes, though, denies this: 'A difference in an object may make a difference in a picture of it simply by affecting the artist's experience and thus the way she drew'.[52] So it is experience that guides one's drawing-actions, not beliefs, and beliefs drop out as playing no necessary role. But consider how, on this account, the artist is supposed to adjust the drawing in order to capture the appearance of its subject. Since only experience may be

---

[48] Lopes, *Understanding Pictures*, pp. 163–5.   [49] *Ibid.*, p. 184.

[50] Note that the non-conceptual content claim is modal: it holds that one *could* have an experience of something, while entirely lacking concepts which pick out that thing; this is consistent with the claim that one does, as a matter of fact, possess these concepts.

[51] Though it certainly has been disputed. For an influential argument against the view, see John McDowell, *Mind and World*, Lecture III.

[52] Lopes, *Understanding Pictures*, p. 187.

involved, she just *sees*, presumably, that, say, a cat drawing is not as black as the cat, and then alters the drawing appropriately. But this claim occludes the role of beliefs and desires in the drawing process. To see that *P*, a picture, is blacker than *O*, its object, is to make a type of judgement: *seeing that* involves a judgement, in a way that simply *seeing* an object does not. Moreover, in order to make the alteration in the drawing, the artist must want to make it, and therefore has to have a desire. Intentional states are necessarily involved in the act of drawing.

There is a general reason why this is so. Drawings, by definition, are the product of an action, the act of drawing something. An action is distinct from mere behaviour (such as a spasm), because the action is intentional under some description and is therefore brought under a concept by the agent. So a drawing must be produced under some intentional description, such as, for instance, *drawing a cat*. Actions have intentional explanations: every action is to be explained by the agent's beliefs and desires. Beliefs and desires are constituted by concepts. So if a drawing is made, the process of its making must be governed by concepts. One wants to draw a cat, for instance, and believes that by making such-and-such marks, one will do so; so one's actions are governed by the cat-concept. Drawing typically consists not in a single action, but in a whole series of co-ordinated actions: to draw the cat, one has to draw the parts of the cat, and correspondingly has a set of desires to draw the cat's parts. And to draw, one must compare the drawing with the cat, which involves deploying further beliefs and desires: perhaps one believes that part of the drawing is less black than the cat, desires that this not be so, and therefore darkens the drawing. Thus drawings, the products of the action of drawing, have their content explained in part by an ineliminable appeal to the artist's beliefs and desires, which explain why the drawing has the content that it does. So the depictive content of drawings is partly dependent on concepts, those concepts that constitute the relevant beliefs and desires of the artist that explain her actions. And this is true of necessity, since drawing is an action. So Walton is correct: drawings, being the products of actions, exhibit counter-factual dependence on visible properties of things, where this dependence must be mediated by the artist's beliefs and other intentional states, such as desires. The mediation cannot be by the artist's experience alone, as Lopes supposes, otherwise she would not be engaged in the *action* of drawing.

As we noted, Lopes also gives several examples of cases where, he claims, the artist does not need to deploy, and is even highly unlikely to deploy, concepts: she does not need to know that it is Piccadilly Circus that she is drawing, nor need she possess the concept of a particular shade of colour to paint it, nor of that particular trapezoidal shape required to draw a square in perspective from a certain angle. In the latter two cases the number of possible colours and shapes far outreaches our available concepts for them, so we usually do not have concepts of them, even though we can draw or paint them. So how can my account of drawing be correct?

I do not claim that *every* feature of a scene needs to be conceptualised by an artist. It is not true in general that every feature of an action is intentional: my action of turning on the lights may disturb the cat, but I did not intend to disturb her, nor did I even know of her presence. Likewise, not every feature of a drawing-action need be intended, so drawings can have some depictive content that is not intended. But the claim that *some* content must be brought under concepts by the artist is enough to undermine Lopes' argument, since to secure belief independence, he has to claim that it is possible that *no* concepts at all are brought to bear by the artist, as indeed he does claim: 'I see no reason why an artist *must* bring to bear *any* concepts about the content of the picture he is making'.[53]

In any case, the particular examples do not prove that no concepts are brought to bear by the artist. An artist may draw Piccadilly Circus without knowing it to be such; but she has to conceptualise it in some way in order to draw it, if only to bring it under general concepts of something with a certain size, shape and look. An artist may, prior to seeing it, have no concept of a particular shade of pink. But in attempting to reproduce something similar on paper, she does employ a concept, and indeed one linguistically expressible: she thinks of *that* particular shade of pink, picking it out indexically. This does not entail that colour experience lacks non-conceptual content: prior to seeing the colour, she may have had no concept of it. But having seen it, she now possesses a concept of it, and can employ it in the judgements, deployed in her picture making, about the relation of the colour of her painting to the colour of its subject. And likewise, an artist can produce a shape, conceptualise it as *that* shape, and then by changing it, discover whether it looks like a square would from a certain angle. So there are concepts that can be deployed in such cases, and indeed must be deployed, for reasons we have given, if the artist is to engage in a drawing-action.

2.4.3 *Opaque pictures*

Since the three arguments for the transparency of handmade pictures fail, and since the view is extremely counterintuitive, we should reject it. But

---

[53] *Ibid.*, p. 186.

where, then, on the slippery slope, should we draw the line that separates those things through which we see, such as mirrors and telescopes, from those things through which we do not? Walton draws it between photographs and (the great majority of) handmade pictures. Is he right to do so?

There are many objections to Walton's view, but I will pick out here only what seems to me the most decisive one. Consider two clocks, A and B, which are completely similar and A controls the position of the hands of B by an automatic radio link. Thus looking at B satisfies Walton's conditions for seeing A through it: B's dependence on A is belief independent, and similarity relations are preserved. Yet when I see B I am not thereby seeing A.[54] Walton has objected that the counterfactual dependence of B on A is not rich enough: only the position and movement of the hands of B depend on those of A. If we increase the number of features of B dependent on those of A, then we do see A through B.[55]

However, it is not true that even extremely rich belief-independent counterfactual dependence suffices for seeing one object through another. Suppose that due to the gradual depletion of African gorillas' habitat, it is decided sometime next century to ban all tourists from visiting them in the wild. Instead, an enterprising showman sets up in the bush several robots which are visually indiscriminable from members of the real colony of gorillas, and has these robots' movements, size, shape, etc., controlled by a computer so that they exactly mimic the movements, size, shape, etc., of the real gorillas a hundred miles away. Then tourists looking at the robots will have an experience that is visually indiscriminable from that of seeing the real gorillas, and this experience will be as richly counterfactually dependent on the features of the gorillas and their movements as one could wish. But is it true that in seeing the robot one is seeing the real gorilla? Not so: one may be genuinely and reasonably disappointed to discover that what one is seeing is not real gorillas, as one had supposed, but only extremely realistic and detailed copies. Or consider a real-life example. The Victoria and Albert Museum in London possesses extremely detailed plaster copies, stained to the correct colours, of historical artefacts, such as Trajan's Column. Since these casts are mechanically produced and preserve real similarity relations (and do so much more faithfully than do photographs), then in looking at the plaster cast of Trajan's Column, I am looking, through the copy, at Trajan's Column itself, according to Walton. Again, that seems deeply counterintuitive; one is looking at a mere copy, and not seeing the original.

---

[54] Currie, *Image and Mind*, pp. 64–5.   [55] Walton, 'On Pictures and Photographs', p. 75 n. 47.

Walton might simply dig in his heels at this point and insist that we really do see the gorillas and Trajan's Column. But there is another, less counter-intuitive, response open to him. In introducing the claim that we literally see through photographs, he wonders whether this is the ordinary use of 'see', or whether it is an extension of it. He remains agnostic about this, but remarks 'if it is an extension, it is a very natural one'.[56] Now, in one sense, an extension is natural, if it is reasonable, preserving the central sense of the term, while adjudicating borderline cases. This sense of 'natural' is not promising here, since many of us are very clear that we don't see the gorillas or Trajan's Column: these are not borderline cases. Any extension of the term 'see' would simply add a different sense to the ordinary one, just involving a kind of belief-independent causal contact, and the claim that we see through photographs would then lose most of its interest. However, there is another, more promising, sense in which an extension to a term is natural. Walton discusses a case of someone's seeing fossils, and considers the objection that she does not thereby see the ancient animals that have been fossilised. His response is that perhaps we should simply talk of being 'in contact with' the ancient animals, since it is possible that the ordinary sense of 'see' does not capture any natural kind at all. One has to extend the notion of 'see' to capture a natural kind distinction, between being in contact with something in a non-belief-mediated way (such as with the fossils, or things seen in photographs), or being related to it in a belief-mediated way (such as one's relation to someone depicted in a painting). So there may be no important distinction between perceiving things in the ordinary sense and not perceiving them. To capture the real, natural kind distinction, perhaps we have to reorganise our concept of seeing quite radically.[57]

So Walton could reply to the objections that in the ordinary sense of 'see' we perhaps do not see the gorillas or Trajan's Column; but the ordinary sense of 'see' doesn't capture any interesting distinction, and certainly not one based on a natural kind difference. On his successor notion of being 'in contact with', we are indeed in contact with the animals and the Column, and that is all that we need to show.

Now there is an obvious danger of triviality here, since we seem to have eviscerated the transparency claim of most of the substance that made it interesting in the first case. Nevertheless, it is a promising reply if indeed the ordinary sense of 'seeing' captures no important distinction. And it also fits well with Walton's characterisation of his argument as constituting

[56] Walton, 'Transparent Pictures', p. 252.   [57] *Ibid.*, p. 275 n. 13.

a 'challenge' to those who wish to stop the slide down the slippery slope before one reaches photographs. The challenge is in part to find a relevant natural kind distinction that allows this.

So here is a response to that challenge: the ordinary sense of 'see' does capture a clear distinction, and indeed one that involves a natural kind distinction.[58] The idea of seeing involves that of being in *unmediated* or *direct* contact with an object. Mediation here is understood in natural kind terms: we see an object only if rays of light pass uninterruptedly from it to our eyes. I saw my computer as I wrote this book, since rays of light from the computer passed uninterruptedly to my eyes. I see objects in optical telescopes and mirrors because the rays of light from the object pass through a lens or are reflected off a surface and those same rays reach my eye. I do not see my dead grandmother in a photograph, since the rays of light that impinged from her onto the negative in the camera are different from those that impinge on my eye when I look at her photograph. I likewise do not see the gorillas or the Column or the ancient animals, since there are no uninterrupted light rays passing between them and me. The ordinary sense of 'seeing' is robust, and rules out seeing through photographs, or indeed seeing through any other kinds of picture.

This account has been denied, and surprisingly by someone who agrees that all pictures are opaque. Gregory Currie objects that light is not essential to seeing: one can imagine bat-like creatures that have visual experiences of objects caused by sonar, and so which see. Also, suppose that one weakened the claim to hold that it is *uninterrupted transmission* that is the key notion, which could be of something that is not light, but only functionally equivalent to it. That view, says Currie, should also be rejected: for there could be a transducer screen, which had a pattern of light falling on one side of it from an object and the other side simultaneously emitted different light rays to produce a qualitatively identical pattern. Surely in this case one would admit that one saw the object on the other side of the screen, even though no single ray of light is emitted from the object to the viewer.[59]

I think it extremely doubtful that Currie's example of bat-like creatures "seeing" by sonar is coherent. Think of those qualities sensitivity to which constitutes sight: we see sizes of things, shapes, distances, tones and colours, for example. Some of these it is possible to detect by sonar: for

---

[58] Note that seeing *involves* a natural kind distinction: I am not claiming that 'seeing' *is* a natural kind term: more is required for seeing than direct contact.

[59] Currie, *Image and Mind*, pp. 58–60.

instance, one can establish the distance, size and shape of things by echo location. But one cannot establish by sound their tones (relative luminance) or their colours. And that is because relative luminance and colours are properties of light, and therefore one needs sight, the faculty that involves sensitivity to light, in order to detect them. Also, if these creatures really saw, they would be able to make true statements, such as 'I can see in the absence of light'; 'There was so much noise, I couldn't see a thing'; 'Visibility conditions are excellent, since it's so quiet'; and 'It's a vacuum – I can't see anything!'. It's clear that the occurrences of 'see' in these contexts would have to occur in heavy scare-quotes; and what this shows is that these creatures would be at best quasi-seeing, or para-seeing, not 'seeing' in the ordinary sense, but in a new, extended sense. So, despite Currie's objection, it is highly plausible that it is a conceptual requirement that seeing involves uninterrupted light transmission.

However, even if that were false and Currie's thought experiment were coherent, it need not undermine the condition of uninterrupted light transmission for seeing. For we could concede instead that what we *mean* by the term 'seeing' involves the broader idea of unmediated or direct contact. The appeal to uninterrupted light transmission would be a claim about what is a *physically necessary* condition for us to see something. Constituted biologically as we are, that necessary condition is uninterrupted light transmission. If the bat-like creatures were possible, then the physi-cally necessary condition for them to see would be something different, concerning sonic properties. But that this were so would not prove that the physically necessary condition for when *we* see is not uninterrupted light transmission. Understanding the uninterrupted light transmission con-dition in this way would suffice for showing that we do not see through photographs, but do see through telescopes, mirrors, and so on.

Currie also objects that lack of interruption cannot be necessary for seeing, since we see objects through the transducer screen. However, this screen is in effect a television screen, where the camera records live what is right in front of one, even though the screen blocks one's line of sight. People who deny that we see through photographs have just as good a reason to deny that we see things on live television. Both photography and television are mechanical forms of image making, which break one's unme-diated contact with objects that is required if one is to see them. Since the transducer screen is just a variation of a television screen, those who deny the transparency of photographs should deny that we see through the transducer screen too.

2.4.4 Objections considered

Let us consider some objections to the view just outlined. First, why assume that there is one sense of 'see' that we are trying to analyse? 'See' is a multiply ambiguous term: for instance, we talk of seeing face to face, of seeing someone's point, and even of 'blindsight', where patients with certain kinds of cortical damage deny that they can see anything, but nevertheless can say what is in front of them with a good degree of accuracy. Given these and many other senses, what is illegitimate in talking of seeing people in photographs or of seeing people on live television? And if this is legitimate, then there seems to be no interesting substantial issue addressed in the transparency debate.

There are many senses of 'see', but that does not eviscerate the conceptual debate of interest. For multiply ambiguous terms, one can still attempt to analyse each of these senses. And the core sense of 'see' that is at issue in this debate is that in which we univocally talk of seeing people face to face, through eyeglasses, through binoculars and in mirrors. The question is whether, understood in this sense of 'see', whatever it is, it is the case that we see people in photographs and handmade pictures? I have argued that we do not. It is compatible with this claim that there are other senses of 'see', distinct and perhaps metaphorical or loose, in which we can talk of seeing people on live TV or of seeing Henry VIII when we look at Holbein's portrait of him.

Second, it may be objected that the analytic project of finding out what we mean in this core sense of 'see', and then establishing whether we see objects in photographs and paintings, has no point and what matters is theory construction. In his most recent reflections on the issue, Walton states that 'My project is theory construction, not conceptual or linguistic analysis'.[60]

We should agree that theory construction is important – but so is conceptual analysis, and whatever Walton's intentions, there is an interesting question to raise about what we *mean* by 'see' in its core sense, and whether we see through photographs in that sense. Suppose that this sense did not feature in any interesting theory, epistemic or aesthetic, about photographs: this would show merely that we had, by extension of the ordinary use of the term or by stipulation of a new use, to decide on a term that figured in the most explanatorily powerful theories. The conceptual project of analysing what we ordinarily mean by 'see' would still have

---

[60] Kendall Walton, *Marvelous Images*, p. 111.

point. But matters are better than this for the opacity theorist. For, as we have seen in criticising Lopes' position, Walton is correct in thinking that photographs, unlike paintings and like ordinary seeing, stand in belief-independent counterfactual relations to their objects. So whatever explanatory power this distinction possesses is also available to the opacity theorist. I have also claimed that there is a further necessary condition for genuine seeing: the uninterrupted transmission of light from the object to the viewer's eyes. This condition not only contributes to the conceptual analysis, but also plays a role in theories of the aesthetics of photographs. Looking at a photograph is very different from seeing the object face to face and affects our appreciation in several ways: the sense of voyeurism in looking at a sexually explicit photograph, for instance, is far less acute than seeing that scene face to face. And the natural explanation is that in the former case we are not really seeing the scene but in the latter case we are, and that this is how it seems to the viewer. The opacity view not only addresses the conceptual issue, but is also more theoretically powerful than its rival.

A third objection questions the adequacy of the argument by noting that an equivalent issue can be raised about sound. Presumably the opacity theorist will hold that we are not literally hearing actors' voices in cinema, but only hearing audio recordings of them, in the same way that we are not literally seeing them, but only seeing visual recordings of their appearance. However, it seems far more plausible to hold that we are hearing the actors than that we are seeing them. So our intuitions are in conflict and do not favour the opacity theorist to the degree that we have assumed.

One should acknowledge that the intuitions for sound transparency are stronger than for visual transparency. One reply is to accept that sound transparency is true. If so, that need not impugn anything argued here for visual transparency: the uninterrupted light transmission condition for genuine seeing does not require that we think there is an uninterrupted sound transmission condition for genuine hearing. That is a defensible view. But the price we pay is to destroy the unity of the account, holding a mixed transparency/opacity theory for the overall cinematic sensory experience. A better response is to argue for opacity of both sensory dimensions, and then seek an explanation for why the intuitions for sound transparency are stronger. That explanation is not hard to find. First, a visual image, such as a picture or photograph, has a surface, located at some definite point in relation to us with a definite size and shape. But a sound image (the recording of a sound) has no surface, and it surrounds us or is at best only vaguely spatially located. So there is no image surface to attend to in the case of the sound image, as there is the case of the visual image. Thus we more easily think of the experience as hearing the source of the sound, rather than merely hearing a sound image. Second, one can in almost all instances visually distinguish between a depiction of a thing and the thing's visual appearance: for instance, I can visually discriminate between a photograph of an apple and the apple itself when I look at it. But with good sound recordings it is almost impossible to discriminate by auditory means between, say, an audio recording of someone speaking and actually hearing that person speaking. So for both reasons the phenomenology of hearing a sound image is closer to that of hearing the source of the sound than is the phenomenology of seeing a visual image to seeing the source of that image. So our intuitions are stronger for sound transparency than visual transparency. But this grounding does not entail or even strengthen the argument for sound transparency. For consider a partial visual analogue of the sound case: a virtual reality image of a scene has no surface to its image (it looks as if we are seeing the scene not its image) and one cannot visually discriminate between that image and the scene; yet the argument for the opacity of pictures developed above applies just as well to virtual reality images as it does to regular photographs. Hence the opacity theorist can hold that the grounding of the intuitions for the sound case does not undermine an opacity argument for sound.

A fourth set of objections targets the uninterrupted (direct) light transmission condition directly. One can see black holes and matte black objects or surfaces; but such things do not produce or reflect light, so according to the condition, one cannot see them; and that is simply false. The reply is that in real cases there is always some light reflecting off the surfaces of matte black objects, so one sees them by virtue of that light. And if there were no light reflected at all (as would be the case with a black hole), then we would not really be seeing this ultra-black object: what we would be seeing is the surrounding matter and the edge where it meets the object. Suppose that a reduction screen were made by making a hole in a card and the hole is smaller than the ultra-black object, and one looked at the object through the hole. If one focused one's attention on the hole and not the surrounding card, one would see nothing at all. And that is what the opacity theorist correctly claims.

Fifth, it may also be objected that I can see with a prosthetic eye and therefore that the condition for uninterrupted transmission to my eye is not necessary for me to see.[61] But that is false: *my eye* is a functional concept and

---

[61] David Lewis ('Veridical Hallucination and Prosthetic Vision', p. 280) takes it that one can genuinely see through a prosthetic eye, or at least that saying so is a legitimate resolution of an indeterminacy within the ordinary sense of 'see'.

is not fixed by its material constituents. My current eye is a natural eye; if it were removed and successfully replaced with a prosthetic eye, then my new eye would be a mechanical one. I would still see objects through it by virtue of the direct light transmission from objects to my eye.

A final worry is that the uninterrupted light transmission condition is a piece of folk physics, which not only may be (and perhaps already has been) undermined by progress in physics, but is also an empirical claim that ought not to feature in the concept of seeing. For if the claim were undermined – if the natural kind difference identified by folk physics turned out not to exist according to scientific physics – then we must conclude that none of us could see, which is absurd. Moreover, since the notion of light transmission is relatively recent, it would follow that we do not have the same concept of seeing as did people in the distant past, which is also implausible. These objections also apply to the weakened conceptual condition of unmediated contact (with no reference to light), which I suggested for those folk who agree with Currie that the bat-like creatures can see: this condition could still be undermined by theory change, with the same absurd or unacceptable results.

However, appeal to folk physics is exactly what one wants if one is engaged in conceptual analysis: after all, few of the folk know about modern scientific physics at other than a rudimentary level, so the conceptual connection would not be to it. And it is easy to exaggerate the dangers of empirical refutation of folk physics: light is on any plausible theory required for seeing and the notion of direct or uninterrupted transmission is compatible with a wide range of physical theories. But suppose that it turned out that modern physics did refute those claims of folk physics required in the conceptual analysis. The best response would be to opt for the nearest successor-concept to 'see' that is compatible with physics. We would be like the dwellers in the Malebranche-world, who discovered that their visual experiences did not stand in belief-independent counterfactual dependence to objects, and so chose the nearest successor-concept to 'seeing' in their world.

This reply, however, sparks the other worry: the proposed analysis entails, together with observed empirical differences in physical theories, that we do not have the same concept of seeing as people in the Ancient World. Aristotle, for instance, held that light does not travel, but is a state, being the actualisation of what is potentially transparent.[62] Since he did not have the notion of light transmission, he did not have our concept of seeing.

---

[62] Aristotle, *On the Soul*, 418^{b}10–27.

However, that is not an absurd result: it is a highly plausible one, since Aristotle's notion of *psuchē* is famously different from our notion of mind, even though that is the closest translation, and sight is one of the faculties of the mind. So, rather than the appeal to folk physics rendering my account problematic, it yields plausible results about our notion of sight.

So a wide range of objections can be answered. We should conclude that, on the slippery slope that starts with unaided vision, then seeing with eyeglasses, then seeing through mirrors and telescopes, then seeing things on television, then through photographs and finally through handmade pictures, we have reached a point at which we can dig in our heels. Lopes' halting point that includes handmade pictures as transparent is counter-intuitive and based on arguments that should be rejected. Walton's stopping point, which includes photographs but not (most) handmade pictures as transparent, falls to counterexamples. It has emerged that there is a simple and intuitively plausible necessary condition for when we really see something: we do so only when rays of light from the object pass directly into our eyes. So we do not see through any pictures: all pictures are opaque. It follows that both traditional and digital cinematic images are opaque.

CHAPTER 3

Cinematic authorship

This book is about cinematic art. If there is an art form, there must, it seems, be artists working in that art form. If that is so, what can we learn about cinematic art by studying the cinematic artist, the so-called 'cinematic author'? This chapter investigates that question, arguing that cinematic authors play a role in the understanding and evaluation of films and that all traditional films made by more than one person in the key production roles are multiply authored. I then argue that the multiple-authorship thesis also applies to digital cinema, and that the latter medium enhances possibilities for collaboration between different film artists. Finally, I show how multiple authorship is also true of interactive digital cinema, but argue that the audience are not among the authors of interactive works, though they do count as co-authors of interactive works' instances.

3.1 TWO PUZZLES

The notion that certain films are authored is one of the most powerful and pervasive views in current thinking about cinema. The enthusiast who looks forward to the film she thinks of as the new 'Scorsese', 'Allen', 'Rohmer', or 'Tarantino' is paying homage to the idea of the director-as-author. Rooted in the writings of Truffaut and other French critics in the 1950s, the view was transplanted to the United States by Andrew Sarris in the early 1960s, and dubbed by him 'the auteur theory'. The figure of the film author, sometimes supposed to have been engulfed by the tides of semiotics and post-structuralism which swept over film studies in the 1970s, yet managed to survive, bobbing up again not as an actual person but as a constructed entity. The notion of director-as-author remains powerful to this day.

Yet the notion of film authorship – so appealing to lay intuition and scholarly understanding alike – is oddly mysterious and deeply elusive. It has been held that the film author is the director, the screen writer, the star, or the studio; that the film author is an actual individual, or a critical construct; that there is not one film author, but several. The claim of film authorship has been held primarily as an evaluative one, or an interpretive one, or simply as the view that there are authors of films as there are authors of literary works. And each of these claims has been challenged, each challenge producing a new defence or reformulation of the thesis. One explanation of this state of affairs, this unclarity in formulation but continuing intuitive appeal, is that the variations of the thesis draw on some core truths for their appeal. Or is a more sceptical conclusion to be drawn: that there is no truth to be found in the claim of film authorship, its capacity endlessly to mutate merely allowing it to stay one step ahead of its critics? That is the first puzzle of authorship.

If, as I shall argue, there is in fact a core truth in the claims of authorship, then we face the question of whether any more substantial claims can be added to it. The most fruitful way to answer this question is by addressing a second puzzle. The dominant view of authorship has been that many films have a single author, usually held to be the director. Yet it is a commonplace that most films are highly collaborative, and collaborative in ways that affect their artistic properties: actors, screen writers, producers, cinematographers, and so on, all leave their marks on the way a film looks and sounds. Yet how can there be a single author if there are very many artists involved in film production? How can a film be like a novel where always in principle there could be and usually in fact is a single author? Various strategies have been developed by auteurists to show how this is possible: it will be shown that they all fail. We must acknowledge that collaborative films have multiple authors. The multiple-authorship view is, I will argue, more theoretically sound and critically fruitful than the dominant view of single authorship. And the notion of multiple authorship will give us another reason, in addition to the rejection of film language in Sections 2.1 and 2.2, to question the literary paradigm that still has considerable influence in cinema studies.

3.2 VARIETIES OF AUTEURISM

We first need to regiment the gaggle of claims constituting auteurism. Any adequate taxonomy of authorial claims must distinguish at least five dimensions on which they can vary:

1. The kind of claim: (i) An *existential* claim: when Truffaut made his claims on behalf of the film author, he contrasted the *auteur* with the *metteur-en-scène*, who merely adds the pictures to a literary text without adding any significantly new dimension of meaning to it. His aims were polemical: to show that there are film artists in the way that there are

literary artists.[1] So we can make an existential claim: film artists exist.
More particularly, this should be understood to require that certain films
are the products of film artists. (ii) A *hermeneutic* claim formulates the
most general claim of auteurist criticism, the kind of criticism that
interprets films by construing them as products of their makers (usually
taken by such critics to be the director): to interpret a film requires
understanding what its maker(s) did. Some more specific versions of this
hold that it is the makers' intentions that determine how films are to be
understood, while others deny intentionalism.[2] (iii) An *evaluative* claim:
early auteurists, pre-eminently Andrew Sarris, were concerned largely
with the problem of the evaluation of films, which Sarris construed in
terms of a 'pantheon' of directors.[3] Such an auteurist might hold that a
good film is the product of a good director. But it is under dispute
whether there are one or several film artists per film (dimension 5) and
also who occupies the role or roles (dimension 4). Moreover, auteurists
ought to acknowledge the possibility that a group of untalented filmmakers might inadvertently produce a masterpiece.[4] So the most general
version of the evaluative claim would hold that a good film is typically the
product of good filmmaker(s). Under this general doctrine we can
distinguish many variations. For instance, there are different theories
about how the film artist makes her film good: either in terms of an
expression of her distinctive personality, or in terms of the overthrow of
established codes and ways of looking so as to open up new ways of
reading and seeing.[5] Clearly, these three kinds of authorial claims –
existential, hermeneutic and evaluative – can consistently be held
together.

2. The ontology of the author: (i) An *actual* person: the kind of entity who
   is the author was supposed in early auteurism to be an actual individual:
   John Ford, Jean Renoir, etc. (ii) A critical *construct*: with the rise of
   auteur-structuralism in the early 1970s, it came increasingly to be held
   that the author was a construct, generated by critics in order to grasp and

---

[1] François Truffaut, 'A Certain Tendency of the French Cinema'.
[2] For instance, V. F. Perkins, *Film as Film*, is a nuanced defender of the authorial thesis, but he is also a formalist, denying the importance of intentions to meaning (p. 173).
[3] See Andrew Sarris, 'Notes on the Auteur Theory in 1962' and 'Towards a Theory of Film History'.
[4] Perkins (*Film as Film*, p. 185) acknowledges the possibility of a 'fluke masterpiece', in the sense of a film that is a masterpiece, even though its overall coherence is not due to directorial control, but says that he knows of no actual examples.
[5] See respectively Sarris' remarks on 'the distinguishable personality of the director as a criterion of value' in 'Notes on the Auteur Theory in 1962', p. 537; and Peter Wollen, *Signs and Meaning in the Cinema*, pp. 171–2.

evaluate films better. On this view the critical task is 'to locate an *author of the fiction* who is by no means dispersed but who in 'his' notional coherence provides the means for us to grasp the text in the moment of its production before us'.[6] More recent theorists are also often attracted to the picture of the author-as-construct. Stephen Heath writes that 'The author, that is, may return as a *fiction* … Grasped thus, the author … now becomes part of an activity of writing-reading'.[7]

3. Authors and artists: (i) *As an artist*: a major objective of auteurism was to help advance the claims of film to be an art, and that required showing the existence of a film artist. Though the literary paradigm was of immense influence on auteurism, early auteurists often did not hold that the author was a textual author, i.e., the producer of a *text*. Sarris mentions Shakespeare, Beethoven and Bach as examples of *auteurs*. On this view, the author is simply an artist.[8] (ii) *As a textual author*: later, with the rise of interest in semiotics in the 1970s, theorists came increasingly to think of a film as literally a text, for they held that there is a language of film. On this view, the film author is the author of the film text.

4. Occupiers of the authorial role(s): Theorists have made differing claims over who counts as the author(s) of a film: (i) the *director* is favoured by most, including Sarris and Perkins; (ii) the *screen writer* by some, e.g., Corliss; (iii) for some films, the *star* is held by some to be the auteur, e.g., McGilligan and Dyer; and (iv) some theorists favour the *producer* or the studio, e.g., Thomas Schatz.[9] These claims are most naturally construed as being about the author as an actual individual, but their analogues exist for the author as a construct (so one might talk about the implied director, screen writer, etc.).

5. The number of authors: (i) *Single authorship*: the dominant view of auteurists appears still to be that there is a single author of a film in most cases (evidently, there will be exceptions where two or more individuals work together very closely, sharing key roles, such as the Coen brothers, or Powell and Pressburger). (ii) *Multiple authorship*: this view holds that there are many authors of a film, plausibly occupying some or all of the main production roles (director, screen writer, actors, cinematographer,

---

[6] Geoffrey Nowell-Smith, 'Six Authors in Pursuit of *The Searchers*', p. 222.
[7] Stephen Heath, 'Comment on "The idea of authorship"', p. 220.
[8] Sarris, 'Notes on the Auteur Theory in 1962', p. 529.
[9] *Ibid.*; Perkins, *Film as Film*, chapter 8; Richard Corliss, 'The Hollywood Screenwriter'. See also Richard Dyer, *Stars*, pp. 174–5, for a discussion of McGilligan and for Dyer's claims about Garbo, Burstyn and Streisand; and Thomas Schatz, *The Genius of the System*, Introduction.

composer, etc.), who may or may not be in harmony on the purposes of the production. This view, at least held unambiguously and explicitly, is less common than the claims of single authorship: it is defended by C. Paul Sellors, and Richard Dyer seems to hold that it applies to many films.[10]

These five dimensions of variation are logically independent of each other; together a selection of one item from each of them makes up a distinct auteurist thesis.[11] For instance, one can hold that (1i) there is a film author, who is (2i) an actual person, (3ii) a textual author, (4i) the director, and (5i) there is just one for a film. Or one can hold that (1i and 5ii) there are multiple authors, who (2ii) are critical constructs, (3i) are artists rather than textual authors, and (4i–iii) are directorial, screen writer, and star-constructs. Or one can hold that (1ii) to understand a film requires understanding what the author did, construing the author as a (5i) single (4i) directorial (2ii) construct and (3ii) a textual author. Evidently, very many other variations are possible. Within each dimension further subdivisions of options could also be made, some of them already mentioned (e.g., the differences in views over how value is conferred on a film, and the role of intentions in the hermeneutic thesis). Hence the taxonomy could further be refined, but the illustration of the wide variety of authorial claims is sufficient for present purposes.

3.3 MINIMAL AUTEURISM

This recipe for making up one's own authorial theses, even with the fairly basic ingredients on offer, gives succour to the sceptic who alleges that auteurism is a sham. This sceptic thinks auteurism is so diverse that it escapes criticism simply by changing its formulation: when criticised, a new theory is offered in the place of the old discredited version, a new theory that will in turn eventually be disproved. For the sceptic, the dominance of authorial views is simply a by-product of the fact that they have no fixity. But, contrary to the sceptic, there are some true auteurist theses.

To address these, we need briefly to discuss the notions of the author and artist. Of the two authorial notions in the auteurist tradition, we can set aside the concept of the textual author, since we argued in Chapter 2 that

---

[10] C. Paul Sellors, 'Collective Authorship in Film'; and Dyer, *Stars*, pp. 175–6, on the 'voices model' of film.

[11] An exception to the 'one item' rule occurs under (4), where if one believes in multiple authorship, more than one item must be selected from this dimension.

there is no language of film and therefore that a film is not a text. So consider the other notion, of the author as an artist. One might suppose that an artist is simply someone who produces a work of art. However, someone could fluke a masterpiece, and one might therefore reasonably deny that he is an artist. Consider a news reporter, filming a short item for the evening news about domestic violence. He operates his own video camera and microphone, but the camera jams repeatedly, its sensitivity to light varies uncontrollably, and the microphone operates in an unpredictable fashion. Returning to the studio, he runs his video report and discovers that through these technical problems and his attempts to overcome them the report has an original and intricate shot-rhythm, the sound alters in ways that highlight the anguish of the victims, and the varying lighting levels complement the dramatic effect. The whole is original, powerful, intriguing, so much so that it qualifies as a little work of art. The reporter has produced an artwork, but he is not an artist, since the report's artistic aspects were produced accidentally: he can take no credit for it as a work of art. So an artist is someone who *non-accidentally* produces a work of art. What does this involve? Works of art have both artistic and non-artistic properties (for instance, in the case of a painting, the properties of the wooden stretcher on which the canvas is tacked are not artistic properties of the work). Works are works of art in respect of their artistic properties, not their non-artistic ones. So the non-accidental production of a work of art requires one to produce a work non-accidentally with artistic properties. More than one artist can make a work, and in such cases each artist non-accidentally endows the work with some artistic properties. An artist, then, is someone who produces a work of art by virtue of non-accidentally making a work with some artistic properties. (It is not required that all of these artistic properties are intentionally produced, since that would require an implausible mastery to be ascribed to the artist: only some of them need be intended.[12]) So an artist is a non-accidental producer of a work of art in the sense just explained. This account of the author as artist naturally generalises to an account of authors in general (who need not be artists), who are non-accidental producers of works, where these need not be artworks. For instance, authors of scientific works are non-accidental producers of scientific works, by virtue of non-accidentally making works with scientific properties, ones that describe

---

[12] The notion of intention is here referentially transparent: i.e., the agent intends to produce a work with some property, which is an artistic property (perhaps, some expressive quality), even if she does not bring that property under the concept of an artistic property; for there can be artists in societies that lack the concept of art.

scientific data or theories. It is the author as artist who will, however, be under discussion here.

Now consider the following argument:

(a) Some films are works of art.
(b) Some of these films are non-accidental works of art.
(c) Non-accidental works of art are products of artists.
(d) So, some films are products of film artists.
(e) So, there are film artists.

The conclusion gives us a version of the existential claim (1), holding for actual authors (2), but underdetermined with respect to formulations of 3, 4 and 5 – the artist might in addition be a textual author (if a film is a text), the role or roles occupied are unspecified, and it is open whether there are one or more authors of a film.

This argument – the argument for the *minimal existential claim* – is sound. (a) Some films are works of art: *Rules of the Game* (1939), *Rashomon* (1950) and *Pulp Fiction* (1994), for instance, are clear examples of works of art; and we have already defended the status of cinema as an art in Chapter 1. (b) The makers of these and many other films did not make them accidentally, but knew what they were doing (as witnessed by their abilities to make other artistically good films, for instance). (c) Since an artist is someone who non-accidentally produces a work of art, a non-accidental work of art must be the product of an artist. So (d) those films that are non-accidental works of art must be the products of artists. And since a film artist is construed here simply as an artist whose product is a film, these artists are film artists. So (e) there are film artists.

This result is not trivial: after all, it is certainly no trivial matter that (a) is true: making films which are works of art is a difficult task, and (b) many skills, much thought and planning are required to avoid making films with many accidental features. But this is an achievement of filmmakers, not of the film theorist. And (c) rests on a conceptual point about the notion of an artist: conceptual points are not trivial either (else there would be no informative analyses of concepts). But there is no disguising the fact that the minimal existential claim falls well short of the ambitions of auteurism: it follows conceptually from the existence of films which are works of art and non-accidental products that there must be film artists, but that is all. Even Truffaut's claim that there are film artists whose contribution lies in more than adding pictures to the text does not follow from this.

The *minimal hermeneutic claim* holds that to interpret a film requires understanding what its maker(s) did. This follows from the general claim that to interpret a work of art requires one to understand what its maker(s) did, since works of art are artefacts and therefore are the products of actions, together with the point already acknowledged that some films are works of art. The minimal hermeneutic claim accepts (1ii) and (2i), and leaves open the options under the remaining dimensions. Intentionalism does not follow from the minimal claim: there are many aspects of understanding what someone did that go beyond explaining it (even if all explanation is intentionalistic, which may be disputed), such as characterising the action in various ways, and not all features of actions (or of films) need be intended. Nor, conversely, is intentionalism ruled out by the hermeneutic claim (though we will argue against intentionalism in Chapter 4).

The *minimal evaluative claim* holds that a good film is typically the product of good filmmaker(s). This claim, by appealing to what is typically the case, allows for the possibility of a fluke masterpiece, and more broadly for a good film that is not the product of good filmmaker(s), since its quality results partly from accidental factors, such as unanticipated interactions between untalented collaborators. The claim is plausible, given that it specifies what is typically the case, since fluke masterpieces are relatively rare and even though, as we shall see, artistically significant properties can arise unintentionally because of interactions between collaborators, these collaborators are usually talented. However, though the claim is plausible, again it is not of much use for elaborating film theory and criticism. For instance, nothing follows from it about *how* the makers give the films the value they possess (whether by the expression of their personalities, or by the creation of complex or subversive structures, for example).

These three theses show that there is a minimal core truth in auteurism, in respect of all three kinds of claims listed under dimension (1). That is enough to refute the sceptic, and also explains the ineliminability of some of the intuitions that make auteurism so attractive. But the theses are fairly minimal, having little substantial contribution to make to film theory and giving very little guidance to critical practice. If this is all that can be shown for auteurism, it is a limp doctrine indeed. The question is, can we specify any of these theses more precisely, cutting down on the indeterminacies, carving out more substantive doctrines? I will now show that we can, by arguing that all versions of the single-authorial thesis (5i) are false.

3.4 THREE STRATEGIES FOR SINGLE AUTHORSHIP

As noted earlier, the dominant view of film authorship has been that there is generally at most one author of a film. We have seen that the second puzzle expresses a *prima facie* difficulty for this view: there is an evident tension between the highly collaborative nature of most films and the claims of single authorship. This puzzle needs to be clarified before it is addressed.

Two kinds of cases are not under dispute between the supporters of single and multiple authorship. First, there are some films, such as Stan Brakhage's *Mothlight* (1963), which are the products of a single individual. Both sides agree that these cases are ones of single authorship, since only one person makes the film. Second, some of the collaborators of highly collaborative films are not authors on either side's account, for though they may be causally responsible for the film's existence and some of its properties, they are not responsible for any of the film's artistic properties. For instance, the catering crew, the production accountants, the personal assistants to stars and the grips (assistants who move props and equipment on set) would feature in any complete causal account of the making of a film and may be responsible for some of its properties (without them the film might have been released much later, for instance). But they are highly unlikely to endow the film with any of its artistic properties. So the dispute over authorship concerns those who are plausibly *artistic* collaborators on films, those who endow it with its artistic properties.

Let me introduce some terminology. I will define a *mainstream* film as one that has at least two people in the key production roles. The key production roles I will take to include at least directing, acting, screen writing, production design, editing, cinematography, animation, composing, and music performance, where these are applicable to a film. These roles are selected because plausibly their occupants endow the film with artistic properties; but I do *not* claim that only these roles matter artistically. However, we need a list of plausible artistic collaborators on which to focus discussion.[13]

In considering mainstream films much of my discussion will concern the actor and his relation to the director, for two reasons. First, the directing role is the one most commonly construed as authorial by auteurists, yet the difficulties of single-authorship views are especially evident in the relation of the actor to the director. (However, I develop several arguments for multiple authorship and many apply to each of the key production roles.) Second, actors are ubiquitous in fiction films, far more so than is commonly realised. It is often thought that animated films lack actors: however, animated films, both traditional and digital, almost invariably incorporate

[13] Note that I say *plausible* artistic collaborators, i.e., there is some prima facie reason to believe that these roles matter artistically. I am not simply assuming that they really do matter artistically. That would be to beg the question against some variants of single-authorship views, which I will argue against.

not computer-generated voices but recordings of actors' voices, and this is of considerable artistic importance to the films. For instance, *Shrek* (2001) is a digitally animated film, but the characters' voices are recordings of actors' vocal performances. And not just *how* the actors produce those vocal performances, but also *who* the actor is who is playing the role is often important: the humour of Donkey in *Shrek* depends in large part on Eddie Murphy's vocal performance and on the audience's knowledge that it is Murphy, with his particular comic *persona*, who is playing the role. So animated films are in almost all cases animated only in respect of the visual track, not in respect of the sound track – they are only half-animated, as it were.

The pressure to acknowledge multiple authorship in mainstream cinema is considerable. Indeed, supporters of single authorship sometimes hedge their views with so many caveats about the collaborative nature of film production that they end up embracing convictions that stand in tension with each other. Sarris acknowledges the input of many people besides the director to a film, and holds that 'the cinema could not be a completely personal art even under the best of conditions', but nevertheless thinks that 'Ultimately, the auteur theory is not so much a theory as an attitude, a table of values that converts film history into directorial autobiography'.[14] Victor Perkins gives a convincing and detailed account of the collaborative elements that enter into a film, but nevertheless thinks that the director is 'the author' of the film (i.e., *the* author: there is just one).[15] Thus, two prominent auteurists are prepared to speak of a single author of a film, but display such sensitivity to the complexities of film production that with only a little violence one could represent their positions as multiple-authorship views, albeit ones that hold that a worthwhile film has the director as the dominant author. Since my concern is not with the details of textual exegesis, but with the tenability of the claim of single authorship, I will draw on the work of these auteurists, without seeking finally to determine what their own view is.

There are several ways in which the single-author theory can address the challenge of artistic collaboration in mainstream film.[16] First, it may be

---

[14] Sarris, 'Towards a Theory of Film History', pp. 247 and 246. [15] Perkins, *Film as Film*, p. 181.
[16] One response from the single-author theorist would be to hold that the author is the maker of the film text (thus construing the film author as a textual author), all other artists contributing to its non-textual elements. But this supposes that film can be thought of as literally a text, and therefore that film conventions constitute a language, which is a view that we have already rejected. And even if we were to think of film as a text, the textual elements, as objects of interpretation, would have to include such items as nuances of acting, of camerawork and of music that are the contributions of artists other than the director. Thus the claims of others to be textual co-authors, even if films were texts, could not be undermined by this strategy.

argued that only one of the key production roles, usually taken as the director (or a combined role such as writer-director), is responsible for the artistic properties of films, despite the appearance that other roles matter artistically too. Second, it may be maintained that the occupant of one of these roles (again, usually identified as the director) has sufficient control over the occupants of the other roles to have their artistry count as an extension of his own. Third, it can be maintained that a film is properly thought of as the product of a single, constructed artist, so that the fact that several actual people occupy the key production roles is irrelevant. Finally, it may be held that the notion of the author of a film is not simply the notion of a film artist (when the film is an artwork), but of a particular kind of artist, perhaps one who is responsible for the properties of the work as a whole, so the existence of a multitude of artists in filmmaking is compatible with there being a single author of the film. These four responses are not mutually exclusive. I consider variants of them in the remainder of the current section and in the next one. I argue that all these responses fail, and that we should acknowledge that mainstream films that are works of art are invariably the products of multiple authors.

3.4.1 The restriction strategy

Summarising the view of his classic auteur study, *Hitchcock's Films*, Robin Wood writes that its premise was that 'the films – insofar as they are significant – belong exclusively to Hitchcock'.[17] Wood's view was therefore that the role of Hitchcock's collaborators did not affect the artistic significance of the film, merely its non-artistic features. The view is analogous to the claim that an assistant may construct a wooden framework and stretch canvas over it, but the sole artistic input of the artist for the resulting painting is not thereby compromised. Authorship, as we noted earlier, concerns the artistic properties of works: the restriction strategy holds that, once we acknowledge that authorship is restricted to artistic properties, we can maintain that a single author, usually the director, controls the artistic properties of a film. The input of the director's collaborators concerns only the non-artistic properties of a film. More developed versions of Wood's thought are deployed by Wollen and Perkins. The former distinguishes between the structure of a film, which the director can control, and

---

[17] Robin Wood, *Hitchcock's Films Revisited*, p. 5. This work incorporates the earlier study, originally published in 1965. On the same page Wood writes that his current view is that Hitchcock's films 'do not belong *only* to him'.

the 'noise', irrelevant to criticism, which may be produced by actors and cameramen forcing themselves to prominence; the latter argues that a director can make a film his own, despite the contributions of others, by controlling the synthetic relationships that constitute a film's essence.[18]

The restriction strategy in its simple version founders as soon as it leaves port. As we saw, there are some collaborators, such as accountants and personal assistants, who do not affect the artistic properties of a film. But occupants of the key production roles in a mainstream film do contribute to its artistic properties. Almost any aspect of a film as seen and heard, if produced by a good print using adequate projection equipment, is potentially significant in judging the meaning and value of a film. The occupants of the key production roles, such as actors, composers and cinematographers, contribute to the properties of the film as seen and heard, so their contributions are artistically relevant. (The few exceptions to the artistic relevance of all aspects of the film as seen and heard, such as reel-change marks and scratches on prints, do nothing to show that the contributions of those in the key production roles are artistically irrelevant.) A further basic difficulty with the restriction strategy bulks large, for there is no aspect of the finished film that can be attributed solely to the director's activity by virtue of his directorial role. The director is someone who directs and supervises others. When we survey artistically significant aspects of the film – whether the acting, editing, screen writing, or whatever – we see the results of others' actions, actions supervised by the director and not attributable to him alone. If he is a writer-director, the script may be his; but the script is a single strand in the intricate web of a film, and if the film is mainstream, at least one of the other key production roles, usually the acting role, must be taken by someone else; so there will always be an artistically relevant feature which is not the writer-director's product alone.

These obstacles to the simple restriction strategy also bar the way to the more sophisticated position of Perkins. Distinguishing between the elements of a film and its synthetic relationships, Perkins holds that the style and meaning of a film are the products of these relationships, which constitute the film *qua* film. Since the director controls the relationships, he commands the artistic terrain of the film. 'Being in charge of relationships, of synthesis, he is in charge of what makes a film a *film*'.[19] But Perkins' auteurist endeavour is not advanced by his distinction between elements and relationships. Though he gives no criterion for distinguishing the two,

[18] Wollen, *Signs and Meaning in the Cinema*, pp. 104–5; and Perkins, *Film as Film*, p. 184.
[19] Perkins, *Film as Film*, p. 184.

he does maintain that the director controls the style, meaning and value of a film by controlling its synthetic relations. So we can understand him as holding that any aspect of the film relevant to these matters concerns not its elements, but its relations. So construed, the difficulties adumbrated above resurface, for it is evident that almost any feature of a film should be counted as a matter of its relations: the story, décor, details of the acting, camerawork, and so on, may all be significant determinants of the style, meaning and value of a film; so the contributions of screen writers, production designers, actors, cinematographers, and so on, concern the relations of the film and so are artistically significant. (Similar considerations undermine Peter Wollen's defence of authorship by distinguishing between 'structure' and 'noise', since his construal of film structure appears to equate it with any aspect of a film that is an object of criticism.) So appeal to the distinction between artistically significant and artistically irrelevant properties of a film will not support any claim of single authorship.[20]

3.4.2 The sufficient control strategy

Painters often had assistants who did not just perform tasks such as stretching a canvas over the frame and mixing paint, but were also given the job of painting in some of the background details; yet we still are prepared to call the resulting painting a Rubens or a Tintoretto. Writers sometimes receive a great deal of help from their editors, not just in removing parts, and tightening structure, but in positive suggestions about new ways to develop the story (Maxwell Perkins' help to Thomas Wolfe in this respect is well known). Hence the artist need not be someone who has total control, but merely sufficient control over the artwork. Sufficient control displays itself not just by the artist's direct personal input into his work, but also in the fact that he uses others' talents, absorbing them into his own work.

Perkins deploys this sufficient control strategy: he acknowledges the director's lack of total power over a film, but maintains that he is 'chiefly responsible for the effect and quality of the completed movie', which is enough to make him 'the author' of the film.[21] The director controls a film not just by what he himself invents, but also by what he allows actors, cameramen and others to do: 'The resulting action "belongs" to the director

---

[20] Recall that Perkins himself may not believe in single authorship: my concern with his arguments is merely to see whether the single-authorship thesis can be supported by means of them.

[21] Perkins, *Film as Film*, pp. 179 and 181.

as much as do the details that he himself suggests'. Hitchcock, for example, was able to cast those actors who best fitted into the design of his films, and so was 'able to absorb the strong personalities of Grant and Stewart into the textures of his movies'.[22]

However, even in the case of paintings and novels, if there are others who make a significant artistic difference to the work, then it is only fair to acknowledge them as artistic collaborators, and modern scholarly practice is coming increasingly to do so (consider the attributions of paintings to Rembrandt and workshop, rather than simply to Rembrandt). So appeal to these other arts does not in itself support the claims of single authorship.[23]

Second, consider a parallel in literature to the degree of control that Perkins says directors have over films: suppose it emerged that Dickens did not pen all of *Great Expectations*, but due to the time pressures of serial novel production, had commissioned Anthony Trollope, George Eliot and other writers to produce individual chapters, had rejected some of their drafts, accepted others with editorial changes, and then inserted passages linking the results together. We would not speak of Dickens as the sole author of the novel. The book would be a collaborative work, in which Dickens' contribution was (perhaps) the most important, but where the artistic work of all participants should be duly acknowledged and all should count as co-authors. Indeed, this kind of situation is common in screen writing: if several people work on a screenplay, they are all credited as co-authors, even if one of them was in overall charge of the process.

Third, Perkins' talk of others' actions 'belonging' to the director should not be taken to show that they belong only to him. Should Stewart decide to read his lines so as to make the character he is playing sound neurotic, and should Hitchcock countenance this interpretation, then Stewart has performed an artistic act, even if Hitchcock also performs such an act by agreeing to accept that interpretation of the role. Nor does the fact that a director can cast actors of his choice in a film make him its sole author. Some actors do have a screen image that the director can employ and inflect, but they are not inanimate objects with a fixed meaning, to be collaged by the director into his film. They are performers, and the exact manner in which they perform will depend ineliminably on their own choices. The actors of a film are among its co-creators.

---

[22] *Ibid.*, pp. 181–2.
[23] See Jack Stillinger, *Multiple Authorship and the Myth of Solitary Genius*, for an account of how extensive multiple authorship has been, even in literature.

So the degree of control that Perkins ascribes to the director is insufficient to make him a film's sole author. But what if the degree of directorial control were considerably greater than that which Perkins correctly thinks is the norm; what if it amounted to total control over the film's artistic properties? If a director could exactly specify and control all the artistic properties that he required the occupant of some other role to bring to a film, then that would, it seems, be a reason to think that he was the single author of the film.

However, for most of the key production roles, this is in practice impossible. This is particularly obvious in the case of acting: think of the innumerable ways in which one can say a line like 'Frankly, my dear, I don't give a damn', the way one can shift the stress to different words, insert pauses of varying lengths, convey vastly different emotions from noble resignation to petty-minded spite. No matter how many takes are used, directorial instructions cannot in practice be fine-grained enough to select just one precise way of saying these lines, with an exactly shaded emotional meaning. Any actor will inevitably bring something of his own personality and training to the way he speaks his lines, inflecting them with the nuances derived from verbal mannerism and unique vocal tonalities, colouring his performance with the personal memory and felt experience he uses in imaginatively projecting herself into his role. Given the inability to specify acting tasks exactly, and given the uniqueness of human beings, the way their mode of expression inevitably reflects their personalities (their expressive individuality), it is evident that the director's degree of control is less than total and is insufficient to establish his single authorship. The same point applies to the artistic aspects of many of the other key production roles: for instance, even if a director were closely to supervise the musical performance of the film score, however much he tried to specify the exact timbre, expressive, rhythmic and other artistic qualities he wanted from the musicians, given the individual ways of performing music, reflecting individual personality, skills and histories, their exact artistic specification would escape his complete control.

However, some tasks involved in some key production roles can be exactly specified and monitored by the director, and hence it may seem that in respect of these roles there could be single authorship of mainstream films. Consider editing: a director could specify some tasks precisely, telling his editor, say, to cut a shot after 240 frames. Of course, for a director to specify all the editorial tasks in this way would be highly non-standard and indeed pointless, since then he might as well do the editing himself, which is in fact fairly common. Where a separate editor is employed, it is to bring his artistic advice, judgement and style to the editing process, and so to exercise some artistic discretion. But the possibility of this complete specification suggests that there could be an editor separate from the director, and so the film would be mainstream, but there could be single authorship in respect of editing tasks. Likewise, a director could engage a composer for the film score, and so the film would be mainstream, but the director could exactly specify the score he wanted, stating its complete notational structure. Evidently, this would be a highly non-standard use of a composer, but since it is in principle possible, does that not show the theoretical possibility of some mainstream film having single directorial authors?

This is, however, not so. Consider the case of the composer in the scenario just sketched: a composer has been engaged, but he is not fulfilling the role of the composer. He is, rather, acting as a mere musical scribe or amanuensis, taking musical dictation from the director, who is the composer. So in this case it is the director who is occupying the composer's role, since he is the only one making the musical choices. So the film is not a mainstream one in respect of these two roles (only one person is occupying both). Similarly, if the director exactly specifies all of the editor's tasks, then it is the director who is acting as the editor, and the putative editor is merely a cutter and splicer of the film in the case of the traditional film, or just an operator of the editing machine in the case of a digital film. An editor has been engaged but is not being allowed to fulfil the editorial role. So our concepts of these film roles requires some discretion to be exercisable by a person to count as her fulfilling them: if no discretion is permitted, then it is the person giving the orders who is the real occupant of the role.

In practice, of course, those engaged as editors, composers and in all other roles are given some room for discretion: otherwise it would be pointless engaging them. A director will give some instructions that allow for leeway in choices, such as that he wants a more dynamically edited sequence, rather than always stating that a cut should be made at a certain precise point; and he will say he wants music with a certain expressive and artistic profile, rather than stating the complete notational structure of the score he wants. And we have just argued that if all of his instructions were of the latter, precise type, then he would himself be the occupant of these roles.

Finally, returning to the real world of less than total directorial control, consider, by way of an illustrative coda, Peter Jackson, a director who, from the extensive evidence of the 'making of' material included in the DVDs of *The Lord of the Rings* trilogy (2001–3) and *King Kong* (2005), keeps a very close eye on all aspects of his hugely complex film productions and requires his collaborators to get his approval for their more important contributions, while still being open to their ideas. He thus looks like a director for whom a sufficient control defence of single authorship would be very promising. But Jackson is firmly opposed to such a claim: 'Have a good look at the credits for any of the *Lord of the Rings* movies, or *King Kong*. The one credit you will not see is "A Peter Jackson Film". I refused to allow that, and never will. Movies are collaborations, and I would never make that kind of possessive claim on such a collaborative piece of work'.[24] From the evidence of the credits on many other directors' films, they would disagree with Jackson. But it is heartening to note that there is at least one immensely talented director, who has as much influence over his films as any director of mainstream films does, who is prepared to abjure the possessive claims of single authorship.

3.4.3 *The construction strategy*

The two previous strategies are most naturally construed as being about authors as actual individuals. But as noted earlier, the dominant view since the early 1970s has been of the film author as a critical construct. This view bears a striking resemblance to that of many literary theorists and philosophers, who hold that the author should be distinguished from the writer of a text, the former being a mere postulate in terms of which one can interpret the work, the latter being the actual individual who penned its words. In literature the advantages of the distinction are that one can acknowledge that the author's *persona* as it appears in her work may be radically different from her actual character, and one can maintain that a work is the product of authorial acts, without being thereby committed to believing that the writer's actual intentions determine the correct interpretation of her work.[25] In film the application of the distinction has, in addition, the advantage of affirming that the constructed author may not be the product of a single actual person, but may instead be the outcome of a collaborative effort between several.[26] Acknowledgement of multiple collaboration in filmmaking is thus compatible with holding that there is a single postulated author

---

[24] Brian Sibley, *Peter Jackson*, p. 557.

[25] See Wayne Booth, *The Rhetoric of Fiction*, especially pp. 70–7 and 151–3, for the notion of the implied author; Gregory Currie, *Image and Mind*, p. 245, for a somewhat different notion of the implied author applied to film; and Alexander Nehamas, 'The Postulated Author', for the author as construct. For our purposes in this chapter the differences between these views are not germane; so I shall here use 'postulated author', 'implied author' and 'author as construct' interchangeably.

[26] '"John Ford" is as much present in the work of collaborators who made the film with and for the director (John Ford) in person', Nowell-Smith, 'Six Authors in Pursuit of *The Searchers*', p. 222.

of the film. This construal of the author, then, permits him to lend a welcome helping hand (if only a constructed one) to the single-authorship thesis.

The formulation of the single-authorship thesis as thus construed needs some care. Substituting the notion of the implied author for that of the actual author, the existential thesis would hold that mainstream films sometimes are the products of a single postulated author. But that is incoherent. To talk of the film as a product of an author is to regard the former as an effect of the latter's actions, yet the author as a merely postulated, non-actual, being cannot possess this sort of causal power. Encountering the same difficulty in the case of literature, Nehamas suggests that we think of the author as being manifested in the text, and Wilson similarly holds that the implied filmmaker manifests himself in his films.[27] A promising way to capture this kind of position is as follows: when we talk of the postulated author with certain characteristics manifesting herself in a text, we mean that for the purposes of interpreting and evaluating the text, it should be thought of *as if* it were the product of a single artist with those characteristics (the *persona*). This formulation preserves the fundamental point that we postulate an author in order to understand and appreciate a text properly (the hermeneutic and evaluative theses are what drive author-as-construct views); it allows the notion of the text as product of the author to figure in the view, as something to be imagined; and it also acknowledges the author to be a construct, a being who is imagined to make the text, with a *persona* that may be distinct from the real writer's personality. We will, then, construe the constructivist auteurist position as holding that some mainstream films manifest a single postulated artist, and gloss this in the manner just suggested, with the notion of a film substituted for that of a text.

In his interpretation of *Letter from an Unknown Woman* (1948), Wilson shows how and why one might appeal to an implied filmmaker. The patterns of camera movement and placement, production design, script, music and acting, he argues, are all crafted so as to create a sympathetic but objective point of view onto the actions and character of Lisa, the film's protagonist, and to give the viewer an insight into her condition that she never herself attains. In light of the wide range of variables which are employed to underpin this vision of Lisa, we here have evidence for the viability and necessity of an implied filmmaker: 'It is impossible to escape

---

[27] Nehamas, 'The Postulated Author', p. 145; and George Wilson, *Narration in Light* pp. 134–9, especially p. 134. Wilson points out that his concept is broadly in line with Booth's notion of the implied author (p. 217 n. 11).

the impression of an intelligent and sometimes ironic observer, the implied film maker as it were, who is continuously observing with special insight into the wider patterns that Lisa ostensibly describes'.[28]

Can the construction strategy save the single-authorship thesis? We should acknowledge a constructed author when we can identify an authorial personality, a *persona*, which may be distinct from that of the actual writer. Clearly there is a Hitchcock *persona* which emerges in his films. But equally Stewart and Grant have *personae* – as indeed does the composer, Bernard Herrmann, and other contributors to Hitchcock's films who are not actors – and these *personae* are prominent in the films. So by the criterion of artistic personality to which the constructivist appeals, we should acknowledge such films to involve multiple artists.

Moreover, were we to construct just one author for each film, it would be so different from people as we know them or require such bizarre motivations that its use to interpret and evaluate films would systematically distort our responses to cinema. Responsible for all aspects of filmmaking, the author must be manifested in the screenplay, direction, camerawork, musical score, editing, and so forth; so we would have to think of it *as if* it were the being who had done all of these things. What sort of entity could master the full range of these functions? At the very least, it would have to be a genius, whose ability to fulfil the many tasks of filmmaking exceeded even Chaplin's myriad skills, and the most trite film would have to be judged an extraordinary achievement, the product of a wonderfully gifted and strikingly protean talent. It would thus lead to radically wrong evaluations of films.

It would also lead to radically incorrect interpretations. Consider the list of credits that occurs in virtually all mainstream films. According to the constructivist, we are to think of these films as if they were the product of a single author. But why, then, has the author chosen to credit numerous people in a large numbers of roles, which he himself is to be imagined to have occupied, such as editors, cinematographers, musicians, composers, production designers, and so on? Is this to be understood as an outbreak of modesty (he does not want to be seen as possessing such multifarious talents); an attempt to pad the payroll for expense purposes; a useful advertising directory of all the aliases under which he goes in the film

---

[28] Wilson, *Narration in Light*, p. 123. It is not clear that Wilson should talk of an observer here, however, since that is presumably someone who is part of the same world as Lisa: the notion of the implied author is of a being that we think of as if it produced the film world, and that requires it not to be a part of that world. For more on implied authors, as contrasted to narrators as observers, see Section 5.2.

industry; or an attempt to deceive us about his true power and influence for some underhand purpose? The canvassed answers are absurd, and the absurdity of even needing to raise the interpretative question shows that there is something wrong with the act of imagination required for attribution of a constructed author in respect of film credits. Nor should we think of the credits as something extrinsic to the film proper, and therefore not the object of film interpretation. Not only may the credits be integrated into the rest of the film (this is particularly true of the opening credits, often shown as the film's action is already underway), but even when the credits are separate, they are part of the film as object of interpretation, since if they were altered, our interpretation of the film would properly change. For instance, a film that is in the usual style of one filmmaker might be a radical stylistic departure for another filmmaker, and so would be interpreted differently if credited differently.

Further, consider the application of the single constructed author to acting performances. Viewing mainstream films with actors, we would have to think of their performances as if they were the products of a single artist: strictly construed, the actors' actions would be the artist's, he would move them in the same way in which I move my arm. To think of the actors in this manner would be to forfeit our sense of them as agents, and so radically to distort our experience of these films, which is an experience of seeing representations of agents performing actions. Moreover, the author must be imagined as capable of moving these performers as we move puppets, a capacity far exceeding human abilities. Who knows what such a being would be like? For the constructivist, interpretation involves seeing what qualities are manifested by a film's implied author: but what might be gained by speculating on the psychology of a kind of super-intelligent octopus, whose tentacles control the myriad machines of cinema and reach into the very souls of actors? Given its unknowable psychology, the signs we take to be those of sympathy towards a character might instead be marks of wry amusement, haughty disdain, vehement fury, or emotions utterly unimaginable to us.[29]

Thus constructivism cannot be employed to defend the single-authorship thesis. But Wilson's sensitive analysis of *Letter from an Unknown Woman* is, surely, correct in seeing signs of the intelligent use

---

[29] The supporter of single authorship might reply that on her view actors are still to be regarded as agents, but as agents completely schooled by the author, every nuance of their performance attributable to his tuition. This version, however, runs into the same difficulties of a superhuman filmmaker whose psychology is unknowable, and strips actors of their expressive individuality that we noted is so central to our appreciation of films.

of scene design, script, music, acting and camera work to express a sympathetic view of Lisa. Signs of intelligent production, though, do not require
one intelligence implicitly to do the producing. Rather than a single implied
filmmaker being manifested in the film, an implied *group* of filmmakers
is manifested in it: actors, screen writers, director, composer, and so on.
By virtue of the co-ordination of their activities to achieve common ends,
each manifests sympathy towards the unfortunate protagonist. But one can
readily imagine a film where such co-ordination breaks down, the implied
actor showing sympathy for a character towards whom the implied director
manifests hostility. The possibility of these conflicts demonstrates the
coherence of the view that an implied group is manifested in a film; and
only the multiple-authorship view can adequately theorise such cases of
the film-as-battleground, some real examples of which are discussed later.
A mainstream film does not manifest just one implied artist. It manifests
very many.

3.5 CINEMATIC UTTERANCE AND SINGLE AUTHORSHIP

The philosophically most sophisticated defence of the possibility of single
authorship of mainstream films is due to Paisley Livingston. He holds that
the author is a real entity, not a constructed one. Some films are unauthored, since they are chaotic with largely unintended features (he likens them
to traffic jams), other films are jointly authored, and some mainstream films,
involving actors distinct from the director, have single authors: for instance,
Winter Light (1962). Despite its being produced within the Swedish studio
system, Livingston argues that the single author of this film is its writer-
director, Ingmar Bergman. Livingston's account has evolved over time, and
he has increasingly made explicit elements that were previously conveyed
chiefly through the treatment of examples.[30] His account has two elements –
an author of a work must have expressive or artistic intentions and must
possess sufficient control over the work as a whole.

Turning to the first condition, Livingston in 'Cinematic Authorship'
defines an author as: 'the agent (or agents) who intentionally make(s)
an utterance, where "utterance" refers to any action, an intended function
of which is expression or communication'.[31] Expression is 'a matter of

---

[30] Livingston's original account is in 'Cinematic Authorship'; it is refined in his *Art and Intention*, and
most recently in his *Cinema, Philosophy, Bergman*, chapter 3. The latter discusses a draft of the present
chapter, and the current section was written in part as a response to Livingston's draft. I have updated
the discussion in light of the proofs of Livingston's book, which he kindly made available to me.
[31] Livingston, 'Cinematic Authorship', p. 134.

articulating or manifesting one's attitudes in some medium' and this must be intentional. Communication 'differs from simple expression in that the agent not only intends to make an attitude manifest, but tries to get this attitude, as well as the relevant intentions, recognized by some audience in the right sort of way'.[32] The notion of an utterance, though derived from theories of linguistic communication, is not narrowly linguistic, so Livingston is not committed to holding that there is a language of film. Applying the notion of authorship to cinema, he gives as a partial analysis of cinematic authorship: 'the agent or agent(s) who intentionally make(s) a cinematic utterance; where cinematic utterance = an action the intended function of which is to make manifest or communicate some attitude(s) by means of the production of an apparently moving image projected on a screen or other surface'.[33] This analysis is applied to four cases of films, two of which he holds are unauthored, one of which is partially authored and the last of which has a single author, Bergman's *Winter Light*.

The analyses just given apply to authors in general, including authors of non-artistic productions such as ordinary speech or letters. So this notion of author is wider than the notion of the author as artist, which is the concept that we have been targeting. Moreover, as Livingston acknowledges, art-works need not be expressive, since they may consist in objects that have significant artistic qualities, but not expressive ones (an artwork might simply be very beautiful without being expressive, for instance). Hence an artist need not be expressing anything in his work and this would make the analyses inapplicable to the artists of some artworks. So in his discussion in *Art and Intention* Livingston holds that, for those authors who are artists, one should substitute in place of the intentional expression of attitudes in the above analyses the 'intentional creation of works having artistically relevant qualities'.[34]

As his remarks on examples in 'Cinematic Authorship' indicate, expressive or artistic intentions do not suffice for authorship. Livingston talks of the author as the artist who is responsible for the work 'as a whole'. For instance, he holds that some industrially produced films have no authors, since no person or group 'intentionally produced the work as whole by acting on any expressive or communicative intentions'.[35] And of *Winter Light*, he says that Bergman is 'the author of the film as whole', which he grounds on Bergman's having 'a high degree of control' over the film's features: Bergman was directly responsible for some of them, such as the

[32] *Ibid.*, p. 135.   [33] *Ibid.*, p. 141.   [34] Livingston, *Art and Intention*, p. 89.
[35] Livingston, 'Cinematic Authorship', p. 138.

film's script, and where this was not so, Bergman was 'supervising and exercising control over the activities of his collaborators'; nor was Bergman subject to any coercion in this process.[36] In his recent *Cinema, Philosophy, Bergman*, he explicitly signals that an author must have sufficient control over the work as a whole, and cites with approval Perkins' account of control over the relationships between elements in the film as being crucial in this respect. Bergman has this degree of control over his films, and thus counts as the single author of them, despite the artistic contributions of others.[37]

This account of authorship, with its dual requirements of expressive or artistic intentions and sufficient control of the work as a whole, is sophisticated, interesting and important. It supports the possibility of single authorship of mainstream films, but does not deny the artistic importance of others' contributions: on the contrary, 'appreciation of a performer's artistic contribution to a film can be at least as crucial as appreciation of the director's achievement'.[38] Livingston also notes that in large-scale commercial films single authorship is not the most common scenario. These points move this version of the single-authorship view closer to the multiple-authorship view I defend. But the point of disagreement remains over single authorship of mainstream films. Is this indeed a possibility?

Consider first the expressive/artistic condition of authorship. Why, one might wonder, do not many of the artistic collaborators in a film express their attitudes in making the film and therefore fulfil a necessary condition for authorship? For instance, an actor will, through her performance, standardly express attitudes towards the particular character that she plays, and those attitudes cannot be entirely traceable to the director, given the nuances that actors bring to a role. An actor's contribution can have more than one source: it may be delivered through the particular way that he plays a character; or a well-known actor may give, though his mere presence, a weight and authority to a character that it would otherwise lack; or aspects of the actor's *persona* may condition the attitudes that are expressed. If the character is an important one, the attitudes expressed by the entire film may depend on how that character is played (we will consider several examples in

---

[36] *Ibid.*, p. 144.

[37] Livingston, *Cinema, Philosophy, Bergman*, chapter 3, see especially p.71.

[38] Livingston, *Art and Intention*, p. 89. Livingston remarks in this context that the disagreement between him and me about single authorship is 'largely verbal'. However, even if this were so, the terminology matters here: talk of single authorship easily tempts those of its adherents less careful than Livingston to occlude the contributions of other cinematic artists in practice, even when they acknowledge them in theory.

Section 3.7). Likewise, composers, set designers, directors of photography, and so on, can express their attitudes through their contributions.

Livingston believes that this view is based on a misconception of the expressive role of actors in particular. For instance, in *Summer with Monika* (1953) Harriet Andersson, who plays the title role, expresses through her acting Monika's attitudes, but does not express her own attitudes. In contrast, Bergman, as writer-director, does express his own attitudes of painful ambivalence towards parenthood and traditional gender roles, which are central themes of his work. So whereas a film can be taken as indicative of its director's attitudes, it is not indicative of the actors' attitudes.[39]

However, even if this were so, the author as artist is someone on Livingston's analysis who intentionally produces artistically relevant qualities, and these include more than expressive qualities; and we can reasonably take a performance by an actor that contributes towards, say, the beauty and originality of a film to be an intentional production of those qualities by her. And there is also no salient difference in respect of the indication of attitudes. If we are talking of the attitudes that the director has in real life, then we are not entitled to take, say, the expression of sepulchral gloomy attitudes in his film as an indication that he really is gloomy (perhaps he thinks that gloomy attitudes make for better films and in reality is quite cheerful); in the same way we are not entitled to take the attitudes an actor expresses in a film to be an indication that he really has those attitudes. However, the relevant attitudes for the artistic assessment of a film are those expressed *in the film*, not those that are held by the filmmakers in real life: a carefree comedy does not cease to be such merely because we discover that the filmmakers were suffering from depression when they made it. And just as directors may express attitudes in their films, so may actors, musicians and other collaborators. An actor may, for instance, find humour in a character that other actors would not, so expressing an attitude of humour to those kinds of situations; and this attitude may be particularly evident where the actor has played other roles in similar fashion or has a particular *persona* (think, for instance, of the way that Cary Grant could find humour and elegance in all manner of roles). Or an actor may find a degree of heroism in even distasteful or disturbing characters, and so express a conception of heroism and an attitude towards it.

Livingston's claimed disanalogy between directors and other contributors also runs into problems given his analysis of joint authorship. He holds

---

[39] Livingston, *Cinema, Philosophy, Bergman*, pp. 79 and 82.

that joint authorship in general occurs, roughly, when an agent intends to contribute to the making of some utterance as an expression of his attitudes and when he intends to do this by acting on sub-plans that mesh with those of other contributors (where the sub-plans govern how the utterance is to be produced and its expressive content); when there is at least one more agent of whom all of the above is true; and when all the agents mutually believe that the above is true of them.[40] Sub-plans mesh when it is possible for them to be simultaneously realised, though this does not rule out significant differences between the plans, nor 'major disagreement' between the co-authors.[41] In respect of this condition, actors and many other contributors should count as co-authors of the film, since they typically have expressive sub-plans that mesh, to varying degrees, with the other contributors to the film, just as the director typically has expressive sub-plans that mesh with theirs; and, in the case of those authors who are artists, they typically also have plans to give the film artistically relevant qualities, such as making it beautiful or original, and so on.

Of course, the director, if he has authority over the other contributors, is likely to be the most important contributor of expressive and artistic properties to a film. But that is entirely compatible with the multiple-authorship view: the view is not that the contribution of all authors must be of equal importance. Just because the director's is the most important "voice" in the film does not mean that others' contributions do not entitle them to count as authors too.

The second condition of authorship on Livingston's account is that of having sufficient control over the work as a whole. For instance, though he acknowledges that Andersson's plans mesh with Bergman's in *Summer with Monika*, he denies that she should count as a joint author, not just because she lacks the appropriate expressive intentions but also because she has insufficient control over the making of the work as a whole. Bergman, in contrast, controls the relationships of the film and can thereby alter the meaning of her performance.

The notion of sufficient control of the film as a whole is somewhat elusive. Livingston says that he employs the restriction and sufficient control strategies and invokes Perkins: control of the film as a whole involves controlling the relationships, as opposed to the elements of a film. As with Perkins, no general criterion for distinguishing between elements and

---

[40] Livingston, *Art and Intention*, pp. 83–4.
[41] *Ibid.*, pp. 79 and 83. Livingston draws here on Michael Bratman's analysis of shared co-operative activity: for further discussion of this, see Section 4.1.

relationships is provided, but Livingston offers properties, such as those of proportion, rhetorical and stylistic patterns, and unity in complexity as examples of relational properties.[42]

However, if the idea of relationships is of patterns in the work, then there are patterns to be found in the acting, set design, music, cinematography, etc.; so on this construal actors, set designers, musicians and cinematographers, etc., should count as co-authors of a film. So on this or any similarly broad understanding of relationships, artistic contributors in general are a film's co-authors. (Again, this is consistent with allowing that the importance of different pattern makers may vary.)

Alternatively, relationships of a film may be construed narrowly. For example, suppose that relationships are taken as the editing relations of the film, since one can alter the meaning of acting performances by changing the editing relationships in which they stand; hence acting performances are a matter of the elements of a film. Recall the Kuleshov effect, discussed in Section 2.3.6: a neutral shot of an actor's face took on very different meanings depending on the shots with which it was joined. So on this proposal artistic meaning is a function of relationships, not of elements, and therefore authorship resides at the editing level. However, the problem is that the meaning of the shots also depends on the actor's expression: it is only because it was neutral that it can be interpreted in different ways, depending on the conjunction of shots: if it had been one of overt anger or fear, for instance, the editing relationships could not have shifted the interpretation in this manner. So the artistic meaning depends on *both* the acting and the editing relationships; since artistic meaning is determined by authors, authorship cannot be restricted to the mere editing relations.

The problems just exemplified are general. If the relationships of a film are construed broadly, as in the pattern making example, then other artistic contributors besides the writer-director must count as co-authors, because of their contribution to the relationships. If, on the other hand, relationships are construed narrowly, as in the editing example, then features of authorship, such as the determination of artistic meaning, are dependent on the elements, and therefore artists who determine these elements must count as co-authors on any adequate understanding of authorship. Either way, multiple authorship is true of mainstream films.

A second and more promising way of understanding the notion of being an artist of the work 'as a whole', can be brought out by considering

---

[42] Livingston, *Cinema, Philosophy, Bergman*, p. 80.

Livingston's discussion of Bergman's role in the making of his films, which stresses his uncoerced supervision and control over the activities of his collaborators. From this one can reasonably assume that authorship of the whole film concerns the role of co-ordinating the contributions of the various artistic collaborators on the film, where co-ordination includes the authority to give orders to them. And one can indeed usefully distinguish between those artists involved in cinema whose role has this feature and those whose role does not. So on this view the *co-ordinating artist*, as we can call her, is the author of the film.[43] But recall the thought experiment of Dickens, who, due to time pressures, farms out the writing of most chapters of *Great Expectations* to Trollope, Eliot and others, while writing a few himself and taking responsibility for co-ordinating the resulting chapters for the final work. Calling Dickens the sole author of the work would be simply false: this is a co-authored work. So discharging the co-ordinating role is insufficient for being the *single* author of a work and, given the authorial roles of Trollope and others, is not necessary for being *an* author of a work. And Bergman's position in his films is akin to Dickens' in this scenario.[44]

Finally, Livingston also defends the idea of an 'unauthored' film, a 'traffic jam' movie, the product of clashing intentions between makers of a film, none of whom has effective artistic control of it. He is correct in calling attention to the existence of traffic jam movies. But while in principle such a film could be unauthored (which on my account would require that each of its makers accidentally produces it), in practice such a situation is highly unlikely to occur. Such a film is better thought of as having multiple authors, but is one in which, rather than being in harmony with each other's intentions, they have severe artistic conflicts with each other. This is in fact a not uncommon situation in filmmaking: perhaps the best-known example is *The Cabinet of Dr Caligari* (1920). So it is not a necessary condition for someone to be an author of a film that she is a co-ordinating artist or that co-ordination occurs spontaneously between participants. Films can be multiply authored without co-ordination.

---

[43] Livingston (*ibid.*, p. 77) endorses this suggestion, holding that the dominant co-ordinating collaborator, provided that she has expressive intentions, is the author of the film.

[44] Livingston objects (*Art and Intention*, p. 88) that my multiple-authorship view exhibits an ambiguity between cases where there are multiple authors of the whole and those in which there are multiple contributors who are not authors of the whole. However, I have distinguished between those artists who are co-ordinating artists and those who are not. This distinction captures what is tenable in the notion of 'as a whole', without holding that mainstream films can have a single author, since the co-ordinating artist is not the single author, as the imaginary case of Dickens shows.

3.6 ONTOLOGY AND MULTIPLE AUTHORSHIP

So some of the more promising strategies and arguments for resolving the second puzzle in favour of single authorship fail. That being so, and in light of the fact of artistic collaboration, we should admit that mainstream films have multiple authors. I will now argue that the failure of the strategies and arguments in favour of single authorship is partly to be explained by a difference between the ontology of traditional films and literature. The discussion here concerns traditional mainstream films that incorporate the recorded performances of actors.[45] Whether the results need to be modified for digital cinema in general and for interactive digital cinema in particular will be discussed in Sections 3.8 and 3.9.

We can approach the issue of ontology by contrasting the role of the author-as-construct in film with its role in literature. The *persona* of Tolstoy as manifested in *Anna Karenina* is very different from the personality of the real man as manifested in his life, and so there is reason to distinguish the former from the latter (though just how sweeping a role this critical construct should play in our understanding of the work is another matter). There is no difficulty in imagining a person with the construct's personality penning the novel: no extraordinary mastery over a wide range of skills and functions would be needed, as it would were a film being made. Nor do actors portray the characters in the novel; so countenancing the single author as critical construct cannot undermine their agency or expressivity, as it does when the single author is introduced into films; nor are the literary author's capacities required to bloat to fantastic proportions so he can be thought of as controlling actors' behaviour. There are thus genuine differences between literature and films, differences which make the construction of a single author in the case of the latter inappropriate in a way they do not in the case of the former.

This question of the disparity between literature and film is worthy of careful scrutiny, for one powerful motivator of the auteurist programme is that the two art forms exhibit a structural similarity. Moreover, many of the arguments deployed above drew on the element of performance in films to attack the single-authorship thesis. But the auteurist may object that theatre similarly involves performances by several actors, yet the playwright's claim to sole authorship goes unchallenged. So what can be said about the relation between literature and film?

---

[45] When in this section I talk of 'films', I should be understood to mean traditional films that incorporate recordings of actors' performances, so as to avoid tedious repetition.

Novels, poems and plays are texts (understanding texts to be semantic entities, rather than simply types of physical marks) produced by writers; but films are moving pictures with sound, which incorporate mechanical recordings of performances. (This is not, of course, to be confused with the claim that films are simply filmed theatre: how the performances are filmed matters a great deal, as was argued in Chapter 1.) This dissimilarity between literary works and films is reflected in their individuation-conditions: literary works are individuated by their texts (and, if we are contextualists, by their writers and times of composition as well[46]), but films are not so individuated, for radically different films can emerge from the same text: the 1922 film *Nosferatu* and the 1978 film of the same name incorporate roughly the same screenplay, but are remarkably different films. Nor are films individuated by their storyboards, if there are any, for very different photographic shots and different performances by actors can be realisations of the same storyboard. Films are, in fact, individuated by their entire range of acoustic and visual properties, and by the causal sources of these.[47] Further, because of their status as texts, literary works can be performed (novels and poems are performable, by being read out, as was common until fairly recently), whereas films cannot be performed, no more than can pictures or photographs. (The screening of a film is not a performance of it, since one cannot, for instance, talk of a screening being a misinterpretation of a work.) Performances in films are, rather, internal to a work: recordings of performances are part of what makes a film what it is.

From these basic ontological differences between literary works and films emerges a difference between the relation of the actor to her role in a play and in a film, which has implications for authorship. There is no difficulty in understanding how Shakespeare can be the sole author of *Othello*, for he can brandish the Bardic plume and inscribe the text. That text specifies the character of Othello, granting him a certain range of determinate features (being a Moor, killing his wife, speaking glorious poetry while proclaiming

---

[46] See Jerrold Levinson, 'What a Musical Work Is' for an influential defence of contextualism. The ontological differences between literature and films remain on this view: a novelist composing a work at a certain time, given the particular text he has produced, could not have composed a different novel using that text, but a director could have produced a different film at a particular time, given a particular screenplay; and evidently it is still true that films cannot be performed, but literary works can be.

[47] We need to refer to the causal sources of the images, because we should count as distinct films those that, though identical in all their perceptible properties, are recordings of different people or objects. Since new copies of films are made by photographing earlier copies, identity of causal source of the images must be understood in terms of the objects which were the source of the images in the first photograph from which later copies were taken.

his simplicity) and leaves a set of other features indeterminate within certain bounds (exactly how he rolls the rhapsodies off his tongue, what his movements and facial expressions are as he does so). The latter gives scope for actors to present their varying interpretations, or characterisations, of his character, by determining these indeterminates in some way within their performance (for instance, speaking certain lines not with heartfelt fervour, but with neurotic unease). But how Robeson or Olivier characterised Othello does not affect the character himself: that is under Shakespeare's complete control.[48] That the *performance* of a play is collaborative, involving many different actors and a director, then, does not undermine the single authorship of the play itself. But whilst a play specifies its characters by its text, a film specifies them by its acoustic and visual features. These features incorporate recordings of actors' performances, so these performances play a part in specifying the characters portrayed in the film. The film actor, then, co-determines (with the screen writer, director, or whomever) the character she plays in a film. How she looks, how she says certain lines are now how that character looks and says those lines; and had a different actor been employed, the character would have been correspondingly different.[49] Imagine a Julie Marston in *Jezebel* (1938) played, not by Bette Davis, but by Claudette Colbert.[50]

The implications for film authorship are evident. In theatre, actors' performances are external to the play itself, whereas in cinema (recordings of) their performances are internal to the film. So, despite the collaborative nature of performance, the playwright can exercise complete control over the characters of her play; but it is a vastly more difficult task for a film's putative author to have the same degree of control over the characters of a film. If the author is construed as an actual individual, she would have entirely to determine the acting of all the actors playing the parts, and we have already seen how implausible is the claim that she could do this. If the author is viewed as a critical construct, she is freed from the constraints on

---

[48] Of course, the actor determines the character-in-performance, i.e., the particular version presented of the character in a particular performance: but the character-in-performance is distinct from the character in the play (for instance, the former exists only for the duration of that particular performance, whereas the latter is not thus temporally bounded).

[49] The film actor will, of course, also leave certain features of her character indeterminate – but they will concern such things as aspects of character motivation, rather than the precise intonation or physical appearance of the character.

[50] For similar considerations about individuation conditions and the difference they make to the relation of theatre and cinema actors to their roles, see Erwin Panofsky, 'Style and Medium in the Motion Pictures', p. 298–9; Stanley Cavell, *The World Viewed*, pp. 27–9; and Arthur Danto, 'Moving Pictures', Sections I and III.

what people as we know them can do. But in thinking of her as if she had control over all the performances, as well as of other filmmaking tasks, both she and the performers must be imagined as radically different from the human beings with which we are familiar. To do this is to speculate on the psychologies of beings so dissimilar from the persons who actually make films that we would warp out of all recognisable shape our understanding and appreciation of cinema. Some of the objections both to the single author as an actual individual and as a construct, then, are rooted in the firm and fertile ground of a basic ontological difference between literature and film.

3.7 THE MULTIPLE-AUTHORSHIP VIEW REFINED

The varieties of auteurism distinguished earlier are susceptible to further subdivisions and refinements. To show the attractions of the multiple-authorship view, in particular its merits in enhancing critical understanding compared to the single-authorship view, it is useful briefly to develop it and to compare films to other collaborative art forms.

Two dimensions of variation may usefully be distinguished in collaborative artistic activities. The first concerns the degree to which creative power in determining the artistic properties of a film is centralised or dispersed. In some films a person or small group of persons may be the dominant collaborator (who will typically, though not always, also be a co-ordinating artist), having power by virtue of their organisational role or by the force of their artistic presence; in other films there may be a greater diffusion of power between many roughly equal collaborators. The second dimension of variation concerns the degree to which the different collaborators are in agreement over the aims of the film and their role within its production. This can vary from total agreement to complete failure to agree. The latter may produce a shambles of a film, or may generate conflicts that greatly enhance its artistic merit. The collaborators may also either be aware of, or be completely unconscious of the fact that they are in agreement or in conflict. The variations possible along these two axes, and the interactions between them, can generate complexities within films that the single-authorship view cannot adequately theorise.

The possibility most akin to the single-authorship view of cinema is when one individual has dominant creative control over a film. The most plausible candidates are writer-directors, such as Ingmar Bergman, Preston Sturges, Quentin Tarantino and Woody Allen. Others, such as producers (David Selznick) or stars (Mae West), may sometimes wield artistic power – a circumstance that explains the endless, futile debates within the auteurist camp as to the identity of a film's author (the disputes under dimension 4). But, as we have seen, such an individual, even when he or she exists, is not correctly characterised as the sole author of the film. Sturges' great films at Paramount in the 1940s relied on a stock company of actors, for whom he wrote the parts, and whose performances are indispensable to the character and success of his films. Bergman and Allen similarly relied on a talented group of artists: the role of Sven Nykvist, Bergman's director of photography, was crucial to the look of his films. Indeed, some of these films' features, often ascribed to the directors, are more plausibly traced to the work of other collaborators. The comic mood of Allen's films became more serious and less kooky when Diane Keaton was replaced by Mia Farrow, a change of tone partly traceable to their differing skills as comic actresses. The existence of dominant collaborator films explains why the notion of single authorship has appeared plausible to many.

In other films artistic power is more dispersed. The great musicals produced by the MGM Freed unit are testimony to the skills of a wide range of artists, all of whom stamped their hallmarks on the silver screen.[51] Or consider *Blade Runner*, given an initial theatrical release in 1982 and re-released in 1992 in Ridley Scott's modified 'director's cut' and again in 2007 in a further modified director's cut, the latter two incarnations bearing witness to the ideology of single authorship. But the film is in fact an extraordinary collaborative venture: Philip Dick's source novel; the radical reworking of that material by David Webb Peoples' screenplay, stressing the futility of revenge, a theme shared with his script for *Unforgiven* (1992); Scott's concern with the marginalised and powerless in society, also seen in *Thelma and Louise* (1991); Syd Mead's marvellous visual imagining of a drenched and decayed megalopolis, half post-modern pastiche, half dystopian nightmare; Vangelis' futuristic, ethereal synthesiser score; the worried helplessness of Harrison Ford's acting; and the tense bundling of danger with hopelessness conveyed in Rutger Hauer's performance – the work of all these artists and many more combine synergistically to produce a cinematic masterpiece.

Rather than rigidly categorising films by their directors, films should be multiply classified: by actors, cameramen, editors, composers, and so on. The career paths of all cinematic artists should be traced, showing how their work adapts to new contexts, demonstrating how each interaction alters the ingredients and flavours of the cinematic potpourri. Sometimes

---

[51] See the interviews with the participants in the *An American in Paris* ballet in Donald Knox, *The Magic Factory*.

tracking the trail of a non-director's career will be the best way to follow significant developments in film history: the career of cameraman Gregg Toland, one of the re-discoverers of deep-focus photography in the 1930s, can fruitfully be traced, as he developed his technique under William Wyler, and then radicalised it with neophyte director Orson Welles, who for some time was credited with innovations not entirely his own. An increasing amount of serious work is being done on the role of stars and other non-directors in filmmaking, and the multiple-authorship thesis should serve to sustain and enhance the importance of such studies.

The second dimension of variation mentioned above, and in particular the role of conflict between authors, is important in shaping many films. One of the key ideas of contemporary criticism, both of films and of literature, is that of the 'contradictory text', the idea that works may be riven with tensions between their professed ideology and their actual representation of the world, so that, for instance, the suppressed violence of an actor's performance may detonate the mealy mouthed pieties of a film's official line. The case for such films is strengthened by tracing their conflicts back to the differing projects of the various collaborators. Yet, ironically, recent criticism has not generally availed itself of this thought; indeed, one of the key sources of the notion of the contradictory film appears to work within a constructivist single-author view.[52] Here again the multiple-authorship version shows its superiority. Consider *Do the Right Thing* (1989), perhaps Spike Lee's finest film (see Figure 5). The film has in Sal a character who is surprisingly sympathetic, despite his complicity in a racial tragedy culminating in a horrifying murder. Sal is an important element in the film's richness and complexity, and some have hailed him as marking the subtlety of character creation of which Lee is capable.[53] The truth is otherwise: 'St. Clair Bourne's documentary record of the location shoot, *Making Do the Right Thing* (1989), offers an intriguing glimpse into the way an actor can overwhelm an auteur. In a discussion about Sal's character, Lee declares flatly that he thinks Sal is a racist. Aiello disagrees – and on the screen if not in the screenplay his portrayal wins the argument.'[54]

Other instances of artistically fruitful disagreement abound: James Cameron, who directed Sigourney Weaver as Ripley in *Aliens* (1986), has remarked, 'The thing we always differed on was how much Ripley hated the alien. Sigourney had the response, "The alien is a creature and I can't blame

[52] The editors of *Cahiers du Cinéma*, 'John Ford's *Young Mr. Lincoln*'.
[53] Lisa Kennedy, 'Is Malcolm X the Right Thing?', p. 9.
[54] Thomas Doherty, 'Review of *Do the Right Thing*', p. 38.

Figure 5. Sal (Danny Aiello) gesticulating at Mookie (Spike Lee) in *Do the Right Thing* (1989).

it for the death of my crew," and my feeling was, "You hate that mother******." I was the throttle and she was the brakes. She would always pull back from a moment that was pushing it too far – that's why you get this incredibly modulated performance'.[55] Some of the complexity of *Gentlemen Prefer Blondes* (1953), Richard Dyer has argued, can be traced to Monroe's spirited refusal to conform to Hawks' demeaning conception of the character she plays. And the story is well known of the conflicts of

[55] Sean Macaulay, 'A lover and a fighter', p. 14.

purpose between Mayer and Janowitz, and Lang and Wiene that resulted in the addition of the framing-story to *The Cabinet of Dr Caligari*. Sub-plans can refuse to mesh with each other, sometimes spectacularly, but a multiply authored film can result, and it may be an artistically successful one, sometimes precisely because of this lack of significant mesh.[56]

Given the importance of collaboration in film, much can be learnt from the critical discourse surrounding other areas of artistic collaboration. For those films that incorporate recordings of performances, studies of collaborations involved in performances are particularly germane. Performances of plays, involving the artistic collaboration of playwrights, directors, actors, set designers and others, provide a useful comparison for thinking about filmmaking: the ideology of single authorship is noticeably less compelling in theatre studies, where the cult of the director has not (yet) ballooned to the bulbous dimensions it has assumed in film studies.

Musical performances are also usually collaborative, and when this is so, the musical styles of all the participants affect the outcome. Particularly illuminating is the comparison of mainstream film with jazz. For the most part what matters in jazz is improvised performance, not composition; and just as radically different films can be based on the same screenplay, so can very different improvisations derive from the same tune. Consequently, critical interest centres on the different musical styles, personalities and interactions of the improvisers in the group, interactions still present even when one member of the group is dominant. The modes of such interplay are complex. A musician's playing may vary in response to that of his collaborators, or his tone may simply sound different in diverse musical contexts: Bill Evans never played better than when working with Scott LaFaro and Paul Motian; in the Miles Davis–John Coltrane groups, the fragility of Davis' tone is rendered more poignant through its contrast to Coltrane's searing attack. The ideal implicit in jazz is one of democratic individualism – of a set of strong musical personalities who converse with each other through their playing, and create music richer than any could make on his own. The multiple-authorship theory of films encourages us to look at films the same way as we do jazz: as a product of many individuals, whose work is inflected in a complex manner by their interactions with their colleagues. A mainstream film is no more the product of a single individual than is the music of an improvising jazz group.

---

[56] For an entertaining account of some of the artistic conflicts that can arise between actors and directors, see John Badham and Craig Modderno, *I'll be In My Trailer*.

The multiple-authorship view can be seen as stemming in part from a more general view of film. One of the most influential paradigms for understanding films has been a literary one. The auteur theory was inspired by the comparison of films to literary works, even though the theory also allowed for structural parallels to paintings and compositional music. The connection between films and literature has also been trumpeted by film semiotics, which argues that films are, or are closely akin to, linguistic texts. The literary paradigm has led to serious distortions in our understanding of film, properly regarded as an audio-visual medium, where the exact qualities of images and sounds, dependent on the particular individuals who generated them, are crucial to a film's artistic features. Films are movies, moving pictures which have learned to talk, and are not usefully regarded as text-like. And, as we saw when examining the question of ontology, there are some important differences between literary works and traditional films that record performances, even waiving the question of the language of film.

3.8 DIGITAL CINEMA AND AUTHORSHIP

So far in this chapter we have been discussing authorship in traditional film: do the theories about authorship and collaboration developed also apply to digital cinema? In this section I will discuss non-interactive digital cinema: in the next, interactive digital cinema. The main question to investigate is whether single authorship can occur in mainstream digital cinema, i.e., where at least two people occupy the key production roles. A second question is whether the director (or whoever is the dominant collaborator, if there is one) has increased control, relative to other artists working on the film, in digital cinema compared to traditional film. Let us begin by reviewing some empirical evidence germane to both questions.

Some prominent directors of digital films have made claims that suggest that they believe that single authorship can occur in digital cinema. George Lucas, who played a pivotal role in the development and popularisation of digital cinema, has said, 'It's going to be more like novels or plays; if you have the talent, you can express yourself'.[57] This is partly a remark about the accessibility to new talent of the medium, but also suggests an enhanced authorial role in digital cinema, as is common in novels and playwriting. Lucas has also compared digital cinema to oil painting, which yields a more 'malleable' image, as opposed to traditional film, which he compares to fresco, with its relative lack of control and its need for multiple 'assistants' to

---

[57] Kristin Thompson and David Bordwell, *Film History*, p. 704.

mix paint and lay on plaster.[58] Robert Rodriguez, an early convert to digital cinema through Lucas' influence, has also claimed of digital cinema, 'It's the speed and power of almost having a paintbrush in your hand',[59] a remark that again nods towards single authorship.

These are not just manifesto comments. Lucas put his authorship claim into practice, removing unwanted expressions and eye blinks from some of the actors in *Star Wars: Episode II – Attack of the Clones* (2002).[60] In *Forrest Gump* (1994), directed by Robert Zemeckis, Gump's fictional meeting with JFK was filmed by taking real footage of the president, digitising it, compositing Tom Hanks as Gump into the scene, digitally painting mouth movements and associated facial highlights onto Kennedy's face, corresponding with his fictional speech with Gump, and morphing the painted movements onto the digital image so that there was a seamless moving image.[61] JFK was, of course, not acting in this context, but the techniques employed show how radically one can change the nature of a recorded performance.

More recently, digital characters have been created employing methods that give the director an enhanced role relative to an actor. As noted in Section 1.4, the character of Gollum in *The Lord of the Rings* trilogy was created using Andy Serkis' voice and body movements, which were recorded by motion capture techniques. These recordings were motion-edited, and then key frame animation (akin to traditional animation, but using computer techniques) was used to create Gollum's expressions; these were sometimes closely modelled on Serkis' own, but were sometimes invented by the animators. In *The Polar Express* (2004) motion capture was used to record not just the actors' bodily movements, but also their facial expressions, with key frame animation used to fill in the details, a technique that led to spookily realistic digital animation, and this was pushed to achieve even more eerily realistic effects in *Beowulf* (2007). In *King Kong* (2005) the same technique was employed to record Serkis' facial movements, software programs were developed to translate human into gorilla expressions, and key frame animation was used to record subtleties of expression that either were lost in motion capture or that could not have been achieved by Serkis, given the difference between gorilla and human physiognomy. The motion capture footage was edited to alter aspects of

[58] Brian McKernan, *Digital Cinema*, p. 36.
[59] Richard Waters, 'Hollywood sees power shift from film-set to desk-top', p. 16.
[60] Thompson and Bordwell, *Film History*, p. 704.
[61] See Stephen Prince, 'True Lies', for a discussion of the techniques used.

Serkis' performance – a motion editor talks of 'performance change' and of 'keeping the tension in the eyes' of Kong by using these techniques.[62] So in digital cinema control by others can reach much further into the actor's domain than in traditional film.

The empirical evidence does not all point towards increased directorial control, however. Most obviously, a quick glance at the credits of any big budget digital film shows that there are large numbers of collaborators involved in its making, and these people are highly technically and artistically skilled. In low-budget digital production, while the cheaper cost of digital as opposed to traditional filmmaking frees up directors from some of the constraints imposed by economics, much production practice favours a more collaborative kind of cinema. Two of the earliest commercial digitally recorded films (though they were transferred to celluloid for commercial release) were the Dogma 95 films, *The Idiots* (1998) and *The Celebration* (1998). Both, particularly the former, directed by Lars von Trier, involved extensive improvisation by cast members, which was recorded directly onto digital tape, facilitated by its cheapness and reusability compared to expensive celluloid. More radical improvisation was practised in *Time Code* (2000), where fifteen takes, each the length of the entire movie, were made, and Mike Figgis, the director, encouraged the actors to improvise extensively around a minimal script, which produced radically different versions (both the first and fifteenth takes are on the DVD, and they are significantly different).

In several ways digital cinema is an actors' cinema. The cheapness of digital tape enables improvisation to be filmed without worry about recording costs; the much greater length of a tape reel than a film reel allows performances to be run without waiting for camera reloads; the lighter weight and greater tolerance of poor lighting conditions of the digital camera mean that actors' movements do not have to be so carefully blocked out in advance and thus more discretion is provided to them; the ability to show an actor her performance immediately, rather than waiting for the 'dailies' to be developed means that feedback can be given immediately and she can refine her performance; the capacity cheaply to run several cameras simultaneously and unobtrusively allows complete coverage of a scene without the performer having to repeat her performance for different set-ups and so unique, one-off performances can be captured; and so on. So digital cinema can foster a much more democratic, actor-centred cinema.

---

[62] *King Kong, Two Disc Special Edition* DVD (Universal Studios, 2006): Disc Two, *Post-production diaries*, especially 'Bringing Kong To Life: I & II'.

In light of this brief review of the evidence, what should we conclude about authorship in digital cinema? In answer to our first question, none of the above points shows that single authorship can occur in digital cinema, if we make the same proviso that we applied to traditional film – that the films are mainstream, involving at least two people in the key production roles. In almost all cases, an actor's expressive activity is recorded in performance, and therefore there is at least one expressive agent in addition to the director involved in the film. This is in contrast to the novel, which does not record others' expressive activities, and so the novelist's single authorship is possible. Since mainstream digital cinema, like traditional film, in virtually all cases records actors' performances, the same argument against single authorship, based on recorded performance, applies to both. The evidence about the ability to reduce the actor's input via selective use of aspects of his performance (for instance, only the voice and body motion in the case of Serkis as Gollum) shows that this expressive agency can be reduced by incorporating less of it into the final character. But, if it is still detectable in the final film (as it most certainly is in the case of Gollum), then we are dealing with a mainstream film and multiple authors.

If there is no actor, a perhaps hypothetical case given the ubiquity of voice acting in animated films, then, if the film is mainstream, there is by definition at least one other person involved in the key production roles. Suppose this to be the animator: then we can deploy many of the arguments advanced earlier. In discussing the restriction strategy I argued that almost all aspects of the film as seen and heard are artistically relevant; and in a fully animated film, artistically relevant properties certainly include the contributions of the animators. In discussing the sufficient control strategy, I argued that if there are at least two collaborators and one gives orders to the other to carry out some tasks, the situation is one of multiple authorship, since it is akin to one in which our hypothetical Dickens designates some tasks to others; and this would apply to a director giving orders to an animator. The fact that the artistic tasks in animation are not exactly specified by the director allows ineliminably for individual expression by animators. (In the theoretical case where a director specified pixel-by-pixel what an animated image should look like, he would himself be filling the animator role, and anyone following this type of order would be reduced to the role of a mere computer operator; so the film would not be a mainstream one in this respect.) And in discussing the construction strategy, I noted the importance of a *persona* for individuating the number of authors; and an animator has her own *persona*, displayed in the way that she draws or paints, either with traditional or computational instruments, as a result of the role of individual expression in her activities. Likewise, thinking of a film as if all tasks, including animation ones, were done by one person would lead to misevaluations of the film, since the degree of competence required to do all such tasks would make even everyday animated films seem works of extraordinary accomplishment. Similar arguments apply to the occupiers of other key production roles.

One might respond to these arguments by imagining an extreme case. Suppose that only a director and actor were involved in making a film, and the director gradually pared away the actor's expressive contribution, say, digitally painting over an ever larger part of the actor's image to produce expressive effects more to the director's liking. (This would be taking to an extreme the examples of Lucas removing actors' eye blinks and JFK's mouth movements being painted in.) Would this not result in a single-authored film? It would, but only at the point where the actor's contribution, including the actor's vocal contribution, was entirely painted out or otherwise erased. At that point no trace of the actor's contribution remains; but then this would no longer be a mainstream film, for only the director would have made the final version of the film. In such a case the actor's contribution is entirely removed, just as many actors' contributions have ended up on the cutting room floor. Hence there is no difference between traditional and digital cinema in this respect: a mainstream film, whether traditional or digital, invariably possesses more than one author.

Our second question concerns whether directorial control is enhanced in digital cinema compared to traditional film. Clearly a degree of control over acting (other than by instruction to the actor to alter her performance) is possible in traditional film. Lighting and devices such as editing can change the recorded performance: for instance, as noted in Section 3.5, the Kuleshov effect shows that one can alter aspects of actors' recorded performance through editing. However, as we have seen the devices available to digital cinema to accomplish this are more radical and powerful. Increased control can be achieved over the actor's artistic input to the film by altering features of recorded performance (digitally painting over the actor's image, for instance) or by incorporating only some aspects of the acting into the final image (motion capture, etc.). Whereas equivalents could be attempted in traditional film, the manipulation involved would be much more easily detectable. The ability of digital cinema to alter recorded actorly performance in this way is an aspect of its general ability to manipulate the image, which we discussed in Section I.2. So the actor's contribution to the final recorded performance is potentially reduced.

However, it does not follow from this that the director's control increases. For the problem is that, as noted, a vast number of collaborators are required to make the kind of high-budget digital film in which actors' performances are attenuated in this fashion. And that means that, while the artistic input of the actor may diminish, the artistic input of other collaborators, such as animators and motion capture editors, increases. So the director's control may not overall grow, and it may even lessen, given the much greater number of artists involved in generating the final recorded performance. Of course, technological progress might lead one day to a single individual being able to undertake all of these artistic roles, as software systems become capable of performing tasks that currently only skilled artists can do. Since it is impossible to predict technological change, one cannot rule this out a priori. So the claim that the director's control has not been enhanced relative to other artists working on the film is an empirical one about the current state of digital cinema and is not a priori establishable.[63]

Although the degree of directorial control, as opposed to the possibility of single authorship, in digital cinema is an empirical matter, the evidence above reveals that digital cinema allows collaboration to enter realms where it would not before have been possible or not been possible to such artistically high standards. Consider digital cinema relative, first, to traditional, live-action film. Collaboration can penetrate far more radically into what was traditionally the actor's role: it can be unbundled, so that different performers control different aspects of it and each aspect can in turn be controlled by more than one artist. Gollum would, within a traditional live action film, have been acted by a single performer, whose voice, movements, facial expressions, bodily expressions and physiognomy were recorded by the camera, the director would have instructed the performer in the acting style required and perhaps modified that performance by cinematic devices such as editing and lighting. In digital cinema something much more radical is possible. Serkis' voice was used (though digitally manipulated) and aspects of his motion were recorded by motion capture, as we have seen. He contributed to the role whatever of his expressive properties survived that process. But motion editors then adjusted the recorded motion for artistic purposes and key frame animators filled in and altered the character's expressions. Animators are often called within

---

[63] This point is consistent with our a priori answer to the first question. If technological changes led to the director being able to make a film entirely by himself, perhaps by using highly realistic avatars instead of actors, then he would be its sole author. But the film would not be a mainstream one.

the profession 'actors with pencils' and in this case they had the opportunity to act, in a sense, with Serkis in the Gollum role: animators, editors and the actor all collaborated in that role. And these artists worked in teams, so that, for instance, several animators collaborated to get the expression right on Gollum's face from moment to moment. More than a hundred people helped produce the final actions and characteristics of the character, and since some of the most effective moments in the film are Gollum's dialogues with himself as Sméagol, over one hundred people collectively managed to deliver a performance that equalled or excelled that of actors of the calibre of Ian McKellen and Cate Blanchett.

It is worth developing this point, since it shows in what ways animators can take on many of the functions of actors. In what sense are animators 'actors with pencils'? As a rough characterisation, an actor is (1) an agent who makes something fictional for an audience by the use of his body and/or voice, where (2) his audience can perceive his body and/or voice, or recordings of them. Condition (1) is also true of an animator: he is an agent who makes something fictional for an audience by the use of his body and/or voice – he employs his body in drawing and painting or he could use a voice recognition system to control a computer's activities of drawing or painting. However, (2) is false of him: we do not perceive his body and/or voice, or recordings of them. Instead, what we perceive are the drawings or paintings that are the *products* of his body and/or voice, or recordings of these products. Call (1), which is the common element in the two roles, the performance role. Actors are performers whom we see and hear, or recordings of whom we see and hear; animators are performers, whose products we perceive, or recordings of them. Animators are strictly speaking performers with pencils, rather than actors with pencils; but they can in digital cinema deliver a performance in what is traditionally the acting role. Thus Serkis, the animators and motion editors jointly delivered a performance as Gollum, but only Serkis, strictly speaking, was acting. Nevertheless, the actions of all these performers were artistically important.

So the roles of actors and animators are closely analogous, with animators taking on many of the functions of actors in live action cinema. And what digital cinema enables is the substitution for the traditional acting role of a broader performance role, in which the actor is only one kind of performer and where only aspects of his acting need be used (for instance, his voice and bodily movements).

Relative to traditional animated film, digital cinema also allows for enhanced collaboration, but here it is in respect of the actor's role growing at the expense of the animator's. For instance, had *The Lord of the Rings* been shot as a traditional animated film, Serkis' role would have been confined to voice acting, with at most his outline shape being used to control the character's outline shape by use of manual rotoscoping (drawing around the edges of the actor's photographed image to create the character's outline). But in digital cinema, motion capture allows the actor far more precise control of the character's motion, and if his facial expressions are also motion captured, to control the character's expressions too. The use of immediate feedback by showing the actor how his expression looks on a real-time wireframe digital "puppet" also permits far more nuanced performance from him. The fact that animators can then edit and adjust this performance and add key frame elements allows them finely to modulate this performance and so to collaborate more intimately with the actor than would be possible within traditional animated film. So, in this respect too, there is the possibility of reconfiguring the relationship between animators and actors and for allowing more nuanced collaboration between them.

So digital cinema has made possible a broadening out of the realm of filmmaking activities in which collaboration is possible, with new artistic possibilities either being made available or being rendered more artistically powerful. And there is now a seamless blend between live action and animated material, reflecting the capabilities of the mélange image, so that the kind of collaboration we have discussed can enter into any digital film. Collaboration has spread wide and far in the digital domain to artistically fruitful effect.

3.9 INTERACTIVITY AND AUTHORSHIP

The two questions that we posed in the last section – concerning the possibility of single authorship in mainstream digital films and whether directorial control is enhanced in digital as opposed to traditional films – need to be posed for interactive digital cinema too. And there are two additional issues raised by interactivity that require separate treatment. Many writers have found it plausible that in interactive works the audience achieves a share in authorship. For the images shown depend in part on the audience's decisions, and that seems to place the audience firmly in the authorship position. In the case of computer games Michael Hammel holds that 'the artwork becomes co-created by the user and the artist' and Barry Atkins writes that 'Every one of us is author, every one of us is artist'. Talking of interactive, networked computer systems, Roy Ascott holds that 'The emerging new order of art is that of interactivity, of "dispersed authorship" ... Creativity is shared, authorship is distributed'.[64] If these claims are correct, multiple authorship is even more radically dispersed in interactive than in non-interactive cinema, since the audience are co-authors of the interactive work. A second position holds that the audience of interactive works are not authors, but are more like performers of traditional works. Authors create the work, but users perform it, in the sense of making choices that instantiate it. Jay Bolter and Diane Gromala hold that for digital interactive works, such as *TEXT RAIN* (2000), 'As users, we enter into a performative relationship with the digital design: we perform the design as we would a musical instrument. Digital artists and designers create instruments that the user will play'.[65] This performance view does not hold that authorship is dispersed, but it does radically reconfigure the relationship between author, performer and audience.

3.9.1 *What is interactivity?*

To assess these claims we need to have a clearer idea of what interactivity is. Some influential writers on digital media have been deeply suspicious of the concept. Espen Aarseth writes that the word 'interactive' 'connotes various vague ideas of computer screens, user freedom, and personalized media, while denoting nothing' and holds that it plays no useful role in discussing digital media.[66] Lev Manovich argues that 'In relation to computer-based media, the concept of interactivity is a tautology', since modern computers allow real-time user input when a program is running, as opposed to older batch processing methods by which information could be input only before a program ran; he concludes that to say that computer media are interactive is 'meaningless'.[67] However, if a statement is a tautology, its constituent components cannot be meaningless; and, while the notion of 'interactivity' is often employed in a vague fashion, we should not conclude that it lacks a precise denotation.

A promising proposal, which was at one point defended by Dominic Lopes, is that 'a work is interactive just in case it prescribes that the actions of its users partly determine its instances and their features'.[68] The proposed

---

[64] Michael Hammel, 'Towards a Yet Newer Laocoon. Or, What we Can Learn from Interacting with Computer Games', p. 64; Barry Atkins, *More than a Game*, p. 153; and Roy Ascott, 'Is There Love in the Telematic Embrace?', pp. 237–8.

[65] Jay David Bolter and Diane Gromala, *Windows and Mirrors*, p. 147.

[66] Espen Aarseth, *Cybertext*, p. 48.   [67] Lev Manovich, *The Language of New Media*, p. 55.

[68] The proposal was in an early draft of Dominic McIver Lopes, *A Philosophy of Computer Art*. He later amended the definition, but his book was still in an evolving draft at the time of writing, so I will not discuss his more recent position. Rather, my purpose in citing his original definition is simply to employ it as a starting point for developing my own account, on which it was a significant influence.

definition has considerable merits. It clearly distinguishes between a work and its instances: interactive works (or at least those cinematic ones with which we are concerned here) are types of which their interaction-instances are tokens.[69] And the notion of interactivity requires not that user input *does* modify the work's instances or features, since, as Lopes notes, vandalising a work and so changing its appearance does not make the work interactive. Rather, the notion of prescription is required – i.e., that the changes made by users are *authorised*.

However, there is a problem with the proposal as it stands. Consider Beethoven's *Eroica* symphony: the musicians who perform it partly determine its instances (they play it) and their features (they play it in different ways to bring out different aesthetic properties) and they are authorised to do this; but the *Eroica* is not an interactive work. The same problem arises for every musical work, and for all those performing arts where there is a work distinct from its instances, such as ballets and plays. So from the definition it seems to follow that all performing artworks are interactive; and that is false. There are interactive dramas and interactive musical works, but not all dramas nor all musical works are interactive.

In an earlier article Lopes distinguishes the role of the user from the role of the performer based on their differing knowledge: 'To perform a [musical] work is to have beliefs about how the work should sound and to enjoy a reasonable measure of success in bringing it about that the sounds one produces are those one believes the work has. But only those who are familiar with the full range of possible interaction-instances of a work satisfy this condition'.[70] One way to develop this is to hold that whereas performers *must* know a lot about the work to perform it, users (interactors) *need not* know anything non-trivial about the work to interact with it, so performers are distinct from users. However, even if this claim about users were true, it would be unsuccessful as a solution to the definitional problem, since it is compatible with a performer being a user (i.e., someone who determines instances of a work) who in addition must know something about the work: i.e., a performer is a type of user.[71] So according to the definition performing

---

[69] Some interactive works are particulars: imagine a one-off installation piece that modified its states according to audience input; so for full generality the definition needs to be modified to hold that an interactive work prescribes that users' actions partly determine the work's instances and their features, *or states of the work*.

[70] Dominic McIver Lopes, 'The Ontology of Interactive Art', p. 80; see also his *A Philosophy of Computer Art*, chapter 4.

[71] Compare: a genetic woman is someone who *must have* a particular sexual chromosomal structure; a genetic human is someone who *need not* have that particular chromosomal structure (since some humans are male); but it would be invalid to conclude from this that women are not humans.

artworks are still interactive. An alternative strategy is to hold that a user is someone who *does not* know anything about the work, but a performer *must* know a lot about the work. This does entail that users are not performers: but it is straightforwardly false of users. The user of a videogame has learned a great deal about the game after he has played it for a while, but he does not thereby cease to become a user or otherwise change his status: he is now an expert user of the game, whereas before he was only a novice user. Also, *any* user of a videogame has to know something about the game to play it: he has to know that it is a game, has to know about the control systems and how to produce changes in the game world, and so on.

A better response is to identify the roles involved in terms not of the knowledge required to fulfil them, but in terms of their part in the appreciation of a work. Consider non-interactive musical and dramatic works. The role of the audience is to appreciate the work; the role of the performer is to instantiate the work for appreciation by the audience; so the two roles are distinct, though the performer role presupposes the existence of the audience role. In non-interactive works the audience has no role in contributing to the performance: audience coughs in the performance of a symphony do not count as part of the musical performance; and audience members running onto the stage do not count as part of the traditional theatrical performance, but as interruptions of it. But in an interactive work audience contributions *do* count as part of the performance: the audience noise during John Cage's 4′ 33″ is part of the performance and audience members who go on stage in Augusto Boal's Theatre of the Oppressed are part of the performance of the work. So the key difference between the non-interactive and the interactive cases is that in the latter audience members participate in the performance, that is, they take on the functions of performers too. The audience role is thus expanded to encompass the performer role. This does not involve merely putting the two roles together without one conditioning the other; rather, the audience role in the interactive case is to appreciate the work *by* instantiating it; merely watching the work while someone else instantiates it does not count as fully appreciating it.

One might suppose that this requires the interactivity definition to be amended to refer not to users but to audience-performers. However, the original definition already states that users' actions instantiate the work, i.e., that users have the key capacity of performers. So all that is required is to substitute reference to the audience for reference to users in the definition, where we understand the audience as those whose role it is to appreciate the work. Hence a work is interactive just in case it authorises that its *audience's* actions partly determine its instances and their features. So traditional musical and other performing works are not interactive, for the audience is not authorised to determine their instances and features; the performers do that. But in interactive works, it is the audience that determines the works' instances and their features.

3.9.2 Authorship

With this account of interactivity on board, we can address our questions about authorship.

First, are the audience members of an interactive work the work's co-authors along with the maker of the work, as Hammel, Atkins and Ascott claim? The answer is 'no', since the concept of interactivity distinguishes between a work and its instances: audience members determine the instances of a work and their features, but they do not alter the work itself.[72] Each instance of the work may go differently due to audience choices, but the work itself is not altered. The authors of *Façade* (2005) are Michael Mateas and Andrew Stern, along with their computing and acting collaborators; the person who plays this digital interactive drama alters features of its instances (for example, by typing in text to which the characters respond), but the work itself remains the same after the audience's engagement with it.

Are audience members co-authors of the work's instances? By definition, audience members are part determiners of an interactive work's instances; so they are co-makers of those instances. But an author in our targeted sense is an artist, a non-accidental producer of an artwork, and not all instances of an artwork are themselves artworks. George Eliot's *Middlemarch* is an artwork, but my battered paperback copy of the novel is not. Likewise, not all performances of an artwork are themselves artworks, since they may be too humdrum and devoid of an interesting interpretation to count as such. But some instances of artworks are themselves artworks. *Eroica* is an artwork, and some of its performances are artworks too: they are judged artistically and are considered in their own right as artworks and may be recorded for posterity. Some performances of plays are also sufficiently accomplished to count as artworks in their own right. And there is no in-principle reason why a playing of *Façade* could not be an artwork. A talented writer might use the game to create an interesting dramatic performance: there is a facility in the work to print out a text of what the player has written and how the two computer-generated characters, Grace and Trip, with

---

[72] Relatedly, see Lopes, *A Philosophy of Computer Art*, chapter 5.

which she has interacted, responded. This printed text is not *Façade*: it is a partial record of an instantiation of it. But this playing of *Façade* could be an artwork in its own right. So, though interactors are not co-authors of interactive works, they are co-authors of their instances where these are themselves artworks. In the same way musical performers are co-authors of artistic performances, but not of the musical works that they perform. Hence the audience co-authorship thesis is false of works as types, but is true of their instances if these instances count as artworks.[73]

Second, what is the relation of the audience of interactive works to the performer of traditional works? I have already argued that in interactive works audience members take on the role of the performer as well as of the audience. And this performance aspect of interaction fits naturally with the importance of role-playing in many interactive works, from the minimally specified role of the Guest character in *Façade* to the richer roles of the player characters, Jack Ryan in *Bioshock* (2007) and Niko Bellic in *Grand Theft Auto IV* (2008). Nevertheless, there is something correct in Lopes' thought that generally the depth of knowledge of the work required by performers of a non-interactive work is greater than that required by users of interactive works. Why is this and is the difference, despite what I have argued, sufficient to mean that the latter are not performers?

Performance of a work has two aspects: compliance and interpretation. Compliance involves making sure that the events that one is producing have the properties that are required for them to instantiate the work: for instance, the musician must hit the right notes in order to play the symphony. Performance interpretation involves further determining the events' properties, beyond those required by compliance, so as to suggest or ground a critical interpretation: for instance, a musician may play the *Eroica* in such a way as to bring out the sense of disillusionment as opposed to heroism in the work. Interpretation is not required, but it must always be possible, for performance to occur. That is why screenings of a non-interactive film are not performances of it: standard projection techniques do not permit the projectionist by her choice of projection methods to provide an interpretation of the film.

The audience of an interactive computer work need not worry about compliance in basic respects: compliance is assured, since the computational processes, if working correctly, assure that every event generated by

---

[73] Where I need to make it explicit that I am referring to works that are instances of other works, rather than works-as-types, I will, for sake of economy, talk of 'instance-works'. Generally, however, I will simply talk of works and their instances.

the processes is compliant: so each image and sound generated by, say, *Façade*, is compliant with it.[74] Let us call this *automated compliance*. That is a typical use of technology – to help us to do things that we would otherwise find it hard to do. Automated compliance explains why the audience need not know many of the features of the interactive work, unlike the situation of the performer of a traditional art form who has to secure compliance through her own skills and so needs to know the features that are required for compliance. But automated compliance still leaves available to the user the more interesting part of performance – interpretative performance. Unlike with compliance, talk of exploring a work is appropriate with interpretative performance, since one is finding out what additional determinations of a performance are permitted once it is compliant and how these ground various interpretations and evaluations of the work. Traditional performers can explore works once they have secured compliance. The same is true of users of computer works; the user of *Façade* can explore what she can do to save Grace and Trip's marriage or alternatively to see how she can undermine it. *Assisted performances*, performances where compliance is automated, are still performances, in the same way that technology-assisted drawing is still drawing. And both traditional and assisted performances are valuable chiefly because they afford the possibility of performance interpretation.

So here there is a difference, but not one that undermines the claim that the audience takes on the performer's role. Moreover, automated compliance must have its limits if the audience is to have a satisfying experience. For instance, the most salient rules from the player's perspective in video-games are the ones that she must follow in order to win the game or more generally to achieve desired results – she must learn how to control her character so as to shoot the alien or find the treasure or save a failing marriage. When successful in her aims, she is following a rule to bring about these results; if compliance with these rules were automated, there would be no challenge and no enjoyment. So there is a large role for skill-based following of rules in interactive cinema, in respect of those rules adherence to which brings about success: rules with automated compliance in contrast mainly govern the basic constitution of the game world that sets the framework within which skill-based compliance can occur.

---

[74] It is possible to use the game engine of a videogame to produce animated films that are not compliant with the videogame, as in the genre of machinima. But a game engine is only part of a videogame program – it is responsible for such things as the physics, artificial intelligence and rendering of the game. Machinima animations, though not compliant with the videogame from which the game engine was extracted, are compliant with the game engine itself; so they do not form a counterexample to automated compliance.

Let us now turn to the two questions that we posed about digital cinema in general in Section 3.8. First, can there be single authorship of mainstream interactive works? (Note that we are now talking about the authorship of the interactive *works* themselves not of their *instances*, which we discussed above.) There are videogame designers, such as Hideo Kojima, Shigeru Miyamoto, Ken Levine and Will Wright, who have been granted auteur-like status by some commentators; and this seems to favour single authorship.

Mainstream works require more than one person to take on the key production roles. Some of these roles, though not exactly the same in interactive and non-interactive cinema, are similar. For instance, the director's role is similar to that of the lead designer; cinematographers in the usual sense do not exist (cameras are usually virtual), but technical directors take on many of their functions. Many roles remain just the same: writers, animators and musicians are present. One might suppose that there are no actors in interactive cinema. But in fact there are live-action interactive works – in *I'm Your Man* (1992) the viewer can select which way the action proceeds at various points by choosing from the DVD menu. And most interactive cinema involves recordings of vocal performances: actors are voice cast to play the roles of both player and non-player characters; and motion capture technology can be used to generate recordings of actors' movements in interactive cinema, just as in non-interactive digital cinema. In *Grand Theft Auto IV*, for instance, Michael Hollick plays the part of the main player character, Niko Bellic: Hollick's voice was recorded for the dialogue and his facial expressions and movements (as well as those of specialists for fight sequences) were motion captured to animate the character; voice acting and motion capture were also employed to generate the non-player characters.[75] So actors exist and are important in interactive cinema.

Hence there are mainstream interactive works, and the key production roles are the same as or similar to those in non-interactive cinema. Given that fact, the arguments against single authorship developed earlier apply here too – indeed, the arguments of Section 3.8 were targeted on digital cinema in general, which includes interactive digital cinema. Since we are talking about mainstream cinematic works, in which more than one person

---

[75] One might wonder whether this point about the importance of the recording of performers is consistent with my claim that the interactive audience adopts the performance role. The answer is that some performances incorporate recordings of other performances: think of rap artists using pre-recorded segments of records, or consider synthesisers, which allow the performer by pressing a single control to trigger a steady beat or a sampled segment of melody. In the case of interactive cinematic works, the recordings triggered can include those of actors' vocal performances of sentences or sentential components, sequences of their motion-captured behaviour, and performances of musical pieces or motifs.

occupies the key production roles, we have to acknowledge the existence of multiple authors, whether they are animators, actors, musicians, and so on, for the reasons we examined earlier.

It might be objected that there is a disanalogy between the interactive and non-interactive cases that undermines this claim. The ontology of interactive cinema differs from non-interactive cinema: interactive works are constituted by a set of rules (and, in the case of computer works, algorithms) that take an initial state, combine it with user input and produce some new state; and one person can write a rule. Non-interactive cinematic works, in contrast, do not involve these kinds of rules (state-transition functions), but are constituted by a fixed structure of images, usually both visual and auditory.[76] So given its constitution by rules, could not a designer-programmer be the single author of an interactive work? The interactive case is like that of a play, where the playwright can produce a work as a single author, despite its performances being collaboratively produced and acted.

However, while the ontological difference between interactive and non-interactive cinema is real, it does not ground single-authorship claims. Though the existence of algorithms comprised of state-transition functions and their implementation in programming is essential for interactivity, it is also essential that both initial and output states occur, and in the case of cinema these are, by definition, moving images – user input transforms one moving image into another according to an algorithm. Interactive digital cinema requires capacities in addition to those of non-interactive digital cinema; but it still requires the capacities of the latter. If the recording of actors (including voice actors) is involved, then the argument of Section 3.6, concerning traditional mainstream films with recorded performances, applies here too: the relation of the actor to her role in such cases is partly a constitutive one, unlike the role of the actor in a play, where the actor's performance does not partly constitute the character as specified in the play, as opposed to the character-in-performance. So in such cases, whether interactive or not, the actor counts as one of the authors of the cinematic work. And if there are no actors, there are, since we are talking of mainstream cinema, at least two people in the other key production roles, such as animators, designers, musicians and so on. Their activities will partly determine artistically relevant properties; they will inevitably exercise discretion in their artistic choices if the film is a genuinely mainstream one; they possess artistic *personae*; and imagining their actions as if they were the

---

[76] See Jesper Juul, *Half-Real*, chapter 3, and Lopes, *A Philosophy of Computer Art*, chapter 4, for discussions of the role of rules and in particular algorithms in enabling computer interactivity.

products of a single constructed author would falsify the interpretation and evaluation of cinematic works. So the arguments against single authorship drawn from consideration of the failures of the restriction, sufficient control and construction strategies still apply to interactive cinema.

The second question we posed is whether the artistic control of the dominant collaborator, say, the designer, is greater in interactive than in traditional cinema. Again, the same points made about digital cinema in Section 3.8 also apply to the interactive case. In practice, artistic collaboration has increased, not diminished: for instance, *Grand Theft Auto IV* credits several hundred people who worked on the game, including producers, art directors, technical directors, writers, character artists, level designers, graphic designers, audio designers, programmers, animators, actors, motion capture directors, and so on. We could imagine a technological future in which software had advanced to the point where one person could fill all of these roles, so the question of degree of control is an empirical matter. Here again, though, we should note that the possibility of collaboration in performing what was traditionally the acting role has been enhanced, since the same technical possibilities are available in interactive as in non-interactive digital cinema.

However, there is a significant difference in degree of control between interactive and non-interactive cinema; but it is in respect of the *instantiations* of the work. By definition, interactive works authorise their audiences partly to determine their instances and their features. Different audience members will make different choices, so a considerable variety in instances of the work will result, in the same way that different players of conventional games such as chess produce very different playings of that game. In contrast, in non-interactive cinema instantiating the work is a matter merely of screening it, and screenings are not dependent on the audience and are, provided that they are technically competent, pretty much the same everywhere; moreover, the respects in which they vary (screen size, and so on) are not of significance to judging the work itself. And, as we noted, screenings do not incorporate interpretations. So the makers of a non-interactive film can exercise almost comprehensive control over the instantiations of their works, assuming technical competence in screenings; but the makers of an interactive work exercise very little control over how their works are instantiated, other than making those instantiations *possible* through their design of the work. We will see some of the implications that this has for interactive narration in Section 5.7. Moreover, since interactive works are not screened but performed, there can be performance interpretations of works; for instance, playings of some narratively rich videogames can incorporate interpretations of the games, with different playings bringing out different possibilities for plot and character traits. So makers of interactive cinema surrender control of work-instances to their audience in ways that the makers of non-interactive cinema do not, and this has artistic importance.

Finally, it has been argued that even non-interactive films have seen a shift of control to the audience due to the advent of interactive media. The film critic Terrence Rafferty, for instance, sees the interactivity of DVDs as a threat to the integrity of film, since, he holds, it shifts control away from the director to the viewer.[77] However, there is no threat here to the integrity of traditional films: the structure of the film is fixed and non-interactive, and the viewer is merely choosing how to access that structure. The *DVD* itself is interactive, since by choosing menu options the viewer can access different parts of the film and so partly determine the DVD's instances; but the *film* itself, which is incorporated in the DVD and for which the DVD is a kind of wrapper, is not interactive.[78] Indeed, anyone with a copy of a traditional film and her own projector or, even better, an editing table, has a similar control over the viewing of the film, though access is somewhat less efficient. Yet it does not follow that, because someone has access to such resources, the control of the filmmakers over traditional film is under threat. Rather, these viewing technologies are frequently employed simply to understand better what the filmmakers have done. This used to be common in well-resourced university film studies departments; and the Kuleshov group in 1922–23 had a copy of D. W. Griffith's film, *Intolerance* (1916), which they viewed so frequently, in order to understand how it was constructed, that they destroyed the print.

So the advent of interactive DVDs offers no in-principle difference to earlier conditions of film viewing. However, there is an important practical difference, since traditional films, projectors and editing desks are very expensive to buy, and very few viewers had access to them. In contrast, digital viewing technology and DVDs are cheap and widely available.[79] And

---

[77] Terrence Rafferty, 'Everybody Gets a Cut: DVDs Give Viewers Dozens of Choices – and that's the Problem'.

[78] Lopes in 'The Ontology of Interactive Art' argues for two types of interactivity – weak (of which DVD menus are an example) and strong (of which computer games are an example). But both DVDs and computer games are fully interactive on the definition given: a better way to handle the different cases is by distinguishing two objects in the case of a DVD of a non-interactive film: the interactive wrapper of the DVD menus and the incorporated non-interactive film to which the wrapper gives access.

[79] The favourable economics of interactive wrappers and the capacity to view films repeatedly are not unique to digital videos, since many of their features are available through analogue video tape: tapes are cheap and one can view them at different speeds, pause and go forwards or backwards, though access is somewhat less efficient, since there is no chapter structure. So my claims about the aesthetic possibilities opened up by the economics of repeated viewing and the interactivity of wrappers apply to analogue video too. I focus on the digital case, though, since this is the main comparator to traditional film throughout this book.

economics matters to what is in practice aesthetically possible. Because one can now view a film repeatedly and control its viewing order and speed, films can layer in enormously complex visual storytelling possibilities, which, if these films could not be seen repeatedly, would escape almost all viewers.

The prize exhibit here is *Memento* (2000), a film which employs a backward narrative structure in its colour segments, a forward narrative path in its black and white segments, and interleaves the two kinds of segments together in order to give the viewer imaginative experience of someone who no longer has a properly functioning short-term memory. The film is so complex in its narrative structure that even its director and writer, Christopher Nolan, has admitted that he does not always know of any one sequence what will next follow it. Moreover, crucial to resolving some important story issues is the ability to interpret very short clips of a fraction of second's duration that are scattered through the film and represent flashbacks of memory or of false memory. The central instances concern whether Sammy Jankis really did kill his wife or whether Leonard Shelby, the film's amnesiac protagonist, killed his own wife and is in the grip of a semi-willed false memory of Jankis' condition. Repeated viewings of the film are necessary to identify the relevant extremely short clips, some lasting less than a fraction of a second each, and also the ability to pause and inspect these images in order to answer such simple but crucial questions as those about whose hands are being depicted in some of the scenes involving Jankis (or Shelby) injecting his wife repeatedly with insulin and so killing her. In practical, communicative terms, this degree of intricate and abbreviated visual storytelling demands a viewer who can watch the film repeatedly and control its movements, at times, frame-by-frame. The changed economics of repeated viewing and the arrival of interactive wrappers have unlocked new aesthetic strategies in cinematic storytelling. So, though control is not lost to the audience in the case of non-interactive films, despite the interactive wrapper commonly employed to package them, the wrapper is still of aesthetic significance in permitting new aesthetic strategies in non-interactive films.

CHAPTER 4

Understanding cinema

Having discussed cinematic authorship, the question arises of how one is to understand films, the products of authorial actions. I begin by discussing the most influential theory of interpretation, intentionalism, and criticise it particularly in respect of its account of collaborative arts, such as cinema. In Section 4.2 I discuss one of the best and most influential theories of interpretation developed by a film theorist, David Bordwell, and show that his global constructivist account should be rejected, but argue that there is a limited role for construction in some films. In Section 4.3 I defend my own account of interpretation, the patchwork theory, in the context of cinema and illustrate it with a discussion of *Rashomon* (1950). Finally, in Section 4.4 I argue that intentions are likely to be subject to some different defeaters in digital as compared to traditional cinema, and show how interactivity makes possible a new kind of constructivism in cinema.

4.1 INTENTIONALISM

I will argue that intentionalism as a theory of interpretation of collaborative art forms, such as cinema, is false. I will also briefly argue that intentionalism fails as a theory of interpretation of art in general. But I will focus mainly on the collaborative case and show that collaborative art forms, compared to solo (non-collaborative) forms, present extra hazards that undermine the artist's intentions and provide extra grounds for unintended but meaningful features of works.

A collaborative artwork I will understand as one in which two or more artists interact to produce the work. Collaborative art forms are art forms in which the artworks are standardly collaborative. Film, as we have seen, is such an art form. Collaborative art forms present a threat to intentionalism, since on the face of it the intentions of collaborators can clash with each other, so some or all of them may be defeated and give rise to features that are unintended but meaningful. Multiple-author theorists who are intentionalists must confront this difficulty. But so too must single-author theorists, for these theorists do not deny that there are cases of co-authorship, as when two people co-direct a film, or share both the writing and directing duties. The most promising way to mitigate the threat of clashing intentions for the intentionalist is by developing a theory of collaborative art making as involving effective, joint intentions, and arguably the best version of such an account is embedded in Michael Bratman's analysis of shared co-operative activity.[1]

According to Bratman, a shared co-operative activity (SCA), such as singing a duet, has three main features. First, the agents must be committed to the joint activity: they must intend to perform it in accordance with and because of meshing sub-plans (plans which are co-realisable) that are not coerced and where this commitment is a matter of common knowledge between them. (This condition is sufficient for the agents to have a joint or shared intention.) Second, they are committed mutually to support each other, at least at a minimal level, provided it does not undermine their own contribution to the joint activity. And third, they are mutually responsive to each other's intentions and actions. Their joint activity is a SCA if and only if the first two commitments lead to the joint activity by way of mutual responsiveness. Though all these features must be present for an activity to be a SCA, the sub-plans may mesh only at one level, and not at another. For instance, two chess players' sub-plans mesh at the level of agreeing on following the rules of the game, but not at the level of agreeing who is to win; nevertheless, they are engaging in a SCA.[2]

Bratman's account provides a promising framework to understand how collaborators' intentions can interact in a collaborative art form such as film. But such an account does not support the truth of intentionalism; on the contrary, it provides the opponent of intentionalism with a framework with which to show how intentions can be defeated in collaborative art. The notion of a SCA covers activities that are relatively harmonious: even in the chess case the players are completely agreed on the rules of the game, though they are competing in it. Clearly, a film that is a SCA would be a harmonious shoot, with actors, cameraman, directors, producers, and so on, co-operating so as to realise their shared intentions in a way that involves

[1] Paisley Livingston, *Art and Intention*, pp. 75–89, calls attention to the importance of Bratman's account and applies it to develop an account of joint authorship in film, as noted in Section 3.5. However, though Livingston describes himself as an intentionalist, he is not, as we will see later, an intentionalist in the sense under discussion here.

[2] Michael Bratman, 'Shared Cooperative Activity'. I have slightly simplified Bratman's intricate analysis, but in a way that does not affect the present discussion.

mutual support and responsiveness. What happens, though, when this harmony starts to break down? I defined a collaborative artwork as one in which two or more artists interact to produce the artwork. That condition is captured by the third condition on a SCA, that the agents are mutually responsive. So failures could occur in respect of the first two conditions, and the artwork would still be collaborative. And Bratman's framework provides a useful way of categorising in what respects these failures may occur.

The commitment to the joint activity may be flawed in various ways. First, coercion of one form or another may occur. Bratman gives, as an example of coercion, my coercing you by pointing a gun to your head. The director Sam Peckinpah was famous for his love of guns and drunkenness, as well as being irascibly demanding: coercion was not too far away. More mundanely, censors placed constraints via the Production Code on film production through most of the history of classical Hollywood cinema. And producers and financiers have routinely seized control of films when they were deemed to be uncommercial. *The Magnificent Ambersons* (1942), directed by Orson Welles, was edited in his absence in a way that triggered his vehement but futile protests.

Second, and even more commonly, the sub-plans of the participants in films may fail to mesh, in that the participants have non co-realisable intentions. Recall the case, discussed in the previous chapter, of *Do the Right Thing* (1989), where Sal is a character who is surprisingly sympathetic, despite his complicity in a racial tragedy culminating in a horrifying murder. That character arose out of the non-meshing sub-plans of director Spike Lee and actor Danny Aiello. Likewise, the modulated character of Ellen Ripley in *Aliens* (1986) arose out of the non-meshing sub-plans of the director James Cameron and the actress Sigourney Weaver. And the conflicts of purpose between the screen writers Mayer and Janowitz, and the directors Lang and Wiene resulted in the addition of the framing-story to *The Cabinet of Dr Caligari* (1920), which radically altered the film's meaning.[3] Sub-plans can grind against each other, sometimes spectacularly.

Third, the common knowledge condition may fail: in the case of Aiello and Lee, neither seems to have realised that the other had a very different conception of Sal's character.

Finally, the second condition on a SCA, the mutual support condition, is frequently violated. Bratman describes the case of unhelpful singers singing

---

[3] Siegfried Kracauer, *From Caligari to Hitler*, pp. 61–76. For a discussion that relocates the conflict in light of new documentary evidence, without nullifying it, see David Robinson, *Das Cabinet des Dr. Caligari*.

a duet, who, though they do not try to undermine the other's actions, are not prepared to provide help when it could easily be provided. Given the intensely competitive nature of film careers, the tendency to 'abandon you to the wolves', as Bratman puts it, when things are not going well, is lamentably common.[4]

So collaborative art making may fail to be a SCA in at least four respects. And in these respects the intentionalist account of interpretation of collaborative art is under pressure: for one can no longer appeal to the intentions partly constitutive of a SCA to show how the intentions of several collaborators mutually co-exist to determine work meaning. Rather, in such cases intentions conflict and clash and produce unintended features of works that partly constitute the works' meanings.[5] So not all meaning properties of works are determined by the artists' intentions. And that, in a nutshell, is the claim that undermines intentionalism.

To examine this threat and consider how the intentionalist can respond to it, we need to get clearer about what intentionalism is and the general kinds of problems that afflict it. Intentionalism I will understand as the doctrine that some subset of the artist's (or artists') intentions wholly determine the meaning of an artwork. Actual intentionalism holds that it is the actual intentions of the artists that wholly determine the meaning of a work: some, but not all, actual intentionalists hold that these intentions must be successfully realised if they are to be meaning determining.[6] Hypothetical intentionalism holds that it is the hypothetical intentions of the artist that wholly determine the meaning of a work: hypothetical intentions are those that a relevant audience would be justified in ascribing to the artist.[7]

Intentionalism generically faces two kinds of challenge. First, it is a feature of our agency that our intentions sometimes misfire: we not infrequently fail to do what we intend to do. An artist may intend to produce some feature in his artwork, but fail, perhaps through lack of skill. These factors are the defeaters of intention. Second, it is also a common feature of our agency that our actions and their products have many features that

---

[4] For many gruesome examples, see John Badham and Craig Modderno, *I'll be in My Trailer.*

[5] A partial exception to this claim is in respect of coercion: if the coercer is one of the filmmakers, rather than an external agent, then the dominance and perhaps effectiveness of the coercer's intentions against the other collaborators may be enhanced, as in the case of the tyrannical director. However, if the coercer is not one of the filmmakers, as in the case of censors, it is more likely that a clash of intentions will result.

[6] E. D. Hirsch, *Validity in Interpretation*, is an instance of the former; Richard Wollheim, *Painting as an Art*, chapter 1, of the latter.

[7] See, for instance, Jerrold Levinson, 'Intention and Interpretation in Literature'; and Gregory Currie, *Image and Mind*, chapter 8.

are not intended. An artist may, for instance, not intend to produce a particular pattern of alliteration in her poem, even though that pattern is present and partly determines the meaning of her work. So there are sometimes happy accidents in respect of artistically meaningful properties. (An accident is happy by virtue of its producing an artistically meaningful property of the work: it may also be happy in respect of this feature being artistically valuable, but that is not a necessary feature of the term as I am employing it here.)

Conflicted collaborations can produce both kinds of features. Some or all of the collaborators' intentions will be defeated, when they are not co-realisable. Lee intended a straightforward denunciation of a racist character; Aiello intended a more sympathetic portrait of the character. Though Aiello is closer to achieving his aim on screen, Lee's denunciatory tone is still present in the film. Mayer and Janowitz intended in the original screenplay of *Caligari* vehemently to criticise social authority, as being in the hands of madmen; Lang and Wiene attempted, through their interpolation of the framing story, to show that it was the critics of social authority who were mad; and Janowitz passionately criticised the change. But the Expressionist décor, by virtue of continuing into the framing story, suggested something different – that there is a subtle questioning of authority in the film. For if authority were vindicated at the end of the film, how is it that the Expressionist sets, purportedly the expression of madness in the contained story, are still present? So in these cases intentions were defeated by the hazards of collaboration, the conflicts and lack of co-ordination that can occur in highly complex collaborative art making. Moreover, not only were intentions defeated, but also unintended and interpretatively important properties were instantiated in the films, i.e., there were happy accidents. The sympathetic portrait of a character that is yet inflected with criticism of him as a racist, the subtle questioning of social authority, and the particular modulations of Ripley's character are genuine, interpretatively relevant features of the films mentioned, yet were not intended individually by the agents nor were they the products of a shared intention embodied in a SCA.

As noted earlier, intentionalism fails as a theory of art in general, not just collaborative art. So it is worth briefly justifying this claim in terms of the two kinds of general challenge that intentionalism faces. First, there are many kinds of defeaters of intention. They can be classified into two types: general and specific. General defeaters apply to all art forms: these include lack of skill by artists, and their attempts to achieve what is simply too difficult or even impossible in their work. Specific defeaters apply only to some art forms (they may apply to more than one, but not to all). Specific defeaters for film include economic factors – filmmakers may be unable to achieve their aims because they lack the economic resources to do so, a factor that also applies to other expensive art forms, such as architecture, but not to low-budget art forms, such as poetry. Specific defeaters also include what we may call the *hazards of the real*: taking a photograph exposes one to whatever is in front of the camera, and this may not always accord with the filmmakers' intentions, as when a film about ancient Rome inadvertently shows railway tracks running in the background. As the American independent filmmaker Maya Deren noted, films are 'controlled accidents'.[8] And sometimes, we can add, the accidents overwhelm the control. The hazards of the real are shared with still photography, but are not a problem for painting, with its ability to produce an image that stands only in an intentional relation to its object. The hazards of collaboration are also a specific defeater of intention, since they do not apply to solo arts. Collaboration increases the ability of artists to achieve their ends in many respects, but also exposes them to the danger that those ends will be defeated through conflicts between the collaborators.

Second, many art forms can embody happy accidents. To take a much-discussed example in a solo art form, Henry James' novella *The Turn of the Screw* can be interpreted as a tale of sexual hysteria told by an unreliable narrator, the governess; but it can also be interpreted as a traditional ghost story. The former interpretation was not intended by James, the latter was; but the hysteria interpretation can be justified in terms of features of the text, since there is no independent corroboration of the governess' narrative claims and (in the real world) they could not be true. So the fact that the text grounds the hysteria interpretation is a happy accident. There are also examples in film where there are happy accidents not grounded on conflicts between collaborators. *Rashomon*, for instance, can be understood as a film about the relativity of truth. However, it was intended by Kurosawa as an account of moral degradation, as an illustration of the fact that everyone will lie in order to protect their own sense of self-worth. The degradation interpretation in fact fits the film better, but the relativity interpretation is a reasonable one; and as such it is a happy accident grounded on features of the film's narrative structure.[9]

---

[8] Maya Deren, 'Cinematography: The Creative Use of Reality'.
[9] See Parker Tyler, '*Rashomon* as Modern Art', for the relativity interpretation and Akira Kurosawa, *Something Like an Autobiography*, for the degradation interpretation. Section 4.3 provides a fuller discussion of this film.

Some reasons for happy accidents are, however, specific to particular art forms: for instance, happy accidents can be the outcome of conflicted collaboration: the subtle criticism of authority in *Caligari* and the nuanced exploration of racism in *Do the Right Thing* are examples, as we saw. Of course, sometimes conflicted collaboration leads merely to a mess, an unhappy accident, without instantiating any meaningful artistic properties – a situation that Livingston has likened to a traffic jam, in discussing a case modelled on *Waterworld* (1995).[10]

How might an intentionalist respond to these threats? Actual intentionalists hold that a work's meaning is determined wholly by the actual intentions that produced it; and some, like Hirsch, hold that this is so, whether or not the intentions were successfully realised. So on this view there can be no accidents, happy or unhappy: *The Turn of the Screw* and *Rashomon* each possess only the one, intended meaning.

However, that judgement does not accord in general with established critical practice and would in the case of many artworks, including the two under discussion, lead to works being judged to possess less artistic value than they otherwise would have. The actual intentionalist of this ilk is also committed to holding that, whilst intentions may be defeated, that is irrelevant to a work's meaning, since meaning is determined by the operative intentions, whether or not they are successfully realised. This claim should be rejected for art in general. It is true that I need to grasp the unsuccessful intentions that led to the production of a work in order to *explain* it. However, in order to *characterise* it, I need to know what features it actually possesses, not those that the artist was trying to give it. A sonnet is a sonnet by virtue of its formal structure; if the artist intended it to be a sonnet, but through ignorance or ineptitude did not achieve that structure, it is not a sonnet. Turning to collaborative art, the problem of defeated, because conflicting, intentions is particularly acute for the actual intentionalist, for if intentions conflict, *whose* intentions are supposed to determine meaning? None of the possibilities is enticing. Mayer and Janowitz intended a straightforward denunciation of authority: but *Caligari* certainly isn't that. Lang and Wiene intended a robust defence of authority: but the film isn't that either, because the Expressionist design is present in both contained and framing stories and so calls into question the authority of the framing story. Nor can one simply disjoin both sets of intentions and say that *Caligari* is either a straightforward denunciation or a robust defence of authority, since both disjuncts are false.

[10] Paisley Livingston, 'Cinematic Authorship'.

Some actual intentionalists, such as Wollheim, hold that meaning is wholly determined only by *successfully realised* intentions. However, that claim also disallows the possibility of happy accidents. And where, because of conflicts, none of the collaborators achieves her intended ends, the film would have to be judged as without artistic meaning. This may be true in some cases (the traffic jam cases), but in others, such as *Caligari*, intentions are defeated, yet the work is meaningful. Further, if one is concerned to *explain* how a film came about, then knowledge of intentions, even when not successfully realised, may be crucial, as in the case of *Caligari*.

Hypothetical intentionalism holds that it is the hypothetical intentions of the artist that wholly determine the meaning of a work. The doctrine comes in a variety of stripes; in the philosophy of film its most prominent defender is Gregory Currie, who terms his version of the view *Implied Author Intentionalism* (IAI). Currie argues that interpreting something is a matter of hypothesising about its intentional causes, and is thus a species of explanation.[11] For instance, interpreting a piece of behaviour is a matter of hypothesising about the mental states that caused it.[12] Interpreting works is a species of the interpretation of behaviour, since works are structured traces of complex behaviour. Currie focuses on narrative interpretation – working out what story a work tells; and he holds that such 'interpretation is explanation by reference to causally efficacious, story-telling intentions'.[13] In the case of literature, the evidence for the assignment of these intentions is the text, understood as a sequence of words and sentences with literal meanings. In the case of films, the evidence is the appearance meaning of a shot, roughly, what a shot appears to depict to someone who lacks knowledge of the rest of the film, cannot identify the actors in the film and knows nothing about its construction.[14] The interpreter of film narration asks herself: 'why is that shot, with just that appearance, inserted in the film just at this point, between these other shots? The answer will be: because the insertion of that shot was intended to tell us something about what is happening in the story'.[15]

The intentions thus assigned are not those of the actual author. That would be to hold Real Author Intentionalism (RAI), i.e., actual intentionalism, which Currie rejects. Instead, he supports IAI, a type of hypothetical intentionalism. This holds, in respect of narrative interpretation, that what story a work tells is given by what its implied author intended. Because the

---

[11] Currie, *Image and Mind*, p. 227.   [12] *Ibid.*, p. 235.   [13] *Ibid.*, p. 240.
[14] *Ibid.*, pp. 255–6.   [15] *Ibid.*, p. 256.

intentions of the implied author are inferred from the text, IAI appears to avoid the difficulties to which RAI succumbs, for the implied author cannot, it seems, fail to do what she intended to do, nor can there be features of the text that were unintended by her. So the account can ascribe hypothetical intentions whose content matches the meaning of films even where that meaning was actually unintended: for instance, on this view Sal's character is that of a sympathetic racist, because the implied author of the film so intended it.

There are three difficulties with this view. First, there is a problem for Currie in both rejecting RAI and maintaining his general account of interpretation. For he holds that interpretation in general is a species of causal explanation. But only *real* intentions, real mental states, can be causally efficacious in bringing about features of artworks. So what the general account of interpretation supports is RAI, not IAI – indeed, for the same reason the general account is actually incompatible with IAI, insofar as the intentions assigned to the implied author are not the author's real intentions. And Currie explicitly notes that the intentions we impute to the implied author may differ from those that we know actually produced a film or text – we may for instance properly disregard the evidence of actual intentions as shown in diaries and provided by acquaintances.[16] He says that this is so because authors may fail to enact their narrative intentions. And that is correct – but it is the intentions that were unsuccessfully acted on that are nevertheless the causally efficacious ones. Suppose I intend to hit a ball, yet miss; the explanation of my action is my acting on this intention, even though it was unsuccessful. The explanation of the action is not given by an intention to miss the ball while swinging the bat wildly, even though this is what I did. In like manner, we have already seen that the actual intentions that were not successfully realised figure in the explanation of films such as *Caligari*.

Currie has replied to this objection that interpretation is a matter of *either* actual causal explanation *or* imagined causal explanation. His account of art interpretation is not just intentionalist, but is also hypothetical and instrumentalist. We can ask ourselves what intentions *appear* to have caused an artwork or we can *imagine* these intentions producing an artwork: for instance, we can think of the heavy brushstrokes of an artwork as produced by an angry artist, even though we know the artist was calm at the time; this gives us a clue, he maintains, to what it is for a work to express anger. So there is a necessary conceptual connection between interpretation

---

[16] *Ibid.*, p. 246.

and attributing intentions, but these intentions need not be actual, but only imagined.[17]

However, this reply fails. Appeal to imagined intentions in the explanation of phenomena such as expression (the angry painting case) must be incomplete. For there must also be a real explanation for why the artwork has the brushstrokes that it does, otherwise the work would not have those features. So the argument, if successful, would prove that there is a necessary role for both actual and hypothetical intentions, and does not favour hypothetical over actual intentionalism. Moreover, the argument holds that interpretation is a matter of either actual causal explanation or imagined causal explanation, and motivates art interpretation as a species of the latter. But this disjunctive account loses the connection, which motivates the account, between interpreting actions and interpreting those of its products that are artworks. For the interpretation of action, in the sense of explaining it, involves appeal only to actual mental states. Consider, for instance, the belief–desire model of the explanation of actions, according to which actions are to be explained by appropriate belief–desire pairs. What matters for explanatory purposes is the actual beliefs and desires possessed by the agent. We could, taking an instrumentalist approach, *imagine* any number of different possible belief–desire pairs that could motivate an action, but they would all be irrelevant to its explanation, if they differed from the belief–desire pair that really motivated it.

There is a second difficulty for Currie, in addition to the tension between IAI and the general account of interpretation, for there are problems with IAI itself. These partly depend on how the thesis is formulated, about which there is some unclarity in Currie's presentation. At one point he states that 'the implied author intends *P* to be fictional means just that the text can reasonably be thought of as produced by someone intending the reader to recognize that *P* is fictional'.[18] It is natural to construe what can 'reasonably be thought' in epistemic terms, what we have reason to believe; on this construal, IAI is a thesis involving what we can term the *epistemic* implied author. So understood, the problem with the thesis is that it would be unreasonable to continue to think of the film as produced by one set of intentions when we know that the actual intentions which produced it were different. And, as we earlier noted, Currie does allow for what it is reasonable to think about intentions and what one knows about them to differ, since he thinks we should ignore evidence of actual intentions in some cases.

---

[17] Gregory Currie, 'Reply to My Critics', pp. 359–60.   [18] Currie, *Image and Mind*, p. 245.

So, on this construal of the implied author, we ought to abandon IAI and adopt RAI on epistemic grounds.

Currie at some points presents IAI as a thesis about the author who *seems* to have produced the text: the *apparent* implied author. 'We may explain the text, and explain it adequately, by reference to a personality that *seems* to have produced it'.[19] This is distinct from the epistemic notion, since something may appear a certain way, even though it is not reasonable to believe that it is that way: in a fairground mirror hall, a person may appear to be 20 foot tall, and 2 inches thick, but it is not reasonable to believe that she is. On this construal of the implied author, the problem of how a merely apparent artist could have causal powers surfaces. In addition, where an apparent artist can be invoked, what the actual artist intended will often be relevant as well, so IAI cannot be an adequate account. Consider an example Walton employs in his discussion of the notion of the apparent artist. The humour of Mozart's *A Musical Joke* depends partly on the fact that it appears to have been written by someone who is an egregiously incompetent composer.[20] Note, however, that what Mozart *actually* is doing, not just apparently doing, also matters: if he were actually competent, and merely pretending to be incompetent, then we would laugh *with* him: if it turned out that he were actually incompetent, but trying his hardest, then if we laughed, we would laugh *at* him.[21] So the notion of the apparent artist may figure in some interpretative contexts: but one may also have to appeal to the actual artist in order to give an adequate account of interpretation.[22]

Currie has also replied to the main thrust of this criticism in respect of the epistemic implied author, which is his favoured view of authorship. He holds that it can be reasonable to suppose that the work was produced by an intention, even when one knows, perhaps from looking at her diary, that its author really had a different intention. The reason for this is that he is

[19] *Ibid.*

[20] Kendall Walton, 'Style and the Products and Processes of Art'.

[21] In *ibid.*, pp. 95–6, Walton in fact understands a *Musical Joke* so that at a superficial level of appearances its composer is incompetent, whereas at a deeper level of appearances he is competent, and thus there may seem no need to appeal to actual features of the composer to ground the distinction between kinds of humorous response. However, imagine we discovered that, despite this deeper level of appearances, Mozart really were an incompetent composer, then we would still, if we laughed, laugh at him. So what the artist is really like can still matter to interpretation. (The supporter of the apparent artist account might reply that all this shows is that at a third, even deeper, level of appearances the composer of the piece is incompetent: but it should be clear by this point that appearances are being invented so as to conform to reality.)

[22] Currie, *Image and Mind*, also discusses the implied author as 'a figure who may in a sense be fictional or imagined', p. 262. IAI construed in terms of a *fictional* implied author would succumb to the same problems as does IAI construed in terms of an apparent implied author – namely, the absence of this author's causal powers and the relevance of actual intentions to interpretation.

a relativist about interpretation: what it is reasonable to believe is relative to the evidence, and what counts as relevant evidence is dependent on one's standpoint. He offers the following consideration (call it the *pre-eminence argument*) for why it is reasonable to exclude some evidence, such as a diary, as irrelevant to interpretation:

the diary entry might give you a view of the author's intention quite different from and contradictory to that you would get from reading the text and knowing nothing about the diary. But if the diary is to overrule the text, then the next [*sic*] has lost its rightly pre-eminent place, and becomes just one more bit of evidence for authorial intention. And we should not treat the next [*sic*] of the work as *just more evidence of an interpretation*.[23]

However, relativism is false of the interpretation of action, Currie's paradigm object of interpretation: the correct interpretation of the content of one's motives is not dependent on the evidential standpoint of one's interpreter, nor therefore relative to it. So, again, the general paradigm of interpretation offered is inconsistent with the hypothetical intentionalism defended for art. Moreover, we can present Currie's view with a dilemma. Suppose, on the one hand, that all evidence is counted as relevant. Then the interpretation generated by hypothetical intentionalism is co-extensive with that generated by actual intentionalism: so, if actual intentionalism is inadequate, as Currie maintains, then so is hypothetical intentionalism. Suppose, on the other hand, that not all evidence is counted as relevant. Then we require a rationale for excluding some evidence as irrelevant. This is something that the pre-eminence argument fails to do. For it is mistaken to suppose that if the evidence of authorial intention in the diary overrules the evidence obtained from consulting the text, then the text becomes *merely* evidence for an interpretation. The art text, crucially, is the *object* of interpretation and not just the *source* of evidence for interpretation. Consulting other texts for evidence of authorial intention does not threaten the art text's status as the object of interpretation. Worse, if the motivation for hypothetical intentionalism is that interpretation is explanation by intentions, then there can be no rationale for excluding some evidence as irrelevant, for what matters on the explanatory account is the *existence* of the intentions that figure in the explanation, not the *evidential sources* we use to learn about them. And any evidence might potentially be relevant to establishing the existence of intentions.

[23] Currie, 'Reply to My Critics', pp. 360–1.

The third and final objection is that hypothetical intentionalism does not, despite its claims, solve either of the two general problems for intentionalism that we noted earlier. For the first general problem, that of unsuccessful intentions, the analogue problem for hypothetical intentionalism is that we are justified in ascribing an intention to an artist, even though he failed to realise it in the work. Such a case is easy to imagine: the artist expresses frustration at his failure, either in the work or in some public forum. We are justified in thinking that he failed to do what he intended to do, so the work does not have the meaning fixed by the content of his intentions. For the second general problem, that of unintended meanings, the analogue for hypothetical intentionalism is that we are justified in ascribing to the artist no intention to produce a certain feature of the work, even though the work has that feature. The justification for the ascription might be public evidence: Henry James might, for instance, have announced in the Preface to *The Turn of the Screw*, rather than in his private notebooks, that he intended the novella to be a straightforward ghost story; and Kurosawa might have announced on the film poster for *Rashomon* that it was about the lies we tell to maintain our self-respect. So hypothetical intentionalism lays itself open to exactly the same structural problems as does actual intentionalism. Despite the elaborate conceptual manoeuvring, it has still failed to escape the basic problems facing all kinds of intentionalism.[24]

So the two most influential types of intentionalism fail as accounts of interpretation, and in particular of the interpretation of collaborative art forms.[25] Collaborative art forms add, through the potential clash of intentions of different collaborators, to the defeaters of intentions and augment the possibility of happy accidents.

4.2 CONSTRUCTIVISM

A very different theory of interpretation has been advanced by David Bordwell and Kristin Thompson. In a series of books and articles they

---

[24] For the general form of this objection, see Robert Stecker, 'Interpretation', p. 331.

[25] One version of intentionalism, partial intentionalism, may look like an attractive option, since it is weaker than the kinds of intentionalism considered so far. It holds that intentions are one factor that figure in determining a work's overall meaning, but that there are other relevant factors, such as features of the text and context. So it can agree that there are unintended meanings and that some intentions fail (see Livingston, *Art and Intention*, p. 142). However, it is not a kind of intentionalism according to the definition offered here, since intentions are only one factor in determining the overall correct interpretation. Moreover, it holds that there are different kinds of meaning, and that for some kinds, such as implicit meanings, intentions figure as a necessary condition (*ibid.*, p. 150), whereas for others they do not. So it is in my terms a kind of patchwork theory and is an example of the sort of theory I defend (see Section 4.3), though the specifics of my account differ from Livingston's.

have developed a systematic and detailed theory, neoformalism, which is a kind of constructivism, arguing that viewers and critics construct the meanings of films. The theory has important implications for the criticism and interpretation of films. After an extensive investigation of current interpretive practices, Bordwell comes to the startling conclusion that 'contemporary interpretation-centred criticism tends to be conservative and coarse-grained ... it has become boring', and calls for fundamental changes in the way that it is practised.[26]

Neoformalism, as its name suggests, is an offspring of formalism, but in Bordwell and Thompson's hands, the notion of form is an elastic one. They reject the form/content distinction, so that questions of meaning and interpretation become inextricable from those of form.[27] In his understanding of neoformalism as a branch of 'historical poetics', Bordwell also stresses that form must be understood in its historical context.[28] But perhaps the most striking departure from traditional formalism is the constructivist claim that crucial features of a work, including its meaning, are partly constructed by its spectators, who are prompted to perform their task by the systems of cues in the work:

the neoformalist critic will not treat its [the film's] devices as fixed and self-contained structures that exist independently of our perception of them ... all those qualities that are of interest to the analyst – its unity; its repetitions and variations; its representation of action, space, and time; its meanings – result from the interaction between the work's formal structures and the mental operations we perform in response to them.[29]

Hence Bordwell and Thompson are committed to constructivism about meanings: 'films "have" meaning only because we attribute meanings to them' and 'Meanings are not found but made'.[30]

As Bordwell notes, the metaphor of construction has its place in opposition to a view of interpretation, according to which 'The artwork or text is taken to be a container into which the artist has stuffed meanings for the perceiver to pull out. Alternatively, an archaeological analogy treats the text as having strata, with layers or deposits of meaning that must be excavated'.[31] Call the view that the meaning of a film is

---

[26] David Bordwell, *Making Meaning*, p. 261.
[27] David Bordwell and Kristin Thompson, *Film Art*, pp. 40–1 and 48.
[28] David Bordwell, 'Historical Poetics of Cinema', especially section 3.
[29] Kristin Thompson, *Breaking the Glass Armor*, pp. 25–6.
[30] The first quotation is from Bordwell and Thompson, *Film Art*, p. 49; the second is from Bordwell, *Making Meaning*, p. 3.
[31] Bordwell, *Making Meaning*, p. 2.

there to be found, i.e., that it is determined independently of the viewer's opinion about it, the *detectivist* view of interpretation. Detectivist views take a wide variety of forms. Intentionalists count as detectivists, since they believe that the meaning of a film is determined independently of what the viewers think about it, for they believe that its meaning is fixed by some sub-set of the filmmakers' intentions. However, (classical) formalists are also detectivists, since, in arguing for the autonomy of the artefact, and against the so-called 'intentional' and 'affective' fallacies, they hold that the meaning of a work is determined by its intrinsic, formal features, and not by its audience. Similarly, the view that interpretation is a matter of grasping what filmmakers did (whether or not they intended to do it) is also detectivist. So anti-constructivists need not be intentionalists, but may occupy a wide swathe of positions about interpretation. Bordwell explicitly rejects two detectivist models of interpretation: the communication model, which understands interpretation in terms of sender, message, and receiver, so that the problem of the interpreter becomes grasping what message the sender transmitted; and the signification, or semiotic model, in terms of which the interpreter's task becomes the decoding of a previously encoded message.[32]

The notion of construction, on the other hand, is based not on a metaphor of opening-up or digging-down, but on the idea of interpretation-as-building: 'An interpretation is built upward, as it were, gaining solidity and scale as other textual materials and appropriate supports ... are introduced'.[33] But, clearly, this does not yet distinguish the doctrine from detectivism, since the detectivist could happily acknowledge the building metaphor, but claim that the building must be constructed according to the plans provided by the architect, or by some other source which is independent of the builder (e.g., by the intrinsic properties of the film). So the real source of the appropriateness of the metaphor is the thought that the builder has some degree of latitude or discretion in how he constructs his building: he need not slavishly follow some external source of authority in his activities.

Constructivism is a popular and influential doctrine in literary theory, where Stanley Fish is a leading proponent of the doctrine. E. H. Gombrich also endorses a version of constructivism, albeit weaker than the one that Fish countenances, in his theory of 'the beholder's share' in the interpretation of

---

[32] *Ibid.*, p. 270; see also Thompson, *Breaking the Glass Armor*, p. 13.
[33] Bordwell, *Making Meaning*, p. 13.

pictures.[34] Given the existence of constructivist theories of other arts, then, a constructivist theory of film may appear a promising prospect.

Bordwell construes 'meaning' in a commendably broad sense, distinguishing four types of meaning. The referential meaning of a film concerns the film's *diegesis*, that is, the world represented by it, so the spatio-temporal details of the represented world are part of a work's referential meaning. The *fabula*, or story, of a film is also an aspect of this kind of meaning. The explicit meaning of a film covers its stated 'moral', such as the announced meaning 'There's no place like home' at the end of *The Wizard of Oz* (1939). These two sorts of meaning are the objects of what Bordwell calls 'comprehension'. The objects of interpretation proper are implicit and symptomatic meanings. The former are meanings that are the objects of explicatory or thematic criticism, and are suggested or implied by the film, without being explicitly stated. Symptomatic meanings are repressed meanings, which reveal the film's ideology and which the film evinces 'involuntarily'.[35]

Though there are problems with this exact typology of meanings (particularly with the category of repressed meaning, which threatens to endow films with consciousness), the question of whether the divisions Bordwell countenances are accurate does not matter for present purposes, since he upholds a constructivist theory about all these sorts of meaning, so he need not defend any sharp boundaries between them. The key point is that his notion of meaning is extremely comprehensive, and that constructivism applies to all types of meaning. Hence both *Narration in the Fiction Film*, which deals with comprehension, and *Making Meaning*, which analyses interpretation, are relevant to the issue of constructivism.

Bordwell's most general claim about how meaning is constructed is that it is made by *mapping* sets of concepts onto cues in films, employing one's background knowledge about films and the world.[36] The background knowledge is given by schemata, which are 'organised clusters of knowledge [which] guide our hypothesis making'.[37] Many of these schemata are applied using our knowledge of film norms.[38] As Bordwell notes, this theory about the application of concepts to sensations is quite general, holding for our perception of the external world, besides applying to our perception of art.[39]

[34] Stanley Fish, *Is There a Text in This Class?*. E. H. Gombrich, *Art and Illusion*, part III. Bordwell appeals frequently to Gombrich's work: see, for instance, David Bordwell, Janet Staiger and Kristin Thompson, *The Classical Hollywood Cinema*, p. 7.
[35] Bordwell, *Making Meaning*, pp. 8–9, and Bordwell and Thompson, *Film Art*, pp. 40–3.
[36] Bordwell, *Making Meaning*, p. 129.   [37] Bordwell, *Narration in the Fiction Film*, p. 31.
[38] *Ibid.*, chapter 8.   [39] *Ibid.*, pp. 30–2.

The doctrine can be briefly illustrated with respect to cinematic space, narration and interpretation.

When we look at a film, what we are really seeing is a surface with intermittent 2D stationary pictures flashed onto it, and for half of the time we are in darkness. Yet what we experience are moving pictures in a continuously lit room. Moreover, on the basis of these 2D pictures we, in some sense, "see" characters moving in a 3D space. So the viewer constructs a rich 3D world on the basis of exiguous cues. Much of this construction is automatic ('bottom-up'), as in the perception of continuous light and movement. Depth cues, such as perspective, the overlapping of objects, texture differences between objects in the foreground and those in the background, and movement parallax prompt the viewer to construct a 3D space out of the 2D image. Such images are inherently ambiguous, for there are a vast number of arrangements of objects which would produce the same 2D image: 'Instead of a costumed man, [there could be] a scatter of garments flung up and frozen, with a huge head miles off that happens to coincide, on our view, with the top edge of a collar'.[40] The viewer has to use her knowledge of likely object configurations to disambiguate the image: what she sees goes far beyond what she is given. She also constructs offscreen space, and intershot space, neither of which is shown by the camera, by means of cues provided in the images, using the schemata that she possesses.[41]

The viewer also constructs the *fabula* (story) of the film out of the *suzhet* (plot), which the film directly provides. The *suzhet* consists of the events that are shown in the film in the order in which they are shown; the *fabula* is the complete set of relevant events, arranged in chronological order as causes and effects. The viewer's aim is to construct the *fabula* with all the relevant events in the correct order, since the *suzhet* will generally omit significant events, creating gaps, and will show actions out of chronological order. In the detective film, for instance, we are shown the criminal investigation before we learn the full details of the crime (who did it), which in the fictional world came first. Thus the *suzhet* temporal order is different from the *fabula* order. The viewer constructs the *fabula* by employing narrative schemata of many sorts. These include prototype schemata (which allow us to recognise people, places, etc.), template schemata (such as the schema which expresses the canonic story format), procedural schemata (which concern the reasons for the presence of elements in the film, such as the characterisation of what counts as realistic) and stylistic schemata (which we

---

[40] *Ibid.*, p. 102.   [41] *Ibid.*, chapter 7.

need in order to grasp, for instance, that a shot of a person looking, followed by a shot of an object, is to be understood as the person looking at the object).[42] These schemata are themselves governed by historically variable norms. What counts as realistic differs between the classical Hollywood cinema and art-cinema, and the spectator must know the appropriate norm for the film in order to understand it properly.[43] In short, in narrative construction the viewer goes massively beyond what is given, by using her background knowledge to construct a story out of exiguous cues.

Whereas space and narration are objects of comprehension, my final illustration of constructivism concerns interpretation in Bordwell's sense. The basic theory of concepts being applied to cues using background knowledge is the same, though Bordwell refines and elaborates the terminology of the theory. He terms conceptual structures 'semantic fields', and characterises the difference between explicatory and symptomatic critics in terms of the fields they employ: the former tend to appeal to concepts such as suffering, identity and alienation, the latter to concepts concerning sexuality, politics and signification.[44] Relevant cues are identified by two criteria (assumptions) – that they be effective in viewers' responses to films, and that the tradition of interpretation recognises them as capable of bearing meanings. The interpreter also uses two hypotheses – that the film should cohere into a whole and that it bear some relation to the external world – and uses heuristics, such as punning, and appealing to reflexivity. Finally, various schemata are employed to structure these interpretations.[45]

Bordwell stresses that all of these processes are guided by norms that are part of the institution of criticism: 'The critical institution … defines the grounds and bounds of interpretive activity, the direction of analogical thinking, the proper goals, the permissible solutions, and the authority that can validate the interpretations produced by ordinary criticism'.[46] The plurality of meanings that is traditionally ascribed to films is, in fact, a product of institutional practices – both of the plurality of different interpretive schools (though Bordwell argues that they share far more in common than is normally supposed), and of the looseness and variety of the interpretive procedures themselves (such as the punning heuristic, which allows an almost endless proliferation of meanings). Here, then, we seem to have a paradigm case of construction: not films, but interpretive practices are the source of the pluralism of meanings: 'If we all agreed to limit our procedures, *Psycho* or *Rules of the Game* or *Last Year at Marienbad* might

---

[42] *Ibid.*, chapters 3 and 4.   [43] *Ibid.*, pp. 153–4.
[44] Bordwell, *Making Meaning*, pp. 107–9.   [45] *Ibid.*, chapter 6.   [46] *Ibid.*, p. 33.

seem as univocal as a shopping list or a telephone book'.[47] Bordwell is certainly critical of much of the output of 'Interpretation, Inc', but insofar as he is a constructivist about interpretation, his proposed reforms in the practice of interpretation would simply encourage the replacement of the semantic fields characteristic of current criticism with more historically sensitive, nuanced and precise semantic fields.[48] While the semantic fields would change, the basic constructivist mechanism of mapping fields onto cues guided by institutional norms would remain.[49]

It should now be apparent how wide-ranging and impressive are the considerations Bordwell provides for the view that meanings are made, not found. However, we need to distinguish four different notions of construction that can be extracted from Bordwell's arguments, and to consider whether any of these notions prove that the audience makes the meanings of films.

Bordwell's most general claim is that in experiencing films we map concepts onto cues using our background knowledge. Call this idea of concept-application guided by background knowledge 'conceptual construction'. As Bordwell is well aware, conceptual construction is an entirely general phenomenon, applying as well to our experience of the external world.[50] 'Constructivist' psychology stresses that perception is an active process, involving the application of concepts to sensory stimuli, employing preconscious inferences. It is opposed to the doctrine of sensationalism, which holds that perception involves passively experiencing a set of sensations, produced in the mind by external objects. Bordwell talks of making as a process of mapping, and appeals to constructivist psychology as a model for his constructivist theory about aesthetics.[51] But does conceptual construction, argued for by constructivist psychology, really give any reason to suppose that meaning is made by a work's audience?

The constructivist theory of perception shows that *perception* is an active process, involving judgements that go beyond what is immediately given (sensory stimuli), but it does not in the least show that the *objects* of perception are constructs. For if constructivist psychology showed that the objects of perception were constructs, then its application to external objects would yield idealism, the theory that the external world is merely a mental construct. But one need not be committed to idealism simply because one

---

[47] *Ibid.*, p. 245.   [48] *Ibid.*, p. 266.

[49] As we shall see shortly, however, Bordwell's positive proposals for reforming the methodology of interpretation stand in a complex relation with his desire to show that meanings are made.

[50] Bordwell, *Narration in the Fiction Film*, pp. 30–2.   [51] *Ibid.*, p. 32.

embraces a constructivist account of perception: indeed, despite the importance of such theories in both psychology and philosophy, idealism is not rampant in academia. One can be a staunch realist about the external world, but a constructivist about the mind's activities, as is the philosopher Karl Popper. Failure to see that this position is coherent would simply be to conflate the activity of perception with the objects of perception.

Turning to works of art, it is clear that the most committed detectivist can acknowledge without inconsistency that our experience of works of art is to be understood in terms of an active process of concept-application using background knowledge. Thus intentionalists can allow that in order to grasp the filmmaker's intentions (or filmmakers' intentions if they believe in multiple authorship), we must actively engage in hypothesis making about what he intended to achieve, using our background knowledge of his other films, of generic practices at the time, and so on, to make the best estimate we can of what he intended to say in the film. But they hold that the audience nevertheless *finds out* about the meaning of the film, for meaning is determined independently of them, by what the filmmaker aimed to convey in his film. Finding, in short, is often an active *process*, but that does not mean that the *objects* of one's search are constructs.[52] The detective is the paradigm of an active, concept-applying, hypothesis-making seeker after truth, but what he is looking for – who committed the crime – is not constructed by the search process.

Indeed, if the mark of an object being a construct were that one applied concepts to the object using one's background knowledge, then the neo-formalist would have to conclude that even the cues, which are supposed to be objectively there, are themselves constructs, since we identify them by the process of applying concepts using background knowledge. Thus neoformalism would be self-refuting, for there would be no aspect of the artwork which was not a construct.

Finally, appealing to the role of norms in governing some of our schemata does not show that the objects of our knowledge are constructs. For, again, applied to the external world, the argument is fallacious. Scientists and detectives work within institutions, governed by norms for the proper conduct of investigations, but that goes no way to demonstrating that micro-particles or criminals are constructs. So the existence of conceptual construction in respect of perception and the mind's activities in general provides no grounds for concluding that the objects of perception or meanings are constructs.

[52] For related criticisms, see Allan Casebier, *Film and Phenomenology*, especially pp. 99–105.

There is a second sense of 'construction' that can be extracted from Bordwell's examples, and this seems to offer a more promising route to showing that meanings are made by a work's audience. It centres on the claim that artworks are 'incomplete' and that viewers must 'flesh out' the work.[53] Consider the construction of space. Bordwell's discussion covers two distinct sorts of processes. Our perception of apparent motion, and the fact that we seem to see the projector producing a continuous stream of light, are cases of genuine perceptual illusions: we cannot see the pictures as stationary, and we believe (unless we are informed about cinematic mechanisms) that the pictures are really moving. Talk of 'constructing' apparent motion and continuous light means that we are subject to perceptual and, for many viewers, cognitive illusions, as we argued in Section 2.3.2. But this sense of 'construction' will not serve for a general theory of cinematic constructivism, since we are not prone to all the relevant perceptual illusions in watching a film. For instance, we do not have a perceptual illusion of directly (face-to-face) seeing 3D objects when watching a film: we can easily perceptually discriminate between looking at a film and looking at what it is a film of.

In what sense, then, do we "see" 3D objects when watching a film?[54] The answer is that imagination enters into our perceptual activities; and we will discuss in detail how this happens in Chapter 5. Let us agree for the time being that we *visually imagine* 3D objects, even though we know that we are looking at 2D images. In respect of onscreen space, the viewer 'constructs' space by *visually imagining* what she knows that she is not actually seeing. In the case of offscreen space we are to *imagine* that (say) a room continues offscreen, though we are not required visually to imagine it, for it lies beyond the area which we are shown (so here the imagining can be imagining *simpliciter*, without any visual or other sensory mode of presentation). So, in general, the sense in which space is constructed is that the viewer *imagines*, visually or *simpliciter*, what she knows she is not actually seeing. The constructive aspect enters because the viewer imagines something more or other than what she is actually seeing. Moreover, this imagining is something that the viewer is *supposed* to do: if she does not imagine a 3D space, then she is not responding to the film as she ought. So the film viewer *ought* to imagine things (visually or *simpliciter*) that she is

---

[53] Bordwell, *Narration in the Fiction Film*, p. 32.

[54] The transparency theorist holds that we are really indirectly seeing recorded objects when we look at the screen, but I argued against transparency in Section 2.4. The transparency theorist also of course denies that we are really seeing *fictional* objects, so he will have to allow a role for imagination in these cases.

not actually seeing when looking at the screen.[55] Call this second sense of construction 'normative construction'.

Normative construction is a widespread phenomenon in films. Cinema provides us with images of actors, but one is to imagine the fictional characters that they play: one is to imagine not Bela Lugosi, but Dracula. When Lugosi places his mouth on an actress' neck, and red paint runs down, one is to imagine Dracula biting into his victim's throat and blood gushing out. Thus we are visually to imagine 3D characters performing actions, whereas what we are really seeing are 2D images of actors performing often quite different actions. We construct not only space, but also the fictionality of the events *per se*.

The notion of normative construction also captures Bordwell's account of constructing the *fabula*. Gaps in the *suzhet* are filled by imagining that events occur, which we do not see, as when we imagine that a woman has climbed a set of stairs, even though we only see images of the beginning and of the end of her ascent. Adjustment of temporal order from *suzhet* to *fabula* can similarly be captured by the notion of normative construction: when we see the commission of the crime in a flashback at the end of a detective film, we imagine the crime occurring before the other events shown in the film, even though the images of the crime are shown after the images of its solution. It is clear, moreover, that in these cases even the *suzhet* is a construct, since it involves fictional events, which themselves are merely imaginary entities.

Does this notion of normative construction show that viewers make, rather than find, the meaning of films? Certainly, film spectators ought to imagine things that they do not actually see on the screen: but it does not follow that the *spectators* determine what they ought to imagine. Recall the photograph of the costumed man, which could, consistently with what is shown, be interpreted as a photograph of a scatter of garments flung up, with a huge head miles off. If spectators chose to see it in the latter fashion, they would simply be wrong: how they *ought* to understand the photograph is determined in this case by facts about the object, light from which entered the camera at the time the photograph was taken. That is something that is in no way dependent on the audience. But the question of whether meaning is made by the audience is a question about whether they play any role in determining what they *ought* to imagine. The mere fact that they imagine

---

[55] Rather than using the idea of visual imagining, the second sense of 'construction' could be formulated using the idea of imagining seeing; but there are good reasons to reject the claim that audiences imagine seeing cinematic fictions, as I will argue in Chapter 5.

something other than what they see does not show that what they ought to imagine is (partly) up to them.

The case of a photograph is, of course, a simple one, and what we ought to imagine will in general be determined by other factors: in the case of filling gaps in the *suzhet*, for instance, it will generally be determined by what would have happened in the real world during the time we are not shown (when, for instance, the woman climbs the stairs). Different theorists have different views about how what we ought to imagine is determined. Intentionalists hold that what ought to be imagined is determined by the filmmakers' intentions. In general, communication-theorists believe that what the audience ought to imagine is determined by the 'sender' of the message, whilst semioticians maintain that it is determined by the 'code' of the film. So these theorists should concede that imagining more than is shown plays a central role in understanding film and representations in general; but this does not in the least undermine their own favoured theories, showing that audiences make meaning. Bordwell's examples merely prove that film spectators ought to imagine things that they know they do not see. But they do not show that spectators play a role in determining what ought to be imagined – they do not prove that the audience makes the meaning of films. Normative construction is therefore compatible with the claim that the audience is *directed* to imagine what it does, and, indeed, we have seen that Bordwell's examples discussed above are cases of directed construction. Hence, though there are many instances of normative construction in films, its existence does not prove that the audience makes the meaning of films.

Bordwell's claims about the nature of interpretation seem to support a version of constructivism stronger than any considered so far. He believes that the norms governing interpretation are shaped and constrained by the institutions of criticism. Call such institutions 'critical schools'. Critics within such schools map semantic fields onto films by using schemata, heuristics, assumptions and hypotheses. Call any critical school that uses some set of the semantic fields, and so forth, that Bordwell lists, a 'qualified critical school'. Then a third kind of constructivism – critical school constructivism – can be defined as the doctrine that if members of a qualified critical school, acting within the norms of that school, interpret a film as having a certain meaning, then the film has that meaning. Bordwell never explicitly formulates this doctrine, but much of what he says in *Making Meaning* about the importance of institutional norms in shaping interpretations suggests that he may endorse it. Unlike the two versions of constructivism just discussed, it is a version that really does entail that meanings are made, not found. For the (explicatory and symptomatic) meanings of films would be determined by the critics operating within qualified schools, and films could gain new meanings simply by new qualified schools coming into existence. And if critics within qualified schools changed their minds about what films meant, then the films would have different meanings.

A strong version of such a doctrine is endorsed in literary theory by Stanley Fish. Fish holds that, for texts considered independently of an interpretive context, 'there are no determinate meanings and that the stability of the text is an illusion'.[56] For 'it is interpretive communities, rather than either the text or the reader, that produce meanings and are responsible for the emergence of formal features'.[57] In claiming 'formal features ... are the *product* of the interpretive principles for which they are supposedly the evidence',[58] Fish goes beyond neoformalism, which holds that there are systems of intrinsic cues in films existing independently of interpretive communities. But the positions do not differ as radically as might at first appear, since the critical school constructivist holds that what cues count as relevant partly depends on traditions of interpretation.[59]

Critical school constructivism, then, entails that meanings are not found, but made. But is the doctrine true? The main problem is that the constraints on interpretation acknowledged by the theory are either too weak or are inappropriate. For instance, the theory holds that cues are relevant to interpretation if they fulfil two conditions: they are effective in spectators' responses (that is, spectators notice them as significant – this is an output of comprehension) and there is a tradition for countenancing them as suitable for interpretation.[60] But these constraints are too weak, for we can imagine a tradition of interpretation gradually evolving over time, so that any feature of the film at all, however irrelevant (such as the reel-change marks, which Bordwell mentions), would come to be held to be of interpretive significance. The requirement that such cues be effective in spectators' responses would not provide an independent brake on such a process, since spectators over the long-run are influenced by what critics say (think of how the *auteur* theory has come to be widely accepted amongst film enthusiasts). Other weapons in the interpretive armoury, such as the punning heuristic, are simply untenable in many cases. Bordwell mentions a critic who uses the chequered patterns on a tablecloth and on a female character's dress in *Ordet*

[56] Fish, *Is There a Text in This Class?*, p. 312. [57] *Ibid.*, p. 14. [58] *Ibid.*, p. 12.

[59] Bordwell, *Making Meaning*, pp. 132–3. There are, however, some other explicit points of disagreement between Bordwell and Fish. For instance, Bordwell argues against Fish's view that all interpreters use a theory in their critical practice (*Making Meaning*, p. 5).

[60] *Ibid.*, pp. 132–3.

(1954) to argue that the character is held 'in check', i.e., is repressed.[61] But *Ordet* is a *Danish* film, and therefore the visual-linguistic pun does not work in the language of the film.

In many cases, the norms that are correctly applied in interpretation are not the norms of the critical institution, but the norms that govern the film in its historical context (including the tradition of filmmaking of which it is a part). Recall an example discussed in Section 1.2. In films made in the West low-angle shots of a character are often 'power shots', connoting the power or threat of a dominant character, as in the shots of the eponymous hero of *Citizen Kane* (1941). Were a critic, using the norms of his school, to interpret the low-angle shots in *Rashomon* as typically expressing a similar view of the characters, he would be wrong. Here the low-angle shots are merely instances of the *tatami* shot, a shot taken as if from a seated position on a mat, the traditional mode of seating in Japanese society, and they have no special expressive force. Here the norms relevant to the interpretation of the film are those of Japanese society and filmmaking, not of the critical institution. Critical school constructivism is a false theory of interpretation.

However, the criticisms I have made of this doctrine are of a piece with the positive proposals Bordwell makes in the last chapter of *Making Meaning* for reforming the practice of film criticism. Bordwell wishes to reinstate a historical dimension to film interpretation, by understanding norms in their historical context, and wants to describe and explain how films are put together, and how they function. In particular, he wants critics to provide 'explanations, of an intentionalist, functionalist, or causal sort'.[62] But intentionalist explanations, for instance, are precisely ones that show that the audience does *not* make the meanings of films, since these meanings are fixed by the filmmakers' intentions.

From his remarks at the end of the book, then, Bordwell may not wish to support critical school constructivism. On this view, his remarks about interpretation are merely about how critics as a matter of fact proceed (compare his statement about his ethnographical approach[63]), and how they *ought* to proceed is given by his own positive proposals. But, if this is so, then the constructivist theory he advances is not a theory of meaning at all: it is a theory about how critics, as a matter of fact, form *judgements* about the meaning of films, and these judgements are often false. A detectivist could agree that critics often ascribe to films, by the mechanisms Bordwell explains, meanings that films do not possess (as the detectivist would put it, critics sometimes 'make up' meanings that films do not have). But,

---

[61] *Ibid.*, p. 139.   [62] *Ibid.*, p. 269.   [63] *Ibid.*, p. xii.

nevertheless, the meanings that films do have are there to be found. Indeed, the detectivist might well endorse Bordwell's appeal to history, and say that what Bordwell shows is that constructivism is false: meanings are to be found in part by patient historical research and are not to be conjured up by critical schools. So reading Bordwell as an opponent of critical school constructivism makes his position more attractive, but it deprives it of any claim to be a constructivist theory of meaning.

On the other hand, Bordwell may believe that his positive proposals are consistent with critical school constructivism, provided that one adds the proviso that the members of a qualified school should use the sort of descriptions and historical explanations mentioned above. But, as we have just seen, to believe that interpreting is a matter of giving such descriptions and explanations is incompatible with holding that meanings are made by the work's audience.[64] It is true that critics will proceed by applying interpretive concepts to films using background knowledge, and will use various inferential processes in developing their interpretations. However, this is merely an instance of conceptual construction, and, as I argued earlier, goes no way to proving that meanings are made, not found. So, however we understand Bordwell's ultimate position on interpretation, it is clear that critical school construction is a false theory, and that mere appeal to the fact that critics apply concepts to films using background knowledge does not show that meanings are made.

Despite the apparently compelling nature of Bordwell's argument, then, it fails to show that genuine constructivism – the thesis that meanings are made by the audience, not found – is true. However, there are other grounds for thinking that there is a modest element of genuine construction in the understanding of films, but this role is a circumscribed one, and does not form the core of a theory of comprehension and interpretation in the way that neoformalists believe. Genuine constructivism holds that the viewers of a film (partially) make the meaning of the film. Let us call this notion of construction *discretionary* construction, since the viewer of the film has (within certain limits) discretion about what she is properly to imagine in respect of the fictional world in the film. The argument thus far has shown that viewers do not have *complete* discretion about what they are properly to imagine: constraints on interpretation are laid down by such

---

[64] Bordwell would probably reply that some of the explanations the historical poetician would give concern the reception of films, and that the audience can use and understand films in ways other than their makers intended (*ibid.*, p. 270). But to acknowledge this is not to agree that the audience is invariably *correct* if they so understand films. The constructivist aspect of interpretation is here simply assumed, rather than argued for.

factors as which objects were photographed, by generic features, by historical norms, and so on. But that still leaves it open that, within the limits specified by such factors, viewers enjoy some discretion over what they properly imagine.

Consider two examples. In the film *M* (1931) Peter Lorre plays a child murderer, but the murders are not shown. He meets a little girl, leads her away, and we see a balloon rising and being caught in some wires. Explaining why he did not depict the murder itself, the director Fritz Lang said 'If I could show what is most horrible for *me*, it may not be horrible for somebody else ... everybody has a *different* feeling, because everybody *imagines* the most horrible thing that could happen to her. And that is something I could not have achieved by showing only one possibility – say, that he tears open the child, cuts her open. Now, in this way, I force the audience to become a collaborator of mine'.[65] A second example concerns the Ealing comedy *Kind Hearts and Coronets* (1949). Its (anti-)hero has murdered eight people to win an aristocratic title and is then arrested for a murder he did not commit. He is acquitted of the killing, but at the end of the film remembers that he has left the journal that records his crimes in the prison cell. As Perkins notes, the film 'leaves the spectator free to complete the action according to his desires', for, though we have reason to think his journal will be found, we do not see his arrest, and it is consistent with the tone of the film that he should evade discovery once more.[66]

These cases are not simply ones where the viewer has to imagine something that she does not see. Rather, they are instances where she has a degree of choice over *what* she ought to imagine occurring. In the first, she can imagine how exactly the murder occurs; in the second, she can imagine how the fictional series of events ends, according to whether she has a temperamental attraction to amoral or to moralistic comedy. So in neither case is the viewer directed to imagine a specific train of events: both cases are examples of genuine, or discretionary, construction. Individual viewers legitimately interpret the films in varying ways, and so properly ascribe varying meanings to them, and the richness of these films is partly to be traced to their capacity to sustain differing interpretations.

Intentionalists may object that even these examples are not instances of genuine construction. For, surely, in the first case the filmmaker clearly

---

[65] V. F. Perkins, *Film as Film*, p. 141. Perkins cites Peter Bogdanovich, *Fritz Lang in America*, as the source of the quote.

[66] Perkins, *Film as Film*, p. 146. Perkins uses these two examples to argue for his theory of 'participant observers', but he does not see the importance of the distinction between normative construction in general and discretionary construction.

intends the viewer to imagine the most horrible thing that could occur. So does not the filmmaker here direct the imaginings of the viewer? However, it is clear that such viewer construction is legitimate, even when the film-makers do not intend the effect: it is consistent with the second example, as described, that the openness of the ending was unintended. Indeed, it is clear that in both cases it is the viewer's search for the version of events which is most aesthetically satisfying to her, which guides her own particular interpretation of the film. So it is the viewer who selects, according to her own temperament and value system, which interpretation of the film she will adopt.

But even here a detectivist may object. For, after all, the viewer can select such interpretations only within certain limits, and those limits are there to be detected (even if they were not always intended). In *Kind Hearts and Coronets* it is permissible to imagine that the new Duke D'Ascoyne is arrested, or gets away with his crimes, but not that he flies to Mars, or becomes a toad, or that the events we see in the film did not occur, but are merely the alcoholic dream of a Thames bargeman. So the limits of legitimate imaginings are there to be found (fixed by whatever constraints her particular version of detectivism countenances). But we can respond to this reply by noting that it concedes to the modest constructivist all that she needs. For she admits that there are limits to the viewer's discretion in construction and that these limits are fixed by such factors as formal and generic features, historical norms, and so on. But within these limits there is genuine construction. Constructivism proceeds within a detectivist framework.[67]

So the neoformalist has failed to prove that genuine construction lies at the heart of the comprehension and interpretation of films. By distinguishing different senses of 'construction', we have shown that conceptual and normative construction exist, but that neither proves that meanings are made by the audience. Critical school constructivism, on the other hand, does entail that meanings are made, but it is a false view of interpretation. There is a genuine role for audiences to make meaning, but this role varies in scope from film to film and is limited within a detectivist framework. Such a limited construction, precisely because of its limits, is incompatible with the neoformalist view that meanings are always made.

---

[67] I will discuss discretionary construction in more detail in Section 4.3, and in Section 4.4 will compare it with another kind of construction, feature construction, which is narrower in scope but stronger.

4.3 THE PATCHWORK THEORY

I have rejected two prominent theories of the interpretation of films, intentionalism and constructivism. So what, then, is the correct theory of interpretation for film? Given my defence of a basic detectivist framework but rejection of intentionalism, one might suppose that it is formalism of a traditional variety. But formalism should be rejected too, if we understand that theory to claim that artists' intentions play no role in interpretation.[68] The most general reason for rejecting formalism is that artworks in general are the products of actions – they are art*works*. An action is necessarily intentional under some description, otherwise it would be a mere piece of behaviour. So a full account of an action must involve appeal to intentions, and therefore a complete interpretation of a work must appeal to intentions, since to understand a film is to understand what its makers did (this is the hermeneutic claim of Section 3.2). But it does not follow from this general claim that every feature of an action, or therefore of its product, is intended; as we saw in Section 4.1, it is true of actions in general that their originating intentions are sometimes not successfully realised and actions can also have unintended features. It would in fact be highly implausible that artists generally had such a degree of mastery that every feature of a work, however, slight, was intended by them. So intentions play some role in the correct characterisation of actions and their products, but are not the only relevant factors.

So the correct theory of interpretation of collaborative art, as of all art, is what I term a *mixed theory* – this holds that several factors figure in determining correct interpretation, of which intentions are only one. A well-known example of a mixed theory is Kendall Walton's view that the artist's intentions, formal features of the work, circumstances of historical context and value maximising all play a role in determining the category under which a work is correctly viewed and therefore its proper interpretation.[69] The challenge for mixed theories is to establish precisely what roles

---

[68] See, for instance, Monroe Beardsley, *Aesthetics*, pp. 17–29; Beardsley distinguishes between speaker meaning and sentence meaning, holds that the latter is the object of interest in the case of literature, and that it is determined by 'public conventions of usage that are tied up with habit patterns in the whole speaking community' (p. 25).

[69] Kendall Walton, 'Categories of Art'. Robert Stecker and Stephen Davies have also developed mixed theories, though they do not describe them using that term. Stecker advances a theory, U, which holds that intentions play a role together with the conventions for interpreting works that obtained at the time of their making (see his *Artworks*, chapter 10). Davies holds that the role of interpretation is to maximise the value of a work, consistent with respecting its identity, and that intentions have a role in determining work identity (see his *Philosophical Perspectives on Art*, Part Two).

these different factors play in interpretation. The type of mixed theory I favour, the patchwork theory, holds that these factors enter differentially into the interpretation of different features of an artwork.[70]

Consider first the major source of the intuition that meaning is unitary and that intentionalism captures it: the semantic paradigm.[71] According to this view, meaning is a linguistic property. Since to interpret a work is to discover its meaning, and since meaning is a linguistic property according to the semantic paradigm, the proper way to interpret all aspects of artworks is via the model of understanding linguistic meaning. It seems plausible that linguistic meaning is fixed by speakers' intentions. Hence to interpret a work is just to discover the intentions with which it was created. So, according to the paradigm, intentionalism is true.[72]

However, while it is correct that to interpret a work is to establish its meaning, this is so only if we understanding 'meaning' in a suitably broad manner. For *meaning* is a concept far wider than that of linguistic meaning. It includes what Grice calls 'natural meaning', that is, the causal relations between natural objects that make the presence of one evidence for the presence of the other (clouds mean rain, spots mean measles).[73] It also includes the sense of 'meaning' used when one talks of the meaning of someone's actions, the meaning of a historical event (e.g., the French Revolution), the meaning of social customs and rituals, and so on. Actions and historical events are not language-like, so it is difficult to understand how the semantic paradigm would apply to them, even if it might be stretched to cover social customs by an appeal to intended conventions. Rather, when one wonders about the meaning of such things, one seeks to assess their significance, to make sense of them, or in the broadest sense to understand them. Such concerns cover a broad range of activities: one looks for an explanation of these actions; one aims to understand the values that they express; one tries to see them as part of a broader social or historical pattern; one aims to characterise the actions in ways that reveal apparently unfamiliar actions as being of a type with which one is familiar, and so on. So the notion of meaning should not be understood on

---

[70] Berys Gaut, 'Interpreting the Arts'.

[71] The phrase 'the semantic paradigm' is inspired by Richard Moran's use of the term 'the linguistic paradigm'. Moran's thoughts about different notions of meaning have influenced some of the remarks I make here about the semantic paradigm.

[72] Paul Grice and John Searle, for instance, are proponents of the view that to grasp the meaning of a sentence essentially involves (but is not exhausted by) grasping the intentions with which it was produced, though Searle, in particular, also stresses the role of rules in fixing linguistic meaning. See Paul Grice, 'Meaning', p. 39, and John Searle, *Speech Acts*, pp. 49–50.

[73] Grice, 'Meaning,' p. 39.

an exclusively linguistic model. And this is particularly germane to cinema: aspects of the content of a photograph (what it is a photograph of) are determined not by any language-like features of photographs, but by the non-conventional, non-intentional causal relations in which the camera stood to its object. As we saw in Chapter 1, there could be natural photographs, which entirely lack intentional features: aspects of photographic content are a kind of natural meaning.

Secondly, even in the case of literature, where the semantic paradigm would seem most at home, what goes under the name of 'interpretation' is much broader than simply discovering linguistic meaning or features that are analogous to linguistic meaning. Features such as assonance, rhythm and rhyme depend on *syntactic* properties and patterns of speech production, not on *semantic* features. But such features are crucial to the correct interpretation of, for example, poetry. Likewise, questions about stylistics are sensitive to facts about sound and the types of different words used. There are also questions about explanation that are germane to interpretation; these include external explanations about why the text was produced as it was (e.g., the effects of serial production demands on the nature of Dickens' narrative techniques); and also internal explanations, explanations about events in the world of the work (e.g., why Hamlet delayed). Issues about the associations of various words matter too, as does an understanding of metaphors – yet such understanding is largely a pragmatic matter and is highly context dependent. 'Juliet is the sun' and 'Achilles is the sun' are both successful metaphors, but do not work by virtue of some fixed metaphorical meaning possessed by 'the sun', since different attributes of the sun are relevant in each case.[74] Classification of narrators as restricted or unrestricted, reliable or unreliable, and distinctions between plot and story rest on identifying features of fictional entities described in or implied by the text, and the understanding of these things is distant from what it is to understand the meanings of words. So even in the case of literature, where the semantic paradigm should find its safest berth, it is in dangerous waters: literary interpretation is sensitive to features such as syntax, pragmatics, explanations and features of real or fictional non-semantic entities. All of these features are normally distinguished from semantic aspects of works. So there is reason to question the extension of the semantic paradigm to such matters, and

---

[74] See Catherine Elgin and Israel Scheffler, 'Mainsprings of Metaphor', pp. 331–5. For a discussion of the role of metaphor in art interpretation and its relation to the patchwork theory, see my 'Metaphor and the Understanding of Art'.

therefore to all aspects of literary interpretation. Given the fact that there is no language of film, as we argued in Sections 2.1 and 2.2, and other dissimilarities between literature and film, there is even more reason to question its application to film.

The upshot of this is that we need to make distinctions in what counts as the meaning or the correct interpretation of a work. Most writers on interpretation have sought *global* theories of interpretation: they have assumed that the meaning of a work is a unitary property, whereas to talk of the meaning of a work is in fact to talk of a very diverse set of properties. The process of interpretation involves ascribing an immense variety of radically different properties to works, and the problem with any global account of interpretation is that the constraints on the correct ascription of one type of property may be different from those on another, so that no theory of interpretation gives the correct grounds for ascription of all of them. Thus different theories of interpretation need to be provided for different properties, and the role of intention in fixing the conditions of ascription of different properties will vary with the type of property, which is what the patchwork theory claims.

It is apparent that the role and importance of intentions in determining the correct ascription of properties to films varies greatly depending on the properties involved. Some features of films are entirely determined by filmmakers' intentions. For instance, *All about My Mother* (1999), directed by Pedro Almodovar, alludes both in its title and its contents to *All about Eve* (1950). A necessary condition for the allusion is that Almodovar or his collaborators intended the reference. If it turned out that none of them had ever heard of the earlier film, then there would be a chance partial coincidence of title, not an allusion. Sometimes works simply happen to resemble other works, rather than alluding to them. Allusions are determined by filmmakers' intentions. The same is true of irony, since to be ironical is to say something while meaning (intending) the opposite. And consider the notion of a remake: something is a remake of a film not by virtue of resembling it (though remakes must resemble the original to some extent), since two films may resemble one another purely by chance. Rather, a remake must be made with an awareness of the original film and an intention to rework elements of the same story into a new film.

Contrast the property of being influenced by something. One film may be influenced by another without its makers intending the influence to occur: in fact artists from at least the Romantic period onwards have characteristically struggled against being influenced by others, but have succumbed, unintentionally, nevertheless.[75] So whether a film is an influence on another film is not determined by the intentions of its makers. Likewise, the property of being an expression of an emotion does not require that the expression be intended. To express an emotion is to provide evidence that one is having that emotion (which is not to say that one is actually having it: evidence can be misleading). As such, it is not a necessary condition that one intends to produce that evidence. I may be at a funeral and, trying to bottle up my feelings, nevertheless weep: I have expressed my grief while intending not to do so.[76]

Other properties are more complex in respect of intentions. At the start of *Bringing Up Baby* (1938), Cary Grant (Dr Huxley) is posed on a platform in the manner of Rodin's *The Thinker*, chin firmly planted on his right fist, while his assistant announces 'Dr Huxley is thinking'. At the end, he and Katherine Hepburn are caught on that same platform in an embrace that recalls Rodin's *The Kiss*, as Stanley Cavell strikingly observes.[77] Suppose that these similarities arose merely by chance. They are still funny, and figure in the correct interpretation of the film as humorous at these points. But instead suppose that Hawks or his screen writers, Dudley Nichols and Hagar Wilde, intended the references to Rodin. What we have then is not just humour, but a display of cleverness in humour, of wit in the proper sense. Not everything that is funny is witty (an unintentional slip may be funny, but is not witty). The existence of the similarity between the film scenes and the Rodin sculptures grounds the humour; the involvement of intention characterises that humour as wit. So the nature of the humour is partly dependent on whether or not intentions figure in its production.

Or consider thematic properties: what, in a broad sense, the film is about. Ascription of themes standardly draws on the ascription of many other properties, such as whether allusions occur, whether certain patterns exist, and so on. Hence a wide range of factors may figure in the correct ascription of themes: their ascription tries to make best sense of films overall, aiming at a comprehensive and coherent interpretation of the work's themes.

To illustrate this point about thematic ascriptions, it is worth considering a detailed example of film interpretation. Consider *Rashomon*, directed by

---

[75] This is one of the points of Harold Bloom's *The Anxiety of Influence*.

[76] R. G. Collingwood, *The Principles of Art*, pp. 121–2, holds that such a case would be one where emotion is betrayed, but not expressed. This seems false as a claim about linguistic usage, as the funeral case shows. Moreover, even if it were correct, one should hold that interpretation is concerned with betrayals of emotion as well as expressions of emotion.

[77] Stanley Cavell, *Pursuits of Happiness*, pp. 117 and 121. The similarity of the closing posture to that of *The Kiss* is more debatable than that of the opening one to *The Thinker*, but I will take Cavell's observation as true for purposes of the discussion.

Figure 6. Tajomaru, the bandit (Toshiro Mifune) and Masago, the wife
(Machiko Kyo) in *Rashomon* (1950).

Akira Kurosawa (see Figure 6). It is often understood as about relativism:
David Cook, for instance, baldly states that it is 'a film about the relativity
of truth'.[78] An alternative interpretation is that it is a tale about moral

---

[78] David A. Cook, *A History of Narrative Film*, p. 784.

degradation – a tale about how people will lie about their actions, however hideous, to protect their own sense of self-worth. As such, this interpretation presupposes the existence of objective truth, which provides a standard against which one can show that people are lying or deceiving themselves. Which is the better thematic interpretation of the film?[79]

The film provides four competing versions of a rape and murder (or suicide) in a forest grove, recounted through flashbacks at an inquest by Takehiro (a samurai warrior), Masago (his wife), Tajomaru (a bandit), and an observing woodcutter. The accounts differ fundamentally about what happened – the bandit says that he raped the wife, though she soon succumbed willingly, and then he killed the warrior in a fair fight with a sword; the wife says that she was raped, her husband scorned her, and that when she awoke from a faint, she saw him with a dagger in his chest (which may suggest that she killed him); the warrior (through a medium) says that he killed himself with the dagger after his wife offered herself freely to the bandit after the rape and begged the bandit to kill him; and the woodcutter says that the warrior and bandit engaged in a cowardly fight, egged on by the shrewish wife who set them to fight over her, and that the bandit killed the warrior with a sword. Though the woodcutter might, as a mere observer, be regarded as the most reliable witness, his testimony is compromised by his implicit admission that he stole the dagger and by his earlier denial that he saw the events at all. There seems no way to reconcile the accounts or to establish which, if any, is true.

The relativity interpretation holds that the film is endorsing or at least exploring the idea of relativism about truth. This was indeed how many of the film's early viewers understood the film: Alain Resnais claimed that *Rashomon* inspired him to make *Last Year at Marienbad* (1961), a film for which a relativistic interpretation is highly plausible.[80] Certainly, there is some evidence for this interpretation in the film: given that there seems no way of reconciling the participants' accounts, this may suggest a genuine indeterminacy about what happened, rather than a mere lacuna in our knowledge about it; and the dream-like atmosphere of much of the recounting of what happened in the forest, supported by the repetitive, bolero-like score, supports the thought that here, as can be the case in the world of

---

[79] There is no need to hold that either is simply false (as would be, for instance, the claim that the film is about the simple joys of family life), since both have some basis in features of the film; also, in the case of the interpretation of artworks, we have an interest grounded in aesthetic value in seeking a plurality of reasonable interpretations, and each of these interpretations is artistically interesting and enriches the film.

[80] Ibid., p. 785.

dreams, there may be no truth about what happened. However, despite the relativity interpretation having some support, the moral degradation interpretation is a better one.

First, the relativity view has a problem with the conclusion of the film: the woodcutter finds a baby at the Rashomon gate, and offers to adopt him. The priest, who has heard these varying accounts and has come close to despair about humanity's capacity to lie, says to the woodcutter in the film's closing lines, 'thanks to you, I think I will be able to keep my faith in men'. On the relativity interpretation this is at best an irrelevance to the film's main theme and at worst an embarrassment. Parker Tyler, a defender of the relativity view, remarks, 'The relation of this incident to the story proper strikes me as the most problematical element of all, if only because the film would have remained intact without it.'[81] But on the moral degradation view, this incident, occurring at the privileged point of the film's ending, fits neatly with the main theme of the film. So the degradation interpretation is more comprehensive in its scope than is the relativity interpretation, since it fits with more (and more important) features of the film. The film also has greater thematic coherence on the degradation interpretation than it does on the relativity view.

Second, if relativity were the theme, then it would be best if all events in the film were relativistically presented. However, the framing story at the Rashomon Gate, the events of the inquest and the incidents in the forest up to the rape are presented in an unambiguous manner. Contrast this with films such as *Last Year at Marienbad*, and Luis Buñuel and Salvador Dalí's *Un Chien andalou* (1928) that do throw reality into question, and in which almost everything is problematic. On the degradation interpretation, in contrast, lies are being told, brought upon by the traumatic events of the rape and murder/suicide: so no other events need to be problematically presented. Hence the interpretation can explain why some events in the film are presented as unknowable or otherwise problematic, while others are not: each person constructs a version of the forest events so as to maintain his or her sense of self-worth.

Third, the degradation view makes best sense within the film's historical context. The wooden Rashomon Gate was the main gate to Kyoto, the mediaeval capital of Japan, and as such was symbolic of the nation. It is shown in a state of near total ruin, and the participants contribute to its

---

[81] Tyler, '*Rashomon* as Modern Art', p. 40. Tyler remarks of the film, 'Within one span of time-and-space, reality (the episode in the forest) has been disintegrated', p. 41. He also touches on the moral degradation interpretation, however.

further destruction by pulling parts off it in order to make a fire to warm themselves. The film was made in 1950, and initially planned in 1948, just after Japan had suffered the most devastating defeat in its history and after its war crimes of rape and murder had been exposed by the occupying Allied powers. Given its historical context, it was natural to understand the film's theme in terms of having to confront hideous crimes, crimes that are lied about and dressed up. In contrast, reflections on the nature of truth looked irrelevant to the contemporary situation.

Finally, the degradation interpretation fits with Kurosawa's intentions. He writes that he explained to his three assistant directors, who complained that they were unable to understand the script, the meaning of the film as follows:

Human beings are unable to be honest with themselves about themselves. They cannot talk about themselves without embellishing. This script portrays such human beings – the kind who cannot survive without lies to make them feel they are better people than they really are. It even shows this sinful need for flattering falsehood going beyond the grave – even the character who dies cannot give up his lies when he speaks to the living through a medium. Egoism is a sin the human being carries with him from birth; it is the most difficult to redeem.[82]

So Kurosawa intended the film to be about moral degradation, and he successfully realised his intentions in the film.

As the example shows, thematic interpretations can draw on formal factors such as internal patterns in the work, contextual factors, such as the historical situation of production, and intentional evidence to support the ascription. The aim is to produce a comprehensive and coherent interpretation by employing the relevant factors.

It should also be noted that, even if Kurosawa had not intended the moral degradation theme but rather the relativity of truth theme, one could still have legitimately ascribed the moral degradation interpretation to the work. For it would still be supported by the factors of coherence and context that we have noted. In this case, it would have been a happy accident, like the hysteria interpretation of *The Turn of the Screw*. As things stand, it is the relativity of truth interpretation that is the happy accident.

Interpretation, then, is a complex matter. Some aspects of works, such as allusions, answer wholly to intentions; other aspects, such as influence, hold independently of intentions; still other aspects, such as the nature of the humour and thematic ascriptions, hold by virtue of a variety of factors.

---

[82] Kurosawa, *Something Like an Autobiography*, p. 183.

Only mixed theories, and in particular patchwork theories, are in a position to respect the complex practice that constitutes interpretation.

The patchwork theory also allows us to acknowledge that there is a legitimate role for restricted, discretionary construction in art interpretation. We argued for the existence of this kind of construction in film in the previous section, and we can now examine in more detail why it occurs and its limits, say something about its role in the other arts and how film compares to these in respect of construction.

Consider painting – for instance, the *Mona Lisa*. Part of the reason why the work is considered great is the figure's famously elusive expression. To some she seems to harbour a deep sadness, others see her as quietly happy, others imagine her as meditating on the secrets of birth and creativity. The painting's capacity to ground such a diversity of reactions is part of its greatness, for it thus speaks to many different states of mind and to a wide variety of situations. We know, in fact, how the painting manages to evoke such a wide range of interpretations of the objects of *La Gioconda*'s thought and of her expression. Leonardo himself developed the theory of how it is done. He uses the device of *sfumato* – by throwing the corners of the figure's mouth and eyes into shadows he deprives the viewer of information that is vital to assessing the face's expression.[83] Yet our drive to interpret human beings is so strong that we do not experience the facial expression as indeterminate within certain bounds, which it in fact is, but seek to resolve it by various interpretative hypotheses. The fact that the information we are given is compatible with several of these hypotheses means that we move from one interpretation to another, consequently seeing the expression as having one determinate characteristic and then as having a different one. Here, even though the expression is in fact indeterminate, it is legitimate to resolve the indeterminacy in various ways by imagining of the figure some determinate facial expression and experiencing it in the light of that imagining. The indeterminacy of works of art in certain respects thus allows the reader or viewer to bring her own values and hypotheses to the work and to construct in imagination features of the work – i.e., properly to imagine of the work properties that it does not really have. The interpreter should certainly note the genuine indeterminacy, but merely to do so without also seeking to resolve it in one way or another would be to refuse to respond to the work in a way that is appropriate to it. The intentionalist can allow this in the case of Leonardo's work, since Leonardo intended the effect. But even if he had not, the possibility of resolution of indeterminacy would be open

[83] See E. H. Gombrich, *The Story of Art*, pp. 227–9.

to the viewer and would be no less legitimate for being unintended by the artist. Resolution of indeterminacy is an important role of the imagination in interpreting works, and imagination plays a justified and indeed central part in our understanding of works.

The role of discretionary construction as well as detection of properties is even more striking in the interpretation of literature. Characters in written fiction are underspecified in many respects – we are often not told the way they speak their words, their emotions, the motivations that they have, even their physical appearance. All of these may be indeterminate (metaphysically, not epistemically, since these are fictional characters). We may legitimately imagine the characters as having certain determinate properties in cases where their properties are indeterminate, seeking out interesting readings of the text, within the bounds permitted by the indeterminacy. Some of the contents of these imaginings will be explanatorily inert, in that they will not affect our interpretation of properties that are explicitly ascribed to characters – for instance, whether one thinks of a fictional character as six foot tall or six foot two inches tall may play no role in one's understanding of his actions or character traits. But some of these constructed properties may be explanatorily active. Whether we think of a character as delivering some crucial lines in an ironical tone of voice or quite sincerely may well transform our understanding of his actions, even though nothing in the text determines or implies what his tone of voice was when he spoke the lines.[84]

The general mechanism for discretionary construction, then, is the determining of indeterminates left open by the work. This kind of construction is restricted, since the determinate boundaries are fixed by the work. Any fictional presentation must be partial, in that it specifies only certain qualities of characters and their actions. There are thus "gaps" in the work, in the sense that certain features of the fictional world are not explicitly specified by the work. Since there are size limits to any work, such gaps are inevitable. But the existence of gaps does not of itself show that the viewer genuinely constructs the meaning of the work, for, given what is explicitly stated and the norms governing the work, the viewer may

---

[84] Discretionary construction is also encouraged insofar as works contain metaphors. Metaphors involve the comparison of one (kind of) thing with another (kind of) thing. Since different sorts of entities are like each other in a vast number of ways, the reader is given wide scope for discretion in choosing the similarities she takes to be salient. Some of these may be inappropriate in the context, or obvious, or trivial; but many are not. Hence the reader can exercise her ingenuity in seeking fresh and illuminating ways in which to understand the metaphor, and so has considerable latitude in its interpretation.

have no discretion about how she is to "fill in" the gaps where these are of significance for understanding the work. That is, she may have no choice about what she properly imagines in respect of the features of the work that are not explicitly stated (i.e., this is a case of normative construction that is fully directed). So global theories of construction are not supported; and, while discretionary construction is reliant on an invariant and inevitable feature of works of art, this feature alone does not suffice for its legitimacy – its legitimacy will also depend on particular features of the work and of the norms applying to it. So the role and importance of discretionary construction may vary from work to work.

This general point applies to films too. For those films that are fiction films, the same point about the metaphysical incompleteness of fiction applies, and allows films to exploit the indeterminacy for constructive purposes. In this respect some films grant their viewers more discretion than others. This is particularly true of many modernist films, such as *Un Chien andalou*, which permit a vast number of equally acceptable (or equally unacceptable) hypotheses about what is going on. As *M* illustrates, films seeking to produce fear or horror in their audience may also rely on discretionary construction to achieve their effects. Some filmmakers, such as Val Lewton and Jacques Tourneur working at RKO in the early 1940s, were masters of using discretionary construction to enhance their effects of menace, often exploiting shadows and suggestion in a similar way to Leonardo's use of *sfumato* techniques.

There is, however, an interesting medium-specific difference between literature and film in respect of construction. Novels have the option not to specify physical features of characters and locations, whereas films are almost inevitably committed to specifying these in great detail but can more easily leave to the viewer's imagination the determination of a character's personality and motivations. In this respect *Citizen Kane* is a supremely cinematic film, since we know how Kane looked, the exact timbre of his voice, and what he did. But, apparently knowing everything, we turn out to be ignorant about what we most want to know: his motivations and personality remain utterly elusive. The richness and greatness of the film, its ability to be apparently open about all that transpires but to hide everything worth knowing, and its capacity to generate innumerable interpretations, all rest on its exploitation of the film medium to show us the physical details of Kane's life, while allowing discretionary construction of his character and motives.

In summary, the patchwork theory considers interpretation as a very diverse set of activities concerned with the ascription of a wide range of

properties to works, with the giving of both internal and external explanations of works and their properties, and permitting a localised kind of
construction. Given this diversity any theory of interpretation will fail that
gives the same ascription conditions to each of the properties that are the
objects of interpretation. The patchwork theory also allows for intentions
to be defeated and for there to be happy accidents. It thus explains the
failures of intentionalism, constructivism and formalism, but allows us still
to generate theories of interpretation, provided these are local to different
kinds of property, not global.

4.4 DIGITAL CINEMA AND INTERPRETATION

How do these conclusions apply to digital cinema? As far as intentionalism
is concerned, the defeaters of intention are often different in digital cinema
than they are in traditional film. Digital cinema (and digital photography),
with its potentially infinite capacity to manipulate the image without
leaving any visible traces of this manipulation, has reduced or even abo-
lished the capacity of the hazards of the real to defeat intention and to create
happy accidents. Unwanted details can be removed from the digital image
with relative ease. However, given the greater role of collaboration in digital
film, the defeaters of intention that are grounded on the collaborative nature
of film, with its potential for clashes between collaborators, have in contrast
increased the probability of the defeat of intentions and of happy accidents.
So while the *sources* of the defeat of intentions and accidents have changed
the *facts* of defeat and accidents have not.

Interactive digital cinema can also defeat intentions in a distinctly new
way, at least in respect of works' instances. The audience of interactive
cinema partly determines the works' instances and their features. The
authors of interactive works standardly have some intentions about the
range of interaction instances, since they aim to provide the audience with a
certain kind of experience – in the case of videogames to make the playing
of the game satisfying. But audience members sometimes play games in
ways that their designers never intended and that may even undermine
some of their aims. A well-known example occurs in the videogame *Deus
Ex* (2000), where players discovered that by attaching mines to the walls
depicted in the game they could climb up them, which the designers had
not intended to be possible.[85] This possibility is known as *emergent gameplay*, gameplay that is not intended or foreseen by the games' designers. It is

---

[85] Jesper Juul, *Half-Real*, p. 76.

an endemic possibility in complex interactive works, since there is a potentially infinite number of ways in which the audience may instantiate a work
and this creates formidable difficulties for the designers in foreseeing all the
possibilities. The phenomenon of emergence applies to interactive works in
general, not just computationally based ones. Chess is interactive, since
audience members are authorised to instantiate the work (the game of chess)
in different ways by playing it. Almost all gameplay in chess is emergent,
since the inventors of chess could not have foreseen all the different games of
chess that have been and could be played.

So the problems with intentionalism that we saw for traditional works
also arise in modified form for digital and interactive cinema and this
reason for adopting mixed theories therefore remains. The patchwork
theory also allows for a role for discretionary construction. The arguments
for it also apply to digital and interactive cinema, but it is also plausible
that interactive cinema enables a new and strong form of constructivism.
For the images seen on the screen in part depend on the choices of the
audience and this looks like a clear case of construction: Grant Tavinor,
for instance, maintains that 'a very real form of constructivism is true of
them [videogames]'.[86]

From the definition of interactivity in Section 3.9, it follows that this kind
of constructivism does not apply to a work but only to instances of a work
(including instance-works, i.e., works that are instances of other works). For
the audience of interactive works partly determines the instances of the
work and their features, not the work itself: so this sort of constructivism
does not have as wide an application as do the other kinds we mooted
earlier, which are applicable to works.

A strong kind of constructivism applies in the interactive case. The
audience of an interactive cinematic work can partly determine the shapes
of images and their sizes by moving the virtual camera, by changing their
position in the fictional world, or by making certain choices about how to
proceed, for instance. They can also partly determine the colours that
appear on screen by, for instance, moving to another part of the environment that has a different colour scheme or by turning on a light in the
fictional world. A visual image on a computer screen (a raster image) is
entirely determined by the colour values of the pixels that constitute it, and
this pixel-colour array can be completely described in terms of shapes, their
sizes and their colours; so interactors can partly determine all the features of
the visual image. On this visual image (together with the sound image,

---

[86] Grant Tavinor, 'Videogames and Interactive Fiction', p. 33.

which the audience also partly determines) and its relations to other visual images, all of the work-instance's other properties supervene. So the sub-venient base of all other properties consists of shapes, sizes, colours and sounds. Shapes and sizes are primary qualities – i.e., qualities that exist independently of our experience of the world: they can be described without implying the actual or possible presence of a subject experiencing them. Colours are secondary qualities, which on a standard conception exist only by virtue of the actual or possible presence of a subject to experience them: were the world devoid of conscious beings, it would lack colours (as well as sounds). So the denotation of 'features' in the definition of interactivity includes both primary and secondary qualities. Let 'features' in the defini-tion pick out only these kinds of properties; and call this sort of construc-tivism *feature construction*.

There are several important points to note about feature construction. First, as we saw, it applies only to instances, not to works. Second, it is indirect in respect of meaning determination: the audience of interactive works partly determines the primary and secondary qualities of work-instances: they specify the image, both visual and auditory. By so doing, they do not directly specify the *meaning* of the work-instance, but they do this indirectly, by specifying its features. If I produce an image on screen and a sound sequence, then it may well have a different meaning (a different correct interpretation) than the different image and sequence that you produce on screen, playing the same game. Third, not all features are experience independent, since some are secondary qualities: but they are in one sense of the term objective, since they are all publicly accessible and the objects of perception: both you and I can see the same shapes and colours. Fourth, since the audience member partly determines the instan-ces, feature construction places him in a similar position to the performer of a non-interactive performing work, and he is also part-author (as artist) of that instance, if the instance is itself an artwork – so feature construction fits neatly with the discussion of authorship and performance in Section 3.9.

So there is a genuine kind of construction that is distinctive of interactive cinema: it is entailed by the basic definition of interactivity; but it is partial in the sense that it applies to instances of cinematic works, not to the works themselves (other than instance-works).

How does feature construction relate to the discretionary construction for which we argued earlier? Recall that discretionary construction occurs when the audience of a work has discretion about what it *properly imagines* about what is fictional – that is, it has a degree of choice within certain limits over what it imagines and this is legitimate, given the features of the work.

For instance, it can properly imagine that the expression of Mona Lisa has a hint of sadness, or that it is one of quiet happiness. The audience does not *believe* that either of these expressions is determinately present, at least if it understands the work, for it knows that the smile is elusive and indeterminate because of the *sfumato* technique: but to interpret the work correctly it must *see* it *as* one expression or another, or as both sequentially.

There are some basic differences between the two types of construction. First, discretionary construction is wider in scope than feature construction. As the example shows, discretionary construction can apply to works, not only to their instances, if they have any (the *Mona Lisa*, being a painting and therefore a particular, has no instances). Also, feature construction applies only in the interactive arena, but discretionary construction can also apply to non-interactive works.

Second, feature construction involves determining the primary and secondary qualities of instances; these are publicly accessible objects of perception and when we perceive them we can (and standardly do) have true *beliefs* that the work has these features. But discretionary construction involves an act of *imagination*: we do not believe that the work objectively has these properties; what we believe is that the work properly sustains certain imaginative experiences. And we may not just imagine, but also *see* the object *as* having these features, in a sense that does not require us to believe that these features are really possessed, in the same way that we can see clouds, if suitably shaped, as whales or hills. The kinds of properties that are ascribed in this way through imagination conditioning experience are sometimes called *tertiary qualities*: we have an experience *as of* objects possessing these properties. The experience is not arbitrary or unconstrained, since we properly imagine these things – the work is correctly interpreted as sustaining these imaginative engagements.

Third, feature construction is a public process, which can be observed by others (for example, you can watch me playing a videogame) and which yields a publicly perceptible object (the changing videogame image); but discretionary construction, being an exercise of imagination, yields only a privately accessible object: you cannot see my act of imagining something; nor can you observe the particular sad smile I experience the Mona Lisa as having, though I can try to get you to have a similar experience.

Finally, feature construction is more basic than discretionary construction, in the sense that one can feature construct something and then perform discretionary construction on it, but not vice versa. Suppose in a videogame version of *Kind Hearts and Coronets* that you happen to play in such a way that the events in the game exactly correspond to those in the film and you finish at the point where the film finishes. You have feature constructed the game-instance; but in addition you could perform discretionary construction on the game-instance, just as you can with the film. For you can properly imagine the continuation of the events as either the Duke's getting caught or going free, and you can have an experience of the game-instance in the light of that imagining, just as you can for the film. But you cannot feature construct on an imaginative experience (the content of your imaginative experience can possess colours and shapes and you can imagine these differently, but the experience itself can possess neither colours nor shapes). What you can do is *objectify* your imaginative experience in the case of the videogame, by producing a game-instance that has the properties that your imaginative experience of the game ascribes to it – for instance, you can carry on playing the game so that the Duke is caught or so that he once again escapes. But that is the production of public features corresponding to a private imaginative experience, rather than feature constructing the experience itself.

So feature construction is in several ways different from and more basic than discretionary construction, but it is also more limited in scope. It represents a genuine new kind of construction, distinctive of interactive cinema.

CHAPTER 5

Cinematic narration

The nature of cinematic narration is a central topic in the philosophy of cinema, and in particular for the project of the present book. Almost all films have a narrative (story) and therefore have a narration (they convey a story). This is true not only of fiction films; most documentaries are also narrative films; and narrative is central to determining viewers' responses to films. Moreover, a central question of this book concerns how the nature of the cinematic medium conditions cinema as an art. So we will examine the similarities and differences between film's narrational capacities and those of other arts, and in so doing will shed light on the nature of cinema and on how it differs from the other arts. Narration is a trans-medium capacity: many works in media besides cinema narrate – narrative works include some dances, musical works and paintings, and almost all comic strips and literature. There has to be some degree of commonalty between these different media by virtue of the fact that they can all narrate, but there may also be interesting differences between them in respect of how they narrate, differences which throw light on their different capacities as media. I will argue that there are some salient differences between cinema and literature in respect of their narrational capacities, particularly in respect of the greater role for implicit narrators in the case of literature than of cinema; and I will trace this to differences between the different media. In the first six sections I discuss narration in traditional film; and in the last section I show that interactive cinema grounds a new possibility for interactive narration.

5.1 SYMMETRY OR ASYMMETRY?

Narration is a matter of telling a story, in a broad sense of 'telling' that is equivalent to conveying something; and stories can be conveyed not just by *verbal* telling, but also by *showing* someone something (pointing out some scene or showing a series of pictures), or by *enacting* it for them (for instance, by miming something that has happened). Thus I will use the terms 'narration' and 'storytelling' equivalently. However, it is important for some purposes to contrast the different ways in which a story can be conveyed, whether verbally, or by showing, or by enactment. I will use 'verbal telling' to signal the verbal mode of conveying; otherwise 'telling' should be understood in the broad sense of conveying something.

Although as we noted, narration occurs in a wide variety of media, we will here mainly be concerned with the relation between cinematic narration and literary narration, particularly narration in novels. What we can call the *symmetry thesis* holds that narration in literature and film is identical in respect of the structural features of narration. Structural features of narration include the basic agents and properties of narration, such as narrators, implied authors, mediation, point of view, and the relation between plot and story. Symmetry theorists hold that these structural features are identical in both media, and that merely the mode of communication of the narrative varies – cinema narrates by showing, literature narrates by verbal telling. The *asymmetry thesis* holds in contrast that cinematic narration differs from literary narration in respect of at least one of its basic structural features – for instance, the asymmetry theorist may hold that whereas narrators are ubiquitous in literature, they are hardly ever found in film, or may hold that cinematic narration is not mediated in the way that literary narration is. The explanation for the asymmetry may be provided in terms of the different modes of communication of the two media, so that in contrast to the symmetry view, the asymmetry view may hold that the mode of communication does affect structural features of narration.

Though the distinction just mentioned is broader than that which most film theorists and philosophers have explicitly applied to themselves, one can plausibly assign several theorists to one camp or another. This is particularly clear in respect of the structural narrational feature that has been most discussed: that of the relative prevalence of cinematic narrators compared to literary narrators. A proponent of symmetry in this respect is Seymour Chatman, who argued at one point in his career that all narratives, whether cinematic or literary, must have narrators; and that in the case of film there is always a (usually implicit) visual narrator, just as in literature there is always an (often implicit) verbal narrator who verbally tells us the story.[1] The issue of whether the narrative is verbally told or shown is for Chatman a secondary one, which does not affect structural features such as the existence of the narrator, the narrator's mediation and point of view.

---

[1] Seymour Chatman, *Coming to Terms.*

Bruce Kawin, along with many other contemporary film theorists, also holds that there is always an implicit cinematic narrator.[2] And Jerrold Levinson supports the symmetry view, at least in respect of the existence of cinematic narrators; he argues that there is always a cinematic narrator, however effaced, in a narrative film, and that this narrator's duties may even extend to the music track of a film.[3]

Asymmetry theorists about narrators include Gregory Currie, Kendall Walton and more tentatively David Bordwell.[4] All of these theorists hold that narrators are to be found less commonly in film than in literature, though, as we shall see, their grounds for this claim differ.

Something of the complexity of the symmetry issue is evidenced by the fact that some of these writers have changed their minds on the topic. Chatman initially (in 1978) argued for a lesser role for narrators in film than in literature, but later (in 1990) came to think that the two domains are symmetrical.[5] And George Wilson shifted from arguing in 1986 for only a very restricted view of narrators in film to a position in 1997 that at least allows for the possibility of ubiquitous narrators in film.[6]

I will argue for the correctness of the asymmetry view about narrators; this will be done by arguing for a very restricted role for narrators in film, and then by showing that the same is not true of literature. I will then trace this difference to differences between the media of film and of literature. These differences in the media also explain several other narrative features of film and literature. In this way we will also strengthen the claim that media-specific explanations are important in film theory, a topic to which we will return in systematic fashion in Chapter 7.

5.2 THE A PRIORI ARGUMENT

Some have thought that there is an a priori argument for the existence of narrators whenever there is narration. This view is maintained by Chatman, and seconded by Levinson.[7] If this argument is successful, the truth of the symmetry view for narrators is immediately established. Chatman writes: 'I would argue that every narrative is by definition narrated – that is,

---

[2] Bruce Kawin, *Mindscreen*, especially chapter 1.
[3] Jerrold Levinson, 'Film Music and Narrative Agency'.
[4] Gregory Currie, *Image and Mind*, section 9.2; Kendall Walton, *Mimesis as Make-Believe*, pp. 357–8; and David Bordwell, *Narration in the Fiction Film*, p. 62.
[5] Compare Seymour Chatman, *Story and Discourse*, with his later *Coming to Terms*.
[6] George Wilson, *Narration in Light*, chapter 7; and his '*Le Grand Imagier* Steps Out'.
[7] Levinson, 'Film Music and Narrative Agency', pp. 251–2.

narratively presented – and that narration, narrative presentation, entails an agent even when that agent bears no signs of human personality.'[8] Narration conceptually entails the existence of a narrator, since narration is storytelling, and this requires a teller of the story.

Bordwell has objected to this kind of view, holding that we do not need to appeal to an agent who tells the story, for every property that can be ascribed to an agent can instead be ascribed to the process of narration itself – including properties such as the suppression of information, the restriction of knowledge, and so on.[9] But the problem with this way of talking is that either it is a personification of a process, which is conceptually confused, or it is merely shorthand for saying that an agent is doing these things, since only an agent can perform actions such as suppressing information.[10]

If there is narration, we must acknowledge a teller of the story. But it does not follow that this is a narrator. To see why, we need to draw on a familiar distinction in narratology and the philosophy of literature between the actual author, the implied author, and the narrator. The actual author of a text is the real person who composed it. The implied author of a text, as we construed him in Section 3.4.3, is a postulated being with a certain *persona*: we think of him *as if* he were the producer of the text, and we ascribe to him the characteristics manifested in the text. As we noted, the actual and implied author need not possess the same characteristics – the real-life personality, say, of Jonathan Swift, might be quite different from that set of character traits that we would ascribe to him on the basis of reading *Gulliver's Travels*. Neither actual nor implied authors are internal to the world of the story, since they are the actual or implied composers of the story, and so must stand outside it. A narrator, in contrast, is a fictional entity internal to the story; he is the fictional person in the world of the story who reports the events of the story. More precisely, we can define the narrator of a text as a particular fictional character of whom it is fictional that he speaks or writes the words that compose the text.[11] For instance, Lemuel Gulliver is the narrator of *Gulliver's Travels*, because it is fictional that he writes a logbook, the words of which compose the novel. Thus it is fictional or make-believe that in reading the novel, we read the text of Gulliver's logbook. Gulliver is distinct from Swift, the implied author of the novel: Gulliver is a hardy seaman faithfully reporting his adventures; the implied

---

[8] Chatman, *Coming to Terms*, p. 115.   [9] Bordwell, *Narration in the Fiction Film*, p. 62.
[10] For this criticism of Bordwell, see also Currie, *Image and Mind*, pp. 247–9.
[11] Walton, *Mimesis as Make-Believe*, p. 355.

author employs these fictional adventures to satirise the beliefs and institutions of eighteenth-century Britain.

With this distinction in mind, we can acknowledge that narration requires a teller of the story, but we can see that this is not the narrator. If there is a story, there must be a teller of it; but the teller who figures in this necessity claim is the actual author. For we require there to be an agent or agents who produced a text for communicative purposes if we are to interpret the text as a story, yet that agent or agents cannot be the narrator who is internal to the world of the fiction, for the text is a real object, and cannot be produced by a merely fictional being. So the a priori argument, if successful, proves the necessity of an actual author or authors, not of a narrator.[12] In many cases, there will be an implied author of the tale as well, but again this does not follow of necessity, since it is a contingent matter whether there is a sufficiently distinct set of characteristics, a *persona*, manifest in the text for us justifiably to count an implied author as present.

Another way of putting this conclusion is by distinguishing two types of narration or storytelling. Actual narration or storytelling involves producing, say, a text or film so as to convey a story (which may be fictional or non-fictional). Since narration is an activity, there must be an agent who performs it. So from the existence of actual narration, it follows that there must be someone who made the text or film to convey the story. That is the actual author. If there is a text or film with a narrative (a story), then there must be an act of actual narration, from which it follows that there is an actual storyteller, the author. For example, Swift is the actual storyteller of *Gulliver's Travels* and the text conveys the fictional story of Gulliver. But in addition some texts and films also have fictional narration: i.e., it is fictional that a story is told by means of them. Since narration is an activity, it follows that there is an agent who narrates, and since this is fictional narration, the agent is fictional; and this is the role of the narrator. For instance, it is fictional in *Gulliver's Travels* that Gulliver tells the story of his adventures, and that is distinct from Swift's role as author. But it is an extra question, distinct from the existence of actual narration, whether fictional narration also occurs in a text or film; and this has to be established by looking at the details of the text or film, not by a priori argument. It is by eliding the two

---

[12] The correctness of the a priori argument that narration requires an actual author might be denied. Walton, for instance, thinks that if cracks which seemed to tell a story appeared by natural means in a rock, then they would tell a story, provided that the audience decided to play a game of make-believe with them in which a story was told (see Walton, *Mimesis as Make-Believe*, chapter 1). However, note that even if this were correct, which I would deny, it would still support the weaker claim that narration requires an agent, and would show that the agents could be the audience, rather than an actual author.

types of narration that the a priori argument assumes from the existence of an actual narration that there is a fictional narration, and hence invalidly concludes that there is a narrator.[13]

There are further reasons for denying that every narrative requires a narrator. As already noted, not all narratives are fictional: there are historical narratives, for instance. Since the narrator is a fictional character, he should have no place in an historical narrative.[14] The teller of the historical tale that is Simon Schama's *Citizens* is Simon Schama, not some fictional entity. Nor does the existence of unreliable narration require the existence of an unreliable narrator. It has been argued for instance that one can analyse such narratives in terms of what the implied author intended.[15]

5.3 THREE MODELS OF IMPLICIT CINEMATIC NARRATORS

Thus one should reject the a priori claim that where there is narration there must be a narrator. But this still leaves it open that one might believe on more specific grounds that there are invariably narrators in film. To consider this claim, we need to examine in more detail what kinds of narrators there might be.

Some films or film sequences have explicit narrators – narrators who are explicitly made fictional in the film. A clear instance is the voice-over narrator, a narrator whose voice is heard over the film's images, usually at the start of the film but often at other points in it as well. Another example is the character-narrator – a character who appears in the film and narrates part or the whole of the film. Often voice-over narrators are also character-narrators; for instance, in *Murder, My Sweet* (1945) Philip Marlowe narrates in voice-over at several points, but also appears as a character in the film. But there are voice-over narrators of films who do not appear in the film, and thus are not character-narrators: for instance, in *Duel in the Sun* (1946) Orson Welles is heard narrating in voice-over at the start of the film, but no character played by him appears in the film. Conversely, some character-narrators do not narrate in voice-over: in *Citizen Kane* (1941) several of Kane's friends narrate sequences in flashback about Kane's earlier career, but their sequences are introduced by their talking within the story-world, rather than in voice-over.

---

[13] See Wilson, '*Le Grand Imagier* Steps Out', p. 297, for the distinction between the actual telling of a story and its fictional telling.
[14] Paisley Livingston, 'Narrative'.   [15] Currie, *Image and Mind*, pp. 269–70.

Explicit narrators have earned comparatively little attention within film theory and the philosophy of film, since their existence is uncontroversial. The debate has centred on whether there are *implicit* narrators of films. Such narrators are held to narrate the film as a whole but not to be explicitly present in voice-over or as characters appearing in it. Since they narrate the film as a whole, but their voices are not heard, they are thought of as visual narrators, somehow making sights or images available to the audience. Believers in such entities usually hold that they are to be found even when there are explicit narrators; in such cases, the implicit narrator stands behind the explicit narrator, controlling the story in which the latter figures. For instance, Sarah Kozloff writes that the 'voice-over narrator is always subsumed by and thus subordinate to a more powerful narrating agent, the image-maker'.[16]

Our question about the ubiquity of narrators will focus on implicit cinematic narrators. There are three main models of such narrators. I will examine each in turn, will raise objections to each, and then consider whether these objections can be answered.

5.3.1 The narrator as invisible observer

The model of the cinematic narrator as invisible observer is the oldest, drawing as it does on the work of the classical film theorist Vsevolod Pudovkin. It is also upheld by several contemporary film theorists, for instance, Jean-Pierre Oudart in his suture theory of cinematic narration.[17] According to this model, the cinematic narrator is to be thought of as an invisible observer stationed at the implied point from which a shot is taken, and through whose eyes we see all of the action. The narrator is the visual presenter of the story; each shot is narrated by him from his subjective point of view. The model thus in a way generalises the point-of-view shot in cinema: all shots are held to be taken from the point of view of the narrator. Just as in a literary tale we learn about a fictional world by reading the narrator's words, so in a cinematic tale we learn about a fictional world by seeing it through the narrator's eyes.

If we try to spell out this view more carefully, we encounter difficulties. One option is to say that we are to imagine that we are the narrator, and so fictionally have his experiences. But, apart from anything else, that gets a basic feature of narration wrong, for it is up to the narrator how he chooses to narrate the story, but it is not up to viewers to choose how the story

---

[16] Sarah Kozloff, *Invisible Storytellers*, pp. 48–9.   [17] Jean-Pierre Oudart, 'Cinema and Suture'.

proceeds. So it is better to construe this account in terms of its being fictional that we have the same perceptual experiences as the narrator does, though we are not fictionally identical with him. However, this version also encounters serious difficulties; for it holds that we make-believedly see the fictional events through the narrator's eyes.

To see why this poses a problem, we need to consider an issue concerning the role of imagination in audiences' viewing of fiction films. As I argued in Section 2.3.2, it is false that fiction film viewers are under a cognitive illusion that they are really seeing and are in the presence of real events depicted on screen, and it is also false that they are undergoing a perceptual illusion with the same content. So if no illusion is involved in audiences' perceptual relation to depicted events, then a plausible alternative is that audiences exercise their imaginations in viewing fiction films. But there is a dispute about how imagination enters viewers' experience. On the one hand, the proponent of personal imagining, the participation theorist, holds that when audiences watch films, they *imagine seeing* the fictional characters and events depicted.[18] This view entails that viewers are, in respect of their perceptual activities, part of the fictional world – fictionally, their seeing is conducted from some point within the fictional world. The proponent of impersonal imagination, on the other hand, holds that viewers *perceptually imagine* the fictional events, but that they do not imagine seeing these events.[19] On this view, viewers visually imagine the cinematic events, but are not fictionally part of the fictional world in respect of their perceptual activities. In imagining the cinematic events, they do not imagine themselves as located within the fictional world, viewing it from some station point inside it.

Suppose that one were to agree with the participation theorist that one make-believedly sees the fictional events, then the narrator as invisible observer model would still fail; for one would have to concede that on the participation view it is fictional in standard film shots that one sees *directly*, not through the eyes of someone else. In viewing such films, it is as if one were looking out through a glass window onto the fictional world.[20] Of course, there are some shots (point-of-view shots) in which it is arguably fictional that one is in some sense seeing through a character's eyes, but such shots are almost invariably clearly marked out as such, and are distinct from the general 'objective' shots that comprise the majority of shots in most films.

---

[18] Walton, *Mimesis as Make-Believe*, chapter 8.
[19] Currie, *Image and Mind*, chapter 6.　　[20] Wilson, *Narration in Light*, p. 55.

However, there are strong arguments against the claim that we make-believedly see fictional events in film. And on the competing, impersonal imagination view, the narrator as invisible observer model fails not because we make-believedly see directly, as claimed by the objection above, but because we do not make-believedly see at all, whether directly or indirectly. We cannot make-believedly see through the narrator's eyes if we do not make-believedly see at all.

There are good reasons to favour the impersonal imagination view. If we make-believedly see the fictional events, then we make-believedly are within the fictional world, stationed at the camera's viewpoint. But as Currie points out, that leads to absurd results. Suppose that a shot is taken from the ceiling of a room; then, fictionally, I must be attached to the ceiling. How did I get there, and how am I managing to stay there? If a shot is taken from outer space, I must make-believedly be at the point. Am I to imagine that I am wearing a spacesuit to keep me alive while floating in outer space? When a shot changes from being of one place to being of a completely different place, am I to imagine that I have the power instantaneously to move from one location to the other? And in other cases it seems that I must imagine not absurdities, but downright contradictions: for instance, if a murder in a film is represented as unseen, then I must imagine that I am seeing something that is unseen.[21]

We can add to these problems. How is one to account for the use of different lenses? The image formed by a wide-angle lens (which produces a 'fish-bowl' effect) is discernibly different from that produced by a normal lens, and both are perceptibly different from that produced by a telephoto lens (which tends to bring distant objects forward and to flatten space). Are we to imagine that we have eyes that can change their focal length so that they can mimic the effects of such lenses? What other things must be true of us for this to be so? How do we account within our seeing for the screen-wipe (a device much loved by Kurosawa), when one image is gradually replaced by another by means of a vertical band wiping across the screen? And how do we explain the split screen: can we fictionally somehow see two different scenes simultaneously – or four scenes in the case of *Time Code* (2000) – with a distinct visual division between their images?

Currie raises his objections against the claim that we make-believedly see fictions (that we are imaginary observers). But if successful, his objections, as well as those just added, work just as powerfully against the idea that the narrator is an invisible observer, for this model requires us make-believedly

---

[21] Currie, *Image and Mind*, chapter 6.

to see through the narrator's eyes and therefore from within the fictional space. Moreover, the oddity of make-believedly seeing through the narrator's eyes is even greater than make-believedly seeing directly. For how are we to imagine that we can see through the narrator's eyes? Are we to imagine that there is some kind of extraordinary technical device, or magical means, by which the narrator's perceptual experience is presented to us directly? But that is ruled out by the fictional worlds of all those films that are broadly realist – i.e., broadly like everyday life, in which these things are impossible. (Indeed, on certain construals of what is at issue it is conceptually impossible that we see through the narrator's eyes, if this involves having the narrator's token perceptual experiences, as opposed to experiences that are qualitatively similar, since token experiences are individuated by reference to the identity of the person having them.) So on the impersonal imagination theory, the narrator as observer model should also be firmly rejected.

5.3.2 *The narrator as guide*

A second model of the cinematic narrator avoids some of the difficulties just adumbrated. This model is similar to the first in that it holds that the cinematic narrator is the fictional visual presenter or shower of each scene, but differs from it, in that it holds that when we fictionally see, we see directly through our own eyes, not his. The narrator is, as it were, a perceptual guide to the scenes, showing us the sights and sounds, pointing them out to us, and directing our attention to what is important. This model of the cinematic narrator is defended by Levinson, who believes that it is 'the best default assumption' for cinematic narration, and also appears to be the model adopted by Chatman.[22]

In support of this model Levinson writes that given that we are make-believedly seeing fictional events, we must be able to answer the question of '*how it is* we are seeing what we are seeing... Reason ... demands an answer to how it is that a world is being made visible to us'.[23] And that answer, he thinks, must involve the narrator as a perceptual guide to the sights seen. In support of this, he argues against Wilson's claim in *Narration in Light* that it is the implied filmmaker that is the agent who performs this perceptual role, rather than the narrator. Levinson correctly points out that if we are to think

---

[22] Levinson, 'Film Music and Narrative Agency', p. 252; and Chatman, *Coming to Terms*. Though he does not defend this version, the model is what Wilson in '*Le Grand Imagier* Steps Out' calls the Fictional Showing Hypothesis in the Face-to Face version.

[23] Levinson, 'Film Music and Narrative Agency', p. 256.

of the agent as fictionally presenting sights to us, then that agent must be internal to the fiction, for the sights are themselves fictional. The implied filmmaker, in contrast, stands outside the fiction, being its author, and thus can make available only *representations* of the fictional events, not the fictional events themselves.[24]

The narrator as guide model has clear advantages over the first model. It acknowledges that in standard cinematic shots we see directly, not through another's eyes, and thus avoids the extra problems of working out how we fictionally could see through someone else's eyes. But, assuming that the impersonal imagination view is correct, the second model is also ruled out; for if we are make-believedly shown, we must make-believedly see, the events depicted; hence Currie's objections against make-believe seeing would tell against this kind of narrator too. And the same point applies to Levinson's claims that we must be able to answer the question from within the fictional world of how we are shown the fictional sights. For this is a demand that we must imagine something else to be fictional if we are to imagine seeing something, and this is precisely the kind of demand that leads to the embarrassing questions rehearsed above, which cause such difficulties for the view that we are make-believedly seeing. If reason demands the existence of a narrator, then, it will also demand answers to these kinds of questions. It seems much better to deny the existence of make-believe seeing at all, and then the question of how we are fictionally shown these events simply lapses.

5.3.3 *The narrator as image-maker*

The third model holds that the narrator does not fictionally present *events* to us, but rather fictionally presents *images* of events to us. It is fictional that we are watching a film about events that actually occurred. The narrator, then, is the maker of that film. The idea seems to have originated with the film theorist Albert Laffay, and was championed by Metz, who talks of each shot being produced by a '*grand imagier*', a great image-maker.[25] A more careful version of the view is championed by Wilson.[26] He defends what he terms the Fictional Showing Hypothesis in its mediated version: that is, he claims that it is fictional that we are being shown images of actual events. He seems to want to leave it for determination at some future point as to whether this requires the existence of a narrator; but for a reason similar

---

[24] *Ibid.*, p. 255.   [25] Christian Metz, *Film Language*, pp. 20–1.
[26] Wilson, '*Le Grand Imagier* Steps Out'.

to that advanced by Levinson (discussed above) against Wilson's earlier theory, it is hard to see how the image-maker could be the implied film-maker. For if it is fictional that we are shown images of actual events, then it is fictional that someone made those images of actual events, and that cannot be a role occupied by the implied filmmaker, since he stands outside the fiction, rather than being a character internal to it. So I will take it that Wilson should be committed to the view that the image-maker is indeed the narrator.

This third model is an improvement on both of the earlier ones. It does not claim that we see through the narrator's eyes, and so sidesteps the problems which we saw that this claim caused. Moreover, since we are fictionally viewing *images* of real events, rather than those events themselves, we can answer some of the embarrassing questions we rehearsed earlier. There is no need, for instance, to imagine that we have eyes which can mimic wide-angle and telephoto lenses, or which somehow can perform the equivalent of a screen-wipe: since we are make-believedly being shown images, it is make-believe in such cases that the images were shot with various lenses, or edited using wipe techniques; and there is no oddity involved at all in imagining these things. Moreover, this view yields the closest analogue to the literary narrator. The literary narrator, recall, is someone whose words it is fictional that we are reading in reading the novel. The strict analogue would not involve sights and sounds, as the first two models of cinematic narration claim, but images that it is fictional that the narrator is producing. Hence the strict analogue would have the narrator as a documentary-maker of events, and it is fictional that in watching a fiction film we are watching the narrator's documentary.

However, if this is the right way of taking the narrator, then we seem to have some even more absurd things to imagine. Why do the characters in the film not notice that there is a documentary film crew present? How could there be such a crew present in scenes when a character is presented as being alone? Or, as Currie notes, if we are to think of the film as a recreation of something that happened earlier, we have to imagine the narrator as someone who has gone to a vast amount of expense, employing actors and technicians to recreate earlier events, something which becomes particularly odd if the narrator is to be considered as living at a time before the invention of cinema.[27]

Wilson believes that these kinds of objection are mistaken. If we assume that it is fictional that we are watching motion picture shots of actual events,

---

[27] Currie, *Image and Mind*, p. 267.

then it may indeed be true by definition that fictionally a camera must be present at the scene. But we need not imagine this; we could imagine that we are watching what he terms 'naturally iconic shots'. These are defined as shots, the features of which exhibit natural counterfactual dependence on the scene; which lack a worked surface (unlike a painting); and which are designed to store or transmit visual information.[28] The point of this definition is that it is not conceptually necessary that such shots are produced by a camera; but they are otherwise as like actual photographic images as is possible. It follows that in imagining that I am viewing such shots of actual events, I need not imagine that a camera was present at the scene, so that no absurd consequences need follow.

If we are to imagine that we are seeing naturally iconic shots, then we are to imagine something far removed from what is fictional in the majority of fiction films, whose represented worlds are overwhelmingly similar to the real world. In the real world, the only way we can produce shots is via the presence of a camera at the scene filmed. So the viewer on this proposal would have to imagine that shots are being taken in a way that is impossible in the world of these fiction films. And it is highly implausible that the proposal captures what viewers imagine, since the concept of a naturally iconic shot is a term of art; it is a concept unlikely ever to have occurred to most film viewers, and perhaps not even be graspable by many of them.

However, the main burden of Wilson's reply is that it may be fictionally *indeterminate* what mechanisms cause these shots to be produced and assembled. Indeed, he notes that there are fictions in which this seems to be so – Flash Gordon's view screen gives him visual access to what is going on elsewhere, though it does not seem to be fictional that a camera is present at the scene, and it is indeterminate how the mechanism operates.[29]

This kind of reply, which relies on fictional indeterminacy or related notions, is open to all of the narratorial models, and we will examine it in the next section. But if this reply is not satisfactory, we can say that the narrator as image-maker, along with the two other models, should be rejected as a general account of film narration.

5.4 ABSURD IMAGININGS AND SILLY QUESTIONS

Several considerations were deployed against the three versions of cinematic narrators, but there was one common objection – that their existence would

---

[28] Wilson, '*Le Grand Imagier* Steps Out', p. 313.   [29] *Ibid.*, pp. 314–15.

require us to engage in absurd or even contradictory imaginings. But is that a good objection?

One worry is that the same kind of argument would rule out the existence of explicit narrators too. For how are we to imagine that these manage to narrate when they do so by visual means? We seem to have a choice of one of the three models discussed above, but the objections to them do not depend on the narrator being implicit, so they work equally against explicit narrators. And that suggests that something is wrong with the objection as it stands.

One can press the point by considering an explicit narrator who seems to be responsible for the sound and images. *All About Eve* (1950) is narrated in voice-over by Addison DeWitt, a theatre critic who introduces us at the start of the film to the characters present at an award ceremony for the actress Eve Harrington (see Figure 7). DeWitt controls the sound – he says of the aged speaker at the ceremony 'it is not important that you hear what he says', and we do not hear the character – until, that is, DeWitt tells us he has decided

Figure 7. Eve Harrington (Anne Baxter) receiving her award in *All about Eve* (1950).

to let us do so. As he introduces each character, including himself, the camera shows us that person. And memorably at one point there is a freeze-frame of Eve about to receive her award. DeWitt's voice continues over this freeze-frame, teasingly implying that we do not know as much about Eve as we suppose. As Sarah Kozloff correctly remarks in discussing this sequence, 'The first thing one notices is that the voice here is actually in complete control of the image... This narrator is also in charge of the sound track'.[30] The sequence points, then, towards DeWitt's being responsible for the sound and images. But if one tries to imagine how this is possible, one is led to imagine absurdities. DeWitt speaks to us from within the story-world: as he looks knowingly at the camera, we hear his voice saying: 'it is perhaps necessary to introduce myself. My name is Addison DeWitt'. But his lips do not move: somehow we seem directly to hear his thoughts, as he controls what we see and hear. Is this fictionally a case of telepathy? And how can DeWitt be controlling image and sound while sitting in front of us, himself part of the story? It does not seem to be fictional that the awards ceremony is being filmed, and that his is a voice-over added to that film later. The sense of the sequence is that we are present; indeed, DeWitt tells us: 'it is important that you know where you are and why you are here'. Yet the fictional world of *All About Eve* is not one filled with magic, it is broadly like the real world; and in the real world this act of narration is impossible. Yet there is no doubt that DeWitt is narrating this sequence, and does so by controlling the sound and images. The argument from absurd imaginings would conclude that DeWitt cannot be the narrator. But he is.

The most powerful response to the argument from absurd imaginings is to hold that it fails since it is an instance of asking *silly questions* about fictions, questions that it is illegitimate to pose and to attempt to answer. How can Othello speak such great verse while holding that he is rude of tongue, and no one notices? Why in Leonardo's *Last Supper* are the disciples all sitting on one side of the table – is it because they are trying to avoid each other's bad breath? Such questions are silly, since there are no answers to them in the fictional world, and we are not supposed to engage in the imaginings that they might prompt; the answers to the question lie, rather, outside the fictional worlds, in the need in the first case to enhance the work aesthetically, and in the second to give us epistemic access to what the disciples' faces look like.[31] In the same way, we illegitimately pose silly questions, if we query how the implicit narrator could have the powers that he fictionally has. That does not mean he does not exist, any more than

[30] Sarah Kozloff, *Invisible Storytellers*, p. 65.   [31] Walton, *Mimesis as Make-Believe*, section 4.5.

posing silly questions about Othello does not show that he does not speak great verse.

There are two kinds of moves behind this general response. First, one can argue that even when one is prescribed by a fiction to imagine some state of affairs, one is not required to imagine its implications.[32] So, even if one is required to imagine a narrator, one need not imagine how he is accomplishing his act of narration – that would be to pose silly questions. Since what is fictional is what one is prescribed to imagine, one can put the point this way: it may be fictionally indeterminate what else is the case, when one imagines some state of affairs – this is Wilson's formulation, as noted earlier.[33] So though it may be fictional that there is an image-maker narrating, it may be fictionally indeterminate how he is doing so. The second kind of move concerns those cases where one is prescribed to imagine contradictions: for instance, that one is seeing a murder and that the murder is unseen. (In this case, one cannot appeal to the fact that one is not required to imagine the implications of one's imaginings, since here one is directly prescribed to imagine incompatible things.) The response is that this introduces no extra difficulties, since imaginings (for instance, dreams) and fictions sometimes involve incongruities of this kind.[34]

This reply, if successful, shows that the main argument against implicit narrators fails and thus leaves it open for us to acknowledge their presence. And it also undermines an objection to the related view that we imagine seeing fictions in cinema, rather than impersonally perceptually imagine them. But is the reply successful?

Consider the second part of the reply – that fictions and imaginings can involve incoherence and inconsistencies, so that no extra kinds of problems are introduced by positing acts or entities that involve imagining contradictions. It is certainly correct that fictions, such as time-travel stories and many fairy tales, may involve incoherence. But we can note as a general heuristic principle that when we interpret fictional worlds we should attempt, other things equal, to render them as like the real world as we can. Very many features of fictional worlds are left implicit – we are not usually told that characters have blood in their veins, that they are not

---

[32] Kendall Walton, 'On Pictures and Photographs: Objections Answered', p. 62. To make this claim sufficiently general, I suggest that implications should be understood in a broad sense: let 'P' and 'Q' range over states of affairs, and suppose that in the real world, if P were the case, then Q would be the case. This might be because P logically entails Q; or more weakly because Q follows from P, given some law of nature; or yet more weakly because P makes it probable that Q. In all such cases I will say that Q is an implication of P.

[33] Wilson, '*Le Grand Imagier* Steps Out', pp. 306–9.

[34] Walton, 'On Pictures and Photographs', p. 65.

robots masquerading as humans, and so on. We assume that these things are so, employing the interpretative principle just mentioned. If we did not assume that fictional worlds were much like the real world, except in those respects in which they explicitly differ, there would be massive indeterminacy as to how correctly to interpret even what is made explicitly fictional. From this point it follows that one should seek, other things equal, to minimise incoherence and contradictions in fictional worlds, for the real world does not have incoherence and contradictions in it. Where there are explicit fictional anomalies, such as singing kettles or time travel, one should obviously accept that these things are fictional. But if the entities are purportedly implicit, such as putative visual narrators, there is reason not to introduce them, unless there are compelling arguments for why we should do so. But we have seen that there are no such arguments: the general a priori argument, and Levinson's argument about what reason demands, both fail. So, insofar as imputing implicit visual narrators to films produces incoherence or inconsistencies, one should reject them.

Now consider the first part of the reply. It may be true that when we are imagining something on our own without fictional guidance, we are not always required to imagine the implications of our imaginings (though this depends in part on the point of our imaginings). But when we appreciate fictions, we generally are required to imagine a wide range of implications of what is explicitly fictional. Comparatively little of a fictional world is made explicit, and we are required to imagine many other states of affairs to interpret what is explicitly fictional correctly. Consider a character's words, reported in a novel: if we seek to understand her motivations, we need to imagine what fictionally are her psychological states that explain her words. So we have to imagine what the implications are of what is explicitly made fictional. In general, we have to imagine the implications of what is explicitly fictional *as part of appreciating a work*. For instance, works can be criticised for having absurd or untenable implications, such as their characters' motivations being implausible, criticisms that may well depend on imagining the implications of what is fictional. So given the general reason to consider the implications of what is explicitly fictional, the argument from absurd imaginings against implicit narrators should stand, for we have seen no good arguments to show that implicit narrators must be imputed to films. Again, however, if narrators are explicit, we have to admit their existence, and either accept the absurd implications, or background them by refusing to dwell on them.

So the outcome of our discussion of silly questions is that we should avoid, if we can, imputing entities to fictions that would ground the asking of such questions of them. Hence we should avoid imputing implicit narrators to films. But this argument has been challenged by George Wilson. Wilson criticises it chiefly by considering its application to literature. For the same basic argument would, it seems, yield the same scepticism about implicit narrators in literature. Consider the case of purported omniscient narrators, such as that in George Eliot's *Middlemarch*. Such narrators are presumably human beings (the fictional teller is not usually an extra-terrestrial or God). How could a mere human being gain access to all this knowledge, often the most intimate thoughts of people, which they do not tell to anyone else? Or consider a novel about someone who dies alone, and we read her dying thoughts; how could the narrator know such things? Clearly, a whole array of silly questions threatens; and a similar argument to that rehearsed against ascribing cinematic narrators should apply to show that implicit narrators are far less common in literature than one might suppose.

Wilson has a response to this example, and he believes that the response shows that the general argument that I have employed is unsound. He notes that the heuristic principle mentioned earlier (that when we interpret fictional worlds we should attempt, other things equal, to render them as like the real world as we can) is defeasible, because of the 'other things equal' clause. In the standard case of omniscience, of which *Middlemarch* is an example, he holds that the principle is defeated. For there is a 'basic prescription of "stipulated" omniscience' operative in such cases, which holds: 'if the narrator fictionally asserts that P, then it is fictional in the story that P, unless that presumption is specifically defeated or otherwise cast in doubt'.[35] And he thinks that in the case of wholly reliable omniscient narration, there is a related implicit stipulation that the narrator knows that *P*. Hence there is no question about how the narrator knows the fictional facts: that happens by stipulation, and hence the heuristic principle gains no traction in such cases. He further supports his position by considering what he says is a related case, modelled on the earlier Othello example, in which a fictional work, written in elegant sestinas (a poetic form), has a narrator who is a plain military man who is reporting on the battles in which he has participated, even though it is fictionally indeterminate how he could have acquired these literary skills, or worse it is fictionally determinate that he could not have acquired the skills. But by the heuristic principle there must be some way that he acquired them: so, here again, the correct conclusion is that the principle is defeated. The first case involves defeat by the machinery of generation of fictional truths, the second case defeat by the form of the narrative: both examples show that the heuristic principle is defeated when it tries to rule out the existence of implicit narrators.[36]

---

[35] George Wilson, 'Elusive Narrators in Literature and Film', p. 85.   [36] *Ibid.*, pp. 85–6.

Wilson's objections are unsuccessful. First, the adapted Othello case is one where the narrator must be explicit, since it is essential to it that we know that he is a plain military man who is reporting on the events in which he participated, so there must be specific evidence within the text for his existence and characteristics. The 'other things equal' clause is intended to allow for explicit narrators, and it would correctly conclude in this case that there is a narrator, and that we just have to acknowledge the inconsistencies in the text. So this case cannot call the principle into question. The standard omniscience case, however, is one where the alleged narrator is implicit and is thus germane. But Wilson's basic prescription of stipulated omniscience does not solve the problem of narratorial knowledge. The principle (ignoring the presumption clause) states: if the narrator fictionally asserts that *P*, then it is fictional that *P*. Now consider the antecedent clause, 'the narrator fictionally asserts that *P*'; if that is true, then we should conclude that the narrator exists. But the narrator does not exist, of course: he is only fictional. So the scope of the 'fictional' operator is too narrow in the principle: the principle should read 'if it is fictional that the narrator asserts that *P*, then it is fictional that *P*'. But now the issue of how the narrator can know that *P* resurfaces. When he was outside the fictional world, he could make it fictional that *P* by stipulation; but he cannot stipulate the existence of facts in the fictional world if he is a participant in it – otherwise he could stipulate himself into existence. So there are two closely related problems with Wilson's stipulation principle: from the principle as stated the narrator would actually exist, rather than fictionally exist, which is false; and once we modify the principle to make the narrator fictional, the stipulation possibility is no longer coherent. In fact, it is the *author* who alone is in the position to bring the fictional truths into existence by stipulation, and, as we noted earlier, the author is a distinct figure from the narrator. Hence Wilson's principle cannot solve the problem of narratorial knowledge.

Wilson has the resources to reply to this objection.[37] For he argues that at least in some cases the actual author is the narrator of a work. He speculates, for instance, that Jane Austen, the actual novelist, is the narrator of *Emma*

---

[37] A different option Wilson might explore is that the narrator is, to employ Walton's terminology, a storytelling narrator rather than a reporting narrator: the former tells a story as fiction, so that it is fictional that the narrator tells a story in which it is fictional that *P* (Walton, *Mimesis as Make-Believe*, pp. 368–72). In such cases the narrator could stipulate that *P*, while still being fictional, though not being a member of the fictional world that includes that state of affairs, *P*. However, this solution would not work for those cases where the narrator tells the story as fact, i.e., for the standard omniscience case, which includes *Middlemarch*, and where the narrator, if he exists, would be a reporting narrator and so a member of the world in which *P* is the case.

and perhaps George Eliot is the narrator of *Middlemarch*.[38] If so, then the entailment that the narrator exists seems correct, since Austen and Eliot existed, and they, as authors, possess powers of stipulation over their fictional worlds.

However, this move does not work. First, as Wilson notes, there are cases where it is explicitly fictional that the actual author is the narrator; but we are of course concerned with implicit narrators in the current debate, and we are given no reason to think that the actual author is the narrator in such cases, other than that they can be used to ground the implicit narrator claim. Without such a reason, a basic principle of ontological parsimony gives us reason not to postulate extra entities.[39] Second, even if we agreed that the actual author could also be the narrator in some cases, it would not rescue the basic principle of stipulated omniscience. For, as we saw in Section 5.2, the *roles* of narrator and author are distinct, so Wilson's claim, if it is to be defensible, can only be that one person may occupy both roles. But if this is so, then we can ask about the person's properties qua author and qua narrator, in the same way that we can ask about a person's properties qua mother and qua academic, if she occupies both roles. So consider S, author and purportedly narrator of a fictional work, W. Qua author, S can stipulate that some state of affairs, P, is fictional in W. But, qua author, she does not know that P, since P is very likely false: what she knows is that *it is fictional* in W that P. Qua purported narrator, she could know that P, because she is fictional, as is the state of affairs that P, so it may be that it is fictional that qua narrator she knows that P. But then the question arises of *how* she knows (has epistemic access to) P. And the answer cannot be that qua narrator she knows because she has stipulated that P, for, qua narrator she has no powers of stipulation over the fictional world. In short, exactly the same problems arise on the dual-occupancy model as arise for the author and narrator considered separately; and the reason for this is plain: the fact that one individual occupies both roles cannot explain how the narratorial role itself has powers both of stipulation and epistemic access. It cannot possess both sets of powers together.

Finally, recall that our main interest is in film rather than literature. Wilson draws a useful distinction between the narrator as a minimal narrating agent (which possesses no powers beyond the ability to narrate) and the narrator as a discernible character (which possesses additional character traits).[40] Wilson is confident that there are narrators as discernible

---

[38] Wilson, 'Elusive Narrators in Literature and Film', pp. 78, and 84 n. 18.
[39] Ockham's razor is also wielded in this context by Thomas Wartenberg, 'Need there be Implicit Narrators of Literary Fictions?', pp. 93–4.
[40] Wilson, 'Elusive Narrators in Literature and Film', p. 76.

characters in literature, but he is noticeably more hesitant about films and seems to hold that these involve only minimal narrating agents.[41] One can see why he thinks this is plausible, since the opportunities for expressing character traits are far greater in the case of literature, with its possibilities of nuances conveyed through the spoken word, than through relatively crude cinematic means, such as camera movement, lighting and so forth.[42] Now if this is so, one must wonder what point there could be to defending minimal narrating agents in film. *Ex hypothesi* they have no traits other their narrating capacities, so their postulation cannot enrich our interpretative insights into films. The only point to postulating them would be to defend the claim of the existence of widespread implicit narrators. But the general arguments for the existence of these entities in cinema fail, and moreover their postulation is inconsistent with a plausible heuristic principle. If postulating them has no advantages and causes unnecessary complications and difficulties, then the rational response is not to postulate them in the first place.

So the replies appealing to the illegitimacy of asking silly questions and to the basic principle of stipulated omniscience fail, and the outcome is that we should acknowledge only explicit narrators in film. We should avoid positing entities that ground silly questions, unless the entities are explicitly fictional. There is another upshot of this discussion. Although it is directly relevant to the issue of narration, Walton's 'silly questions' reply is explicitly directed in defence of his view that we make-believedly see fictions, against Currie's view that we impersonally visually imagine them. Since we have argued that the reply fails, we should similarly conclude the default mode in traditional cinema is that we impersonally imagine visual fictions.[43] But, again, the position must allow for what is made explicitly fictional; and in the case of make-believe seeing, it is plausible that in some cases, such as certain point-of-view shots, it is fictional that we make-believedly see what the character sees. The default mode of the spectator's engagement with traditional film is impersonal visual imagining, but there can be suitably cued episodes of make-believe seeing.[44]

---

[41] Ibid., pp. 76 and 87.

[42] However, even in the literary case, the 'voice' suggested by the work may more plausibly be that of the implied author, rather than the narrator, as we shall see in the next section.

[43] I will argue in Section 6.5 that in interactive cinema the situation is more complex.

[44] For related arguments on this point, see my 'Imagination, Interpretation and Film'. p. 336. Andrew Kania, 'Against the Ubiquity of Fictional Narrators' also argues that we should avoid postulating fictional narrators unless there is specific evidence to favour their presence. His position differs from that defended here, however, in part because I will argue that there is more reason to postulate narrators in literature than in film and also because Kania accepts the legitimacy of Wilson's appeal to indeterminacy, which I reject.

5.5 LITERARY NARRATORS

I have argued that only explicit (voice-over or character) narrators ought to be acknowledged in cinema. I also noted, in discussing Wilson's objection to the argument, that the same basic argument applies to literature, and that this shows that narrators are less common in literature than is usually supposed. However, that does not yet support the symmetry claim about narrators, since it may be that there are other considerations that show that narrators have a greater role in literature than in film, even though they are not as ubiquitous in literature as is often thought. I consider now three arguments in support of this asymmetry.

The first holds that in literature one always has a sense of a "voice" issuing the words of the text. Language is an extremely subtle instrument for expressing nuances and character, so it is natural to think of some personality reflected in the words. One can contrast this with cinema; whilst a sense of personality may be conveyed by lighting, camera movement, and so on, these devices are relatively crude compared to the subtleties of language, as noted earlier. However, though the point about the relative subtlety of language and cinematic technique is correct, the greater sense of a "voice" in deployment of language does not show that this is a *narratorial* voice. It could be that of the implied author. So the point does not prove the ubiquity of narrators in literature.

Second, and more promising, is Kendall Walton's argument that, since we pervasively employ declarative sentences to report or describe events, when we encounter such sentences in a fictional work, we 'almost inevitably' imagine someone using those sentences for declarative (assertive) purposes; since in the context it is only fictional that these sentences are declarative, it must be a fictional entity who reports by means of them, i.e., there must be a narrator.[45] Wilson similarly holds that we imagine and are supposed to imagine when encountering a literary fiction that where there is an assertion, someone is asserting something; and this is the narrator. He rejects Noël Carroll's alternative view that we simply take the propositional content presented as something to be imagined. For this content can be presented in a variety of different modes with different illocutionary forces: it might be fictional that it is asserted that P, or fictional that it is supposed that P, or fictional that it is asked whether P, and so on. So the view that we simply invariably imagine that P is inadequate, since it is insensitive to the variety of modes of presentation of content that are

---

[45] Walton, *Mimesis as Make-Believe*, pp. 365–6.

available.[46] We can add that if these arguments were correct, there would be a contrast with cinema. Since fiction film is the dominant type of cinematic practice, not documentary film, a parallel argument to Walton's would not show that fiction films are to be thought of as fictional documentaries (which would yield a version of the narrator as image-maker). And Wilson's illocutionary force argument, being based on speech acts, would not apply directly to cinema, which, as we saw in Section 2.1, is not language-like in its structure; so at best one would have a strained application to cinema (what, for instance, would count as a cinematic shot that would fictionally be asking whether *P*?). So if the arguments are sound, they would show that we have more reason to believe in narrators in literature than in film, and they would support the asymmetry claim.

Are these arguments sound? Both authors are hesitant in their endorsement of them, and with good reason. It cannot be the case that mere fictional assertion gives grounds for holding that there is an implicit narrator; for, as David Davies has noted, philosophical thought experiments are verbal fictions, but there is no tendency or reason to think of them as involving an implicit narrator: they are put forward merely for us to imagine the propositional content presented and are received as such.[47] The illocutionary force argument is more subtle. There are two kinds of cases to examine. Consider the following extract from a made-up short story: 'Dahlia heard a noise in the house and crept silently down the stairs. Suppose she did not make it to the front door. What would she do? She was very afraid.' Here the supposition and question are most naturally understood as making it fictional that Dahlia wonders whether she would make it to the door and what she would do then. We are to imagine states of affairs that are the contents of Dahlia's consciousness, and this gives no more reason to believe in the existence of a narrator than does the fact that the first and last sentences of the quotation ask us to imagine states of affairs that are independent of her consciousness. What, though, if we took the supposition and the question not to be reports of Dahlia's consciousness? Wilson seems in his example to have this alternative in mind: 'Katie loves Hubble. Many people thought so. But was it true?' In such cases the question seems to be addressed to the reader. But this does not require a narrator either, but only an author: it is fictional that many people thought that Katie loves Hubble; and the author asks the reader to consider whether it is true in the fiction that

---

[46] Wilson, 'Elusive Narrators in Literature and Film', pp. 82–3. Wilson says that this argument is his main reason for believing in minimal narrating agents as narrators in literature.

[47] David Davies, 'Eluding Wilson's "Elusive Narrators"'.

Katie loves Hubble. And in Dahlia's case, on this reading, the author asks the reader to consider what Dahlia ought fictionally to do, and again no narrator is required. In the same way, a philosophical thought experiment might conclude by asking the reader what fictionally the parties in the predicament ought to do; and, as noted, there is no tendency to attribute narrators to thought experiments. So in neither the first kind of case, where the content of characters' mental states is fictionally presented, nor in the second case, where the reader is addressed by the author, is there any need to attribute a narrator to the fiction. So assertion or other speech acts in fiction do not give sufficient grounds for ascribing a narrator, and if we are to do so, we have to appeal to more specific features of the text that are best explained by the presence of a narrator.

So far we have seen no decisive reason to believe in the asymmetry claim. And, as noted in the discussion of omniscience in the previous section, similar arguments against implicit narrators that were developed for cinema also apply to the case of literary omniscience. So we should conclude that the role of the narrator is overestimated in literature; much of the "voice" that we ascribe to a narrator should more properly be ascribed to an implied author. However, while that point moves literary and cinematic narration closer together, it is not correct to conclude that film and literature are exactly alike in this respect, i.e., that the symmetry claim is true. For there is a third argument for asymmetry, which rests on the claim that there is a crucial difference in the epistemic access available to a narrator in film and literature. The easiest way to see this is by considering an example. In *North by Northwest* (1959), Roger Thornhill (Cary Grant) ends up battling on Mount Rushmore, at one point hanging on for his life by one hand from the stony visage of a president, with the heroine, Eve, dangling from his other hand. The shot is taken apparently from a point in mid-space, down and to the right of Thornhill. Clearly a host of awkward questions could be asked: how, fictionally, can the narrator be suspended in mid-air? Is it fictional that he has wings, and can hover around just out of reach of Thornhill? I have argued that it is best to avoid ascribing entities to fictions that could be the objects of such questions. But imagine that the same scene were told in a novel. There would be no similar set of awkward questions to be asked. For the narrator might have observed the battle safely from the ground through a telescope; or he might have been told of it later by Thornhill; or he might have read about it in one of the participants' diaries; and so on. The crucial difference is that the film image has an intrinsic perspective from which it is taken; and in anything remotely resembling the real world, it follows that someone or something was observing the scene from that point of space at the time that the scene was occurring. But the same is not true of language. So it is a difference between a *visual* medium and a merely *lexical* medium that explains why certain absurd imaginings are grounded in the first case and not in the second. This point applies not just to the visual, but to the *auditory* nature of film too. For the sound image presents Thornhill's and Eve's voices from a point close to them; again, we could ask how, fictionally, the narrator (or the spectator) could be in this position floating in space. But the same point does not apply to a report of the characters' words in a novel: we could have been told later what they said, and so on. So the difference is that in cinema there is the *sound* of the words, in the case of the novel there is merely a lexical report. In short, it is because film is an *auditory-visual* medium, and the novel is a *lexical* medium, that there is greater grounding for absurd imaginings in the case of the former than the latter. So there is more reason to believe in implicit narrators in novels than in films; and this difference is to be traced to medium-specific differences – to the nature of an auditory-visual medium as opposed to a lexical medium. We have returned to the importance of the medium in film again.

5.6 OTHER NARRATIVE FEATURES

So far we have concentrated on the question of the existence of narrators in novels and films. Yet the point about medium-grounded asymmetry generalises to other aspects of narration too.

First, if, as I have argued, narrators are less common in film than in novels, due to the differences in the media, then that point also bears on the question of mediation and point of view in film, as compared to novels. Narrators mediate readers' epistemic access to a fictional world in the sense that it is fictional that the words of a narrated text are the words of the narrator, and hence the reader's knowledge of the world depends on the narrator. To allow for the possibility of unreliable narrators, the reader must be prepared to adjust his beliefs about the fictional world in the light of his judgements about whether on various points the narrator can be trusted. The narrator, in the way he describes the events that occur, also exhibits an affective point of view on them, reporting them neutrally, favourably or unfavourably. In the case of those films without narrators, *a fortiori* access and point of view cannot depend on the narrator. So there is a way in which films without narrators are not mediated, i.e., they are more immediate, than literary works with narrators; and this feature depends on properties of the respective media. However, this does not mean that film is completely unmediated: mediation can happen in other ways in film – for instance, implied filmmakers may mediate access; and as we have noted, Currie has argued that unreliable narration in film can be construed in terms of the implied author.[48]

Second, consider the question of access to characters' subjective states. In literature we can be given highly specific and detailed descriptions of the nuances of what characters are thinking and feeling. In film, we have to infer characters' inner states from their looks, gestures and speech – in short, from their behaviour. Even if they speak out loud a description that might have figured in a novel about them, the status of this description is different in the case of film; for here their speaking the words is itself a part of the behaviour that they exhibit, from which we infer their mental states. But a description in the novel would make it directly fictionally true that they were in certain mental states, without the need for inference from their behaviour on our part. Thus novels can give us direct access to subjective states in a way that films cannot.[49] This is a difference in the narrative powers of films and novels; and it too is to be traced to media-specific differences. One can describe someone's mental states, her thoughts and feelings. But one cannot photograph a thought or feeling, nor can one tape-record it; one can only record the outward manifestations of these things. So there is a simple explanation for why film and literature differ in respect of subjective access. It is one reason why Proust's works, with their masterly and extensive nuanced descriptions of inner states, have been so hard to adapt successfully to film.

Third and relatedly, there is a difference in the range of what films as opposed to novels make fictionally explicit, as we noted in Section 4.3. It is sometimes said in criticism of films that they leave less to the imagination than do literary works. For a range of audio and visual facts, this is true. A film shows very precisely how a character looks and sounds, whereas a novel may give only a vague, or indeed no, description of how even an important character looks and sounds. So in respect of the visual and auditory properties of characters and settings, films leave less to the imagination, since they

---

[48] The immediacy of film may also in part be traced directly to differences in the signs that constitute the media: our visual capacities to understand the world are activated much earlier as children than is our linguistic knowledge, and the capacity to read is gained much later, being the result of an extended learning process. It would be unsurprising, then, if part of our sense of the immediacy of films compared to novels is derived from films' being grounded on a less culturally determined capacity. Communication by visual and auditory means is more immediate than communication by written words.

[49] There is one exception: in film a reliable voice-over narrator can make it directly fictionally true that a character is feeling something. But if this device were used as extensively in a film as are descriptions in novels, films would start to approximate literary works being read out, with visuals added to illustrate them.

make the relevant properties explicitly fictional. But, as we have just seen, films cannot give direct access to characters' subjective states, so given the inferences required from behaviour, these subjective states are only implicitly fictional, i.e., they will require inferences from what is explicitly fictional in order to establish them. Or, indeed, they may be left fairly indeterminate: it is not uncommon to have precise knowledge of how a film character looks, yet to be left wondering about his motivations. So though it is true that in respect of visual and auditory appearances films typically leave less to the imagination, it is also fairly common for them to require more imagination in respect of characters' motivations (in the sense of requiring inferences about them, or leaving them indeterminate). And again this difference is grounded on a medium-specific difference: as an audio-visual medium, film must show audio-visual properties of what is in front of the camera, whereas its access to subjective states is indirect and inferential. In contrast, novels, as a lexical medium, have the option of leaving auditory-visual properties relatively underspecified, but they can directly describe characters' subjective states.[50]

Finally, there is a way in which narrational commentary is more indirect in film than it is in literature. In his fine study of *Une Partie de campagne* (1936), an adaptation of Guy de Maupassant's short story of the same name, Chatman points out that whereas de Maupassant simply describes a young girl as 'pretty', Renoir, the film's director, does not have that option. All he can do is to cast an actress whom he hopes that many people would find pretty.[51] The point, of course, generalises: language can be explicitly evaluative; filmed images cannot be, for one cannot photograph a value. So there is a possibility of explicit evaluative commentary in literature that cannot be achieved by the visual images of film.

There are evidently other respects in which the nature of the media affects their narrational capacities – music can contribute narrative information, for instance, in film, but obviously music cannot be heard at all in novels – but the points just noted should serve to illustrate that there is a rich variety of ways in which properties of the media affect narration.

These points further ground one of the main claims of this book – that it is a mistake to think that the issue of medium-specificity should play no role in the philosophy of cinema: medium-specific explanations plausibly figure

---

[50] This is not to say, of course, that novels must specify such states with any precision (some of Hemingway's works, for instance, do not), but only that they *can* directly specify such states, if they choose, and exploit this ability for striking artistic effect.

[51] Seymour Chatman, 'What Novels Can Do that Films Can't (and Vice Versa)', p. 452.

in an account of cinematic, as compared to novelistic, narration. The basis of these claims must be specified carefully – medium-specific features should not, for instance, be understood as ones that are *unique* to a medium, since several explanatorily important features of traditional films are shared with, for instance, digital cinema, and the same is true of properties shared in common by the novel and, say, the short story and poem. Rather, as I shall argue in Chapter 7, medium-specific features should be construed not in absolute terms, but rather as being relative to other media, as differential features, i.e., as features that differ between one group of media and another specified group. For instance, being audio-visual is a differential feature between traditional film and literature, since the former possesses this property and the latter does not. But being audio-visual is not a feature unique to traditional film, since it is also shared with analogue video, digital cinema and indeed theatrical performance. And this differential feature explains, as we have seen, several important differences between the narrative capacities of film and novels. Medium-specific explanations, in the sense of medium-involving explanations that appeal to differential properties between sets of media, are an important class of explanations in respect of narration.

5.7 INTERACTIVE NARRATION

How do these medium-specific claims apply to digital cinema? Non-interactive digital and traditional cinema share the same structural narrative features – they are both audio-visual means of narration, rather than lexical ones, like novels; so the claims about the restricted role of narrators in traditional films that we have defended apply equally to digital cinema. Digital cinema has in certain respects greater storytelling abilities, given its greater representational capacities, as shown by special effects. For instance, though it cannot, any more than can traditional film, photograph subjective states, it can suggest them even more effectively than does traditional film: the startling representation of the eruption of unwilled memory into conscious perceptual experience in *Eternal Sunshine of the Spotless Mind* (2004), in scenes which represent the fabric of reality as visibly coming apart, could not have been achieved so effectively without digital special effects. But, as we noted in Section 2.3.5, digital cinema also pays an epistemic price for its enhanced powers of representation, since one cannot with such confidence assume that it provides evidence of what actually happened in front of the camera. The result is that the aesthetic potency of realism is threatened in digital films: one has epistemic grounds for remaining more sceptical, for instance, about whether some breathtaking stunt involved any real action at all. So there are both gains and losses in narrative capacities in digital cinema compared to traditional film.

I have argued that there are good reasons to deny the presence of implicit narrators in non-interactive cinema: is that also true in interactive cinema? The argument against them rested on the fact that they ground absurd imaginings, and in the case of the narrator as invisible observer and as guide, these imaginings are that I make-believedly see things in the fictional world, which may require me to imagine such things as that I am stuck to the ceiling, or in outer space, or able to jump from one point to another instantaneously in the case of an editing cut. However, as we will see in Section 6.5, interactive cinema can under certain circumstances, particularly in its first-person modes (where the fictional world is shown from a persisting first-person point of view with no jump cuts) and where the character the player controls is only minimally specified, consistently ground a sense that one is directly participating in the fictional world, which standardly involves its being make-believe that one is seeing things in that world through one's own eyes. Hence in these cases there are no absurd imaginings; and so, one might conclude, the player is the implicit narrator in such instances. However, that last inference is mistaken. It is fictional that a narrator possesses story information that she transmits to the audience and the audience learns this information by virtue of the narrator's transmission of it to them. When the narrator performs this kind of action of information transmission to an audience, she performs a storytelling action. But if I directly participate in a fictional world, I am not the implicit narrator. For when I am directly participating in the fictional world, the make-believe actions in which I am engaged are standardly not storytelling ones.[52] They are actions of shooting enemies, searching for buried treasure, solving certain puzzles, and so on, not actions of telling stories about these deeds. In this mode of direct participation one is *exploring* the fictional world, not *narrating* facts about it; in the same way, one can explore the real world without telling stories about it. So there are good reasons to resist the existence of implicit narrators in the interactive cinema case.

However, there is one narrative respect in which interactive cinema appears to be distinctively different from non-interactive cinema: it enables

---

[52] Note that this is compatible with the existence of games in which I am cast as the narrator, where the fictional actions I am called upon to perform are storytelling ones to a fictional audience, distinct from myself. These are cases where there is an explicit narrator, but the issue under consideration concerns the existence of implicit narrators.

interactive narration. Several theorists have celebrated this possibility, particularly in respect of computer games. Janet Murray has argued that Star Trek's holodeck provides a convincing thought experiment for how interactive narration is possible, allowing crew members to 'participate in stories that change around them in response to their actions'.[53] The video-game designer, Chris Crawford, though he concedes that interactive story-telling is 'a Holy Grail that ... remains out of our reach', nevertheless holds that it will eventually be attained.[54] The media theorist, Marie-Laure Ryan, also affirms the possibility of interactive storytelling by computer.[55] And Michael Mateas and Andrew Stern not only defend the coherence of interactive storytelling but claim, in their computer game, *Façade* (2005), to have actually implemented it.[56] So all of these theorists and designers would agree that there is a fundamental medium-specific difference in narration between non-interactive and interactive cinema (including videogames).

These theorists, the narratologists, have met opposition from the ludo-logists, who stress the game aspect of videogames and question whether their narrative aspects are really interactive. Jesper Juul has queried the very coherence of the idea of interactive narration, holding that *'you cannot have interactivity and narration at the same time'*.[57] Gonzalo Frasca has argued that the simulation structure of games is incompatible with narration.[58] Espen Aarseth holds that the mission-based structure of many games gives the merely delusive appearance of narration.[59] And Steven Poole thinks that interactive storytelling must always remain limited and have little value compared to non-interactive narration.[60]

So before affirming that there is an important medium-specific narrative difference between interactive and non-interactive cinema, we need to examine the arguments against interactive storytelling. These fall broadly into two classes: arguments that query the *possibility* of interactive narration and its computational implementation; and arguments that question its *value*. Replying to these arguments will also require us to get clearer about the key concepts in play.

---

[53] Janet Murray, *Hamlet on the Holodeck*, p. 15.   [54] Chris Crawford, 'Interactive Storytelling', p. 272.

[55] Marie-Laure Ryan, *Avatars of Story*, chapter 8. Ryan provides an excellent survey of the literature on this topic, to which I am indebted.

[56] Michael Mateas and Andrew Stern, 'Façade: An Experiment in Building a Fully-Realized Interactive Drama'. The game can be downloaded from www.interactivestory.net.

[57] Jesper Juul, 'Games Telling Stories?', p. 7.

[58] Gonzalo Frasca, 'Simulation versus Narrative: Introduction to Ludology'.

[59] Espen Aarseth, 'Quest Games as Post-Narrative Discourse'.

[60] Steven Poole, *Trigger Happy*, chapter 5.

5.7.1 Objections to interactive narration

The main discussion of the possibility of interactive narration has been in game theory. Some of that debate is specific to computer games, but much of it explicitly or implicitly queries the very possibility of interactive story-telling. We can think of the objections as holding that, where there is interactivity, essential elements of narration are absent, so there can be no interactive narration.

First, though the modern videogame often does narrate, it does so only in its non-interactive sequences: and where it is interactive, in the gameplay, it never narrates. So where there is interactivity there is no narration; where there is narration, there is no interactivity: interactive narration never occurs. Storytelling occurs in cut scenes, which are short non-interactive films that provide exposition before the player is handed control for the gameplay, and only the latter is interactive.[61] Call this the *bifurcation argument*.

This argument, being empirical, could not show that interactive story-telling cannot occur in principle. Moreover, though bifurcation is true of many games, it is not true of all of them. *Bioshock* (2007) has two different, major endings, with some additional minor variations, each comprised of a distinct cut scene, and which is shown depends on the player's choices in the game. *Grand Theft Auto IV* (2008) also has more than one ending, as does *Shadow of Memories* (2001–2), which has no less than six different endings, again depending on the player's choices. More radically, *Façade* allows for continuous interactivity, with the story going in very different ways from moment to moment, depending on user input.

Second, interactivity requires modifying or changing something, and that is only possible for things that are happening now: one cannot change the past. But narration requires a temporal separation between the act of narra-tion, which may occur now, and the events narrated, which happen earlier than the narrational act. Since one cannot change past events, a necessary feature of narration is undermined by the presence of interactivity. Call this the *temporal distance argument*. Juul advances this argument and holds that therefore the events represented in an interactive context must always be represented as being in the present, and hence a fundamental structural feature of narration is lacking in interactive contexts.[62]

---

[61] Aarseth, 'Quest Games as Post-Narrative Discourse'; Crawford, 'Interactive Storytelling'; and Poole, *Trigger Happy*, p. 96. Poole deploys the point in an argument against the possibility of artistically valuable interactive storytelling, for which see Section 5.7.3 below.

[62] Juul, 'Games Telling Stories?'. A related point is made by Poole, *Trigger Happy*, pp. 95–6. Juul in his later work allows for a greater role for narration in games: see Jesper Juul, *Half-Real*, pp. 156–60.

However, it is not a conceptual requirement that the events narrated and the telling of them must be at temporally distinct points: one can tell a story about things that are happening now, which is what sports commentators do.[63] Moreover, some games, such as *Lara Croft Tomb Raider: Legend* (2006), have segments that are in flashback but which are interactive. Suppose that we were required to imagine some temporal incoherence here, such as being able to change the past: that would not show that these events were not set in the past, because it is fully explicit that this is so. The flashback segment in the Peru level in *Legend* is explicitly introduced by a cut scene showing that the events happened in the past. And, as noted earlier, it is possible to imagine what is impossible or incoherent (for instance, conscious, singing kettles), so incoherence does not prove that there is no temporal separation – in the same way that any incoherence introduced by explicit narrators does not prove that they do not exist. However, there need be no temporal incoherence introduced by interactive flashbacks. Consider a novelist writing a historical novel: by writing certain words she makes it fictional that certain events happened in the past. Is it thereby fictional that she has altered the past? Not so: there is a crucial scope difference of 'fictional' between the following propositions: the novelist writes P now and thereby makes it fictional that Q in the past; and it is fictional that the novelist writes P now and thereby makes it the case that Q in the past. Only the latter proposition makes it fictional that an event in the present changes the past. But it is the former that it is the correct formulation: the novelist operates outside the fictional world and constructs it. And the player of an interactive flashback is in this respect in a position analogous to the novelist's.

A third argument holds that interactivity requires a simulation of some situation and simulations are incompatible with narration. There are different variations of this *simulation argument*. One version holds that a simulation is not a representation, but a narrative is a type of representation, so no simulations are narratives. Frasca defends this view. He holds that videogames are simulations and understands a simulation as a *model* of a situation. He notes that whereas a narrative can be understood merely by knowing what happened, to understand a simulation one must experiment, trying it out several times with different inputs. A simulation in a videogame is like Augusto Boal's Theatre of the Oppressed, which involves inviting members of the audience on stage in order to participate in a fictional scenario and solve some problem. In short, 'the potential of games is not to

---

[63] Ryan, *Avatars of Story*, p. 186.

tell a story but to simulate: to create an environment for experimentation'.[64] A related variant of this objection holds that simulations are open-ended: one does not know what will happen (hence the point about experimentation). But in the case of a story, the storyteller must know what will happen. So interactive narration is not possible.

Frasca's point about the kind of repeat play required for understanding videogames is an important one to which we will return. But the simulation argument fails. For even if we think of a game as a simulation, a simulation is a model and a model is not something that structurally resembles and causally responds to something else. Rather, a model is *of* something, i.e., it is a representation. So simulations are kinds of representations and therefore can be narratives; and indeed some of them are. Moreover, the openness of the events and the fact that one can experiment with different inputs does not undermine the narrative component. For when a novelist is writing a story but has not yet decided on how the story will end, the story is similarly open-ended for him at the point of writing and he may try out different options in how it goes, but he is nevertheless telling the story as he writes it. Moreover, the notion of interactive storytelling requires the story to vary with audience input. So to point to the capacity to experiment in such works in order to show that narrative is not present is simply to assume that there can be no such thing as interactive narration. Boal's theatre in fact shows that there can be experimentation in narrative, since the actors vary the story they are conveying, depending on how the participating audience member acts.

A fourth argument holds that narration requires narrators, and in the interactive context there are no such entities, perhaps because the player is partly in control of the process of how the game goes, and hence there is no narrator controlling it. Call this the *no narrators argument*.[65]

We have already argued in Section 5.2 that narration does not require narrators. Narrators are fictional entities internal to the fictional world. Narration entails the existence of someone telling a story, but that person is an actual person, standardly the author or authors. So the no narrators argument is unsound. If interactors partly determine the story, then they are in a position akin to the authorial one, except that their determination is of the particular instance of the work, as we noted in Section 3.9, not the work itself.

[64] Frasca, 'Simulation versus Narrative', p. 225.
[65] Markku Eskelinen, 'The Gaming Situation', for instance, appeals to the absence of narrators and narratees as a reason to be sceptical about the possibility of narration in games.

A final objection is the *error argument*. Many videogames have a quest or mission structure, that is, the player is set fictional tasks and has to overcome obstacles to achieve them – perhaps he has to search for buried gold and fight enemies to secure it. Quest games are the sort of things about which one can tell good stories, for canonical stories have a protagonist who must overcome obstacles to fulfil goals. But to say that one can tell a story about some events does not entail that those events are stories. If I go on a shopping trip and tell a story about it afterwards, this does not show that my shopping trip was a story. In a videogame it is likewise true that one is fictionally engaged in actions, but one is not telling stories, whether interactive or not. But one is easily misled into thinking that one is by the fact that one can recount stories about what one did after finishing playing.[66]

It is certainly possible to confuse the fact that something would make a good story with the fact that it is a good story. However, the argument does not prove an error is being made in this case. What is correct is that in quest videogames, and indeed in almost all videogames, it is not *fictional* that one is telling a story, whether interactive or not (so one is not the narrator of these stories). It is fictional that one is engaged in many actions, none of which is a storytelling action. But the question is whether one is *actually* engaged in storytelling by means of making certain things fictional. A novelist tells a story by making certain things fictional using a written text. It need not thereby be *fictional* that he is telling a story – that is, as we noted, storytelling does not require a narrator. So if nothing in the fiction the novelist writes involves someone telling a story, it does not follow he is not actually telling a fictional story. In the same way, interactive storytelling does not require that it is fictional that interactive storytelling occurs. No error therefore need be imputed to the believer in interactive storytelling.

5.7.2 *The concept of interactive narration*

So some prominent objections to the idea of interactive narration fail. But perhaps there are lurking in the notion other difficulties. So it is time to get clearer about the notion of interactive storytelling. Let us consider a clear, paradigm case.

Jane decides to tell Otis, her bright and very excitable five-year-old son, a story. She makes up a tale called 'Teddy and the Dragon' concerning how

---

[66] This is an elaboration of, and I hope improvement on, an argument given by Aarseth, 'Quest Games as Post-Narrative Discourse'. Aarseth does not discuss canonical stories and holds that actions are quite distinct from storytelling, since stories have meaning and actions do not. The problem with this is that storytelling is one kind of action, so some actions can convey meanings.

teddy goes to the woods and meets a dragon there, with various exciting consequences. She verbally tells it to Otis. After a few tellings Otis starts to get bored and interrupts his mother with demands that teddy does something different this time. She initially ignores these protests, but, as is the way with mothers, eventually gives in. So when teddy is at the edge of the woods, Jane asks Otis whether teddy goes in or not. Otis decides that he does not, but instead heads off to the nearby beach. Improvising rapidly, Jane has teddy hunt for buried treasure on the beach. Does he find it? Otis decides that he does. On opening it, teddy discovers a golden egg. But this, it turns out, is a dragon's egg, and the dragon flies furiously out of the woods to reclaim it. There is no getting away from those dragons. Otis gets to decide whether teddy flees the dragon, or stands and fights. And so it goes.

Otis loves the new storytelling method, since it is to an extent up to him what happens in the story, and he knows it. Initially, Jane always asks Otis what teddy does at certain points; but as Otis gets more familiar with the method, Jane simply pauses at these points, and Otis announces what teddy will do.

Gradually Otis (who as I mentioned is very excitable) decides to act out teddy's decisions, rather than report them; and Jane, entering into the spirit of things, acts the parts of others in the story and sets the scene. Flapping her hands wildly, she becomes the dragon; Otis, wearing a fluffy cap with cute cloth ears, runs screaming from her. The kitchen becomes the beach, the cleaning box under the table the buried treasure; the living room becomes the forest, the rubber plant a tree and the sofa a large hill.

Enacting the story rather than verbally reporting it has two nice features: it makes the story more vivid and exciting; and it also means that Otis can decide what teddy does by acting out his decisions, rather than having to report them: Otis' decisions are thus incorporated into the enacted story.

This dramatic enactment of the story is such a success that Otis cannot have enough of it and he is a very insistent child. Jane is getting tired, particularly since she has a demanding job. Fortunately for her – and *very* fortunately for our example – her job is so demanding because she is a prominent videogame designer. Seeing the success of the story on her young son, she decides to produce a videogame, and working with her talented team of artists and programmers, she releases two years later *Teddy and the Dragon*. The player gets to play the part of teddy, who, depending on the player's choices, gets to meet a dragon in the woods or discovers buried treasure on the beach. Otis loves the game and plays it incessantly. Jane gets to put her feet up and watch television. Everyone lives happily ever after.

The Otis example illustrates a number of points. First, the difference between straight (non-interactive) and interactive storytelling is connected with the fact that the audience's choices partly determine what happens in the story. Mere interruptions, as in Otis' initial indignant demands for something new to happen, even though they affect what is said between him and Jane, do not count as contributions to an interactive story. Second, stories can be told through games of make-believe. Jane and Otis are playing a game of make-believe.[67] But they are also and by means of that game engaged in interactive storytelling, since Jane is using the acts of make-believe in order to tell a story and the content of that story is partly dependent on Otis' choices, a fact that is known to both of them. Jane is the storyteller, Otis is participating in that storytelling by virtue of making choices, either verbally or through his make-believe actions. So the performance of actions of make-believe can be the vehicle for interactive storytelling. Third, there is a close affinity between live-action role-playing games, which is what the enacted version of 'Teddy and the Dragon' is, and videogames, since both can serve as vehicles for make-believe and storytelling.[68] The difference is that videogames standardly use moving pictures for storytelling, whereas live-action role-playing games use enactment, i.e., they make it fictional of the players' bodies that they are the characters' bodies, in the same way that actors make it fictional of their bodies that they are the character's bodies. Otis' body is fictionally teddy's body in the enacted version; in the videogame version it is the moving image, which Otis controls, that is fictionally teddy's body. But in both versions players can play roles in the game and so participate in games of make-believe that can serve as vehicles for storytelling. The underlying similarity can be brought out by imagining Jane telling the story through a series of pictures of what the dragon is doing, and then Otis drawing in what teddy does in response to the dragon's action, rather than their using enactment.

So, in the light of our example, what is interactive narration, that is, interactive storytelling? Start with the question of what is it to *tell* a story. To tell someone something requires that one transmit information to her: to tell someone the time requires one to transmit information to her about the time. Does information transmission suffice for telling? We can say that a stone tells the story of the volcanic eruptions that led to its formation,

---

[67] For the classic treatment of games of make-believe, see Walton, *Mimesis as Make-Believe*, especially chapter 1.

[68] On live-action role-playing games and their relation to narration, see Murray, *Hamlet on the Holodeck*, especially pp. 116–25.

since it stores information about those eruptions. We can say that the thermometer tells the story of the day's temperature changes because it transmits information about them. So in a *minimal* sense telling is simply information transmission. But in the sense in which one person tells another something, telling is an action, so it is intentional under some description. Plausibly, that description is that information is being transmitted. A story is a kind of representation; a representation carries information (I am using 'information' in a sense that does not require it be to be veridical); so stories carry information. So to tell someone a story is intentionally to transmit to her story information.[69] Information can be conveyed by various means, including spoken and written utterances, visual images and make-believe actions. So storytelling covers not just verbal tellings, but also showings of images and enactments.

What is it for a *story* to be told? A story is always about something, so a story is a kind of representation. But not all representations are stories: 'the pot is black' is not a story, since it is a statement about a state of affairs. A story-representation must refer to at least one *event*. So is 'the rain fell' a story? Not in any remotely normal sense. How about 'the rain fell and Jack got very wet'? That is more promising. A story is a representation of a *sequence* of events. How about this: 'my car started when I pressed the ignition, the Japanese stock market fell by 500 points, and the sun came out in Dulwich'? Baffling. This looks like a list of unconnected events; struggling to interpret it as a story, one looks for some connection between them: perhaps there was a causal link between my car starting and the Japanese stock market swan diving, or some symbolic connection between them, or some other kind of connection? So a story is a representation of a series of *linked* events. That is, the story represents them as linked, whether or not they really are. Could this be refined to state what sort of linkage? Probably not: experimental literature could have been designed to undermine any such attempt.[70] So we will stick with *some* kind of linkage being ascribed,

---

[69] Note that this does not entail that the *story-content* conveyed is the content intended: as we saw in Section 4.1, one may intend to convey one content but fail to convey it (one's intentions may be defeated, perhaps through one's incompetence) and one may also convey something in addition to what one intended (the case of happy accidents, such as *The Turn of the Screw*). To hold that an action is categorised as a *type* of action partly in terms of the intention with which it is done is not to hold that the *content* of the action, if it has one, is determined by that intention. Consider a parallel: murder is by definition intentional killing, as opposed to manslaughter, which is non-intentional killing; but if I murder someone, it does not follow that I murdered the person I intended to (maybe his bodyguard got in the way of my shot and I killed him by mistake).

[70] For a discussion about what kind of linkage might be required, see Livingston, 'Narrative'. Livingston is not optimistic on finding a satisfactory answer: as he correctly notes, here 'Intuitions clash and blur' (p. 361).

implicitly or explicitly, by the story; and that will suffice for our present purposes.

What makes a story interactive? As noted, the story content in such a case is partly determined by the audience's actions (in this case, what Otis said). But that does not quite suffice, since Otis' interruptions to the straight story do not count as making the story interactive. Certainly, that is because the interruptions do not count as part of the story; but the question is what makes this so. Suppose Al, a drug-addled and weakly sentimental gangster, attends a performance of *Othello*, gets up on stage when Othello is about to kill Desdemona and threatens the actor playing Othello with grievous bodily harm if he kills her. Not liking the look of Al, the actor complies. Have we just seen an interactive performance of *Othello*? Evidently not. The reason is that the audience's part determination of story content was not *authorised* by the work. (In general, we can speak of authorisation by the work that tells the story, or, equivalently, authorisation by the tellers of the story.[71]) Contrast the case where there is a performance of *interactive-Othello*, an interactive play loosely modelled on *Othello*: here, if Al leapt on stage with the same threat, he would count as partly determining story content, since *interactive-Othello* authorises audiences' contribution to its content.

So an interactive story is a story where its teller (or the work) authorises that the story content is partly determined by the audience's actions. And interactive storytelling is storytelling where the teller (or work) authorises that the story content is partly determined by the audience's actions. On this account story content must be variable, since otherwise it could not be partly determined by the audience. Given the fact that content is variable, each particular determination of the content forms a *story-instance*. So equivalently we can say that interactive storytelling is storytelling where the teller (or work) authorises that *story-instances* are partly determined by the audience's actions. The definition of interactive storytelling, then, is an instance of the interactivity schema defended in Section 3.9.

Applying this analysis, Jane tells Otis a story by virtue of intentionally transmitting to him a representation about a sequence of linked events; that story is interactive because she authorises it that Otis' actions partly determine the story content. Jane could simply play a game of make-believe with

---

[71] I rely here on a general equivalence between things artworks do and what artists do in artworks. For instance, we can say either that a work represents something or that the artist represents something in the work; that a work expresses some emotion or that the artist expresses that emotion in the work; and so on. See my *Art, Emotion and Ethics*, pp. 71–4.

Otis while lacking any intention to transmit story information: in this case no story is told in their game. If she plays the game with an intention to transmit story information, then their game of make-believe is also an instance of storytelling. Some actions of make-believe and the games they comprise are vehicles for interactive storytelling.

One might query the adequacy of this analysis of interactive storytelling: for if storytelling is an action, how can a computer, which is a machine, do it? An action, as we have noted, is intentional under some description; but computers cannot have intentions, so they cannot really act; hence they cannot tell stories, whether interactive or not. So no videogames or indeed interactive cinematic works in general, all of which run on computers, can tell stories, whether interactive or not.

One reply holds that the sense in which videogames tell stories is the minimal sense in which a thermometer tells the story of the day's temperature range: that is, it provides a representation of, and hence transmits information about, a sequence of related temperature events. In the same way, a computer transmits to the player information about a series of linked make-believe events in a videogame. This minimal sense of storytelling as information transmission is certainly applicable. However, the normal sense of storytelling is as well. For when people act they often act by using something. When they speak, they use sentences: their speaking actions are the production of those sentences in certain contexts. When the sentences convey stories, they do so by virtue of people using those sentences to convey stories. Likewise, non-interactive cinema often conveys stories; when it does so, it is by virtue of the filmmakers using the visual and auditory images to convey a story. Unlike in the production of speech, machines, from the camera to the projector, are involved in cinema; but the existence of these machines does not show that cinema cannot tell stories. For these machines are used to make and show images and these images are used to convey a story. So if one asks how interactive cinematic works can tell stories, the answer is that their designers use them to tell stories, in similar fashion to how traditional filmmakers use film images to tell stories. In the case of videogames, the stories are usually interactive, but the principle remains the same. Jane and her team of designers use the videogame *Teddy and the Dragon* to tell interactive stories, just as Jane uses words and actions in her live action telling of the story to Otis (and uses pictures in the version in which she tells the story by drawing what the dragon does). So the answer to the objection is simple: computational processes cannot by themselves tell stories; but it is the *use* of these processes by designers to tell stories that explains how videogames can tell stories. Items like sentences, traditional films and videogames can possess *derivative* intentionality: that is, they can possess intentional properties deriving from the ways in which they are employed by agents.

5.7.3 *The value of interactive narration*

So far we have defended the coherence of interactive narration and shown that interactive cinema can employ it. So there is a medium-specific difference between interactive and non-interactive cinema in respect of its narrative capacities. But does interactive storytelling have any artistic worth? There might be a medium-specific difference, but it could be devoid of artistic interest. Consider three arguments for why this is so.

The argument from *aesthetic distance* holds that interactive storytelling undermines the possibility of aesthetic contemplation, since it requires active intervention by the player to generate instances of the story; yet it is a condition for something having aesthetic value that one be able to maintain aesthetic distance from it, which includes one not having to act towards it or intervene in it in any way.[72]

It is true that interactive storytelling, by definition, requires the interactor to do something partly to determine story content. But it is false that active involvement undermines aesthetic appreciation. An artist making a work is engaged in active intervention, but she can attend to and produce aesthetically valuable qualities in the work. Further, the correct method of appreciating a thing is in part governed by the functional nature of that thing. The correct way to appreciate a meal is not just to look at it but to eat it, since meals are for eating; the correct way to appreciate a knife is not just to contemplate it, but to use it, since knives are for cutting. Similarly, the correct way to appreciate an interactive story is not simply to watch it unfold, but to interact with it and see how one's actions produce its various instances. And this process is actually incompatible with aesthetic distance, understood as the mere contemplation of a work.

A second argument holds that the aesthetic value of great stories depends on their being, like life, *irreversible*. The pity and terror that Aristotle identifies as the core emotions of tragedy require events that cannot be undone: if Oedipus were able to go back and undo his deeds, there would no tragedy. The same applies to comedy: a comic mistake by a character could be avoided by him next time. And certain choices would make bad stories – for instance, if Oedipus decided not to investigate what was the

---

[72] For a defence of the notion of aesthetic distance, see Edward Bullough, 'Psychical Distance'.

source of Thebes' troubles.[73] So interactive storytelling permits users to reverse choices and therefore aesthetic value is greatly diminished.

First, note that it does not follow from the interactivity of a narrative that it is reversible. Reversibility means that the interactor can confront the same choice situation again in the fiction and make a different choice next time. But there could be games in which the same choice situation is never confronted again and the game could only be played once. (Conversely, though, the reversibility of a game does entail interactivity, since one must be able to choose in the fiction in order to be able to make a different choice next time.) So interactivity *per se* is not the source of the alleged lack of tragic possibility, but only the reversibility it makes possible. However, since all or almost all interactive works do permit reversibility, the reversibility objection is not yet answered in practice.

Reversibility would plausibly eliminate or at least reduce some of the tragic effect if some of the choices available did not have tragic outcomes. For then one could choose differently, avoiding the tragic outcome, and it would not be true that one could not undo the tragic event; yet the sense that one could not undo what has been done contributes to the emotional power of tragedy. But even in these cases, and depending on the details of the story, the fact that one could secure non-tragic outcomes in the story-telling, might make the poignancy of the tragic ones all the greater, since one could experience how things would have been had the tragic choices been avoided. In some tragedies, in contrast, all choices lead to tragedy: the point of the Oedipus story is that the gods had decreed his fate, so that *whatever* he had chosen to do, he would be doomed. Perhaps whatever Anna Karenina had chosen – whether to stay with Karenin or not – would have led to a tragic outcome. So all outcomes of an interactive story might end in tragedy; and that would make the power of the tragedy greater, not less: for the sense of tragic oppression would be that much more powerful. Likewise, in a comedy comic results might ensue, no matter what a character did. Indeed, some non-interactive comedies employ reversible choices for their characters for comic effect – in *Groundhog Day* (1993) Bill Murray is in a position akin to that of a game player who must keep attempting to solve a problem until he gets it right. The results are undoubtedly very funny. More broadly, reversibility enables learning through trying things out; and, as we shall see shortly, this is an important component of the value of art.

---

[73] Poole, *Trigger Happy*, pp. 99–100. Poole credits the point about reversibility to Alain and Fréderic Le Diberder.

A third argument querying the value of interactive storytelling is the *branching problem* argument. Interactive storytelling requires there to be choices open to the player, otherwise her actions could not partly determine the story content. But if there are choices about how the story proceeds, then the story will branch at the point of choice, and further down the storyline for each new choice there will be a further branch. The number of outcomes will grow exponentially as the number of choices increases. Soon we will have a *story tree* that represents a vast number of different storylines, each storyline beginning at the trunk of the tree and ending in a distinct twig.[74] But then as the storylines multiply it will be increasingly hard and then in practice impossible to ensure that each of them is artistically valuable. Increase the degree of interactivity and the chances of storytelling excellence diminish rapidly. So interactive storytelling is doomed to be artistically uninteresting.

The branching problem has worried both practitioners and theorists. The designer Chris Crawford notes 'the geometric explosion of the branching tree' and suggests that designers face a dilemma between boring the player, if there are too few narrative choices, or opening up choice and so leaving the game with only a 'a tiny spark of narrative life', as is the case with simulation games.[75] Marie-Laure Ryan similarly identifies the quandary of restricting interactors' choices to such an extent that the story becomes boring, or opening up the story to so much choice that narrative coherence is lost.[76] Steven Poole develops a sustained account of this difficulty, which he calls the *data intensiveness problem*. Typically the burden of narration in videogames is carried by non-interactive cut scenes. Some games determine which cut scene is to be played depending on the player's actions (for instance, if the player has been winning, the cut scene shows his side doing well), but these possibilities for interaction are severely curtailed by the fact that the production of cut scenes is time consuming, and unless there is only an extremely limited number of options they cannot be produced. Poole concedes that the data intensiveness problem can be solved for character interactions through the use of artificial intelligence (AI) algorithms that allow for reasonably lifelike interactions with non-playable, computer-generated characters. But this method does not work for generating the plot; for, though there are heuristic programs that generate plots,

---

[74] A story tree is a representation of all the possible ways the story could develop: it need not be explicitly envisaged and programmed in advance. Procedural simulation techniques, for instance, allow the story to develop in various ways, but the designers need not and standardly do not envisage all of the possible outcomes.

[75] Crawford, 'Interactive Storytelling', pp. 261–2.   [76] Ryan, *Avatars of Story*, chapter 5.

they are devoid of literary value. Given the large number of possible actions available to the player, a good plot response would require the development of a computer that not only was conscious, but also had the consciousness of a creative writer. Absent the development of such a creative computer, interactive storytelling of any interest is not possible.[77]

Though the branching problem is invariably discussed as a computational one, it is in fact a general problem for interactive storytelling and so arises for human storytellers too. If the requirement is that, no matter what the player does, the storyteller must come up with an artistically good response immediately, even creative writers would very likely fail to rise to that challenge.

The branching problem is real, since there is a trade-off, given limited artistic resources, between making storytelling more interactive and having each individual storyline be artistically interesting. However, it does not follow that interactive storytelling is of little artistic worth. First, from the fact that one trades off interactivity against narrative interest, one cannot conclude that no point on the trade-off line has artistic value. For instance, even if one conceded that complete choice by the audience would make it in practice impossible to produce any coherent story, it would not follow that restricting audience choice to some degree would result in the narrative lacking all value. If Otis decides that teddy spontaneously explodes, he will likely be told not to be silly, rather than make Jane feel obliged to come up with an interesting outcome. And Jane can still produce an interesting story while denying Otis untrammelled choice. *Some* choice is required for a story to be interactive: but that does not require, either logically or artistically, that *all* choices be permitted. In general the interactive storyteller should engage in, to continue the arboreal metaphor, *pruning*.[78] This may involve limiting the range of input options available to the audience; it may also involve restricting the structure of the story – the widespread use of levels in videogames ensures that, even though there are several ways the story may proceed in each level, at the start of a new level each player enters at the same point, no matter what her previous actions.[79]

Second, while it is plausible that increasing audience choice makes it harder to make *each individual* storyline artistically interesting, because of the resulting artistic demands, it does not follow that *overall* narrative value diminishes. For narrative ability need not be shown merely by generating

---

[77] Poole, *Trigger Happy*, chapter 5.   [78] Crawford, 'Interactive Storytelling', discusses pruning.
[79] Aarseth, 'Quest Games as Post-Narrative Discourse', describes this as a 'string-of-pearls' structure, where choice is possible within the pearls but not within the string.

rewarding and detailed individual plotlines, but might instead be evinced through making a rich and satisfying *structure* of plots that develop from a wide variety of inputs – it might, that is, be displayed by constructing an overall architectonic of possible plots, rather than through developing the intricacies of an individual plot. Appreciating this structure would require playing through the various possibilities that it generates and comparing them to each other. So the object of aesthetic appreciation would shift in part to the story tree, not just appreciation of each individual storyline.

As noted, Poole argues that there is a particular problem for computational implementations of interactive storytelling, since only a creative writer could, when confronted with any of an indefinitely large number of actions by a player, come up with an interesting plot continuation in response to those actions; and he sees no prospect of a computer attaining true creativity. However, this argument sets the bar for an interesting plot extremely high, requiring it to be something of very great interest or be of extreme literary value.[80] But at the level of everyday interesting plots, the great majority of them in commercial cinema are generic, as witnessed by the plethora of handbooks on how to write screenplays. These look like just the sort of plots where heuristic algorithms might do an effective job.

Façade, which employs AI techniques, demonstrates that interactive storytelling by computer is not just possible but can also have artistic worth. Its creators, Michael Mateas and Andrew Stern, describe it as an 'interactive drama', which generates a situation that is 'akin to being onstage with two live actors who are motivated to make a dramatic situation happen'.[81] A typical playing lasts about 20 minutes (though the range can vary between about 5 and 25 minutes). The player plays a friend of a couple, Grace and Trip, whose marriage is teetering on the edge of collapse. The graphics are 3D with only basic rendering; but the power of the work depends on the interaction between the player, and Grace and Trip. The player sees the apartment from a first-person point of view, can walk freely around it, pick up and move some objects, including a drink that Trip may offer him, and can hug or kiss Grace and Trip. The player can also type in whatever text he likes and that text appears on screen. The couple responds to it as well as to many of the player's make-believe actions, including his hugs, kisses and movements towards or away from them. Their response is

---

[80] At one point, Poole seems to flirt with this idea: he dryly remarks that 'It is hardly surprising, though obscurely disappointing, that no one has tried to make a videogame out of Nabokov's *Pale Fire*' (*Trigger Happy*, p. 95).

[81] Mateas and Stern, 'Façade', p. 3.

provided verbally on the sound track, and since the player chooses a name at the start from a large menu, he is addressed by name by the couple. They respond not just verbally, but also through their bodily movements and facial expressions (including looks of surprise, pleasure, flirtatiousness and anger). They react in very different ways depending on what the player decides to do. By the end, they may declare that things are going better between them, or give a strong indication that their marriage is over, or Trip may walk out, or Grace may walk out, or the player may get thrown out of the apartment quite early on (vigorous flirting tends to produce this). How the conversation goes and the points of tension in their marriage that appear depend partly on what the player writes and does. Different perspectives on the couple's problems emerge: on some runs, Trip accuses Grace of lacking the courage to have become a professional artist, on others Grace accuses Trip of preventing her from becoming an artist. Mateas and Stern suggest that six or seven runs are required to get a sense of the entire range of possibilities, since less than 30 per cent of the available content is displayed on each run.

The effect of all this is extraordinarily involving: you feel as if you are genuinely interacting with the characters, since they address you, and react facially and bodily to what you say and do and will even draw you back to the point of their dispute if you try to change the subject. You can also experiment to see how your interventions shape their relationship, discovering, for instance, what are the best strategies to try to hold their fragile relationship together. This is seamless interactive storytelling by computer and is an artistic success. True, there are strict limits to that success: most notably, the natural language processing is primitive, since there are only about forty basic 'discourse acts' onto which any typed utterance is mapped. So misapprehensions can occur – one reporter, playing a female guest, discovered that his character's announcement that she was pregnant by Trip was treated by the couple as flirting with them.[82] Yet, despite its limitations, *Façade* is a significant artistic achievement.

Computationally, the branching problem is solved by a combination of two methods. First, the work employs procedural simulation, which uses 'agents' (the characters) who are given basic goals and various means to achieve them: this allows for considerable flexibility in their responses and is an illustration of the AI technique that Poole admits can control character actions. The second method employs a 'drama manager' which provides an overall, though highly flexible, structure to the story. The drama manager

---

[82] Jonathan Rauch, 'Sex, Lies, and Video Games', p. 81.

chooses from 200 'beats', little sequences of dramatic action constituted by character behaviours, and orders them in the light of player input and previous events to create a rising tension to the story. So Grace and Trip respond differently to player input depending on which beat of the story they are in. The notion of beats was developed by Robert McKee, a well-known author of screenwriting handbooks, and Mateas and Stern's computational implementation of his theory illustrates the point made earlier that interactive storytelling can work well if the standard of value set is not at that of great creative writing but of cinematic genres, the plots of which can be formulated as a set of rules.

This point prompts our final question: if interactive storytelling has artistic value, including in its computationally implemented forms, just how great is that value? Is it essentially a trivial device or is there at least the potential for an artistically significant new form of cinematic narration to emerge?

Recall my earlier remark that the value of interactive storytelling lies in part in the story tree, not just in the individual storylines: appreciation consists in part in appreciating the architectonic of the plot, not just individual plot lines. A story tree represents all the possible storylines producible by the interactor's choices. Call all the possible scenarios (counterfactual situations) that a story tree describes a *story space*. To appreciate a story space requires one to *explore* a good number of the storylines through it. Exploration is the key method of appreciation for an interactive story, for without it one cannot appreciate the story as what it is, a story tree: one must choose differently at the same fork on different occasions to discover what lies down each branch. Exploration in the case of almost all video-games involves exploration of a make-believe environment, a physical space. In the case of some games, such as *Façade*, it is also exploration of a psychological space: one discovers what would happen if one chose differently, and then sees how the characters react to one's choices. And in other games, exploration is partly of a moral space, exploring what one morally ought to do. In *Bioshock* one is repeatedly confronted with the choice of either 'harvesting' (i.e., killing) genetically modified little girls in order to acquire a serum one needs to ensure one's survival or to rescue them and so secure only half the amount of that serum. The choice becomes increasingly complex and one's feelings even more fraught as one discovers, through the course of the narrative, that the character one plays is genetically programmed and is being manipulated in the same way that the little girls have been.

Exploration is a matter, then, of choosing, on different occasions, to go down different branches of a fork. As such, it requires reversibility, but, as we have seen, reversibility need undermine neither tragic nor comic power. What exploration does require, though, is being able to explore the scenario of what would happen if *P* occurred, as well as the scenario of what would happen if *P* did not occur. So one must evaluate both a counterfactual and also the counterpart counterfactual with the negated antecedent. In contrast, non-interactive storytelling standardly explores only one of those counterfactuals.[83] One gets to learn what would happen, say, if a guest is unsympathetic to a married couple as their marriage is failing, but not what would happen if the guest were sympathetic: only one branch of the story fork is explored. But fully to understand a situation requires one to evaluate *all* of the relevant counterfactuals: for instance, fully to understand the role of a guest in helping to bring about a marital breakdown, one needs to evaluate not just what would happen were the guest unsympathetic, but also what would happen were she sympathetic. For if in the latter scenario the marriage still failed, the guest played no decisive role in its breakdown. Given the ability of interactive storytelling to explore all the relevant counter-factuals, it follows that this kind of storytelling has a structural cognitive advantage over non-interactive storytelling. Those of us who are aesthetic cognitivists believe that the value of art consists in part in its capacity to teach us about the world.[84] As such, the cognitive advantage that inter-active storytelling enjoys is, when implemented through artistic means, a significant artistic value of works. Hence, even though the computational implementation of interactive storytelling is currently fairly simple, this form of art has not just artistic worth, but potentially has very considerable artistic value.

So interactive narration is a coherent concept, it can be and has been computationally implemented in videogames and other kinds of interactive cinema, it has artistic worth and has potentially has considerable artistic worth. Hence there is a medium-specific and artistically important narrative difference between interactive and non-interactive cinema. Some of the implications of this claim for emotional engagement with cinema will be explored in the next chapter.

---

[83] I say 'standardly' because non-interactive stories could explore both forks of the branch sequentially. What they cannot provide, however, is the experience of the viewer choosing these options; and the linear presentation of one scenario after another risks producing unengaging stories.

[84] See my *Art, Emotion and Ethics*, chapters 7 and 8.

CHAPTER 6

Emotion and identification

There is no doubt of the emotional impact that films can have on their audiences. The nature of that impact varies immensely, ranging from the gut-churning fear produced by an effective horror film to the nuanced emotional landscape of the best films within the European art-cinema tradition. The emotional power of cinema is central to its appeal and value as an art form, and the question arises of how it is achieved. I begin by examining how filmmakers employ aspects of the cinematic medium to foster emotional engagement. I then turn to defend the coherence and the role of identification, one of the most important devices of emotional engagement in cinema, and also show how it produces emotional learning. The discussion in the first four sections chiefly concerns emotion and identification in traditional films. In the last section I examine what difference digital cinema, in particular interactive digital cinema, makes to the ways that we can emotionally engage with films.

6.1 EMOTION AND CINEMA

In discussing the emotional power of cinema, I make two assumptions. The first is of the truth of the cognitive-evaluative theory of the emotions. This theory holds that emotions are not simply feelings, as are moods, but that they have an intentional object: I am afraid *of* something, I hope *that* something will relieve me from the danger, I pity *that man*. An emotion essentially incorporates an evaluative thought about this object: to be afraid of something essentially involves evaluating that thing as dangerous, to pity someone essentially involves evaluating him as suffering. This evaluative thought, however, is insufficient for an emotion to exist, for one can imagine or believe that something is dangerous without fearing it. So an affective state, a feeling, is also characteristically required for an emotion to occur. However, emotions are not individuated by these feelings, since the feelings experienced by different individuals in the grip of the same emotion might vary; and there are some emotions, such as shame and guilt, where plausibly the feelings are the same, but the emotions are distinct. So an emotion characteristically involves a feeling, but what particular feeling it is may vary. Finally, emotions typically provide a motivating force for the individual who experiences them, given the presence of the appropriate beliefs: someone who is afraid, if he believes that the object of which he is afraid really exists and is dangerous, will typically be motivated to flee; someone who pities someone will typically be motivated to help him, if he believes he can. (This is to say that the person experiencing the emotion typically has a motivation in the presence of the appropriate belief, not that he will act, since he may have other, countervailing motivations.) The important point for what follows is that on this theory emotions have intentional objects.[1]

My second assumption concerns the possibility and rationality conditions of emotions. It is uncontroversial that objects believed to exist can be the objects of emotions. Watching a horror film, I may be reminded of my old enemy and this triggers my fear of him. I may even be afraid of features of the film itself: if I suffer from epilepsy, I may fear that the strobe lighting effect of the film will trigger an attack. More controversial is the claim that one can rationally experience real emotions towards objects that one knows are merely fictional – that I can rationally fear the fictional monster and rationally pity the fictional heroine in a horror film. Though the claim is controversial, I will assume its truth here.[2] It follows that when we talk about the emotional impact of cinema, this includes the emotions that we are feeling towards the fictional characters and events represented.

One of the major themes of this book is the role of the medium in conditioning the artistic properties of cinematic works; so in assessing the way that cinema can emotionally engage us, we will be discussing, in part, the way that features of the cinematic medium can be mobilised to foster emotional engagement. Not all moving images foster engagement. Watching the CCTV footage of life outside a building which I have been paid to guard at the dead of night may be a singularly boring experience.

---

[1] Examples of cognitive-evaluative theories, which vary in their details, include: Ronald de Sousa, *The Rationality of Emotion*; Patricia Greenspan, *Emotions and Reasons*; and Robert C. Roberts, 'What An Emotion Is'.

[2] See my *Art, Emotion and Ethics*, chapter 9, for an argument for the possibility and rationality of feeling real emotions towards objects believed to be fictional. I discuss the possibility and rationality of emotions directed towards one's make-believe actions in interactive contexts in Section 6.5 below. Though I do not rely on the claim here, I also believe that 'negative' emotions, such as fear and pity, can be experienced as pleasant under certain circumstances, so that it is possible to enjoy the emotions aroused by horror films and melodramas: see my 'The Paradox of Horror'.

So it is in specific *uses* of the cinematic medium that we must seek the answer to our question about how cinema engages emotions. This point has been taken by Noël Carroll to show that there is no role for the medium in explaining the nature of emotional engagement with cinema.[3] But the fact that not all works in a medium possess a certain feature does not show that there are no medium-involving evaluations and explanations of those works. It is in the *use* of a medium that an artistic effect may be achieved, and appeal to the use of a medium obviously involves reference to the medium. And this is indeed how medium-specificity claims were taken by defenders of the view: Arnheim, for instance, does not believe that all films are expressive – on the contrary, he holds that many are not, but his theory locates the expressive power of cinema in the particular use of the medium by a film artist, as we saw in Section 1.2.

Moreover, Carroll takes medium-specificity claims to be claims about features that are *unique* to the medium. Despite his claim to the contrary, some features that are employed for purposes of emotional engagement are in fact unique to the medium – for instance, camera movement is often important in fostering engagement but is unique to cinema, the medium of the moving image. But many features employed are not unique. As we noted in Section 5.6, a better way of taking the notion of medium-specificity is in terms of those features that are *differential*, i.e., that characterise a group of media, of which cinema or a type of cinema is one, as opposed to another group of media, which lack this feature. So understood, features of the cinematic medium that promote engagement are usually differential ones.

Moreover, they very often exhibit the feature of being *doubly differential*. For instance, narrative plays a very important part in engaging one's emotions: curiosity, wanting to know how things turn out, is a powerful motivation for continuing engagement. Having a narrative is a differential feature: some media are not narrative ones (absolute music is not, for instance) and others have very limited narrative capacities (for instance, painting). But in addition, one can ask *how* different media narrate: for instance, one can consider how cinema narrates as opposed to how novels narrate, a topic discussed in Chapter 5. As we saw there, cinema narrates in a rather different way from literature, including there being a more restricted role for narrators in cinema. So not only is narration a differential property, but also the *mode* of narration is: when both a feature and its mode are

---

[3] Noël Carroll, 'The Power of Movies'. Despite my disagreement with Carroll on medium-specificity, I am at several points in this section indebted to his extremely fine discussion of the emotional power of cinema.

differential, we have the feature of being doubly differential. Likewise, identification is a differential feature of media, since identification occurs only when there is some character with whom one can identify. Some media, such as abstract painting and absolute music, lack characters, so identification cannot occur there (setting aside any possibilities of identifying with the makers of the artworks). But one can also examine *how* cinematic identification works, as opposed to, say, identification in literature, through devices such as the point-of-view shot; and if these devices are themselves differential, then we have the feature of being doubly differential again. We will examine identification in cinema in more detail shortly.

Within this framework, which allows us to assess the use of the cinematic medium without focusing only on features unique to it, we will pose our question about how cinema fosters emotional engagement. I focus on four aspects of the cinematic medium that can be deployed to achieve this end.

The first aspect is the pictorial nature of cinema. As we noted in Section 2.1, pictures possess natural generativity, i.e., having seen at most a very small sample of pictures in a style, one can go on correctly to interpret other pictures in that style. Pictures differ in this way from language: if one is given at most a small sample of words in an unfamiliar language, one cannot thereby go on correctly to interpret other words in that language. The best explanation for the difference is that the capacity to recognise objects is employed to recognise pictures of them, but the same is not true of language. So the capacity correctly to interpret pictures is developmentally available when object-recognitional capacities are available, whereas the capacity to interpret language is a later developmental acquisition. As Carroll has argued, this feature explains why films are so accessible to their audiences worldwide, the grasp of their pictorial dimension not requiring any training, whereas grasp of a linguistic work would. Moreover, since the process of picture recognition is a basic visual capacity, employing it to understand a film is less taxing than reading a novel, with its requirement to process language.[4]

We can add that the psychological machinery underlying natural generativity, with its rapid and automatic processing of sensory data, plausibly partly explains some of the differences in emotional impact that moving pictures can have compared to their literary equivalents. There is a greater immediacy of response, a more visceral impact in cinema than is available in novels. Consider the notion of being startled by something. If I am unaware of your presence and you suddenly place your hand on my shoulder from

---

[4] *Ibid.*, p. 83.

behind, I will be startled. The reason for my reaction is that I have an unexpected sensory input which I spontaneously interpret as a potential threat, and it then takes me a moment or two to interpret it in a less threatening manner. Cinema is capable of inducing the startle response in a wide variety of contexts, from action sequences to horror films. Part of the reason for this is that we rapidly and automatically interpret a suddenly occurring visual image, say, of a knife being thrust into a character, as threatening (music and sound effects usually play a crucial role in inducing the response as well). But novels cannot directly induce the startle response, since there is no sudden *sensory* input, either pictorial or sonic, that is liable spontaneously to be construed as a threat. Processing of a novel's content is slower and involves the cognitively higher functions of language interpretation. Novels can, of course, surprise and shock; but both of those reactions are more cognitively grounded and sophisticated than is the primitive startle response – they involve one's expectations being overturned, rather than a sensory input occurring and being spontaneously regarded as threatening. The startle response in cinema is crucial in setting the tone of a variety of induced emotions, including fear, shock, sudden elation, and so forth: it plausibly explains in part the more visceral impact that cinema can have in respect of these states than literature can.

Traditional cinema, our topic in this section, is photographic, a feature that also conditions the emotional impact of films. As I argued in Section 2.4, photographic images are not transparent, but it can sometimes strike one *as if* they were, i.e., *as if* one were looking through a window onto a fictional world; moreover, traditional photographs are correctly seen as providers of good, though defeasible, evidence that what appears to have been photographed really did occur. The result is that the emotional power of a photographed scene is liable to be greater than that of a scene in a painting: for in the former case, it may seem as if one is in direct visual contact with something that one thereby has evidence did occur. Photographs, I have argued, are not transparent and they can be subject to manipulation and fakery, particularly if they are digital; but the immediate emotional impact they can have is grounded on what seems to be the case, not what is really so. Only on reflection may one render it salient to oneself that, after all, the events depicted in the fiction film did not really occur.

There is another aspect to the photographic image, compared to language or painting, that conditions its emotional impact. In linguistic works one can use an indefinite description to refer to something – 'a man came into the room', say, rather than using a proper name for him. Thus it is possible to construct a linguistic work entirely from generalities. In similar fashion, in the case of a handmade picture, one can draw simply a man, rather than drawing a particular man. But in the case of a photograph, one cannot photograph simply a man: one must photograph a *particular* man. Photographs record particulars. Moreover, in the case of a linguistic work one can ascribe to an object attributes that lack a high degree of specificity – it might simply be described as 'red', for instance. But in the case of a photograph, as of a painting, one must record that object as having some very specific shade of red. Call this necessary feature of photographs – the recording of particulars with highly specific attributes – the *density* of the photographic image. Density is an important factor in emotional engage-ment. Our emotional reactions to generalities, such as statistics recording mortality in developing countries, are often muted: but our emotions are triggered, other things equal, much more powerfully by specifics, and the density of the photographic image is thus a powerful elicitor of emotions.

The second aspect of the cinematic medium I will consider is the fact that it is composed of *multiple* pictures, which allow for the illusion of *movement*. Editing is grounded on this multiplicity, and can be used to foster emotional engagement.[5] A standard editing technique, much loved by D. W. Griffith, is the parallel edit, by which two events are shown as occurring simultaneously, and which is designed so that the intercutting between the two scenes accelerates as the climax of the scene approaches. As the shots get shorter, there is an increasing tempo in the rhythm of the cutting, which creates a sense of excitement and anticipation in the viewer. Also important is camera movement, which can focus attention by moving towards something, add to the dynamic impact of a scene and ground a sense of quasi-personality, which draws the viewer emotionally into the film: in *Rules of the Game* (1939), for instance, in the Walpurgis Night scene in the chateau, the camera blunders around like a confused guest at the charade, each movement revealing one comically disastrous scene after another.

Films can also show objects at various distances, either from far away or close up. While close-ups exist, of course, in paintings and still photo-graphs, they are at their most effective in eliciting emotion when employed to record movement. The early film theorist Béla Balázs noted that, by providing a 'microphysiognomy' of the human face, the cinematic close-up can reveal the flow of emotions across a face, emotions that would have likely escaped an observer in real life and so reveal aspects of reality that were

---

[5] Note that one can edit shots that are stills, as is most of Chris Marker's *La Jetée* (1962); so editing depends on the multiplicity of frames, not directly on movement (though the possibility of the latter is grounded on the former).

hitherto unseen.[6] The use of this technique is a strong factor in producing emotions in the audience, and is particularly important, as we shall see shortly, in fostering identification with a character through the reaction shot.

A third important feature of the medium is the way time is related to works in the medium. There are four kinds of temporal properties that are important in film. Story time consists of the entire stretch of the time in which the events recounted occurred, plot time comprises the temporal stretches of the story that are shown, in the order that they are shown.[7] Literary works support stories and plots and therefore their associated temporal properties, but it is not true that works in all media do so: for instance, absolute music (music without words) cannot tell stories, and paintings generally at most merely suggest a story and plot, since they usually represent only one moment in time.[8] Viewing time is a distinct, relational temporal property: it is the length of time that the viewer (or reader or auditor), in order to experience the work, needs to take to view it; and viewing order is the temporal order in which she views the work. The viewing time and order are variable for the viewer of a painting – it is up to her how long she spends in viewing the work and in what temporal order she peruses the parts of the work, and there is no set minimum time required to experience it (it can be experienced in a moment). For the reader of a novel, viewing time is also variable and to a lesser extent discretionary (people read at different speeds) but the temporal order of reading is not: to appreciate a novel, one must read it in the correct order at least once. In the case of a (non-interactive) film, however, viewing time and order are fixed (at least under standard viewing conditions in a cinema). The reason is that, unlike paintings, still photographs and literary works, there is a fourth temporal property – work time – that (non-interactive) films possess. This is the length of time that a work lasts. It makes no sense to talk about how long a painting lasts, nor how long a literary work lasts (as opposed to how many words it is composed of). Interestingly, apart from films, it is only performances that have a work time. For instance, a symphony has no work time (though if it is played extremely fast or slow, it may cease to be recognisable). But a performance

---

[6] Béla Balázs, *Theory of the Film*, chapter 8, especially pp. 65–6.
[7] See the discussion of these notions in relation to Bordwell's views in Section 4.2.
[8] There are exceptions here: absolute 'programme' music exists, but this depends on the existence of a descriptive title for the piece and some independent, written source for the story. There are also paintings (for instance, some *quattrocento* religious paintings) that depict several distinct moments in the same story, so that a minimal narrative is conveyed in a single painting.

of a symphony has a work time, a definite duration. Likewise, a play has no work time, but its performance does.

The existence of work time, with its consequent determination of the viewing time required to experience the work, has important implications for emotional engagement. Since the filmmakers determine the exact length of time and viewing order of the film, the emotional effects can be far more precisely controlled than with media that do not support works with work time. For instance, a series of precisely calibrated emotional shocks can be administered over a short time period with increasing frequency (a feature of many horror films). Most emotions have a natural temporal profile: if one is afraid, for instance, it takes some time for that fear to dissipate, in part because of the physiological disturbances associated with the emotion. In the case of a film, its makers can employ this fact to pile emotion on top of emotion without respite. Also important is the fact that the audience's focus of attention can be manipulated: for instance, so many significant events can be shown in such rapid succession that the viewer cannot grasp them properly as they occur and may be moved in a superficial manner by them; only later, after the film viewing is over, may the viewer reflect, perhaps wryly, that a rather different set of emotional reactions would have been far more appropriate.

The final aspect of the cinematic medium I will discuss is the sound and, particularly, the musical dimension of film. It is hard to overstate the importance of music in eliciting emotional reactions in films. This is not just a matter of musical highlighting at specific points in a film – to underscore the emotional importance of the moment that romance blossoms, or the monster strikes, or the pratfall happens. Several films, particularly in the epic genre, are through-composed and their emotional impact depends centrally on the quality of the score – for instance, Howard Shore's magnificent music for *The Lord of the Rings* trilogy (2001–3) comprises nearly twelve hours of elaborately scored music, employing leitmotifs for many of the characters and cultures, and is absolutely central to the emotional effect of the films. Indeed, it would not be *entirely* perverse to regard these films as the visual illustration of their musical score.

Music does not simply add tonal and emotional colour to a film, but also through its association with the particular events represented, gains greater expressive power and thereby imparts that power to the film as a whole. Music without words can straightforwardly convey moods such as happiness or sadness, since these do not necessarily possess an intentional object (I can simply be happy or sad, without necessarily being happy or sad *about* anything). There is a puzzle, however, about the ability of absolute music to express emotions: as we saw, an emotion has an intentional object and it is essential to the individuation of the emotion that it involves an evaluative thought about that object. But if music lacks words, then it is deeply puzzling how it could express an emotion, for there is no possibility of an evaluative thought being conveyed about the object (or at best, only a very vague thought might be suggested – for instance, an accelerating tempo might convey a thought of something important or exciting happening). But if music has words, and even more if it is associated with visual images as well as words, then it becomes uncontroversially capable of expressing emotions, for the evaluative thoughts can be conveyed by the visual images and the speech of the characters. Music thereby gains expressive power and precision, and can in turn contribute this to the film as a whole (the same is true of opera, where words and actions lend emotional precision to music otherwise incapable of such precise articulation of emotions). Since expression is such a powerful elicitor of emotions, the film audience's emotional engagement is thereby enhanced. So music is a major source of film's emotional power.

I have examined, then, four aspects of the cinematic medium, to show how traditional films can emotionally engage their audiences by employing features of the medium. The discussion is not meant to be exhaustive, since it would be impossible to survey the myriad of possibilities films have for emotional engagement within a short compass. But it does illustrate some of the central ways in which films can engage their audiences. And it is important to note that some of these ways deploy aspects of the medium unique to cinema (for instance, camera movement), but others employ aspects differential to it, so that one should compare and contrast the way films emotionally engage with the ways that works in other media do. We will return to the general significance of the role of the medium in the final chapter. In the next three sections I turn to examine in more detail the role of identification, one of the most important means of fostering emotional engagement in cinema.

6.2 THE CONCEPT OF IDENTIFICATION

When viewers of films are asked to describe their emotional reactions to films they often appeal to the notion of identification. They say things such as 'I could really identify with that character', 'the film was no good: there wasn't a single character I could identify with', or 'I felt so badly about what happened to her, because I strongly identified with her'. It is part of the folk wisdom of responding to films (and to literature) that audiences sometimes identify with characters, that the success or failure of a film partly depends on whether this identification occurs, and that the quality and strength of emotional responses depend on identification. It seems that any theorist interested in our emotional reactions to films must give an account of the nature of this process of identification and explain its importance in shaping responses. And there would appear to be no room for denying the existence and importance of spectatorial identification.

Yet film theory has exhibited a curious reaction to this folk wisdom. On the one hand psychoanalytically inspired theories have responded positively to these claims, but treated them in hyperbolical fashion. Drawing on Lacan, such theories hold that the child is constituted as a subject through an act of identification with her own image in the mirror at the age of six to eighteen months; the power of cinema in giving an impression of reality and as an ideological device lies in its ability to re-enact this basic process of identification. Film identification according to Baudry has a dual aspect:

one can distinguish two levels of identification. The first, attached to the image itself, derives from the character portrayed as a center of secondary identifications, carrying an identity which constantly must be seized and reestablished. The second level permits the appearance of the first and places it 'in action' – this is the transcendental subject whose place is taken by the camera which constitutes and rules the objects in the 'world'.[9]

While they acknowledge the existence of character identification, central to the folk theory, psychoanalytic theories thus demote it to a secondary status. Central becomes the notion of the identification of the viewer with an invisible observer, an identification that constitutes the identity of the viewer as an illusorily unified, ideological subject. And besides this sidelining of the notion of character-identification, the dominant trend in psychoanalytic theories also departs from the folk view in regarding the viewer as becoming a fetishist, sadist and voyeur through his acts of identification.[10]

Those film theorists and philosophers who draw on analytical philosophy and cognitive science generally have little time for such psychoanalytic construals of spectators' responses. But rather than simply stripping out the psychoanalytic components from the notion of identification, they have in most cases rejected the claim that identification occurs at all. Noël Carroll

---

[9] Jean-Louis Baudry, 'Ideological Effects of the Basic Cinematographic Apparatus', pp. 363–4.
[10] For a critique of these claims, see Noël Carroll, *Mystifying Movies*. In Section 5.3.1 I argued against the claim that cinematic spectatorship involves an invisible observer; and in 'On Cinema and Perversion' argue that the film viewer is not *ipso facto* a pervert.

writes that 'identification … is not the correct model for describing the emotional responses of spectators'; Gregory Currie argues that identification does not occur in the point-of-view shot; and even Murray Smith, who has some sympathy with the idea of identification, generally presents his own concept of engagement not as an analysis of identification, but as an improved concept with which to replace it.[11]

This suspicion of the notion of identification by theorists influenced by analytic philosophy and cognitive science is striking, given the widespread use of it in ordinary viewers' reports of their interactions with films, and indeed of the use of the notion more generally in ordinary life, as when we talk of identifying with our friends. And it also fuels the accusation by psychoanalytic theorists that analytic approaches are peculiarly unsuited to account for emotional responses to films. For if they reject appeal to a central notion required to explicate spectators' emotions, how can they give an adequate account of those emotions?

This then is the situation that confronts anyone interested in the notion of identification in film. The task of this and the following sections is to rehabilitate the notion of identification for analytic theories of film, to show that the notion does not suffer from the deep conceptual confusions alleged against it, and to demonstrate that it has explanatory power in accounting for spectators' emotional responses to films. The argument will require several distinctions to be drawn, but these involve refining the notion of identification, not abandoning it.

The notion of identification can seem deeply odd. Its etymological root is of 'making identical'. Thus it would seem that when I identify with a character, I merge my identity with his, which would 'require some sort of curious metaphysical process, like Dr Spock's Vulcan mind-meld, between the audience member and the protagonist'.[12] This is not just deeply odd, but actually impossible: two people cannot be made (numerically) the same without ceasing to exist. But here, as quite generally, etymology is a bad guide to meaning. Any argument exploiting this etymology to show that identification does not exist would be like an argument which noted that 'television' has as its etymological root 'seeing at a distance', then argued that we do not literally see things at a distance when we look at a television

---

[11] Noël Carroll, *The Philosophy of Horror or Paradoxes of the Heart*, p. 96; Gregory Currie, *Image and Mind*, pp. 174–6; and Murray Smith, *Engaging Characters*. Sometimes, as on p. 73, Smith seems to think of the idea of engagement as an analysis of the notion of identification; more generally, as on p. 93, he presents it as a replacement for that of identification.

[12] Carroll, *The Philosophy of Horror*, p. 89. I am not accusing Carroll of embracing the fallacious argument I attack in this paragraph.

screen, but only their images, and concluded that televisions do not exist. The question is not what the etymology of the term is, but of what it means, and the meaning of a term is a matter of its use in the language.

So how do we use the term 'identification' when we apply it to a character in a fiction? One can use it simply to say that one cares for the character. To say that there is no one in a film with whom one can identify is simply in this usage to report that one does not care about what happens to any of the characters. But in such a use, the fact that I identify with a character cannot *explain* why I care for her, for such a purported explanation would be entirely vacuous. The natural thought here is that identification in the explanatory sense is a matter of putting oneself in the character's shoes, and, because one does so, one may come to care for her. But what is this notion of placing oneself in someone else's position?

Psychoanalytic and Brechtian theories, given their belief in popular cinema as a form of illusionism, might naturally hold that just as the viewer is somehow under the cognitive illusion that the cinematic events are real, so she is somehow under the illusion that she is the character with whom she identifies. But that would be to credit the viewer of a film with an extra-ordinary degree of irrationality; it would be to hold that she does not believe that she is sitting safely in the dark, as is clearly the case, but that she believes she is swinging from a rope on a mountain-top, or shooting at villains, or otherwise doing whatever the film represents the character as doing.

A more plausible version of this story would hold that a 'suspension of disbelief' occurs in the cinema: the viewer believes that she is not the fictional character, but this belief is somehow bracketed from her motiva-tional set. In such cases the viewer reacts *as if* she believed that she were the character depicted, even though she does not in fact believe this to be the case. But then the problem is that many of the viewer's reactions to the film make no sense under this assumption: since for instance characters in horror films rarely want to suffer the terrors that torment them, viewers who identify with these characters should storm out of these films, for on this construal of identification they should react as if they believed they were these characters.[13]

A better version of the identification view would hold, rather, that the viewer *imagines* herself to be the character with whom she identifies. This then is part of the explanation of why she comes to care for the character, if she indeed does. But this formulation raises new worries; for it may be

---

[13] See also *ibid.*, pp. 63–8, for a critique of illusionistic and suspension-of-disbelief theories of emotional responses to fictions.

objected that it makes no sense to talk about imagining oneself to be someone else. Arguably there are no possible worlds in which I am identical with some other person – they are simply worlds in which I possess that other person's properties without being him. So how can I imagine being another person? Similar worries apply if one holds that it makes no sense to think that I could be different in some radical way from the person I am (I could not have been a tenth-century female Eskimo, for instance). The reply is that even if one accepted claims of this kind, it would not follow that one could not imagine things that the claims hold are impossible. We can in fact imagine things that are not just metaphysically but even logically impossible – for instance, that Hobbes actually did square the circle (as at one time he thought he had done). And we do that not infrequently in responding to fiction – we may be asked to imagine people going back in time and conceiving themselves, we may be asked to imagine werewolves, or people turning into trees, or intelligent, talkative rats complaining about lordly, overbearing toads.

However, there is still a problem with holding that one imagines oneself to be another person when one identifies with him. As Richard Wollheim has noted, if I imagine myself to be a particular character (say Jeeves), then since identity is a symmetrical relation, this is equivalent to the claim that I imagine Jeeves to be me. But the two imaginings are very different projects: in the former case I imagine myself in Jeeves' position, serving and manipulating Bertie Wooster; in the second case I imagine Jeeves surreptitiously taking over my life, and I become disconcertingly butler-like.[14]

What we should conclude from this is that the act of imaginative identification involves imagining not, strictly speaking, being that other person, but rather imagining being in her situation, where the idea of her situation encompasses every property she possesses, including all her physical and psychological traits (so we imagine the world from her physical and psychological perspective). Hence what I do in imaginatively identifying myself with Jeeves is imagining being in his situation, doing what he does, feeling what he does, etc. And that is clearly different from imagining Jeeves being in my situation.

Wollheim has objected to this construal of identification: he holds that since I do not imagine myself to be identical to Jeeves, the account would allow me while imagining myself in his situation to imagine meeting him, which my imaginative project surely rules out.[15] And it is indeed true that

---

[14] Richard Wollheim, *The Thread of Life*, p. 75; Wollheim's example uses Sultan Mahomet II.
[15] *Ibid.*, pp. 75–6.

my imaginative project rules this out: but that is in fact compatible with imagining myself to be in Jeeves' situation. For as we have understood the notion of a person's situation, it comprises all of his properties; and these include not just his contingent properties, but also his modal properties, such as necessarily not being a number, necessarily having the potential for self-consciousness and necessarily not being able to meet himself. Thus Jeeves (fictionally) has the property of necessarily not being able to meet himself, i.e., necessarily not being able to meet Jeeves. Hence, were the question raised of whether I could properly imagine myself meeting Jeeves when I am imagining myself in his situation, I ought to rule out imagining meeting him. For I ought to imagine possessing those of his properties that are relevant to this situation, in particular the modal property of being unable to meet Jeeves. Thus Wollheim's rejection of the account of identification in terms of imagining oneself in another's situation looks plausible only on an overly narrow understanding of someone's situation that excludes certain of his modal properties.

This account of identification also fits how we talk of imaginative acts. We frequently talk of understanding someone by imagining ourselves in her situation, of putting ourselves in her shoes. We come to understand her by imaginatively projecting ourselves into her external situation, imaginarily altering those aspects of our personalities which differ from hers, and then relying on our dispositions to respond in various ways, so as to work out what other things she might reasonably be supposed to be feeling.[16]

Even on this construal of imaginative identification, however, the idea that identification occurs in films seems to encounter fundamental difficulties. It is often supposed that one of the central cases of cinematic identification is when we are shown a point-of-view shot; here surely we are asked to identify with a character: we literally take up her perspective. But this claim has met with a barrage of objections. Currie has urged that if identification occurred in the point-of-view shot, then the viewer would have to imagine that what happens to the character happens to her, would have to imagine that she possesses the most obvious and dramatically salient characteristics of the character, and would have to have or imagine she has some concern with and sympathy for the values and projects of the character. But none of these, says Currie, need be the case. I often do not imagine

---

[16] This root idea of understanding another by imagining oneself in her place (the idea of *verstehen* as a mode of cognition of others) should be distinguished from the notion of simulation as employed in simulation theory. The latter, as defended by Currie in *Image and Mind*, is a particular theory about how this kind of imaginative act occurs. For a criticism of simulation theory and the development of an alternative account, see my *Art, Emotion and Ethics*, Section 7.3.

any of the events happening to the character happening to myself, nor do I imagine myself having any of his characteristics, nor need I have the least sympathy with him – consider for instance the frequent use of point-of-view shots in horror films, taken from the perspective of the killer.[17] Smith has also noted that the point-of-view shot need not give access to the character's subjectivity: indeed, the point-of-view shot in horror films often functions to disguise the killer's identity.[18]

These observations about point-of-view shots are well taken; but they do not force us to abandon the claim that identification can occur in such cases. Once we construe identification as a matter of imagining oneself in a character's situation, the issue becomes pertinent of *which aspects* of the character's situation one imagines oneself in. As we have seen, we should construe the situation of the character in terms of what properties she possesses. Her physical properties include her size, physical position, the physical aspects of her actions, and so on. Her psychological ones can be thought of in terms of her perspective on the (fictional) world. But that perspective is not just a visual one (how things look to her); we can also think of the character as possessing an affective perspective on events (how she feels about them), a motivational perspective (what she is motivated to do in respect of them), an epistemic perspective (what she believes about them), and so forth. Thus the question to ask whenever someone talks of identifying with a character is *in what respects* does she identify with the character; the act of identification is aspectual. To identify perceptually with a character is to imagine seeing what he sees; to identify affectively with him is to imagine feeling what he feels; to identify motivationally is to imagine wanting what he wants; to identify epistemically with him is to imagine believing what he believes; to identify practically with him is to imagine doing what he does; and so on. What the objections rehearsed above force us to see is that just because one is identifying perceptually with the character, it does not follow that one is identifying motivationally or affectively with him, nor does it follow that one imagines that one has his physical characteristics.

This analysis needs to be refined slightly. First, I have spoken of what a character sees, feels, wants, believes or does; if the character is fictional, then this should be understood in terms of what it is fictional that a character sees, feels, wants, believes or does. Second, suppose that I am watching *Forrest Gump* (1994) for the first time, and have fallen asleep just before the scene in which Forrest meets JFK. This scene includes a point-of-view shot

---

[17] Currie, *Image and Mind*, pp. 174–6.   [18] Smith, *Engaging Characters*, p. 157.

from Forrest's perspective of JFK (this isn't true of the actual film but let us suppose that it is). By sheer chance I happen to dream of JFK from just the same visual perspective as Forrest sees him. It is true that I imagine seeing JFK and that it is fictional that Forrest sees JFK; but I am not thereby perceptually identifying with Forrest – I do not even know that he meets JFK in the film. What is missing is that my imagining seeing JFK is not *guided* by the thought that it is fictional that this is what Forrest sees. So the full analysis of perceptual identification in the case of fiction is that I perceptually identify with a fictional character *C* who sees *O* if and only if I imagine seeing *O*, where my imagining is guided by the thought that it is fictional that *C* sees *O*. And the same applies, *mutatis mutandis*, for the other aspects of identification. However, except where the more exact formulation is needed, I will for the sake of convenience continue to use as a shorthand version the analysis advanced in the previous paragraph.[19]

The appeal to aspectual identification may seem to distort the concept of identification. Surely, it will be urged that the notion of identification is a global concept – that is, we imagine being in that person's situation in all respects – and in talking of aspectual identification we are in effect abandoning the notion of identification.

On the contrary, if identification were global, it could not in practice occur. Even a fictional character has an indeterminately large number of properties (most of which will be implicit, not explicitly stated by the text or film), and a real person has an infinite number of such properties. It would not be possible to imagine oneself as possessing all of these properties. And of course one does not do so: one picks out those characteristics that are relevant for the purpose of one's imagining. Imagining other properties of oneself would simply be idle, performing no useful task in one's imaginative engagement with the work. Nor should someone hold that even though one does not imagine all these properties holding of oneself, one ought to do so. This would on any account be futile, since one could not fulfil the normative command; and if Kant is correct that 'ought' implies 'can', there can in any case be no such norm.

---

[19] A slightly different way of handling the Gump problem is to distinguish between an extensional reading of 'what Forrest sees', which picks out whatever is the object of Forrest's sight (JFK), and an intensional reading, whereby the object of sight, JFK, is brought under a particular thought content (a mode of presentation), namely, that this is what Forrest sees. On the applicable intensional reading I do not perceptually identify with Gump when asleep. This has the advantage of not requiring the addition of the guidance clause but has the disadvantage of being less explicit and some will query the use here of the notion of a mode of presentation of perceptual content.

Some objections to the idea of identification claim that it is much too crude a notion, reducing the possibilities of our relations to characters to either being identified with a character or distanced from her, and thus we need to abandon the notion.[20] Once we recognise the existence of aspectual identification, we can see that recognition of these complexities is well within the grasp of the notion of identification. Since we have distinguished different aspects of identification, we can note that the fact that we are perceptually identified with a character does not entail that we are motivationally or affectively identified with her – the fact that we are imagining seeing from her perspective does not *require* us to imagine wanting what she wants, or imagine feeling what she feels. It then becomes a matter of substantive theorising to investigate under what conditions one form of identification fosters another. It would be surprising, given the complexity of cinematic art in general, if one could find any invariant, law-like principles for linking different aspects of identification together. But that leaves plenty of scope for investigating how one form of identification may tend, other things equal, to promote another form, or for how certain film techniques may tend to enhance some kinds of identification.

So far I have been following out the implications of the thought that identification involves imagining oneself in another's situation. This idea of imaginative identification is, however, not exhaustive of all that people mean when they talk of identification. For consider the idea of empathy, which is naturally thought of as a kind of identification, and a very important one at that. If someone has a parent die, identifying with the bereaved person characteristically takes the form of taking on her feelings, sharing them ('I feel your pain', 'I know what it's like to undergo that loss'). But this is different from the notion of affective identification as we have characterised it. That required the viewer to *imagine* feeling what a person (or a character fictionally) feels; empathy requires the viewer *actually* to feel what a person (or a character fictionally) feels.

Now it is plausible that empathy requires one imaginatively to enter into a character's mind, and to feel with him because of one's imagining of his situation.[21] But that is to say that empathic identification requires some form of imaginative identification; it is not to conflate the two phenomena. It is possible to identify with a character affectively, imagining his sorrow, anger or fear, yet not to empathise with him, since one does not actually feel sorrowful, angry or afraid with him. In fact, it is only those theorists who allow for the possibility of feeling real emotions towards merely imagined

[20] Smith, *Engaging Characters*, p. 222.   [21] See Alex Neill, 'Empathy and (Film) Fiction'.

situations who can even allow for the existence of empathic identification with fictional characters. (Though those who deny the possibility of feeling real emotions towards merely imagined situations can, of course, allow for empathic identification with real people.) For the idea of empathic identification is that one feels towards the situation that confronts the character what the character (fictionally) feels towards it; and since that situation is merely fictional, the possibility of real emotions directed towards situations known merely to be fictional must be allowed.

The final notion we need to discuss is that of sympathy. As earlier noted, sometimes to talk of identification with a character is simply to say that one sympathises with him. But if we want to retain identification as an explanatory concept, we should mark this off as a distinct usage. And, in fact, sympathy and empathic identification are distinct notions. To sympathise with a character is in a broad sense to care for him, to be concerned for him. (We need not care for him merely because he is suffering – sympathy in the narrow sense – since one can talk for instance of having sympathy with the goals of a political party, even though that party is not suffering.) This care can be manifested in a variety of mental states: fearing for what may befall him, getting angry on his behalf, pitying him, feeling elated at his triumphs, and so forth. These states need have no relation to what he is feeling: I may pity him because he has been knocked into a coma in a road accident and is feeling nothing; I may be angry on his behalf for what has been done to him, even though he may be stoical about it; I may fear for what will befall him, even though he is sublimely unaware of the imminent danger in which he stands. Empathy, in contrast, requires one to share in the feelings one ascribes to him: I am empathically angry only if I believe or imagine that he is angry, and the thought of his anger controls and guides the formation of my anger.[22] So if he is in a coma, and not feeling anything, nothing counts as empathising with him. Since most people are concerned for themselves, empathising with them will involve sharing this concern, and hence sympathising with them. But the co-occurrence of sympathy and empathy is contingent on the psychology of the person with whom we are empathising and sympathising, rather than showing that these two kinds of dispositions to feel are the same.

These distinctions also allow us to answer an influential objection to the idea of identification advanced by Carroll. Carroll holds that identification with a character requires one to feel what she is feeling. But, he points out, the correspondence between what the viewer feels and what a character feels

---

[22] See *ibid.* for an illuminating discussion of the differences between empathy and sympathy.

is normally at most a partial one. A woman is swimming in the sea, unaware that she is in imminent danger of attack by a shark: she is happy, we are tense and fearful. Oedipus feels guilt for what he has done: we do not feel guilt, but pity him. And Carroll holds that a partial correspondence of feelings is insufficient for identification.[23]

Insofar as Carroll is discussing the notion of identification here, it must be that of empathic identification, for he is discussing what the audience actually feels, not just what it imagines feeling. So even if successful his critique does not undermine the notion of imaginative identification. Moreover, because we have seen that the activity of identification is always aspectual (and therefore partial), it cannot be an objection to it occurring that the correspondences between what the audience is feeling and what the characters are fictionally feeling are only partial. For identification always is partial.[24] Further, what Carroll's examples show is that our responses to characters' situations are often sympathetic (we are concerned at the swimmer's situation, even though she does not recognise the danger and so feels no fear), rather than empathic. But this point hardly shows that empathy never occurs: for when the swimmer does recognise the danger and panics, we then share her fear.

Carroll objects to this last move: he holds that we do not share the swimmer's fear, because her fear is self-directed, whereas our fear is directed towards her. However, this objection fails to see the significance of the imaginative element involved in empathic identification. That is, we have to place ourselves imaginatively in the swimmer's situation in order to empathise with her. Thus when I imagine the shark's attack on the swimmer, I am imagining the shark's attack on me (since I am imaginarily in her situation), and hence I can share the swimmer's fear, since in both cases it is self-directed.[25]

---

[23] Carroll, *The Philosophy of Horror*, pp. 90–2.

[24] What Carroll says does not in any case support his position: 'if the correspondences are only partial, why call the phenomenon *identification* at all? If two people are rooting for the same athlete at a sporting event, it would not appear appropriate to say that they are identifying with each other. They may be unaware of each other's existence' (*ibid.*, p. 92). But even if the spectators had exactly the same emotional states, they would still not be identifying with each other. Rather, empathic identification requires one to feel what another is feeling, *because* one recognises that he is feeling it. This is why the spectators are not identifying with each other, not because they are not sharing all their emotional states.

[25] Carroll also objects that the swimmer's fear is based on a belief that she is in danger, whereas my empathic fear is based only on imagining that I am in danger. But this does not show that the fear is not shared, since as he has himself argued, the object of fear is a thought content, whether or not it is asserted, and the thought contents are the same in both cases. (For Carroll's 'Thought Theory' of emotional response, see *ibid.*, pp. 79–88.)

6.3 IDENTIFICATION AND FILM TECHNIQUES

So far I have defended the concept of identification from the claim that it is mysterious or incoherent by distinguishing different kinds of identification: on the one hand, imaginative identification (imaginarily putting oneself in another's position) which is in turn sub-divided into perceptual, affective, motivational, epistemic, practical and perhaps other forms of identification; and on the other hand, empathic identification, which requires one actually to share the character's (fictional) emotions because of one's imaginarily projecting oneself into the character's situation. On the basis of these different kinds of identification, one may come to sympathise with the character (this sympathy, as we have noted, is sometimes itself thought of as a kind of identification, but we will treat it as one possible upshot of identification, since one can sympathise with someone without employing any sort of imaginative projection into his position). I have also deployed these distinctions to defend the claim that identification occurs in films against the sorts of objections that are often raised against it. Given these distinctions between different kinds of identification, we can now examine in more detail the role of identification in our relations to films.

As earlier remarked, the point-of-view shot is often thought of as the locus of character identification in film. In fact, it is the locus of perceptual identification (the viewer imagining seeing what the character fictionally sees), and it does not follow that the viewer identifies with the character in all other respects. The example of a shot in a horror film taken from the point of view of the killer shows that there is no necessary tendency to empathise with the character whose visual perspective we imaginarily occupy. However, since we now have the distinction between affective and empathic identification in place, we can see that there may be a tendency to affective identification resulting from this shot: that is, other things equal, this shot may get us to imagine what the character is feeling (though we need not actually feel it ourselves, i.e., we need not empathise with him). Consider the shot in *The Silence of the Lambs* (1991) taken from the point of view of Buffalo Bill, who is wearing green-tinted night-glasses, looking at Starling (Jodie Foster), while she flails around in the dark, desperately trying to defend herself from him. Certainly, we have no tendency here to empathise or sympathise with Bill – our sympathies lie entirely with Starling – but the shot does tend to foster our imagining of Bill's murderous feelings (partly because we can see their terrifying effect on Starling).[26]

---

[26] This shot also doubles as a reaction shot of Starling: for the significance of reaction shots, see below.

The point-of-view shot, besides grounding perceptual identification, and having a tendency to foster affective identification, also fosters a kind of epistemic identification. For the latter requires us to imagine believing what the characters fictionally believe; and some beliefs are perceptual. However, the idea of epistemic identification is broader than that of perceptual identification, since we may occupy the character's epistemic perspective by virtue of having our knowledge of what is happening restricted to her knowledge (this is characteristic of the detective film for instance).[27]

These distinctions also allow us to answer an objection that has been raised to the point-of-view shot as a locus of identification. According to Jinhee Choi, this sort of shot only rarely fosters central imagining (imagining from the inside), i.e., imagining what it would be like to be in the character's situation. This kind of imagining standardly is triggered only when the viewer has incomplete information and that is not true in the point-of-view shot: 'Why should the viewer need to imagine anything when the character's perceptual state is directly available to him or her?'[28] The reply is twofold. First, what the viewer is presented with is a cinematic image: even when she is engaged only in perceptual imagining, the viewer thus still has to go beyond what is presented, since she has to *imagine* this image as representing the content of the character's visual field. Second, as we have seen, imagining has many aspects and just because there is perceptual identification (imagining seeing what the character sees), it does not follow that there is any other sort of identification, including affective identification. So the viewer has the further task of engaging in these other sorts of imagining if they are called for, which go beyond what is shown in the shot: imagining from the inside is aspectual.

However, though the point-of-view shot is the characteristic form of perceptual identification in film, it is not the only type. This is demonstrated by another shot from *The Silence of the Lambs*. Consider the scene in which Starling and the other F.B.I. agents are in the autopsy room with one of Buffalo Bill's victims, who has been partially flayed by him. It is only towards the end of the scene that we are finally shown the corpse itself; up to this point we are confined to watching the investigators' reactions, particularly Starling's. Watching Foster's finely nuanced performance, which registers barely controlled disgust and fear, modulated by pity for

---

[27] This is what Murray Smith terms allegiance with a character: see Smith, *Engaging Characters*, especially chapter 5. He holds that the notion of identification cannot distinguish allegiance from other senses in which we are engaged with a character: but as we have seen, the notion of identification can in fact be refined so as to recognise this case.

[28] Jinhee Choi, 'Leaving It Up to the Imagination: POV Shots and Imagining from the Inside', p. 21.

the victim, we are invited to imagine what she sees, without actually being shown it. The result is that what we imagine her seeing is very likely worse than what we are finally shown, since each viewer, watching the emotions registered on her face, is invited to imagine something that will justify these emotions, and so tends to imagine whatever would make these emotions appropriate to her: each imagines her own private nightmare scenario. Thus the expressive reaction shot, as well as the point-of-view shot, can cue the spectator to imagine seeing from the character's point of view.

Further, as the example also shows, the reaction shot can be a more effective vehicle for affective and empathic identification with a character than is the point-of-view shot.[29] The reaction shot shows the human face or body, which we are expert at interpreting for signs of emotion, and through the art of a consummate actor like Foster, we can obtain a very full sense of what the character is feeling. Hence we are provided with a large amount of information with which to engage accurately in affective identification.

Moreover, if we are confronted with visual evidence of an individual's suffering, we have a strong tendency to empathise and sympathise with her. Tales of mass disasters in distant countries also have the power to move us to empathy and sympathy; but generally more effective is a confrontation with the individual visage, with the particularities of an individual's plight etched in her expression. For instance, aid agencies employ photographs of individuals in states of distress as a way more effectively to convey their message of mass suffering (recall the discussion of photographic density in Section 6.1).

As noted earlier, the point-of-view shot also has some tendency to move us to affective identification. But it has the disadvantage of having less information to convey about what the character is feeling, and, because of the absence of a shot of her face, has less power to move us to empathy and sympathy with her. The point-of-view shot has in fact fairly crude options available for the conveying of feelings (that is, when it is a subjective point-of-view shot, as opposed to a merely optical point-of-view shot). It may employ a shaking camera to convey unrest and uncertainty: think of the handheld, jiggling shots in *A Woman Under the Influence* (1974), written and directed by John Cassavetes, which convey something of the troubled minds of the married couple. It may employ low-angle shots to convey a sense of being dominated by other characters: think of some of the low-angle shots of Kane in *Citizen Kane* (1941). Even more radically, the entire

---

[29] For a fine discussion of this phenomenon, and of Truffaut's thoughts thereon, see Smith, *Engaging Characters*, pp. 156–61.

mise-en-scène may be set up so as to convey a character's troubled state of mind: think of the shot from the crazed artist Borg's perspective of the dinner-guests in Ingmar Bergman's *Hour of the Wolf* (1968). If we contrast these fairly simple options with the subtleties of Foster's reaction-shot in the autopsy scene, we can see that on the whole the reaction shot is more important than the point-of-view shot in mobilising affective and empathic identification.

Epistemic identification also has a tendency to foster empathy, though in more indirect ways than does the expressive reaction shot. If our knowledge of what is fictional in the film corresponds to a high degree with that of a particular character, there is a tendency to identify affectively and to empathise with that character, even if we are not antecedently disposed to do so. Consider a scene in which we follow the movements of a group of criminals, engaged on a job; we watch them being vigilant, stopping lest they be discovered, being alarmed at dangers, being hopeful about the success of the crime, etc. In these cases, where we have the same epistemic point of view on the events as they do, we can easily find ourselves empathising with them and wanting their crime to succeed, even though normally we would not want this.

A more complex example of this phenomenon occurs in *Groundhog Day* (1993) (see Figure 8). Phil Connors (Bill Murray), a TV weatherman, is

Figure 8. Phil Connors (Bill Murray) reporting in *Groundhog Day* (1993).

caught in a comic version of Nietzsche's eternal recurrence, condemned to live the same day over again and again until he gets it right. Our feelings for Phil are initially complex: his humour is hip and funny, but his cynicism is upfront too, and our affections are divided between him and his colleagues. As the film progresses we increasingly empathise and sympathise with him. This is partly because he grows morally and becomes a more attractive figure. But it is also because we are stuck in the same epistemic situation as he is. No one apart from him and the viewer realises that the scenes we are seeing have been played out many times before: we thus share the knowledge about what is happening only with him, and find it increasingly difficult to look at the world from any other point of view than his, because we know that none of the other characters appreciates what is going on. Here epistemic identification tends to foster our empathy and sympathy with the character.

In addition to these factors, there are others that tend to foster empathy and sympathy. First, empathy and sympathy are mutually reinforcing. To empathise with a character involves feeling what fictionally she is feeling; since most characters have a concern for their own welfare, by empathising with them one will also be sympathetic to them, i.e., one will be concerned for them. Conversely, if one is sympathetic to a character, one will tend to align one's emotions with his, feel what he feels, and so empathise with him. Second and more obviously, we tend to sympathise with characters who are represented as having various attractive traits or ones that merit sympathy. A wide range of traits can foster such responses: characters may be witty (as is Phil Connors), physically attractive, interestingly complex, and so forth. In *The Crying Game* (1992), written and directed by Neil Jordan, our sympathies are mobilised towards Jody (the British soldier, played by Forest Whitaker), Fergus (the IRA member, played by Stephen Rea) and Dil (the transvestite, played by Jaye Davidson) by their vulnerability: Jody is vulnerable because he appears to be in imminent danger of being killed by the IRA, yet is in Northern Ireland for no better reason than that he needed a job; Fergus is vulnerable because, as rapidly becomes clear, he does not believe in the credo of violence to which he is ostensibly committed and is himself then endangered by it (his vulnerability is displayed in his remark to Jody that 'I'm not good for much'); and Dil is vulnerable because of her marginal social and sexual situation. Besides these kinds of character-traits that can promote empathy and sympathy, the knowledge of who is playing the character can also materially engage our feelings. Hitchcock, for instance, was a master at deploying this technique. Considered in terms of his character traits, Scottie in *Vertigo* (1958) is a fairly unsympathetic character; but we are encouraged to empathise with him partly because of our epistemic identification (up to the point of Madeleine/Judy's flashback we are unaware of the plot that has been hatched against him, and are largely confined to his knowledge of events), and also because he is played by James Stewart, with his long history of playing folksy, sympathetic heroes.

Thus the notion of identification can be refined so as to avoid the objections frequently levelled against it, and this refinement permits the creation of theories of some complexity by examining the relations between different kinds of identification. The refined notions still allow for an important connection between identification and emotion. This is displayed partly in the constitutive connection between empathic feelings and identification: empathy is feeling what a character feels because one imaginatively projects oneself into his situation. And the connection between identification and emotion is also displayed in some causal connections: for instance, epistemic identification with a character tends to foster empathy with him. Thus the common view that there is an important connection between identification and emotional response to films has received a partial defence, based on distinguishing different notions of identification. However, the theorist's claim that the point-of-view shot lies at the heart of cinematic identification has fared less well. It certainly constitutes a characteristic form of perceptual identi-fication, but it is not the only form: the reaction shot too can invite us to imagine seeing from a character's perspective. And while the point-of-view shot may have some tendency to get us affectively to identify with the character concerned, it is not as effective in this respect as the reaction shot, and the latter is vastly more effective in engaging our empathy and sympathy.

6.4 IDENTIFICATION AND EMOTIONAL LEARNING

Identification, then, plays an important role in our emotional responses to films. It also plays a significant part in teaching us how to respond emo-tionally to fictionally delineated situations. There are at least two basic forms that this kind of learning may take. The first is that through empathy our emotional reactions mirror those of a character, and that as she grows emotionally, we do too, learning to respond to situations in a way that we and she would previously have found inappropriate. The second basic type of learning results from identifying with a character, but coming to realise that her reactions are in some ways inappropriate to her situation, and discovering that there is a deeper perspective on her situation, different from her own. In the first case, both we and the character grow emotionally together; in the second only we may grow, while the character remains much the same. The first possibility is illustrated by *The Crying Game*, the second by *Letter from an Unknown Woman* (1948).[30]

In *The Crying Game* we are led after the traumatic death of Jody to identify (epistemically, affectively and empathically) with Fergus, who is traumatised by Jody's death and eager to escape the IRA. Jody has asked Fergus to take care of his lover, Dil; Fergus has seen a picture of her, and found her very attractive. He falls in love with her, she performs oral sex on him; and at the turning point of the film she appears naked before him: Dil is a man. Fergus is aghast, strikes Dil, throws up in the toilet and storms out. Since the audience has been epistemically closely identified with Fergus throughout, it is also likely to be astounded by the discovery (Jaye Davidson's impersonation of a woman is extraordinarily convincing). The rest of the film is the story of how Fergus comes to accept the fact that he loves Dil, even though Dil is male ('I preferred you as a girl'), and goes to prison for her sake.

The Crying Game is thematically very rich, engaging with issues of race, gender and love. What is interesting for our purposes is how Fergus is represented as coming to accept that he loves Dil, even though his heterosexuality was not previously in doubt. Love transcends mere gender boundaries; not only is that a theme of the film, but the audience is also positioned to *want* Fergus and Dil to continue their erotic friendship, even after it is clear that Dil is a man. Because we are multiply identified with Fergus, and because Fergus comes to accept his love for Dil, we too are encouraged to accept it. Here identification with a character whose attitudes towards homosexuality change fundamentally in the course of the film also, through empathy, encourages the audience to want the relationship to work out, and thus also encourages them to question their attitudes towards homosexuality.[31] This, then, is a particularly clear example of a film that deploys identification to get audiences to reconsider their emotional responses and to learn from a fictional situation.

Letter from an Unknown Woman, directed by Max Ophüls, is on the face of it a film that falls well within the conventions of the 'woman's picture'

---

[30] When employed for promoting moral learning, I term the first of these strategies the *ethical journey strategy*, the second the *seduction strategy*; see my *Art, Emotion and Ethics*, Sections 8.3 and 8.4.

[31] For an insightful discussion of *The Crying Game* to which I am indebted, see Matthew Kieran, 'Art, Imagination, and the Cultivation of Morals', p. 338.

Figure 9. Lisa (Joan Fontaine) and Stefan (Louis Jourdan) in *Letter from an Unknown Woman* (1948).

(see Figure 9). Lisa, the unknown woman of the title, loves Stefan from a distance; she is enamoured of his musical prowess and the sense of culture and mystery that he brings to her cramped bourgeois life, when she first encounters him at puberty. Yet she talks to him only a handful of times and goes to bed with him only once, from which she conceives a son. For the sake of that son, she marries an honourable man, whom she respects but does not love, but throws it all away when she meets Stefan years later. Yet Stefan does not recognise her, and she leaves his apartment distraught, apparently having finally seen through his superficial charm and having grasped the fact that she was no more than another conquest to him. Yet the film is structured around the letter she writes to him while she is dying, a letter that reveals her still hopeless infatuation with him, a letter that avers the great good that could have come out of their love – if only he could have remembered her, if only he could have recognised that she was his true muse, the woman who could have lent meaning to his life. Stefan, reading the letter, apparently accepts his responsibility and his failure, goes off to fight a duel with Lisa's husband, and thus departs to his certain death.

On the face of it, the film is a paradigm melodrama, a picture that intends not so much to jerk tears, as to ladle them out in bucketfuls. The audience is multiply identified with Lisa: hers is the voice-over and almost all the scenes in flashback are those in which she features; she is quiet and beautiful, with a childlike charm and an impressive determination. The audience is thus epistemically, affectively and empathically identified with her, and there is no doubt about the resulting sympathy that they are encouraged to feel for her. Yet in a real sense, Lisa never learns the significance of what has happened to her. Her dying letter is a testament to how if only Stefan had been able to love truly, to dedicate himself to her, their lives would have been immeasurably richer. So identification with Lisa on this interpretation of the film would lead to a reinforcement of the romantic attitudes that many of the original audience members presumably brought with them when they went to see the film.

There is another way to interpret the film, however. Lisa is an obsessive, unable to recognise that she is projecting her romantic fantasies onto a figure who does not in the least conform with them, and she pursues these fantasies literally to the death, even though there is abundant evidence that she is deluding herself in a way guaranteed to culminate in disaster. Much in the film supports this interpretation. Lisa avers things in her letter that are contradicted by what we see: for instance, that 'I've had no will but his [Stefan's] ever', whereas in fact it is transparently clear that Lisa has a very determined will of her own (she is willing to throw away her marriage on a chance of being with Stefan), whereas Stefan wanders through life with little sense of direction (he admits that he rarely actually reaches any place for which he sets out). These and other clues in the film provide the audience with evidence for a counter-perspective in the film, a point of view that is not Lisa's, and which shows us that Lisa's views are partly fantasised distortions of her true situation.[32]

On this second (and I think better) way of interpreting the film, the audience is encouraged to identify with Lisa in several respects, but is also provided with evidence that her actions are in certain respects foolish and self-deluded. If it grasps this counter-evidence, then what it has learnt from the film is that certain of its romantic values are distorted, tending to encourage potentially disastrous self-delusions. And because the audience so much identifies with Lisa, it should take that lesson to heart; it cannot stand back and think that what has been shown about Lisa's values has nothing to do with its own, since it has seen those values enacted in a

[32] George Wilson, *Narration in Light*, chapter 6.

woman with whom it has closely identified. This, then, is the second way that identification with a character may teach an audience about correct emotional responses. On this model, the character does not grow emotionally, but the audience does because of the way it has discovered that its values are flawed. Here identification plays a more indirect cognitive role than on the first model: to learn what it is appropriate to feel, the audience has to be prepared to detect the existence of a counter-perspective to that of the character. But identification functions to drive the lesson home, to show that the values and attitudes under attack are the audience's own, and thus to create the possibility of a real, lived change in its basic commitments. As this possibility illustrates, the Brechtian idea that identification must always function so as to render the audience uncritically receptive to conventional values is false. Identification may work in an appropriate context to drive home some hard lessons.

So, despite the criticisms that have been laid against the coherence and the explanatory power of the concept of identification, it does in fact have a valuable role to play in understanding our emotional responses towards films. As used by audiences to describe and explain their reactions to films, it is undoubtedly somewhat crude. But once we make necessary distinctions, the concept can be refined so that it plays a valuable part in film theory and in the analysis of individual films.

6.5 EMOTION AND INTERACTION

What differences, if any, are there between emotional engagement with traditional film and with digital cinema? In terms of non-interactive digital cinema, there are comparatively few. Given its greater facility for producing special effects, scenes with more visual impact can be created in digital cinema and these may foster greater emotional engagement. However, to recall a now familiar point, the reduction in evidential warrant in digital cinema means that there may be a diminished sense that apparently real events (say, a stunt man taking a tumble from a height) actually happened. This grounds a countervailing loss of visceral impact in some situations.

For films with interactive menu wrappers – films on DVD – the role of emotions is also much the same as for films with non-interactive wrappers – films watched in the cinema. Though one can control one's access to the work in the former case, it is still true that there is a fixed work time and that the viewing time (the time required to experience the work) must be at least as long as the work time, so there are no emotional differences stemming from this source. However, since one can control one's access to the work, so that images can be paused, sequences rewound, and so on, one can have a more analytic relation to the work, as we saw in Section 3.9.2.

With interactive works, however, there are significant differences in respect of the emotions generated and of the role of imaginative participation compared to non-interactive cinema. Further, videogames are often complimented on being 'immersive' and this clearly has something to do with their emotional impact, so this concept needs to be investigated.

Grant Tavinor has argued that some distinctive emotions are felt in videogames, since one can make certain things fictional in them, and hence one can feel emotions about what one has fictionally done in them. He reports having felt guilty for mugging a prostitute in *Grand Theft Auto III* (2001), and holds that 'it is possible in the case of videogames to feel guilty or ashamed for *what one does in a fictional world*'.[33] There is something true and important about this claim, but it needs careful unpacking. In most fictions, it is not fictional that I, as a member of the audience, can do anything in the fictional world. But in interactive fictions it is standardly fictional that I can do things in these worlds. And what I do should be understood to include what my player character does, since this kind of fictional character is controlled by me (I discuss player characters in more detail later in this section). This means that the *objects* of my emotions are widened in this kind of fiction, since the emotions are directed towards states of affairs that involve me (or my player character). In non-interactive contexts I can fear, say, the monster and fear for the characters; but in videogames I can fear that the monster will eat *me* (or my player character). Some emotions, such as fear, can be self- or other-directed: one can fear for oneself or fear for others. But some emotions, if one is rational, can be felt *only* towards *one's own* actions and feelings: these are necessarily self-directed emotions.[34] For instance, I can feel guilty and ashamed only of things that *I* do or feel. I can feel guilty or ashamed about what others do on my command or request, of course: but here one thinks of their actions as extensions of one's own. So, besides the objects of the emotions being self-involving, interactivity also appears to allow certain distinctive kinds of emotion – necessarily self-directed ones – to be rationally felt that cannot be felt in non-interactive contexts.

However, even thus unpacked, the last claim is not quite right. Distinguish between fictions that are audience-*involving* and those that are

---

[33] Grant Tavinor, 'Videogames and Interactive Fiction', pp. 24–5.
[34] Throughout this section when I claim that certain emotions are possible, I should be understood as holding that they are also rational in these contexts.

audience-*generated* (which interactive fictions are, at least in part).[35] In the former case, it is fictional that members of the audience (or their player characters) are part of the fictional world. This is generally the case in interactive fictions but not invariably so: in hypertext stories, for instance, one clicks on one of several links to determine which way a story proceeds. The story is thus interactive, but is not necessarily audience-involving, since the audience may not be able to act in the fictional world, but merely construct an instance of it from outside it. Conversely, a fiction can be audience-involving, but not interactive. Consider the traditional theatrical aside, in which the audience is addressed by a character on stage. The audience is thereby made part of the fictional world, but its actions do not determine any features of that world, since the drama is not an interactive one. If the audience is threatened in an aside, it is thereby fictional that it is endangered, and audience members can fear for themselves; if the character announces that the audience has done heinous acts (for instance, mugging prostitutes), they can feel guilty, and so on. Hence, the fact that the objects of emotion are broader and that necessarily self-directed emotions can be felt here are grounded on the fictions being audience-involving, rather than audience-generated (i.e., interactive). It is true, however, that the majority of interactive fictions, particularly in cinema, are audience-involving as well. And it is also true that if an interactive fiction is audience-involving, the emotions are widened in their objects and self-directed emotions are grounded in the fiction.[36]

So far we have been discussing guilt directed towards what it is fictional that one does in the fictional world. However, another possible object of guilt is what one *actually* does, does in the real world, in relation to the fiction. In the case of interactive works one's actions partly determine instances of the works and their features: if the works are interactive fictions, then one's actions partly determine instances of these fictional worlds and their features. In the case of non-interactive works one can feel guilt and other emotions towards what one is watching: for instance, one may feel guilty about watching a morally problematic film, or ashamed of watching

---

[35] When talking of 'fiction' in the context of the fictions that audience members generate, I am referring to fiction-instances: i.e., the particular instantiations of the fiction that individual audience members generate by their actions. The interactive work creates a fiction that is underspecified in multiple ways: it is filled out in various ways as fiction-instances by the actions of its audience.

[36] As we saw in Section 6.2, it is possible to fear for oneself when one identifies with a character who is under threat, since one is imagining oneself in the character's position. In such cases it is not part of the fiction that one identifies with the character, though one has chosen to do so. The difference in the case of audience-involving fictions is that it is part of the fiction that one is in the fictional world and under threat.

a cheesy melodrama, or afraid that watching an exciting film is raising one's pulse rate to dangerous levels. But if the work is an interactive fiction, then there is an additional object for these emotions: for instance, one can feel guilty about what one has *made* fictional in these works. So, in the prostitute-mugging case, in addition to feeling guilty that in the fictional world one has mugged her, one may also feel guilty that one has *made* it fictional that one mugged her. (These are distinct states: recall that the former is possible in the theatrical aside case without the latter being true.) And it is the latter feeling that is directed at the distinctive kind of actions involved in interactive fictions: i.e., the action by which the audience partly generates the fiction. However, feeling guilty about what one makes fictional seems absurd: a novelist should not feel guilty simply because he has written a fictional work in which something morally bad happens. Rather, it would be morally problematic if he *enjoyed* making morally bad things happen in the work. So the object of guilt about real actions that generate fictions is, at least in part, the *feelings* one experiences towards these fiction-generating actions.

In discussing Tavinor's claim, then, we have seen that the thought that one can feel distinctive emotions about what one does in fictional worlds turns out to be a complex one. There is in fact a double object of guilt (or of other emotions) here: first, guilt can be directed at what it is *fictional* that one (or one's player character) has done, and this is distinctive of audience-involving rather than audience-generated fictions, though the two types overlap greatly, particularly in the case of cinematic works; second, guilt can be directed at what one feels about what one *actually* does in making certain things fictional, and this is distinctive of interactive fictions. So there are objects and kinds of emotions distinctive to interactive contexts, but they are more complex than may at first appear.

There are several other ways in which interactive cinema is emotionally distinctive.[37] Consider again the real action of making certain things fictional. First, each audience member may choose differently about what to make fictional, so the concomitant emotions are particularised – they are directed at different objects for each interactor. When playing *Façade* (2005), I choose to aggravate Grace and Trip's marital problems, you choose to help them, and we each react to the different fictional events that unfold from our choices.

Second, work time, unlike with non-interactive cinema, is not fixed, since the particular images constituting the work-instances are partly

---

[37] See also Torben Grodal, 'Stories for Eye, Ear, and Muscles: Video Games, Media, and Embodied Experiences', especially pp. 150–1, for a good discussion of some of these issues.

276 A Philosophy of Cinematic Art

determined by players' choices and skills, and these vary widely. For the same reason, viewing time is highly variable. That means that the temporal aspects of the work do not provide the degree of control over audiences' emotional reactions that, as we saw in Section 6.1, non-interactive cinema provides.

Third, in choosing we have to exercise practical skills, and thereby we can experience emotions directed towards the exercise of those skills. In *Façade* one has to exercise some skills, such as being able to type fast enough to produce input before the context changes. In commercial videogames, skills of dexterity, reaction speed, planning abilities and very often skills specific to a particular game are required to win. In such cases, frustration at oneself, anger at one's incompetence and elation at finally succeeding are common, and are directed at one's own practical abilities. In non-interactive contexts the relevant self-directed emotions are at most directed at one's cognitive skills (one is pleased that one has figured out who the murderer is before the film reveals him, for instance). So in non-interactive contexts a far wider range of skills can be the object of one's emotions.

Fourth, in non-interactive fictions one cannot bring about changes in the fictional world, so one cannot, for instance, try to rescue a character from a marauding attacker. Fear that one feels for a character, therefore, is in a certain way passive: there is nothing one can do to help her. But with an interactive work, one can try to rescue her; and one can also try to escape or fight back when one is under threat oneself. This brings the role of the emotion closer to its role in real life, since it is not divorced from the possibility of action. This may or may not make the emotion more intense – it certainly moves it closer to real life.

Fifth, as discussed in Section 5.7, interactive stories are almost invariably reversible, so, even if a story is a tragedy, provided that some outcomes are non-tragic, tragic emotions generally have a lesser place. But reversibility allows for learning and for trying things out, and succeeding or failing with them; so emotions grounded on the learning process have a wider role in interactive contexts. There is a wide range of emotions that can be grounded on this process (and not just directed at the exercise of any skills involved): frustration at failure to achieve something, excitement in making progress, elation and satisfaction at success, and so forth. Assuming that non-tragic outcomes are available, a reversible narrative allows one to live as if one had a time machine or a rewind button for one's life, by which one can go back and rectify mistakes that one has made and get them right next time. The tragic emotions would have much reduced power in a reversible life, since in this life any tragedy would be only temporary (unless all possible outcomes were tragic). But this life would instead have increased scope for and intensity of a range of emotions grounded on a process of trying and learning. The same applies to narratives involving the possibility of reversible outcomes. In videogames one's player character's death is an annoyance, not a disaster.

Finally, in commercial videogames there is constant hedonic feedback, either positive or negative, depending on how one acts in the game. This feedback ranges from the pleasures of successfully accomplishing tasks to annoyance at being hopelessly stuck. Hedonic feedback is a significant contributor to the immersion effect of videogames that is part of their emotional power: one talks of being immersed in some task when one is totally focused on it, and rewards and punishments are powerful motivators for keeping attention focused.

In short, the range of emotional objects and even the kinds of emotions one can feel differ and are generally wider in interactive compared to non-interactive cinema.

Is there any difference in the role or limits of character identification in the two types of cinema? A commonly drawn distinction is between player (or playable) characters, also known as avatars, and non-player (or non-playable) characters. Non-player characters can straightforwardly be the objects of identification, just as can characters in non-interactive cinema, since the audience does not control them in either case. Currently, most non-player characters hardly merit identification, since they are not represented as having much if any inner life; but some characters are interesting enough to warrant it, as in the case of Grace and Trip. And in multiplayer games, where some of the characters are controlled by other people, the characters can potentially be as interesting and rich as their players wish them to be.

Turning to player characters, consider one of the most famous of them: Lara Croft. Particularly in the later games in the series, she is reasonably richly characterised, partly through the cut scenes but also in her gameplay radio messages to her assistants, and is represented as danger-seeking, courageous, at times flippant and funny, with a hidden sorrow based on the early loss of her parents. She also, importantly, has a set of capabilities for jumping, fighting, looking, and so on, which further specify her. The *Tomb Raider* games (1996 onwards) are third-person games, so one sees the character and knows what she looks like, and it is part of the attraction of the games that the audience comes to care for her. So identification processes, both imaginative and empathic, can operate here, even for a player character. Player characters by definition can be controlled, and this involves feature construction of their instances (see Section 4.4). In *Lara Croft Tomb Raider* (2001), the first film based on the game series, when Lara is in danger this is entirely outside the control of the audience; but in the case of the game, I as player, may choose to put Lara into danger: I construct some of her relational properties. However, this fact does not undermine my ability to identify with her. If she is in danger, whether in the film or in the game, I can affectively and empathetically identify with her; and the same processes of character identification can occur in both cases. So for both player and non-player characters identification is possible.

Imaginative identification with a character by definition involves imagining seeing, doing, feeling, believing, etc., something, guided by the thought that fictionally the character is seeing, doing, feeling, believing, etc., that thing. However, there is another mode of imaginative engagement possible with interactive cinema. For one may simply imagine seeing, doing, feeling, believing, etc., that thing without this imagining being guided by any thought involving the character. This is the possibility of make-believe *direct participation* in the fiction. The phenomenology of a great deal of videogame playing suggests that direct participation often occurs. I may simply imagine seeing some monster, imagining battling with it, imagine believing that it is very dangerous, imagine feeling that I am about to die, and so on, without the thought occurring to me that it is the player character who is fictionally seeing, doing or feeling these things. The player character is the *vehicle* for my direct participation, but is not the *object* of my imaginings in this case, for my imaginings about my actions are not guided by the thought that the character is doing these things. It is plausibly this kind of direct engagement (as well as that of hedonic feedback discussed earlier) that grounds the sense of immersion – that fictionally one is present in the world of the game – which game players so prize.[38]

What tends to foster this sense of direct participation in interactive cinema as opposed to non-interactive cinema? My direct participation in a fictional world requires my fictional presence in that world – for instance, imagining fighting a monster requires me to imagine that I am present in the fictional world with the monster. In the real world, if I am present somewhere I can make changes to my environment. In the case of non-interactive cinema I cannot make changes to the fictional environment; but

---

[38] Another, distinct sense of immersion is that of *sensory* immersion. In Section 1.4 we discussed sensory immersion in virtual reality: this occurs where sensory input from a virtual reality display representing some world is perceptually indiscriminable from the sensory input from that world itself. However, this is not the sense of immersion that figures in most discussions of videogames, since currently game displays are very far from being virtual reality ones.

in the case of interactive cinema I can. So at the most general level, the grounding for direct participation in interactive cinema is simply the fact that the cinematic works are interactive.

The sense that the audience can have of direct participation is advanced by at least two important techniques. First, the player character may be thin, i.e., minimally characterised. Since the difference between character identification and direct participation is that in the latter case the thought of the character plays no role in my imaginings, having the player character possess fewer characteristics reduces the scope for the thought of her characteristics to play a role in my imaginings. And some player characters are very thin – for instance, in *Façade* the player character has almost no features other than those that the player chooses to construct: even the character's name can be that of the player. Second, first-person games, which involve showing the fictional world from a point of view entirely confined to that of the player character, tend to foster the sense that one is directly participating in the fictional world. This is in part because the technique supports minimal characterisation: for instance, one does not know what the character looks like, since one is observing from her perspective. But it is also because the technique directly fosters one aspect of direct participation, that of imagining seeing the fictional world through one's own eyes, without mediation by a character. Recall that we rejected imagining seeing (personal imagining) as the default mode of non-interactive cinema in Section 5.4 by employing an argument from absurd imaginings. That argument holds that if I make-believedly see something, then I am make-believedly present, but then why, for instance, does no one notice that I am there; how can I flip from point to point instantaneously when the scene changes, etc? The answer for a first-person game like *Façade* is that the other characters most definitely notice that you are there, since they look at you and talk to you, and the scene is temporally and spatially continuous, so here absurd imaginings get no grip. So first-person techniques support direct participation in interactive contexts.

Hence direct participation has a role in interactive cinema that it does not in non-interactive cinema. Extended first-person camera techniques employed in the latter, for instance, do not foster the sense of one's make-believe presence. The most radical attempt to use extended first-person camera in traditional cinema is *Lady in the Lake* (1946), a film almost entirely shot from the first-person perspective of Philip Marlowe. The results are famously unsuccessful: George Wilson memorably remarks that the film 'gives the impression that there is a camera by the name of "Philip Marlowe" stumbling around Los Angeles and passing itself off as the well-known human being of the same name'.[39] Whatever the intended effect, the technique does not create a sense of one's direct participation in the fictional world and this is in part because one cannot alter that world and so has no sense that one is present in it.

So direct participation is a viable and important alternative to character identification in interactive cinema. As noted, which of these two imaginative modes of engagement occurs will tend in part to depend on the thinness or fullness of the characters and on whether a first-person or third-person point of view is used. However, these are only tendencies, so let me close with two observations about the complexity of these cases: the first is about the relation of thinness to player characters, the second about the relation of first-person point of view to direct participation.

One might suppose, for instance that all player characters must be very thin. Thin characters have few traits ascribed to them by the fiction, independently of what the player chooses to make fictional; full characters have many more. Player characters tend to be thin. In the *Lara Croft Tomb Raider* film the character of Lara is far fuller than in even the later videogames in the series, even though the film is only a basic adventure story. And Lara in the games is a fuller character than player characters in most other games. As noted, characters tend to be even thinner in first-person games where the player make-believedly sees from a continuous first-person perspective, so that she may not be aware of even what the character looks like. In *Façade* the player character of the guest is devoid of almost all characteristics, other than being a friend of Grace and Trip; and even in as narratively rich a first-person game as *Bioshock* (2007), the player character of Jack Ryan has relatively few characteristics. But are player characters inevitably thin? Hideo Kojima, the distinguished designer of several games, including the *Metal Gear Solid* series (1998 onwards), remarks of the player character, Solid Snake, in that series that '[w]e tried not to give him [Snake] too much character because we want players to be able to take on his role'.[40] So Kojima explains thinness by the need for role-playing. However, a film or stage actor takes on a role, but that does not mean that film characters or characters in plays have to be thin. Rather, the problem seems to be that commercial videogames aim to be enjoyable to a wide variety of players. The fuller a character is, the greater is the danger that some of his characteristics may annoy or grate with players. But there is no reason in principle why player characters should not have fuller characteristics, and this would

[39] Wilson, *Narration in Light*, p. 86.
[40] Interview with Hideo Kojima, quoted in James Newman, *Videogames*, p. 133.

be easier if designers tailored them to narrower audiences. Then identification could play a larger role in these audience's responses to the characters. Alternatively, some games now give audiences the tools to feature construct characters themselves almost from the ground up, and in these cases audiences can ensure that characters are full without grating on them; examples of such games are *The Elder Scrolls IV: Oblivion* (2006) and, more radically, *Spore* (2008).

One should also avoid oversimplifying the role of first-person as opposed to third-person games. For while first-person games tend to foster direct participation more strongly, third-person games can also provide a sense of direct participation, because they too share in the basic feature of the player being able to make changes in the fictional world. Consider this typical passage from a *Tomb Raider* walkthrough: 'Jump to the horizontal bar in front of you, swing on it and jump to the next pole. As soon as you grab it, Lara's momentum makes it swing by ninety degrees. Now quickly swing backwards (the wooden board enables Lara to jump from this position) to reach the horizontal bar behind her'.[41] The passage switches repeatedly between third-person and second-person modes (the latter acknowledges the sense of direct participation). And that switch captures much of what one experiences in playing this third-person game. One can either focus attention on what the character is doing or focus on those aspects of the fiction that ground one's direct participation in the fictional world. So games with fuller characters and third-person games can also support a sense of direct participation, but in such cases awareness of the player character's personality, and attention to her actions and appearance, observed from a third-person point of view, give greater grounding for character identification.

So interactive cinema, besides allowing for a greater range of objects of the emotions and kinds of emotions, also allows for the distinctive possibility of sustained direct imaginative participation, in addition to the character-identification possibilities that it shares with non-interactive cinema.

---

[41] Piggyback Interactive Limited, *Lara Croft Tomb Raider*, p. 121. Walkthroughs are guides that provide detailed instructions about what to do in a game.

CHAPTER 7

The role of the medium

At many points in this book I have invoked the notions of medium-specificity and of a medium; and the notion has structured our discussion of many of the artistic features of cinema. It is now time to examine these notions in greater detail and defend them from their critics. Medium-specificity is a concept that has figured in the discussion of many art forms besides cinema, and it helps to defend its application to film if we draw on examples from other media, to show that its use in cinema is not a mere product of the idiosyncrasies of the history of film theory. So this final chapter will range more widely than a discussion of cinema and deploy examples of how medium-specificity applies in other art forms too.

I begin by briefly examining some of the historical background to medium-specificity claims, particularly in the work of Gotthold Lessing. The second section distinguishes between three different versions of the medium-specificity claim. It also discusses and defends the notion of a medium and of differential properties, expanding on the brief discussion of these notions in earlier chapters of the book. The next three sections argue for the three versions of the medium-specificity claims, relating them back to the discussion in earlier chapters of the book. I conclude with a brief summary of the main claims of the book, highlighting how cinematic art is grounded on the features of the cinematic medium.

7.1 TWO TENDENCIES IN THE PHILOSOPHY OF ART

One can usefully distinguish between two broad tendencies in the philosophy of art. The globalising tendency looks for theories that cover all art forms: general theories of the nature of expression, of aesthetic properties, of the role of imagination in appreciation, and so on. The localising tendency, in contrast, looks for theories that apply to particular art forms, seeking respects in which each art form may differ from others: for instance, it looks for theories of cinematic expression and authorship, as distinct from theories of expression in painting or authorship in literature.

Both of these tendencies are rooted in the birth of modern aesthetics in the eighteenth century. In 1746, Charles Batteux, in a book that Paul Kristeller has identified as the founding document for the modern notion of the fine arts, *The Fine Arts Reduced to a Single Principle*, defined the fine arts as the imitation of beautiful nature. Twenty years later, in 1766, Gotthold Lessing in his *Laocoön* argued that the visual arts of painting and sculpture are subject to quite different principles of evaluation than is poetry. Those two tendencies in aesthetics have continued to the present day, with, on the one hand, works such as Kendall Walton's *Mimesis as Make-Believe* attempting a general theory of representation for the arts, and, on the other hand, Peter Kivy's *Philosophies of Arts* pleading for greater attention to the peculiarities of individual art forms, holding that, for instance, 'profundity' when applied to music should not be understood to have the same meaning as when applied to literature.[1]

In deciding which of these tendencies aesthetics should adopt, the plausible reply, of course, is that it should adopt both. One should try for the most general theories, when one can find properties that genuinely are invariant across different art forms; but one should also be sensitive to those cases in which properties, such as narration, representation, and expression, have structurally different forms in different arts. If one were a dogmatic globaliser, and thought that all artistic properties are the same across all the arts, then there would be little or no room for philosophies of the individual arts. For instance, there would be no role for a philosophy of cinema, strictly speaking, but only for the application of a general philosophy of art to individual films. On the other hand, if one were a dogmatic localiser, and held that one could philosophise only about the individual arts, and that nothing whatsoever of interest could be said about art in general, then one would wonder what role there could be for a philosophy of art, other than as a mere compendium of the philosophies of the individual arts.

So far, so sensible. Things get more interesting when one distinguishes between different options within the localising tendency. For if one believes that there are significantly different artistic properties possessed by the individual arts, then the question arises of why this is so, and at that point one begins to enter the domain of seriously contested and therefore seriously interesting matters. For example, some commentators have lamented

---

[1] Paul Kristeller, 'The Modern System of the Arts'; Gotthold Lessing, *Laocoön*; Kendall Walton, *Mimesis as Make-Believe*; and Peter Kivy, *Philosophies of Art*.

what they regard as the conservatism of the modern novel, rooted, they claim, in an eighteenth-century Enlightenment view of reality that was further ossified by Victorian realist thought. They contrast this with the explosion in formal possibilities that marked the emergence of modern painting in the late nineteenth and early twentieth centuries: the rupturing of form that characterised analytic Cubism, the liberation of colour that marked expressionism, the abandonment of representation that defined the emergence of abstract art. In contrast, the novel is still stubbornly stuck, it is alleged, in outdated realist forms, and the mainstream of literary practice has untenably spurned the centrality of originality that its visual cousin has enthusiastically embraced.

Suppose that this view is correct. It still leaves open the question of why this difference exists between the two art forms. Several possible explanations spring to mind. Perhaps it is due simply to a difference in the way that the two traditions have developed, with more conservative artists drawn to literature than were attracted to the visual arts. Perhaps it is due to the entrenched expectations of the two different audiences for the art forms. So historical and sociological explanations might be sought for the difference. But there are other possibilities. One is that the difference is to be explained by differences in the media involved. For instance, visual depiction engages natural recognitional capacities, as we saw in Section 2.1, and it might be argued that these capacities are sufficiently plastic and adaptable to cope with the radical distortions of modernist depictive techniques: one can still recognise Ambroise Vollard in Picasso's portrait of his dealer, despite the Cubist distortions.[2] In contrast, similarly disruptive strategies for literature would be scuppered by the fact that the written word bears an essentially conventional relation to its referent, so that radical distortion of the lexical sign would undermine the possibility of communication – or at least render it so difficult and draw on so large a range of assumed knowledge that it would undermine its ease and directness. Thus, one might argue, *Finnegan's Wake*, which is as revolutionary a departure in literature as is *Les Demoiselles d'Avignon* in painting, is far less successful as a work of art because its comprehension imposes the requirement of having so intimate an acquaintance with several European languages and so extraordinary a facility for word play and puns as is possessed by very few people, other than James Joyce. This explanation of the alleged difference in the conservatism of the art forms would appeal to the nature of the different media – a lexical one as

---

[2] For a discussion of this plasticity (or, as he terms it, *dynamism*) of recognitional capacities, see Dominic McIver Lopes, *Understanding Pictures*, chapter 7.

opposed to a visual one – and to the associated interpretative capacities that engage with these different media.

So believers in medium-specificity are more than localisers: they are localisers who hold that the differences in artistic properties or evaluations that apply to artworks are to be explained, at least in part, by the different features of the media in which these artworks occur. Hence medium-specificity introduces an interesting and substantive thesis into what would be an almost trivial debate about methodology. Lessing himself was an arch-defender of medium-specificity. He held that the visual arts of painting and sculpture ought to imitate beautiful bodies; in contrast, poetry ought to imitate actions. The reason derived from differences in the respective media. The visual arts consist of signs that co-exist in space, and so, on the principle that 'incontestably, signs must have a proper relation to the thing signified', are properly suited to represent things whose parts coexist in space, that is, bodies.[3] And poetry, which consists of articulate signs in time, is properly suited to represent things that similarly extend in time, particularly human actions. On the basis of this medium-grounded difference, Lessing advocated that poetry should be governed by a principle of frugality of description, according to which poets should describe bodies and objects only in the course of their occurrence in actions, as when Homer describes Agamemnon's clothes in the course of describing his action of dressing. According to the frugality principle, then, Ernest Hemingway would come out well as a novelist and the later Henry James would come out *very* badly.

I do not invoke Lessing here in order to defend the particular details of his view (for many of those details are indefensible), but rather to call to attention the general structure of his medium-specificity claims. And that general structure has been of enduring influence on several later theorists. The art critic and theorist Clement Greenberg argued that painting is distinctive in being the art of flat, coloured surfaces and that this feature sets the proper goal and course for the development of the art; hence Abstract Expressionism and Colour Field painting were, he argued, the highest contemporary fulfilment of the art of painting.[4]

However, it was of course in early film theory that the most sustained advocacy of medium-specificity claims found, in the early twentieth century, its home. As we saw in Section 1.2, Arnheim, in *Film as Art*, argued that film is an art by virtue of its divergence in a way distinctive of the medium from what he called the complete recording of reality; and

[3] Lessing, *Laocoön*, p. 349. [4] Clement Greenberg, 'Modernist Painting'.

Arnheim identified himself self-consciously as an heir to Lessing: one of the chapters of his book is entitled 'A New Laocoön'. As noted in Section 2.3.6, André Bazin, perhaps the greatest of film theorists, appealed to the nature of the medium to argue for the superiority of cinematic styles that he believed to be realist, paradigmatically Jean Renoir's use of deep focus, moving camera and extended takes in films such as *Rules of the Game* (1939). Bazin pithily maintains: 'The realism of the cinema follows directly from its photographic nature'.[5] But medium-specificity claims have encountered opposition from some, notably Noël Carroll, whose philosophical career has been marked by a sustained and fervent hostility to specificity claims. The tenor of Carroll's animadversions against medium-specificity is aptly summed up in the title of one of his articles: 'Forget the Medium!'[6] So we need to determine whether the medium-specificity view can be defended.

7.2 MEDIUM-SPECIFICITY CLAIMS

7.2.1 *Three claims*

So what exactly is the medium-specificity claim? That is by no means a simple question to answer, for very many different claims have been launched under the medium-specificity flag of convenience and several of them are holed below the water line. Rather than criticising those that fail, I will distinguish three main versions that, I will show, can be defended.

First, consider an evaluative claim:

(MSV) Some correct artistic evaluations of artworks refer to distinctive properties of the medium in which these artworks occur.

This version of the claim grounds evaluations, or more ambitiously evaluative principles, that apply to artworks and refer to distinctive features of a medium. For instance, Lessing's principle of frugality applies to works of poetry, not to the visual arts, and cites features, such as being signs successive in time, that are distinctive of the medium according to Lessing. In contrast, paintings and sculptures are not bound by this principle, since they involve signs co-existing in space.

---

[5] André Bazin, *What is Cinema?*, p. 108.

[6] Noël Carroll, 'Forget the Medium!' Carroll has some localising sympathies and even within film theory is sceptical of the attempt to find general theories, favouring instead what he calls 'piecemeal' theorising. Nevertheless, he opposes all medium-specificity claims.

Second, there is an explanatory version of the claim:

(MSX) Correct explanations of some of the artistic properties of artworks refer to distinctive properties of the medium in which these artworks occur.

This differs from the previous claim in two respects. First, it goes beyond simply identifying evaluations or evaluative principles by citing distinctive features of the medium: it tries to *explain* why these evaluations have the form they do in terms of the distinctive features of the medium. For instance, Lessing employs a general mimetic principle, which holds that things properly imitate objects that they structurally resemble. It is *because* poetry consists of signs successive in time that it properly imitates actions, which are successive in time. The second difference from the first, evaluative, version of medium-specificity is that 'artistic property' will be construed to cover not just artistic evaluative properties, but all those properties that can figure in the grounds of artistic evaluations: i.e., that can figure in reasons for making artistic judgements. For instance, narrative structure counts as an artistic property on this understanding, since one may cite a work's narrative structure as a reason for its artistic success; but having a particular narrative structure is not in itself an evaluative notion.

Finally, we can distinguish a version of the medium-specificity claim that applies not, as do the earlier two, to artworks, but to art forms:

(MSF) For a medium to constitute an art form it must instantiate artistic properties that are distinct from those that are instantiated by other media.

This claim is similar to that defended by early film theorists, such as Arnheim, who wanted to show that the new medium of film was not just a scientifically useful means for recording the world, but was itself a new art form. And such theorists thought that the way to do this was to show that film could do artistically important things that other art forms, such as theatre, did not or could not do at all.

I will argue that all three kinds of medium-specificity claims are true of cinema, and indeed will show that they apply to several other arts. So, while Carroll is correct in thinking that many versions of medium-specificity claims are false, he is wrong in thinking that all versions fail.

7.2.2 *The concept of a medium*

Critics of medium-specificity sometimes express scepticism about the very notion of a medium. Monroe Beardsley, for instance, holds that the idea of a medium is 'almost useless for serious and careful criticism' in the arts.[7] Carroll agrees: he thinks that the notion is so unclear that one ought probably to abandon it.[8] And, certainly, adherents of medium-specificity had better get clear about the concept.

A tempting thought is that a medium is the kind of stuff out of which artworks are made. Paintings are made out of paint and canvas: so the medium of painting is paint on canvas. Drawings are made of graphite and paper: so the medium of drawing is graphite on paper. Yet that cannot be right: we should follow Richard Wollheim in distinguishing between the *material*, the stuff of art, and the *medium*.[9] The material does not invariably determine the medium. Consider drawing: graphite on paper is employed not just for drawing, but to write stories in pencil, and it could even be used to make sculptures. Conversely, there are many different materials with which one can draw: graphite, chalk, silverpoint, and so on. Rather, the medium is how one *uses* the material; so the medium is constituted by the set of practices that govern the use of the material. In the medium of drawing, one uses various materials to produce lines; and many different sorts of material can be used for this purpose. Indeed, there is an analogy here with functionalism in the philosophy of mind: the functionalist holds that there are several different physical and even non-physical states that can realise the same mental state, a state that is functionally individuated. In similar fashion, a medium is constituted by a set of practices, and these determine which physical materials can realise it. Graphite on paper can instantiate a line, but milk on paper would be near useless for drawing, since it would be very hard to form lines. Sculpture is a medium of three-dimensional shapes; so materials that can realise the sculptural medium must be able to retain three-dimensional shape. Hence liquid water cannot constitute the material of sculpture; but ice could. However, the functionalist analogy has its limits, for when we *finely* individuate media, the materials employed sometimes play a role in this finer individuation. For instance, the media of printing are partly individuated by the materials employed in the production of the prints – as shown in the classifications of woodcut printing, as opposed to lithographs or etchings. Materials also play a role in finely individuating the media of painting – as instanced by oil painting, as opposed to watercolours or frescos.

The material of art is not always physical. If a medium is a set of practices for organising a material, then it requires some material or other. But if all

---

[7] Monroe Beardsley, *Aesthetics*, p. 82.   [8] Carroll, 'Forget the Medium!' p. 6.
[9] Richard Wollheim, *Painting as an Art*, chapter 1, especially p. 23.

material were physical, then one must conclude that there is no medium of literature, since a literary work is not constituted by any physical materials that may realise it; for a literary work is not a physical type. Likewise, digital imagery would have to be ruled not to be a medium, if material must be physical.[10] Rather, one should allow that some material is not physical, but symbolic, made of signs – lexical signs in the case of literature or numerically constituted bitmaps in the case of the digital image.

This view leads to the conception of a medium that is similar to that articulated by Dominic Lopes: 'Artworks standardly belong to the same art medium when and only when they are produced in accordance with a set of practices for working with some materials, whether physical, as in sculpture, or symbolic, as in literature'.[11] A similar account of the notion of a medium has been defended by David Davies.[12]

Lopes' individuation condition is restricted to an *art* medium. But the notion of a medium is more general, and it is important to see this in order to forestall an objection. For if one characterises a medium in terms of a set of practices, then it is easy to suppose that the notion of a medium and the notion of an art form are one and the same: drawing is a medium, drawing is an art form. That would mean that one could not pose any interesting questions about the relation of a medium to an art form. For instance, Carroll in effect proposes that one abandons the idea of a medium, and simply talks of art forms. But the notion of a medium is different to and extends wider than that of an art form. This is partly because not all media are used in art. Telephonic communication is a medium, but while some conceptual artist has doubtless at some point used telephones for art, telephonic communication is not an art form. And even when a medium is standardly used for art, not all uses of that medium count as art uses. Many drawings are art, but there are also technical drawings, and if I draw you a route plan to show you how to get to my house, I do not thereby produce a work of art. So the *art form* of drawing is not to be identified with the *medium* of drawing. Rather, the art form is a particular *use* of the medium: a use that either aims to realise artistic values or that does realise those values. So one cannot substitute the notion of an art form for that of a medium; hence one can pose non-trivial questions about the relation of an art form to its medium, which is precisely what deliberation on MSF calls for.

---

[10] This view is in fact defended by Timothy Binkley, 'Computer Art', who claims that 'The computer is neither a medium nor a tool', p. 413.

[11] Dominic McIver Lopes, 'Digital Art', p. 110.   [12] David Davies, 'Medium'.

Finally, it is important to note that media can incorporate other media, or as I termed it in Section I.2, media *nest*. Consider printing, which is a medium. There are many kinds of printing: woodcuts, etchings, engravings, lithographs, and so on. Each of these kinds can properly itself be called a medium. So one medium can contain several media. There can be many levels of nesting. Pictures are a medium, but there are many kinds of pictures: paintings, photographs, moving pictures (cinema), prints, and so on. Each of these can properly be described as a medium. And within cinema, the medium of the moving image, there are many different kinds of images. The most common are traditional (photochemical) photographs; but there are also analogue video moving images, digital moving images, and, as we noted in the Introduction, there have been films, such as those of Émile Reynaud, which were composed of handmade images projected onto a screen. So the medium of the moving image contains several other more specific media, such as traditional photographic cinema, digital cinema, analogue video cinema and handmade cinema.

It follows from the phenomenon of nesting that one has to specify the *level* at which one is making a medium-specific claim. For instance, if one cites some feature of the cinematic medium in discussing a film, one should be clear as to whether one is appealing to the fact that the medium incorporates photographic images, or to the more general fact that it incorporates visual images.

7.2.3 *The notion of specificity*

So medium-specificity claims are not void because of the incoherence or unclarity of the notion of a medium. But the other part of the claim, that of specificity – or, as I have put it, of distinctness – also calls out for clarification. One common understanding by both proponents and opponents of the view is that specificity should be understood in terms of what is *unique* to a medium. This may be construed as either a contingent truth or as a modal claim – that is, construed in terms of those features that are *as a matter of fact* possessed only by the medium in question, or, more strongly, in terms of those features that *could only* be possessed by the medium in question. The latter would yield the view that is sometimes identified with medium-specificity, namely, medium essentialism.

Carroll employs the notion of uniqueness in criticising medium-specificity. For instance, he considers and objects to the claim that each art form should explore *only* those avenues in which it *exclusively* excels above other arts.[13] Narration is common to both films and novels, so from this version of the specificity thesis it follows that neither films nor novels should narrate, since both do; or that films should not narrate (since novels were in place first); or that novels should not narrate, but should cede priority to the newcomer; and all of these options, Carroll correctly notes, are absurd.

There is more than one thing wrong with this objection if it is directed against medium-specificity arguments in general, since Carroll simply saddles the specificity theorist with the view that an art form should do *only* what is unique to it: the theorist could instead hold that an art form should *always* do what is unique to it but can *also* pursue other features that are shared with different media, such as narration. But, even setting this point aside, why should one insist that the favoured activities are those that are *exclusive*, i.e., unique, to the art form (or to the medium, now that we have rescued the notion from the accusation of incoherence)?

Lessing, for instance, does not hold that art forms must pursue only activities that are unique to them. For he treats sculpture and painting together, as both involving signs that co-exist in space: so co-existence of signs in space is not unique either to painting or sculpture. Rather, this property is what I termed in Section 5.6 a *differential* one: it distinguishes one group of media, the target class, from another group of media, the contrast class. In Lessing's theory, the group of media that constitutes the target class is the group of visual media, consisting of signs co-existing in space, which is distinguished from the contrast class of lexical media, consisting of the group of those media involving signs successive in time, such as poetry. The notion of uniqueness is simply the limiting case of the differential, when there is only one member of the target class and the contrast class consists of all other media. This notion of the differential can do useful work, since a feature of a medium may figure in an explanation or evaluation, even though it is possessed by more than one medium. And it also fits naturally with the point that media nest. For instance, in discussing a film, I may explain some of its features by appealing to the fact that it is in a visual medium, and other of its features by the fact that it is in a photographic one. Both of these features are differential and involve nesting.

So, while there are cases where distinctness (specificity) should be understood in terms of uniqueness, the general understanding of this claim should be in terms of differential properties – properties that distinguish one group of media from another group, but that are not necessarily unique to any particular medium.

It might be thought that the substitution of differential for unique properties would eviscerate medium-specific claims of all interest, perhaps rendering them trivial. For if one can group media as one wishes into target and contrast classes, then it may appear that there are no constraints on theory, unlike the uniqueness case, where only one grouping (one medium, contrasted with all other media) is mandated.

However, this triviality worry is misplaced. The notion of differential properties provides a useful analytic framework for discussing the relations between different media, and provides us with the capacity to locate precisely which features figure, for instance, in explanations of the artistic properties of different art forms (we will see several examples of the usefulness of this framework in Section 7.4). Moreover, there is no reason to assume that a feature of a medium in order to be genuinely explanatory must be unique to it. On the contrary, even if one held that uniqueness were a prerequisite for genuineness of explanation, then one would have to admit that differential properties must also be genuinely explanatory, since differential properties are unique to *groups* of media. So triviality concerns should be set aside.

7.3 EVALUATING ARTWORKS

Having clarified the key terms involved in medium-specificity claims, we can now defend these claims. Carroll successfully shows that many versions of medium-specificity are untenable. Some are trivial, such as 'only aspire for effects that are possible in the medium'; others are unacceptable, such as 'do not pursue effects that are difficult in the medium', which would be a recipe for artistic mediocrity.[14] And the lack of clarity that specificity theorists have often shown in their formulations gives Carroll good grounds to raise objections against many of them. But to say that there are many false versions of the view is not to say that no version of the view is correct.

Consider first the evaluative version of the medium-specificity claim, MSV, which holds that some correct artistic evaluations of artworks refer to distinctive properties of the medium in which those artworks occur. There are at least two reasons to think that this version is correct.

---

[14] Noël Carroll, 'Medium Specificity Arguments and the Self-Consciously Invented Arts: Film, Video, and Photography', pp. 8–13.

First, consider the following argument. Artworks are by definition works, not natural products: they are the products of action. And appreciating them involves in part appreciating them as an *achievement*. That involves understanding what the artist was aiming at, and what difficulties she had to overcome to reach her goal. Some of these difficulties are due to distinctive features of the medium, and hence a correct evaluation of those artworks must involve an understanding of, and therefore reference to, these distinctive features.

Consider Lorenzo Bernini's extraordinary sculpture, *Apollo and Daphne* (Borghese Gallery, Rome). The sculpture shows Daphne, who is being pursued with sexual intent by Apollo, at the moment that she begins to metamorphose into a tree in order to escape his amorous advances. Her legs are being engulfed by bark, her fingers are transmuting into twigs. The delicacy of the sculpting is breathtaking: the twigs are so finely delineated that the marble is honed to a point where a single false move would have cracked the piece. This is sculpting of technically the highest order, employed for gripping and poignant artistic effect.[15] To appreciate the scale of this achievement, one must grasp some differential features of the medium. For this is *carved* sculpture, carved in marble. Suppose that a counterpart of *Apollo and Daphne* had been made as *cast* sculpture, cast perhaps in bronze. With cast sculpture one can use materials such as wax or clay to build up a mould around an armature to form a shape from which the final statue is cast. Certainly, the cast version of *Apollo and Daphne* would be an impressive achievement, but it would lack that extraordinary sense of reckless danger that the carved version possesses; for if the artist broke part of the mould in modelling the twigs, he could easily have repaired it before casting the final statue. So one must know not just that this is a work of sculpture to appreciate it, but also must grasp some of the distinctive features of the media of carved, as opposed to cast, sculpture.

The same point applies to many other artistic achievements. To evaluate correctly Michelangelo's achievement in painting the Sistine Chapel one must understand the nature of fresco painting: since it is a quick-drying medium, the artist has to act decisively and boldly in order to make an image. Opportunities for touching-up are limited, and these must be added later as separate, localised layers (and in the case of the Sistine Chapel it is

---

[15] Interestingly, it was not Bernini who sculpted the most delicate passages, but his assistant Giuliano Finelli, to whom Bernini gave no credit. Finelli walked out of Bernini's studio for twenty years because of this slight. (See Simon Schama, *Power of Art*, p. 100.) Not only in cinema does collaboration occur – and not only in cinema is a failure to acknowledge the artistic contribution of a collaborator an ethical as well as an aesthetic slight.

famously controversial to what extent Michelangelo did this). But this feature of the medium is a differential one: it is true of some painting media, but not of others, such as oil painting. Understanding this feature of fresco painting makes Michelangelo's achievement all the more extraordinary: he had to get it pretty much right first time and to work extremely rapidly. The same medium-involving point applies to watercolour painting, where there are even fewer opportunities for revision: and that makes even more impressive Turner's achievement in his watercolours.

Returning to film, consider achievements in digital animation. As we saw in Section 2.3.3, the ideal of photoreal animation has been important in recent cinematic practice: that is, the ideal that a digital image of some object should be visually indiscernible from how a photograph of that object would look, if the object had existed with the ascribed properties. For instance, a digital image of King Kong is photoreal just in case it looks visually indiscernible from how a photograph of Kong would look, if he existed with the ascribed properties. The photoreal ideal can be achieved in digital animation: and that is a very considerable achievement. But suppose that one were told that the animation in *King Kong* (2005) was not in fact accomplished by digital means, but produced by each frame being hand drawn by animators using coloured ink in traditional fashion. What was before an impressive achievement would now become an almost superhuman one: the skill, dedication and time involved would make it scarcely conceivable that the animators had achieved the photoreal ideal. So, again, understanding how a medium differs from others is required to make some correct evaluations of artworks.

This point about medium-involving evaluations is closely related to Kendall Walton's argument in 'Categories of Art' that to appreciate an artwork correctly, one must know the category under which it is correctly perceived: so, for instance, Picasso's *Guernica* is dynamic and vibrant if it is viewed (correctly) as a painting, but is dead and dull if it is viewed as falling under the category of a *guernica*, where guernicas are three-dimensional works, with different varying heights and topographies in the third dimension, all of which look like Picasso's *Guernica* when viewed head-on. The relation of MSV to Walton's point is that, whereas Walton confines his claim largely to artistic categories, MSV holds that the notion of a medium plays a similar role in evaluating at least some aspects of works.

There is a second kind of reason for thinking that MSV is correct. There are terms of critical appraisal that refer to differential features of the medium in which a work occurs. A film can be praised for being

cinematic, or criticised for being uncinematic. A painting may be celebrated as being very painterly, or condemned (as is true of many of
Magritte's works) for displaying no interest in painterly facture. A work
of literature may be honoured for being very literary, or derided for being
written in flat and halting prose. These terms are all evaluative, and they
claim that the works in question are good in part because they exploit
features that are distinctive to the medium. And, interestingly, artists do
think in these terms. Quentin Tarantino, for example, holds: 'Violence is
one of the most cinematic things you can do with film. It's almost as if
Edison and the Lumière brothers invented the camera for filming violence. The most cinematic directors, they're taking cinema and exciting
you. I really do think about it like that.'[16]

In a nice critique of Carroll's rejection of medium-specificity, Murray
Smith recalls that his wife once remarked that the film *My Dinner with
André* (1981) is not very cinematic, even though she thought it a good film.
The film is a straightforward recording of the eponymous André Gregory
and his friend, Wallace Shawn, having dinner together and talking for
nearly two hours. It is riveting because of the nature of that conversation,
the personalities of the two protagonists and the narrative arc of their
interaction. But it could have been done as a stage play, and the result
recorded by a film that, qua film, lacked any artistic pretensions. The
actual film is uncinematic because it does not exploit in any interesting
fashion any distinctively cinematic devices, such as montage, elaborate
framing techniques, camera movement: it uses these devices only for
recording purposes. So, as Smith notes, it makes sense to say that the
film is overall good, but that it is uncinematic; so some evaluative terms
refer to the distinctive capabilities of the medium.[17] And, we should add,
we can regard the uncinematic as a certain kind of defect: it is a kind of *pro
tanto* merit that a film is cinematic, and a *pro tanto* defect that it is
uncinematic. Similar remarks apply to those other evaluative terms that
are medium-involving, such as the painterly. I can criticise Magritte's
paintings as not being painterly, since they show no interest in the
distinctive capabilities of making images through paint (most of them
could have been done as photographs of mocked-up installations), but
nevertheless I can hold that Magritte's paintings are overall good, because
of the interest of the ideas that he uses these flat and toneless paintings
to convey.

[16] Quentin Tarantino, 'I Call the Shots Here', p. 8.
[17] Murray Smith, 'My Dinner with Noël; or, Can We Forget the Medium?'.

7.4 EXPLAINING ARTISTIC FEATURES

So one should believe in MSV, the evaluative version of medium-specificity. The explanatory version, MSX, is also true: that is, correct explanations of some of the artistic properties of artworks refer to distinctive properties of the medium in which these artworks occur. In fact, we have seen numerous instances of its truth in the previous chapters. The following examples are a selection from them.

First, recall the discussion in Chapter 1 of still photographs and traditional, photographic films. One artistic property, in my favoured sense of a property that can feature in the reasons for an artistic evaluation, is fictionality. Roger Scruton has noted the 'fictional incompetence of photography', the fact that one cannot photograph a fiction.[18] One can photograph a real object that represents a fiction, such as an actor playing a fictional character, but that is not the same, of course, as photographing a fiction – for instance, photographing a fictional character. The fictional incompetence of photography contrasts with other media, such as painting and literature, which can and do represent fictions. The explanation of this photographic incapacity is, as we saw, straightforward: the photographic relation is a causal one and one cannot have a genuinely causal relation with a non-existent object. Painting and literature, in contrast, have an intentional relation to their subject matter, and therefore can represent non-existent objects. The point is enough to show that the explanatory version of medium-specificity, MSX, is true: one can explain why photographic artworks lack this artistically relevant fictional capacity by appealing to differential features of the photographic medium. So there is at least one true instance of MSX.

A second example rests not on a feature of the photographic medium, but on a differential feature of visual media as opposed to lexical media. As we saw in Chapter 2, a common view amongst film theorists is that there is a language of film, in the sense that film images are structured like a language. According to this view the relations of images to each other, or the relations internal to an individual image, have a structure that is grammar-like, and the relation of the image to the world is like that of a word to its referent. Communication can be an artistic property, and the mode of communication of an artwork can be one too. But, given the nature of the visual medium, visual images do not have a language-like relation to the world. For, as we noted, the relation of the visual image to its referent is not conventional, unlike the relation of the verbal sign to its referent:

---

[18] Roger Scruton, 'Photography and Representation', p. 112.

interpreting visual images deploys object-recognitional capacities, but interpreting verbal signs deploys one's knowledge of conventions. So, again, one can explain an artistic property of film images, their mode of communication, by appeal to the differential features of the (in this case visual) medium in which they figure.

In Chapter 2 we also discussed several notions of realism, and some apply only to works in visual media, as opposed to lexical media. For instance, photorealism applies only where a representation of an object is visually indiscriminable from a photograph of it; but literary representations of objects can always be discriminated from photographs of them. And perceptual realism involves a representation looking in salient ways like what it represents; that is true of some visual representations, but not of sentences, which do not look saliently like the state of affairs that they describe. Photorealism and perceptual realism and their associated styles are artistic properties of some cinematic works, and the explanation for why this is so draws on differential features of visual as opposed to lexical media. So here again, MSX is true.

Another example of MSX was discussed in Chapter 3. The single-authorship view in its classic form, the *auteur* theory, holds that mainstream films can be the product of a single author. I rejected this theory on several grounds. One of them involved appeal to the photographic medium, which includes digital photographs, and more broadly to the recording medium. If cinematic works incorporate recordings, as they almost invariably do, of actors' performances (whether bodily, vocal or motion), then the film's director, if he does not act all the roles, is reliant on the expressive activities of these agents. He seeks to shape the performance of the actors through his direction and can cut scenes together in ways that modify their performances, but their expressive agency is still their own, not his. So a film in which the director is distinct from the actors recorded must always be multiply authored: the single-authorship thesis is false in such cases. Now this claim rests on a differential feature of recording media: they produce causal imprints of what is in front of the camera or is picked up by the microphone. But literary works, including plays, do not causally record actors' performances, or indeed anything else. Hence an actor in a play does not partly determine the character he plays: Robeson does not determine Othello's character by acting it, though he does determine the character-in-performance. But the film actor is a co-determiner of the character in the film he plays: Bogart is co-determiner of Marlowe's character in *The Big Sleep* (1946), for casting a different actor in the role would have produced a different Marlowe character. So, again, one can partly explain an artistic property of artworks, concerning the role of multiple authorship in them, by the differential features of a photographic recording medium, as opposed to a purely intentional medium.

There were two further examples of medium-involving explanations in Chapter 3. We saw how digital cinema creates new possibilities for enhancing collaboration in acting (an artistic property in our sense) through technologies such as motion capture, which require computer techniques that are not part of the technology of traditional film, but which are native to the digital medium. And we saw how the audiences of interactive works are co-makers of the works' instances and their features (though not of the works themselves); but this is not true of non-interactive cinema, where audiences cannot determine works' instances and their features. So, again, differences in authorship are to be explained by differential features of interactive as opposed to non-interactive media.

In Chapter 4 we saw several examples of medium-involving explanations. Intentionalism concerning the interpretation of artworks is, I argued, in general, false, but its defeaters vary. In the collaborative arts, such as cinema, the hazards of collaboration not infrequently defeat intentions; but in the solo arts, such as literature, where most works are the products of single artists, collaboration plays little role as a defeater of intentions. Also, to consider another ground of defeat, in traditional, photographic cinema intentions are subject to defeat by the hazards of the real, something that plays no role in purely intentional media such as literature, and a greatly diminished role in digital cinema, with its potentially limitless capacity to manipulate images. We also saw that in interactive digital cinema, such as videogames, constructivism of a strong kind (feature constructivism) unproblematically applies in general; but only a weaker kind of constructivism (discretionary constructivism) applies to non-interactive cinema, and its application is dependent on the details of individual films. So, again, features of the medium condition artistic properties of works.

Chapter 5 argued that implicit narrators play no role in cinema, even though they play some role in literature. This argument rested on a differential feature of the two media: if there were an implicit visual narrator in film, that narrator would have to be located, fictionally, at the point of view of the image showing the scene. In many cases that would ground absurd imaginings, as in the case of *North by Northwest* (1959), in which the narrator would have to be imagined as floating in midair. In contrast, the literary medium lacks a visual point of view on the action, and so we can think of the implied narrator not as present, but as learning about the events some other way, such as being told about them by the participants later. Again, there is a medium-involving explanation of an artistic property (the structural features of narration) of artworks resting on distinctive features of the two media. We also defended the coherence of the idea of interactive narration and showed how it is possible in interactive cinema; evidently, this kind of narration is not possible in non-interactive cinema, and so rests on a differential property of interactive media.

Finally, in Chapter 6 we gave many examples of medium-involving explanations concerning the emotional impact of cinema, of which the following are some. First, cinema can generate a more immediate and visceral response than can novels, and this is in part due to the fact that it can produce the startle response and novels cannot, which in turn is grounded on the capacity of moving pictures, music and sound effects to be spontaneously interpreted as threatening, whereas the same is not true of the sensory input associated with novels. Second, photographs are prone to have a greater emotional impact than paintings, because photographs can seem as if they were transparent and have more evidential warrant than do paintings. Third, camera movement and editing can be used to create emotional impact, perhaps generating a rising sense of excitement by increasing editing rhythm, and this rests on the fact that cinema is composed of multiple pictures; so the same mechanisms are not available in literature. Fourth, the fact that non-interactive films have a work time conditions the emotional control that filmmakers can exert over their audience. Performances (which are themselves sometimes artworks, as well as being *of* artworks) have a work time, but works in other media, such as painting and literature, do not, and consequently cannot control the timing of the flow of emotions so precisely. Fifth, sound film, unlike literature, can have a musical track and music in film is central to its emotional impact, achieving greater emotional precision through its associations with words and images. Music lacking such associations, such as absolute music (music without words), either can convey only moods and not emotions, or at best can convey emotions only in an imprecise manner. Finally, interactive digital cinema displays differences from non-interactive cinema in respect of emotional engagement or its grounds: the range of emotional states one can rationally experience is increased in interactive cinema, and the scope of identification is partly limited by the audience's make-believe direct participation in the fictional world in some modes of interactive cinema. These differences are to be explained by the differences between interactive and non-interactive media.

This range of examples shows the usefulness of the analytic framework provided by speaking of differential properties, rather than of properties unique to individual media. First, some explanations of some artistic properties refer to the differences between audio-visual as opposed to lexical media: this is true of the properties of the type of communication (whether it is language-like), of the existence of implicit narrators, and of the emotional differences grounded on the presence or absence of the startle response and of music. Second, some explanations of some artistic properties refer to the differences between photographic media as opposed to non-photographic media, such as painting and literature: these include explanations of the fictional incompetence of photographs, the explanation of the impossibility of single authorship where actors' expressive actions are photographically recorded, and some aspects of emotional impact, such as those grounded on the seeming transparency and greater evidential warrant of photography. Third, some explanations of some artistic properties refer to the differences between traditional photography, and digital photography and recording: for instance, the greatly diminished role of the hazards of the real as defeaters of intention and the increased possibility of collaboration in the actor's role in digital cinema. Fourth, some explanations of some artistic properties refer to the difference between interactive and non-interactive media: the role of feature constructivism, of interactive narration, and the breadth of emotional responses that are possible and rational in interactive cinema are of this kind. So the differential framework provides a powerful way in which to understand the relations between features of the media and the artistic properties of cinematic and other artworks.

7.5 MEDIA AND ART FORMS

The final version of the medium-specific claim, MSF, governs the conditions under which media constitute art forms, rather than being a principle that applies to individual artworks. It states that for a medium to constitute an art form it must instantiate artistic properties that are distinct from those that are instantiated by other media. It can be employed when a theorist tries to show that an emerging medium constitutes an art form, and indeed something very like it was invoked by Arnheim in his claim that film to be an art must diverge from the complete recording of reality in ways distinctive to the medium. We discussed the divergence aspect of Arnheim's claim in Section 1.2; the distinctiveness aspect is captured by MSF. MSF also fits naturally with the perspective of an artist confronted with a new medium: what, she might wonder, can she do now that is of artistic interest that she could not do before? That thought has continued to resonate with the developers of more recent types of moving image. Shigeru Miyamoto, inventor of the platform game and one of the most important designers in videogame history, remarked in 1999: 'The beauty of interactive media is it is different from other types of media, so we need to concentrate on those differences'.[19]

It may seem that there is no need to invoke a principle of this kind to show that a medium constitutes an art form. Carroll thinks that one can show that a medium is an established art by pointing to works of art in that medium; and that is surely a seductive thought.[20] But it is one whose blandishments should be resisted. Recall the argument from CDs, discussed in Section 1.1. Suppose someone maintains that CDs are an art form, and supports this by pointing to all the great works that are on CD – works by Bach, Beethoven, Coltrane, the Beatles, etc. That would be a bad argument: the fact that a medium contains great works does not show that the medium constitutes an art form. For a medium can contain *recordings* of great works, but is not thereby itself an art form; in the same way, the fact that there are photographs of great paintings does not show that photography is an art form.

What more is required for a medium to achieve art status? Someone might point out that the audio recording medium can itself constitute an art form. After 1964 Glenn Gould played only in the studio, and put together his final recordings from snippets of sound taken from a large number of recording sessions, so achieving effects that he could not obtain from any single recording or live session. And the Beatles' *Sgt. Pepper's Lonely Hearts Club Band* is a studio album that uses a wide range of electronic manipulation and effects that would have been very hard or impossible to achieve live at the time of its release in 1967. It was widely hailed as proof that the recording studio can be a tool of artistic exploration. These examples, albeit in a different medium, fit smoothly with the argument of Section 1.3 that cinema is an art in part because of the plasticity of its recording capacities. In parallel fashion, the ability to record sounds in different ways in part determines the audio recording medium as an art. But note that the examples also show something more. For we noted in these cases that the audio recording medium can create *distinctive* artistic effects and values that would be impossible or very hard to achieve without employing the medium; and that is the full answer to why audio recording is an art form. And that is what MSF holds.

---

[19] Quoted in Steven Poole, *Trigger Happy*, p. 218.
[20] Carroll, 'Medium Specificity Arguments and the Self-Consciously Invented Arts', p. 19.

This argument shows that audio recording as a medium constitutes an art form, but it does not show that CDs are an art form. They are merely a storage medium; the recordings may instead be stored on vinyl records, audiotape, and so on. What more would our hypothetical defender of the CD as an art form have to demonstrate? He could try to show that there is something artistically distinctive about digital recordings, because, for instance, of their greater capacity to manipulate sound compared to analogue recording, thus allowing greater freedom and possibilities for the artist. So MSF would have to be invoked again. But, again, though this argument helps to show that digital recording is an art form, it would not show that CDs are an art form, because there are many different ways to store digital recordings, not just on CDs, but in MP3 players, and so on; so there is nothing artistically distinctive that the CD as opposed to the MP3 player could do. The CD remains a storage medium, not a medium that instantiates an art form. So MSF does give intuitively acceptable results in this hypothetical argument, and thereby gains reasoned support.

How does MSF apply to cinema? In Chapter 1 we showed that cinema possesses a plasticity of recording capacities and argued that it is an art form in part because of its ability to vary the mode of presentation of its content, for instance, the scene recorded. The ability to vary its mode of presentation is also possessed by other art forms, such as literature, where the same scene can be described in many different ways. What, then, makes it the case that literature and cinema are two art forms, rather than merely two instances of a single art form (say, a general narrative art form)? The answer is that the modes of presentation of content differ between the two media (lexical as opposed to moving image modes of presentation), such that different artistic properties can be instantiated by these media. (Recall that artistic properties include both artistic evaluative properties and properties that figure in the grounds of artistic evaluations.) So let us consider what is artistically distinctive to the cinematic mode of presentation.

Cinema is the medium of the moving image; so moving images are unique to it; and certain of its devices are also distinctive, and indeed unique to it. Editing (in the sense of the editing together of motion shots) and camera movement occur only in cinema, for instance. A scene can be edited in different ways – the editing mode of presentation of a scene can be varied – so that artistic properties can be achieved that are distinctive to the medium. For instance, by accelerating the editing rhythm one can generate increasing emotional tension and excitement. Likewise, a scene can be shot with different camera movements (or none), so varying the mode of presentation in a way distinctive to the medium. For instance, camera movements can be used to pick out one part of a scene as important; or movements can be created to suggest a personality or a presence; or the camera may be held stationary for long periods so as to suggest a sense of being entrapped – recall the discussion of *Jeanne Dielman, 23 quai du Commerce, 1980 Bruxelles* (1975) in Section 1.2. And in general visual styles in cinema are partly constituted by particular choices about editing and camera movements.

Unique devices can be combined with other features of the medium that are not unique to it, such as acting, to create composite effects that are distinctive to the cinematic medium. For instance, the Kuleshov effect combines editing with acting to create artistically meaningful properties that depend on both components; camera movement can also be combined with acting to create distinctive effects, such as the complete circular camera movement around Scottie and Madeleine/Judy in *Vertigo* (1958), which expresses Scottie's disoriented and wrenching imaginative return to his embrace with Madeleine in the livery stable. The ability to use different lenses is common to still photography and cinema, but because moving images are unique to the cinematic medium, distinctive artistic possibilities can be realised by the use of varying lenses. For instance, the zoom shot and the rack-focus shot are unique to cinema (the latter involves changing the focus of the image within one shot) and can be employed to create various effects, from disorientation to a shifting in the focus of attention. A long lens used for a shot, where an actor is moving towards the camera but is at a distance, can create a sense of hardly any motion occurring at all, and so can create a sense of stasis or futility. Close-ups of a person's face when we can observe it in motion are very different from close-ups of a face in a still photograph, for we can observe the flow of emotion in the former case but not in the latter. Sound is common to a variety of media, but by combining it with editing, for instance cutting to the rhythm of the music, distinctive artistic effects can be achieved; and the same is true of the combination of camera movement with sound which can create cross-modal rhythmic effects, either reinforcing each other or standing in complex counterpoint. Likewise, narrative is common to a variety of media, but by narrating by moving images, distinctive artistic properties are instantiated, such as the absence of implicit narrators in cinema, as distinct from their greater presence in lexical media, which grounds in one respect a greater immediacy of cinematic storytelling.

The distinctiveness of the cinematic mode of presentation was implicit in many of the examples discussed in Chapter 1, but in the light of MSF we can now see its importance. Not just the capacity to vary its mode of presentation matters to making cinema an art form, but also the distinctiveness of this mode of presentation is essential. So the cinematic medium is an art form because of its ability to instantiate distinctive artistic properties, rather than merely being one instance of a more general narrative art form.

To illustrate this point further, consider an example of what makes cinema distinctive relative to theatre, a traditional concern for theorising about film, as we noted in Chapter 1. A rather awful genre of films, known as *films d'art*, flourished in cinema between 1908 and 1912. These films consist of recordings in long shot of great actors of the day, such as Sarah Bernhardt, emoting (silently) in a conventional theatre-like setting, while the camera sits stationary, like a spellbound spectator agog at the thespian brilliance enacted before him. As the name of the genre suggests, these films had the ambition of showing that film could be an art because of the artistry of what is shown. But, of course, these films show no such thing: they are only *recordings* of an art, not art themselves. In contrast, developments, particularly those associated with the director D. W. Griffith, that were simultaneously unfolding in despised commercial films, gave reason to believe that the film medium could constitute an art form. These films employed cinematic innovations such as montage, moving cameras, opening up the action to the outside world and the melding of sight gags with cinematic techniques.[21] The contrast shows again that it is the plasticity of recording capacities demonstrated by the latter group of films that in part grounds the claims of film to be an art form. But note what the example of *films d'art* also brings out: these films do not add any artistic value to what could be achieved simply by being in the auditorium, watching an equivalent play; so there are no distinctive values realised by the recording medium in such cases. But Griffith's films showed that new, distinctive artistic possibilities were available in the cinematic medium through exploiting the plasticity of its recording capacities, and therefore that the medium could constitute an art form. So a full account of the cinematic medium's status as an art form invokes MSF.

Consider too a hypothetical case. Suppose that someone maintained that acetate cinema is a new art form, compared to nitrate cinema. Acetate film is 'safety stock', which became widespread in feature film

---

[21] Recall Arnheim's nice example of a sight gag that rests in part on using the camera to occlude important information – Charlie Chaplin's response to being deserted by his wife. Observing Charlie from behind, we think that he is shaking with grief; when he turns around we see that he is vigorously manipulating a cocktail shaker (see Rudolf Arnheim, *Film as Art*, p. 51).

production from 1952 as a replacement for older nitrate stock, which was both highly combustible and also prone to disintegrate over time. This person might hold that acetate films and nitrate films are different media, albeit at a very fine level of individuation, perhaps because the practices that govern production using nitrate film are slightly different from those governing acetate films (one must take greater care to avoid fires in making nitrate films, for example). Even if this were accepted as constituting a difference in media, it would not prove that there are two different art forms. For nothing artistically interesting and distinctive can be accomplished in acetate film that cannot be accomplished in nitrate film, and vice versa.

Contrast this with the case of someone who holds that digital cinema is a new art form compared to traditional, analogue cinema. Here the claims for there being a new medium are far more robust, since the nature of the digital image and its associated production practices are very different from those of the analogue image. But this would not suffice to show that this is a new art form. For it might be that digital cinema is merely a more convenient way of achieving what could be done before. What makes plausible the claim that digital cinema is a new art form is that one can show the achievability of distinctive artistic properties and values in it. For instance, as we noted in Section 1.4, digital cinema can directly create expressive content through using the hand construction ('painting') mode of the mélange image, without needing to record some actual object, as is required in traditional cinema (traditional animated films are, recall, recordings of drawings and paintings). And probably anything that is visually imaginable is now filmable, as witnessed by the emergence of films that successfully film what was deemed by previous generations of filmmakers to be completely unfilmable, notably Tolkien's *The Lord of the Rings*, spectacularly filmed by Peter Jackson. Digital cinema also allows collaboration to enter into the actor's domain in ways that were not previously possible, through techniques such as motion capture. Moreover, several styles are possible in digital cinema that are in practice unachievable in traditional film. As noted earlier, photoreal animation is now possible, but was not practically possible before. A distinct style is what might be called the *storybook style*, which melds together aspects of animation with photography in one image. *Sin City* (2005) and *300* (2007) are both good examples: based on the graphic novels of Frank Miller, they blend seamlessly together photography with handmade digital elements, the effect being (particularly in the latter film) eerily as if someone had somehow painted a photograph. In blending both elements together they overtly exploit the features of the mélange image.[22] There is also what might be called the *toy style*, most associated with Pixar, which has gradually edged towards – and in *Ratatouille* (2007) actually achieves – photoreal animation of what look like living toys, complete with uncannily accurate representations of that most difficult material to animate, wet fur. These three styles are in practice impossible to achieve outside digital cinema. So distinct artistic properties and values are achievable in digital cinema and this grounds the claim that it constitutes a distinct art form.

Finally, the claims of interactive digital cinema to be a distinct art form to non-interactive digital cinema are well grounded (art forms as well as media can nest). As we have seen, audiences are co-authors of instances of works when these instances are themselves artworks, interactive narration becomes possible, the range of emotional states audiences can rationally experience increases, identification has a somewhat different scope, and immersion as direct participation is an important feature in conditioning emotional reactions. In instantiating this range of artistic properties, interactive digital cinema shows itself to be an art form in its own right, and not merely an instance of the more general art form of digital cinema.

Hence the claims of cinema, of digital cinema and of interactive digital cinema to be art forms are all well grounded on MSF. More generally, we have also seen that though there are many false or uninteresting versions of medium-specificity claims, there are nevertheless at least three substantive and true versions of them. We should accept variants of the localising tradition in aesthetics that holds that the notion of a medium plays a role in evaluating artworks, in explaining works' artistic features and in determining whether a medium constitutes an art form. Lessing, Arnheim and Bazin, I like to think, would have been pleased.

7.6 CONCLUSION

Cinema was born as a technology but rapidly grew into an art. This book has traced the relations between those two aspects of film – its technological features, particularly as they are embodied in the cinematic medium, and its artistic qualities.

We saw how cinema becomes an art, in part, by exploiting the plasticity of its recording capacities; we argued that its representational capacities are

---

[22] The storybook style is distinct from setting photographed elements, such as actors, next to animated characters or against an animated background, which is an effect that is easily achievable within traditional film, and is to be seen as early as Walt Disney's *Alice in Cartoonland* series (1924–7).

not language-like but are grounded on its pictorial nature, and that the various kinds of realism that pictures permit are to be found in cinema; it was shown that mainstream films are always multiply authored; we argued that the correct interpretation of films is not intentionalist, and that constructivism, outside interactive cinema, plays a limited role; the role of the cinematic narrator, it was argued, is much restricted compared to literature; we showed how cinema engages the emotions in various ways, some distinctive to it, and defended the importance of identification in fostering such engagement; finally, it was argued that these artistic features of films are conditioned by the features of the medium, either of cinema itself or of its contained media.

Cinema, the medium of the moving image, comes, we have seen, in a wide variety of kinds from the simple object-generated images of Javanese shadow plays to the high technological achievements of interactive digital cinema. Classical film theorists were focused on what was distinctive of the medium, since they had witnessed the birth of photographic film. But with the dominance of traditional film for most of the one hundred years after the 1890s, it was increasingly tempting to take the properties of the medium for granted and to lose sight of their role in making cinema an art. More recently, however, there has been an explosion in the kinds of cinema available to us – not just digital cinema *per se*, but also the interactive cinema of videogames – and of emerging types of cinema, such as 3D cinema (of a type vastly superior to the experiments of the 1950s) and it is likely that truly immersive virtual reality will be achieved in the not too distant future. Given this variety of moving image technologies, the need to focus attention once more on the medium of cinema and its contained media has become pressing, to explore again the manifold relations between medium and artistry. Philosophers of cinema have for the most part been surprisingly uninterested in these new and emerging media, but understanding and appreciating them is vital to understanding the artistic qualities of cinema. This book has, I hope, gone some way towards remedying the relative neglect of new cinematic media by analytic philosophers, and has shown that in discussing cinema as an art, we had better not forget the medium.

Bibliography

Aarseth, Espen, *Cybertext: Perspectives on Ergodic Literature*, Baltimore, Md.: Johns Hopkins University Press, 1997.

'Quest Games as Post-Narrative Discourse' in Marie-Laure Ryan (ed.), *Narrative Across Media: The Languages of Storytelling*, Lincoln: University of Nebraska Press, 2004.

Abell, Catherine, 'Pictorial Realism', *Australasian Journal of Philosophy*, 85 (2007): 1–17.

Allen, Richard, *Projecting Illusion: Film Spectatorship and the Impression of Reality*, Cambridge University Press, 1995.

Allen, Richard and Murray Smith (eds.), *Film Theory and Philosophy*, Oxford: Clarendon Press, 1997.

Aristotle, *On the Soul*, in Jonathan Barnes (ed.), *The Complete Works of Aristotle: The Revised Oxford Translation*, vol. I, Princeton University Press, 1984.

Arnheim, Rudolf, *Film as Art*, Berkeley: University of California Press, 1957.

Ascott, Roy, 'Is There Love in the Telematic Embrace?' in Roy Ascott, *Telematic Embrace: Visionary Theories of Art, Technology, and Consciousness*, ed. Edward A. Shanken, Berkeley: University of California Press, 2003.

Atkins, Barry, *More than a Game: The Computer Game as Fictional Form*, Manchester University Press, 2003.

Badham, John and Craig Modderno, *I'll be in My Trailer: The Creative Wars between Directors and Actors*, Studio City, Calif.: Michael Wiese Productions, 2006.

Balázs, Béla, *Theory of the Film: Character and Growth of a New Art*, trans. Edith Bone, New York: Dover Publications, 1970.

Baudry, Jean-Louis, 'Ideological Effects of the Basic Cinematographic Apparatus' in Leo Braudy and Marshall Cohen (eds.), *Film Theory and Criticism*, 6th edn, New York: Oxford University Press, 2004.

Bazin, André, *What is Cinema?*, vol. I, trans. H. Gray, Berkeley: University of California Press, 1967.

'The Evolution of the Language of Cinema' in his *What is Cinema?*, vol. I, trans. H. Gray, Berkeley: University of California Press, 1967.

'The Ontology of the Photographic Image' in his *What is Cinema?*, vol. I, trans. H. Gray, Berkeley: University of California Press, 1967.

Beardsley, Monroe, *Aesthetics: Problems in the Philosophy of Criticism*, 2nd edn, Indianapolis, Ind.: Hackett, 1981.

Binkley, Timothy, 'Computer Art' in Michael Kelly (ed.), *Encyclopedia of Aesthetics*, New York: Oxford University Press, 1998.

Bloom, Harold, *The Anxiety of Influence: A Theory of Poetry*, Oxford University Press, 1973.

Bolter, Jay David and Diane Gromala, *Windows and Mirrors: Interaction Design, Digital Art, and the Myth of Transparency*, Cambridge, Mass.: MIT Press, 2003.

Booth, Wayne, *The Rhetoric of Fiction*, 2nd edn, University of Chicago Press, 1983.

Bordwell, David, *Narration in the Fiction Film*, Madison: University of Wisconsin Press, 1985.

'Historical Poetics of Cinema' in R. Barton Palmer (ed.), *The Cinematic Text: Methods and Approaches*, New York: AMS Press, 1989.

Making Meaning: Inference and Rhetoric in the Interpretation of Cinema, Cambridge, Mass.: Harvard University Press, 1989.

Bordwell, David and Noël Carroll (eds.), *Post-Theory: Reconstructing Film Studies*, Madison: University of Wisconsin Press, 1996.

Bordwell, David, Janet Staiger and Kristin Thompson, *The Classical Hollywood Cinema: Film Style and Mode of Production to 1960*, London: Routledge, 1985.

Bordwell, David and Kristin Thompson, *Film Art: An Introduction*, 6th edn, New York: McGraw-Hill, 2001.

Bratman, Michael, 'Shared Cooperative Activity' in his *Faces of Intention: Selected Essays on Intention and Agency*, Cambridge University Press, 1999.

Braudy, Leo and Marshall Cohen (eds.), *Film Theory and Criticism: Introductory Readings*, 6th edn, New York: Oxford University Press, 2004.

Buchler, Justus (ed.), *Philosophical Writings of Peirce*, New York: Dover Publications, 1955.

Bullough, Edward, 'Psychical Distance' in Alex Neill and Aaron Ridley (eds.), *The Philosophy of Art: Readings Ancient and Modern*, New York: McGraw-Hill, 1995.

Carroll, Noël, *Mystifying Movies: Fads and Fallacies in Contemporary Film Theory*, New York: Columbia University Press, 1988.

Philosophical Problems of Classical Film Theory, Princeton University Press, 1988.

The Philosophy of Horror or Paradoxes of the Heart, London: Routledge, 1990.

'Towards an Ontology of the Moving Image' in Cynthia A. Freeland and Thomas E. Wartenberg (eds.), *Philosophy and Film*, London: Routledge, 1995.

'From Real to Reel: Entangled in Nonfiction Film' in his *Theorizing the Moving Image*, Cambridge University Press, 1996.

'Medium Specificity Arguments and the Self-Consciously Invented Arts: Film, Video, and Photography' in his *Theorizing the Moving Image*, Cambridge University Press, 1996.

'The Power of Movies' in his *Theorizing the Moving Image*, Cambridge University Press, 1996.

Theorizing the Moving Image, Cambridge University Press, 1996.

'Forget the Medium!' in his *Engaging the Moving Image*, New Haven, Conn.: Yale University Press, 2003.

Comedy Incarnate: Buster Keaton, Physical Comedy and Bodily Coping, Malden, Mass.: Blackwell, 2007.

Casebier, Allan, *Film and Phenomenology*, Cambridge University Press, 1991.

Cavell, Stanley, *Pursuits of Happiness: The Hollywood Comedy of Remarriage*, Cambridge, Mass.: Harvard University Press, 1976.

The World Viewed: Reflections on the Ontology of Film, enlarged edition, Cambridge, Mass.: Harvard University Press, 1979.

Chatman, Seymour, *Story and Discourse: Narrative Structure in Fiction and Film*, Ithaca, NY: Cornell University Press, 1978.

Coming to Terms: The Rhetoric of Narrative in Fiction and Film, Ithaca, NY: Cornell University Press, 1990.

'What Novels Can Do that Films Can't (and Vice Versa)' in Leo Braudy and Marshall Cohen (eds.), *Film Theory and Criticism: Introductory Readings*, 6th edn, New York: Oxford University Press, 2004.

Choi, Jinhee, 'Leaving It Up to the Imagination: POV Shots and Imagining from the Inside', *Journal of Aesthetics and Art Criticism*, 63 (2005): 17–25.

Cohen, Jonathan and Aaron Meskin, 'On the Epistemic Value of Photographs', *Journal of Aesthetics and Art Criticism*, 62 (2004): 197–210.

Collingwood, R. G., *The Principles of Art*, Oxford University Press, 1938.

Cook, David A., *A History of Narrative Film*, 2nd edn, New York: Norton, 1990.

Corliss, Richard, 'The Hollywood Screenwriter' in Gerald Mast, Marshall Cohen and Leo Braudy (eds.), *Film Theory and Criticism: Introductory Readings*, 4th edn, New York: Oxford University Press, 1992.

Crawford, Chris, 'Interactive Storytelling' in Mark J. P. Wolf and Bernard Perron (eds.), *The Video Game Theory Reader*, London: Routledge, 2003.

Currie, Gregory, *Image and Mind: Film, Philosophy, and Cognitive Science*, Cambridge University Press, 1995.

'Reply to My Critics', *Philosophical Studies*, 89 (1998): 355–66.

Danto, Arthur, 'Moving Pictures', *Quarterly Review of Film Studies*, 4 (1979): 1–21.

Davies, David, 'Medium' in Jerrold Levinson (ed.), *The Oxford Handbook of Aesthetics*, Oxford University Press, 2003.

'How Photographs "Signify": Cartier-Bresson's "Reply" to Scruton' in Scott Walden (ed.), *Photography and Philosophy: Essays on the Pencil of Nature*, Malden, Mass.: Blackwell, 2008.

'Eluding Wilson's "Elusive Narrators"', *Philosophical Studies*, forthcoming.

Davies, Stephen, *Philosophical Perspectives on Art*, Oxford University Press, 2007.

Derakhshani, Dariush, *Introducing Maya 2008*, Indianapolis, Ind.: Wiley, 2008.

Deren, Maya, 'Cinematography: The Creative Use of Reality' in Leo Braudy and Marshall Cohen (eds.), *Film Theory and Criticism: Introductory Readings*, 6th edn, New York: Oxford University Press, 2004.

De Sousa, Ronald, *The Rationality of Emotion*, Cambridge, Mass.: MIT Press, 1987.

Doherty, Thomas, 'Review of *Do the Right Thing*', *Film Quarterly*, 43, no. 2 (1989–90): 35–40.

Dyer, Richard, *Stars*, London: British Film Institute, 1979.

Editors of *Cahiers du Cinéma*, 'John Ford's Young Mr. Lincoln' in Gerald Mast and Marshall Cohen (eds.), *Film Theory and Criticism: Introductory Readings*, 3rd edn, New York: Oxford University Press, 1985.

Eisenstein, Sergei, 'Beyond the Shot [The Cinematographic Principle and the Ideogram]' in Leo Braudy and Marshall Cohen (eds.), *Film Theory and Criticism: Introductory Readings*, 6th edn, New York: Oxford University Press, 2004.

Elgin, Catherine and Israel Scheffler, 'Mainsprings of Metaphor', *Journal of Philosophy*, 84 (1987): 331–5.

Eskelinen, Markku, 'The Gaming Situation', *Game Studies*, 1 (2001), www. gamestudies.org.

Fish, Stanley, *Is There a Text in This Class?: The Authority of Interpretive Communities*, Cambridge, Mass.: Harvard University Press, 1980.

Frasca, Gonzalo, 'Simulation versus Narrative: Introduction to Ludology' in Mark J. P. Wolf and Bernard Perron (eds.), *The Video Game Theory Reader*, London: Routledge, 2003.

Friday, Jonathan, 'André Bazin's Ontology of Photographic and Film Imagery', *Journal of Aesthetics and Art Criticism*, 63 (2005): 339–50.

Gaut, Berys, 'Interpreting the Arts: The Patchwork Theory', *Journal of Aesthetics and Art Criticism*, 51 (1993): 597–609.

'The Paradox of Horror', *British Journal of Aesthetics*, 33 (1993): 333–45.

'On Cinema and Perversion', *Film and Philosophy*, 1 (1994): 3–17.

'Metaphor and the Understanding of Art', *Proceedings of the Aristotelian Society*, 97 (1997): 223–41.

'Imagination, Interpretation and Film', *Philosophical Studies*, 89 (1998): 331–41.

'"Art" as a Cluster Concept' in Noël Carroll (ed.), *Theories of Art Today*, Madison: University of Wisconsin Press, 2000.

'The Cluster Account of Art Defended', *British Journal of Aesthetics*, 45 (2005): 273–88.

Art, Emotion and Ethics, Oxford University Press, 2007.

Gombrich, E. H., *Art and Illusion*, 5th edn, London: Phaidon Press, 1977.

The Story of Art, 14th edn, Oxford: Phaidon Press, 1984.

Goodman, Nelson, *Languages of Art: An Approach to a Theory of Symbols*, Indianapolis, Ind.: Hackett, 1976.

Grau, Oliver, *Virtual Art: From Illusion to Immersion*, trans. Gloria Custance, Cambridge, Mass.: MIT Press, 2003.

Greenberg, Clement, 'Modernist Painting' in Francis Frascina and Charles Harrison (eds.), *Modern Art and Modernism: A Critical Anthology*, London: Harper and Row, 1982.

Greenspan, Patricia, *Emotions and Reasons: An Inquiry into Emotional Justification*, London: Routledge, 1988.

Grice, Paul, 'Meaning', *Philosophical Review*, 66 (1957): 377–88.

Grodal, Torben, *Moving Pictures: A New Theory of Film Genres, Feelings, and Cognition*, Oxford: Clarendon Press, 1997.

'Stories for Eye, Ear, and Muscles: Video Games, Media, and Embodied Experiences' in Mark J. P. Wolf and Bernard Perron (eds.), *The Video Game Theory Reader*, London: Routledge, 2003.

Hammel, Michael, 'Towards a Yet Newer Laocoon. Or, What We Can Learn from Interacting with Computer Games' in Anna Bentkowska-Kafel, Trish Cashen and Hazel Gardiner (eds.), *Digital Art History*, Bristol: Intellect Books, 2005.

Harman, Gilbert, 'Semiotics and the Cinema: Metz and Wollen' in Leo Braudy and Marshall Cohen (eds.), *Film Theory and Criticism: Introductory Readings*, 5th edn, New York: Oxford University Press, 1999.

Heath, Stephen, 'Comment on "The idea of authorship"' in John Caughie (ed.), *Theories of Authorship*, London: Routledge, 1981.

Heim, Michael, 'Virtual Reality' in Michael Kelly (ed.), *Encyclopedia of Aesthetics*, New York: Oxford University Press, 1998.

Hirsch, E. D., *Validity in Interpretation*, New Haven, Conn.: Yale University Press, 1967.

Jarvie, Ian, *Philosophy of the Film: Epistemology, Ontology, Aesthetics*, New York: Routledge & Kegan Paul, 1987.

Juul, Jesper, 'Games Telling Stories? A Brief Note on Games and Narratives', *Game Studies*, 1 (2001), www.gamestudies.org.

  Half-Real: Video Games between Real Rules and Fictional Worlds, Cambridge, Mass.: MIT Press, 2005.

Kania, Andrew, 'The Illusion of Realism in Film', *British Journal of Aesthetics*, 42 (2002): 243–58.

  'Against the Ubiquity of Fictional Narrators', *Journal of Aesthetics and Art Criticism*, 63 (2005): 47–54.

Kawin, Bruce, *Mindscreen: Bergman, Godard, and First-Person Film*, Princeton University Press, 1978.

Kennedy, Lisa, 'Is Malcolm X the Right Thing?', *Sight and Sound*, 3, no. 2 (NS), (1993): 6–10.

Kerlow, Isaac, *The Art of 3D Computer Animation and Effects*, 3rd edn, Hoboken, NJ: John Wiley, 2004.

Kieran, Matthew, 'Art, Imagination, and the Cultivation of Morals', *Journal of Aesthetics and Art Criticism*, 54 (1996): 337–51.

King, William L., 'Scruton and Reasons for Looking at Photographs', *British Journal of Aesthetics*, 32 (1992): 258–65.

Kivy, Peter, 'Music in the Movies: A Philosophical Enquiry' in Richard Allen and Murray Smith (eds.), *Film Theory and Philosophy*, Oxford: Clarendon Press, 1997.

  Philosophies of Arts: An Essay in Differences, Cambridge University Press, 1997.

Knox, Donald, *The Magic Factory: How MGM Made An American in Paris*, Westport, Conn.: Praeger, 1973.

Kozloff, Sarah, *Invisible Storytellers: Voice-Over Narration in American Fiction Film*, Berkeley: University of California Press, 1988.

Kracauer, Siegfried, *From Caligari to Hitler*, Princeton University Press, 1947.

  Theory of Film: The Redemption of Physical Reality, Princeton University Press, 1997.

Kristeller, Paul, 'The Modern System of the Arts', *Journal of the History of Ideas*, 12 (1951): 496–527, and 13 (1952): 17–46.

Kulvicki, John V., *On Images: Their Structure and Content*, Oxford: Clarendon Press, 2006.

Kurosawa, Akira, *Something Like an Autobiography*, trans. Audie E. Bock, New York: Alfred Knopf, 1982.

Lessing, Gotthold, *Laocoön*, extracted in Hazard Adams (ed.), *Critical Theory Since Plato*, San Diego, Calif.: Harcourt Brace Jovanovich, 1971.

Levinson, Jerrold, 'What a Musical Work Is' in his *Music, Art, and Metaphysics: Essays in Philosophical Aesthetics*, Ithaca, NY: Cornell University Press, 1990.

'Film Music and Narrative Agency' in David Bordwell and Noël Carroll (eds.), *Post-Theory: Reconstructing Film Studies*, Madison: University of Wisconsin Press, 1996.

'Intention and Interpretation in Literature' in his *The Pleasures of Aesthetics*, Ithaca, NY: Cornell University Press, 1996.

Lewis, David, *Convention*, Cambridge, Mass.: Harvard University Press, 1969.

'Veridical Hallucination and Prosthetic Vision' in his *Philosophical Papers*, Volume II, Oxford University Press, 1986.

Livingston, Paisley, 'Cinematic Authorship' in Richard Allen and Murray Smith (eds.), *Film Theory and Philosophy*, Oxford: Clarendon Press, 1997.

Art and Intention: A Philosophical Study, Oxford: Clarendon Press, 2005.

'Narrative' in Berys Gaut and Dominic McIver Lopes (eds.), *The Routledge Companion to Aesthetics*, 2nd edn, London: Routledge, 2005.

Cinema, Philosophy, Bergman: On Film as Philosophy, Oxford University Press, 2009.

Livingston, Paisley and Carl Plantinga (eds.), *The Routledge Companion to Philosophy and Film*, London: Routledge, 2009.

Lopes, Dominic McIver, 'Pictorial Realism', *Journal of Aesthetics and Art Criticism*, 53 (1995): 277–85.

Understanding Pictures, Oxford: Clarendon Press, 1996.

'Imagination, Illusion and Experience in Film', *Philosophical Studies*, 89 (1998): 343–53.

'The Ontology of Interactive Art', *Journal of Aesthetic Education*, 35 (2001): 65–81.

'The Aesthetics of Photographic Transparency', *Mind*, 112 (2003): 433–48.

'Digital Art' in Luciano Floridi (ed.), *The Blackwell Guide to the Philosophy of Computing and Information*, Malden, Mass.: Blackwell, 2004.

A Philosophy of Computer Art, London: Routledge, 2010.

Macaulay, Sean, 'A Lover and a Fighter', *The Times*, 23 August 2001, 14 and 19.

Manovich, Lev, *The Language of New Media*, Cambridge, Mass.: MIT Press, 2001.

Mateas, Michael and Andrew Stern, 'Façade: An Experiment in Building a Fully-Realized Interactive Drama' (2003), www.interactivestory.net.

McDowell, John, *Mind and World*, Cambridge, Mass.: Harvard University Press, 1994.

McKernan, Brian, *Digital Cinema: The Revolution in Cinematography, Postproduction, and Distribution*, New York: McGraw-Hill, 2005.

Metz, Christian, *Film Language: A Semiotics of the Cinema*, trans. Michael Taylor, New York: Oxford University Press, 1974.

The Imaginary Signifier: Psychoanalysis and the Cinema, trans. C. Britton *et al.*, Bloomington: Indiana University Press, 1982.

Mitchell, William J., *The Reconfigured Eye: Visual Truth in the Post-Photographic Era*, Cambridge, Mass.: MIT Press, 1992.

Monaco, James, *How to Read a Film*, 3rd edn, New York: Oxford University Press, 2000.

Morrison, Michael, *Beginning Game Programming*, Indianapolis, Ind.: Sams Publishing, 2005.

Munsterberg, Hugo, *The Photoplay: A Psychological Study* in Allan Langdale (ed.), *Hugo Munsterberg on Film*, London: Routledge, 2002.

Murray, Janet H., *Hamlet on the Holodeck: The Future of Narrative in Cyberspace*, Cambridge, Mass.: MIT Press, 1997.

Nehamas, Alexander 'The Postulated Author', *Critical Inquiry*, 8 (1981): 133–49.

Neill, Alex, 'Empathy and (Film) Fiction' in David Bordwell and Noël Carroll (eds.), *Post-Theory: Reconstructing Film Studies*, Madison: University of Wisconsin Press, 1996.

Newman, James, *Videogames*, London: Routledge, 2004.

Nowell-Smith, Geoffrey, 'Six Authors in Pursuit of *The Searchers*' in John Caughie (ed.), *Theories of Authorship*, London: Routledge, 1981.

Oudart, Jean-Pierre, 'Cinema and Suture', *Screen*, 18 (1977/78): 35–47.

Panofsky, Erwin, 'Style and Medium in the Motion Pictures' in Leo Braudy and Marshall Cohen (eds.), *Film Theory and Criticism: Introductory Readings*, 6th edn, New York: Oxford University Press, 2004.

Perkins, V. F., *Film as Film: Understanding and Judging Movies*, Harmondsworth: Penguin, 1972.

Piggyback Interactive Limited, *Lara Croft Tomb Raider: Legend: The Complete Guide*, Piggybackinteractive.com, 2006.

Plantinga, Carl and Greg M. Smith (eds.), *Passionate Views: Film, Cognition, and Emotion*, Baltimore, Md.: Johns Hopkins University Press, 1999.

Poole, Steven, *Trigger Happy: Videogames and the Entertainment Revolution*, New York: Arcade Publishing, 2004.

Prince, Stephen, 'The Discourse of Pictures: Iconicity and Film Studies' in Leo Braudy and Marshall Cohen (eds.), *Film Theory and Criticism: Introductory Readings*, 6th edn, New York: Oxford University Press, 2004.

'True Lies: Perceptual Realism, Digital Images, and Film Theory' in Leo Braudy and Marshall Cohen (eds.), *Film Theory and Criticism: Introductory Readings*, 6th edn, New York: Oxford University Press, 2004.

Pudovkin, Vsevolod, *Film Acting and Film Technique*, trans Ivor Montagu, London: Vision Press, 1958.

Rafferty, Terrence, 'Everybody Gets a Cut: DVDs Give Viewers Dozens of Choices – and that's the Problem' in Noël Carroll and Jinhee Choi (eds.), *Philosophy of Film and Motion Pictures: An Anthology*, Malden, Mass.: Blackwell, 2006.

Rauch, Jonathan, 'Sex, Lies, and Video Games', *The Atlantic Monthly*, 298 (November 2006): 76–86.

Roberts, Robert C., 'What An Emotion Is: A Sketch', *Philosophical Review*, 97 (1988): 183–209.

Robinson, David, *Das Cabinet des Dr. Caligari*, London: British Film Institute, 1997.

Rothman, William, 'Against "The System of the Suture"' in Leo Braudy and Marshall Cohen (eds.), *Film Theory and Criticism: Introductory Readings*, 5th edn, New York: Oxford University Press, 1999.

Ryan, Marie-Laure, *Narrative as Virtual Reality: Immersion and Interactivity in Literature and Electronic Media*, Baltimore, Md.: Johns Hopkins University Press, 2001.

Avatars of Story, Minneapolis: University of Minnesota Press, 2006.

Sarris, Andrew, 'Towards a Theory of Film History' in Bill Nichols (ed.), *Movies and Methods*, vol. I, Berkeley: University of California Press, 1976.

'Notes on the Auteur Theory in 1962' in Gerald Mast, and Marshall Cohen (eds.), *Film Theory and Criticism: Introductory Readings*, 3rd edn, New York: Oxford University Press, 1985.

Sartwell, Crispin, 'What Pictorial Realism Is', *British Journal of Aesthetics*, 34 (1994): 2–12.

Savedoff, Barbara, 'Transforming Images: Photographs of Representations', *Journal of Aesthetics and Art Criticism*, 50 (1992): 93–106.

'Escaping Reality: Digital Imagery and the Resources of Photography,' *Journal of Aesthetics and Art Criticism*, 55 (1997): 201–14.

Schama, Simon, *Power of Art*, London: BBC Books, 2006.

Schatz, Thomas, *The Genius of the System: Hollywood Filmmaking in the Studio Era*, New York: Pantheon, 1988.

Schier, Flint, *Deeper into Pictures: An Essay on Pictorial Representation*, Cambridge University Press, 1986.

Scruton, Roger, 'Fantasy, Imagination and the Screen' in his *The Aesthetic Understanding*, London: Methuen, 1983.

'Photography and Representation' in his *The Aesthetic Understanding*, London: Methuen, 1983.

'The Photographic Surrogate' in his *The Philosopher on Dover Beach*, Manchester: Carcanet, 1990.

Searle, John, *Speech Acts*, Cambridge University Press, 1969.

Sellors, C. Paul, 'Collective Authorship in Film', *Journal of Aesthetics and Art Criticism*, 65 (2007): 263–71.

Sesonske, Alexander, 'Cinema Space' in David Carr and Edward S. Casey (eds.), *Explorations in Phenomenology*, The Hague: Martinus Nijhoff, 1973.

'Aesthetics of Film, or A Funny Thing Happened on the Way to the Movies', *Journal of Aesthetics and Art Criticism*, 33 (1974): 51–7.

Sibley, Brian, *Peter Jackson: A Film-maker's Journey*, London: HarperCollins, 2006.

Smith, Murray, *Engaging Characters: Fiction, Emotion, and the Cinema*, Oxford: Clarendon Press, 1995.

'My Dinner with Noël; or, Can We Forget the Medium?', *Film Studies: An International Review*, 8 (2006): 140–8.

Sparshott, Francis, 'Basic Film Aesthetics' in Gerald Mast and Marshall Cohen (eds.), *Film Theory and Criticism*, 3rd edn, New York: Oxford University Press, 1985.

Spellerberg, James, 'Technology and Ideology in the Cinema' in Gerald Mast and Marshall Cohen (eds.), *Film Theory and Criticism*, 3rd edn, New York: Oxford University Press, 1985.

Stecker, Robert, *Artworks: Definition, Meaning, Value*, University Park: Pennsylvania State University Press, 1997.

'Interpretation' in Berys Gaut and Dominic McIver Lopes (eds.), *The Routledge Companion to Aesthetics*, 2nd edn, London: Routledge, 2005.

Stillinger, Jack, *Multiple Authorship and the Myth of Solitary Genius*, New York: Oxford University Press, 1992.

Tarantino, Quentin, 'I Call the Shots Here', *Sunday Times Magazine*, 4 March 2007: 8.

Tavinor, Grant, 'Videogames and Interactive Fiction,' *Philosophy and Literature*, 29 (2005): 24–40.

The Art of Videogames, Malden, Mass.: Blackwell, 2009.

Thompson, Kristin, *Breaking the Glass Armor: Neoformalist Film Analysis*, Princeton University Press, 1988.

Thompson, Kristin and David Bordwell, *Film History: An Introduction*, 2nd edn, New York: McGraw-Hill, 2003.

Truffaut, François, 'A Certain Tendency of the French Cinema', in Bill Nichols (ed.), *Movies and Methods*, vol. I, Berkeley: University of California Press, 1976.

Tyler, Parker, '*Rashomon* as Modern Art' in his *The Three Faces of the Film*, New York: Thomas Yoseloff, 1960.

Walton, Kendall, 'Categories of Art', *Philosophical Review*, 79 (1970): 334–67.

'Style and the Products and Processes of Art' in Berel Lang (ed.), *The Concept of Style*, Philadelphia: University of Pennsylvania Press, 1979.

'Transparent Pictures: On the Nature of Photographic Realism', *Critical Inquiry*, 11 (1984): 246–77.

Mimesis as Make-Believe: On the Foundations of the Representational Arts, Cambridge, Mass.: Harvard University Press, 1990.

'On Pictures and Photographs: Objections Answered' in Richard Allen and Murray Smith (eds.), *Film Theory and Philosophy*, Oxford: Clarendon Press, 1997.

Marvelous Images: On Values and the Arts, New York: Oxford University Press, 2008.

Warburton, Nigel, 'Photographic Communication', *British Journal of Aesthetics*, 28 (1988): 173–81.

'Seeing through "Seeing Through Photographs"', *Ratio*, N.S. 1 (1988): 64–74.

Wartenberg, Thomas, 'Need there be Implicit Narrators of Literary Fictions?' *Philosophical Studies*, 135 (2007): 89–94.

Thinking on Screen: Film as Philosophy, London: Routledge, 2007.

Waters, Richard, 'Hollywood sees power shift from film-set to desk-top', *Financial Times*, 20 June 2005: 16.

Wicks, Robert, 'Photography as a Representational Art', *British Journal of Aesthetics*, 29 (1989): 1–9.

Wilson, George, *Narration in Light: Studies in Cinematic Point of View*, Baltimore, Md.: Johns Hopkins University Press, 1986.

'*Le Grand Imagier* Steps Out: The Primitive Basis of Film Narration', *Philosophical Topics*, 25 (1997): 295–318.

'Elusive Narrators in Literature and Film', *Philosophical Studies*, 135 (2007): 73–88.

Wollheim, Richard, *Painting as an Art*, Princeton University Press, 1987.

The Thread of Life, Cambridge, Mass.: Harvard University Press, 1984.

Wollen, Peter, *Signs and Meaning in the Cinema*, 3rd edn, Bloomington: Indiana University Press, 1972.

Wood, Robin, *Hitchcock's Films Revisited*, London: Faber and Faber, 1991.

Index